Hidden Histories of

Gender and the State in Latin America

D1051188

Hidden Histories of

Gender and the State in

Latin America

Elizabeth Dore & Maxine Molyneux, editors

Duke University Press   Durham & London

2000

© 2000 Duke University Press

except chapter 12 (© Institute of Latin American Studies).

All rights reserved

Printed in the United States of America on acid-free paper ∞

Designed by C. H. Westmoreland

Typeset in Dante by Keystone Typesetting, Inc.

Library of Congress Cataloging-in-Publication Data appear on the
last printed page of this book.

Permission was granted by Cambridge University Press to use
Elizabeth Dore's chapter, "Property, Households, and Public Regulation
of Domestic Life, Diriomo, Nicaragua, 1840–1900."

Permission was granted by the Institute of Latin American Studies,
University of London, to use Maxine Molyneux's chapter, "State, Gender,
and Institutional Change: The Federación de Mujeres Cubanas."

From E. D. and M. M.

for Alex, Matthew, Rachel

Variants of this approach differ in how they treat the state; sometimes it is viewed as a power broker between competing interests, sometimes its discursive interventions are the object of analysis, and sometimes it is ignored altogether. Consequently, explicit definitions of the state are rarely found in this approach. Culture, discourses, and civil society replace the state as the meaningful sites of the social analysis of power relations.

Neoliberalism, the economic creed of the 1980s and 1990s, was the third analytic influence to marginalize the state. A central proposition of this approach is that the state represents a potential threat to economic and other freedoms. Its activities should be curtailed because markets allocate resources most efficiently when freed from state intervention.[5] Notwithstanding neoliberalisms' doctrinaire antistatism, it is worth noting that in practice this creed is often associated with strong states of a particular kind: states that regularly intervened to enforce neoliberal policies, to maintain law and order, and to guarantee the "freedom" of the market.

The fourth body of work to marginalize the state was concerned with the analysis of globalization. At the end of the millennium, many academics and policymakers held that capitalism had reached a new globalized stage in which the power of states had declined irreversibly vis-à-vis transnational corporations. They argued that as a consequence of deregulation, nation-states were withering away, their powers appropriated by multilateral agencies that presided over an increasingly globalized civil society.[6] Although critics of this literature pointed to the ways in which states were still influenced by economic and social policy,[7] the locus of scholarly interest was in the main on transnational processes, in which states were largely ignored.

Although these four approaches in one way or another have turned attention away from the state, Latin American history and gender studies have been in some ways out of step with this trend. On the one hand, historians have analyzed processes of state formation, in particular how forms of rule were normalized through everyday customs, practices, and rituals. On the other hand, feminists, often reflecting the experience of Latin American women's movements, have engaged in theoretical and political debates over the state and over whether women should work in, with, or against it. In this perspective, the state remained a central term of reference.

The essays in this volume emerge from these two areas of shared concern. They represent a work of collaboration between social scientists from various disciplines and examine the changing modalities of state / gender relations across a period of some two hundred years in Latin America. In doing so, they offer a number of different approaches to and treatments of particular states. Some emphasize ways in which states have intervened in the gender order; others examine the ways in which states have deployed gender discourses; and still others are concerned with the relationship between states and social actors, especially women's movements.

The chapters on the colonial state emphasize two themes: (1) the close link between family and public patriarchy, and (2) the formation of a social hierarchy formally demarcated by criteria of race and gender. Both aspects of state-society relations endured long after Spanish and Portuguese rule ended in the Americas. After independence, states set about reconstituting more absolutist models of patriarchy that had relaxed as a consequence of social upheaval and war. In the latter part of the nineteenth century, liberal states intervened to modernize patriarchy, often through reform of the legal system. Many of these apparently modern measures undermined women's historic rights to property and formal sexual parity within marriage.

The chapters on the later variants of Latin American state forms suggest that among the significant changes during the twentieth century, three were particularly salient: the rise of the women's movement, which placed new demands on the state; the emergence of states that actively and explicitly sought to intervene in the gender order through legislation; and the slowly increasing presence of women within the apparatuses of the state as members of the government and in official women's organizations. The mobilization of women was part of the broader incorporation of citizens and new social classes into politics. Women thus became both social actors and objects of state policy, with contrasting results in different political contexts.

The focus of this study, the gendered character of states, is an ongoing one, the terms of which are repeatedly redefined by domestic, continental, and global processes. In this sense, the chapters in this volume offer not only a historical context for understanding contemporary processes but also contain implications for the formulation of current and future policies. It is our hope that this book will contribute to the dialogue that began in the 1980s among those in Latin America and beyond who are concerned with promoting gender justice there. That this dialogue will continue in the new millennium is beyond doubt. It is as much as a contribution to unfinished business as in its reformulation of the past that this volume will be tested.

Notes

1 Karl Marx and Friedrich Engels, *Manifesto of the Communist Party,* in *The Marx Engels Reader,* 2d ed., ed. Robert C. Tucker (New York: W. W. Norton, 1978), 475.
2 The regulation approach is one school that continued to develop theories on political economy and to focus on the state. See, for example, the collection edited by R. Burrows and B. Loader, *Towards a Post-Fordist Welfare State* (London: Routledge, 1994).
3 See Sonia Alvarez, Evelina Dagnino, and Arturo Escobar, eds. *Cultures of Politics / Politics of Cultures* (Boulder, Colo.: Westview, 1998), and Dagnino's essay on Gramsci's appeal to the Latin American left, 33–63.
4 Michel Foucault, *The History of Sexuality,* vol. 1, *An Introduction* (London: Allen Lane, 1979). Feminist theory shares in the view that power is dispersed, and it has developed critiques of normative theories of political power as residing only in the public domain. For a feminist engagement with the work of Foucault, see Caroline Ramazanoglu, ed., *Up against Foucault: Explorations of Some Tensions between Foucault and Feminism* (London and New York: Routledge, 1993). For a Foucauldian interpretation of peasant resistance, see James C. Scott, *Weapons of the Weak: Everyday Forms of Peasant Resistance* (New Haven: Yale University Press, 1985).
5 For a periodization of the Latin American state and critique of neoliberalism, see Peter Smith, "The Rise and Fall of the Developmental State in Latin America," in *The Changing Role of the State in Latin America,* ed. Menno Vellinga (Boulder, Colo.: Westview, 1998), 51–73.
6 Frances Fox Piven and Richard A. Cloward, "Eras of Power." For a critique of this view, see Ellen Meiskins Wood, "Class Compacts, the Welfare State and Epochal Shifts." Both appear in *Monthly Review* 49, no. 8 (January 1998): 11–43.
7 For a critical analysis of the role of the states in the context of globalization, see Paul Hirst and G. Thompson, *Globalisation in Question* (Cambridge: Polity, 1996).

Acknowledgments

We would like to thank the participants in the original conference that launched this project: Sylvia Chant, Mary Goldsmith Connelly, Deborah Levenson-Estrada, Susana Novick, Ruth Pearson, Carmen Ramos Escandón, Judith March Sánchez, Jean Stubbs, Ingrid Vargas Guell, Sarah Bradshaw, Carolee Benglesdorf, María del Carmen Feijoó and the contributors to this volume. In our title, we also acknowledge the pioneering work of Sheila Rowbotham, whose book *Hidden from History* was such an inspiration to feminist historians. We discussed this project with many colleagues at the Institute of Latin American Studies (ILAS), University of London and the University of Portsmouth, who were generous with their time and expertise. In particular, we appreciate the research assistance of Anne Worden, Latin American librarian, and Paul Wright, computer technician, Elizabeth Clifford, and Rebecca Platt, all at the University of Portsmouth; Tony Bell, Anna Hayes, Alan Biggens and others at ILAS for help with the conference and the manuscript. We thank Pam Decho for translating a chapter; Tim Girven for indexing; Annie Barva, copyeditor; Patricia Mickelberry, managing editor; and Cherie Westmoreland, designer—all at Duke University Press. We appreciate the comments on our chapters we received from Nikki Craske, James Dunkerley, María Carmen Feijoó, Robbie Gray, Elizabeth Jelín, Asunción Lavrin, Silvia Arrom, Muriel Nazzari, Carmen Ramos, Susan Besse, Elizabeth Kuznesof and the anonymous reviewers. Elizabeth Dore acknowledges ongoing support from the History Research Centre and the School of Languages and Area Studies of the University of Portsmouth, as well as research grants from the Fulbright Commission, the British Academy, the American Philosophical Society, and the American Council of Learned Societies. Maxine Molyneux thanks ILAS for supporting research on Cuba. We are grateful to Valerie Millholland, whose experience and professionalism proved invaluable in guiding this project through its different phases. Finally, Fred and John helped in the many ways they always have done, and more.

I

State and Gender in

Latin America

Elizabeth Dore

One Step Forward,

Two Steps Back

Gender and the State in the Long Nineteenth Century

This book is a response to Joan Scott's call to examine how politics constructs gender and gender constructs politics.[1] Its purpose is to analyze how politics of a particular type—state politics—affected gender relations and how gender conditioned state formation in Latin America from the late colony to the twenty-first century. Each chapter is a study of ways in which the state influenced gender relations and vice versa in a particular country at a specific historical conjuncture. Like all anthologies, this one aspires to be more than the sum of its parts. Its aim is to contribute to the elaboration of a systematic account of the interaction between state politics and gender politics in Latin America.

Periodizations of the state in Latin America are fairly common, typologies even more so.[2] They highlight agreement regarding the importance of historicizing state forms and disagreement regarding how to differentiate states. Notwithstanding their diversity, the existing periodizations do not take gender into account: neither the gendered nature of states nor how states regulated gender.[3] In light of this absence, the two introductory chapters in part 1 of this volume analyze major changes in gendered state making across Latin America.

Until recently this endeavour would have foundered on a paucity of empirical research and an underdevelopment of theory. The former obstacle has been partially overcome by a number of excellent monographs on what could broadly be called state-gender relations in Latin America; the latter has been redressed by the growth of an analytical literature concerning gender and the state.[4] These contributions made our project not only possible, but necessary. Drawing on the twelve case studies presented in this volume and on recent scholarship in the field, the introductory chapters analyze the ways states constructed gender and how gender conditioned state making over a period of 250 years. In light of the heterogeneity of states and gender cultures in Latin America and of the time span under review, the objective of these two essays is to identify major turning points and historical continuities in the interface between state politics and gender politics.

Years ago, historians of Europe and the United States assessed the fit between "traditional" history and "gender" history.[5] They questioned, in particular, whether conventional periodizations corresponded to major turning points in women's lives. Joan Kelly, for instance, asked, "Did women have a Renaissance?"[6] More recently, feminist scholars in the United States have debated whether state-sponsored research and development in the field of contraception, which culminated in the Pill, were more important in the transformation of gender relations in the late twentieth century than, say, the Cold War. Maxine Molyneux and I embarked on this cross-disciplinary project after realizing that scholars of Latin America rarely have addressed issues of long-term regional trends and turning points in the ways states influenced gender.[7] Our conclusions, which form part 1 of this book, were written in the spirit of discovery and recovery. We hope they make a contribution to the fruitful dialogue between feminists working to transform the state and those of us studying the formation of gender relations in Latin America.

How Latin American states sought to govern gender relations during the long nineteenth century, from the late colony to the twentieth century, is the subject of this essay.[8] It focuses on the legal regulation of gender, especially changes in family and property law. Although states enact laws to promote certain social practices and to discourage others, it goes without saying that governments are not always successful in reforming societies in accordance with their laws. Consequently, this account of long-term transformations in the legal foundations of gender relations should be read as a history of state policy, not as a history of gendered practices.

Latin American historians have tended to view the long nineteenth century as an era in which the state gradually dismantled major structural inequalities in gender relations. Studies of legal reform, education, employment, and social policy have emphasized the incremental elimination of restrictions on women's participation in the public domain. In particular, historians have stressed the emancipatory effects of secularization, arguing that the declining prerogatives of the church and the rising powers of the state generally resulted in an expansion of women's rights. Overall, these analyses have supported the orthodox interpretation of liberalism in Latin America, which claims that liberal states ushered in "Order and Progress."

Yet evidence from a number of countries casts doubt on this account. Transposing Kelly's question regarding women in Renaissance Europe to the Latin American context, I ask, "Did liberal states usher in 'Order and Progress' in gender relations?" I assess the implications of legal reforms and secularization for women, keeping in mind that their effects varied along lines of nation, class, and race. I conclude that, on balance, state policy had more negative than positive consequences for gender equality, which suggests the need to reassess the view that the long nineteenth century was a period of progress for women. Some legal reforms and some aspects of secularization did reduce gender inequalities for some, maybe most, women. Nevertheless, I propose that the general direction of change was regressive rather than progressive. My interpretation of the relationship between state politics and gender politics in the long nineteenth century can be summarized in the phrase "one step forward, two steps back."

States act in myriad ways on gender relations. It is necessary, therefore, to clarify what this chapter is not about. During the long nineteenth century, Latin American states moved on a number of fronts to normalize elite, predominantly male, ideals of femininity and masculinity, especially in areas of health, education, employment, and charity-social work. This normalization provided the opportunity for national, regional, and local officials to exert pressure on men and women to conform to what the elite regarded as "proper" behavior. As a number of chapters in this volume demonstrate, "proper" was a highly fluid notion that varied by sex, class, race, marital status, age, and so on.[9] Furthermore, state policy regarding gender has never been limited to the exercise of government. Art, literature, and cultural ceremonies in every country and in every epoch have played a central role in the construction of the official politics of gender.[10] Despite their importance, these nonlegal and nonlegislative forms of regulation are not treated in this chapter, except in passing.

My argument—that changes in state policy increased more than decreased gender inequalities—is developed in six parts. I begin with a brief discussion about how to study the state and with a characterization of Latin American states as they emerged over the course of the long nineteenth century. The second part examines and rejects the myth of the supersubordinated female in the colonial era; the third part analyzes the early republics; and the fourth part treats the reform of property and family law enacted by liberal states. What this essay stresses and what has not been adequately explored before is that the liberal assault on the historic privileges of the church and Indian Communities was accompanied by a similar assault on the privileges of women. At a time when landed property and other resources gradually became commodities, women lost much of the legal protection to family property that they had enjoyed "from time immemorial." The fifth part assesses secularization and its implications for marital rights, and finds that, contrary to the prevailing view, secularization of married life tended to expand inequalities between women and men. The conclusion contrasts this interpretation to the view that history is a story of progress.

Part One: Understanding the State

To understand the state, we must begin by posing three interrelated questions: What is the state? Why does it exist? How does it rule? Answering these questions involves a theoretical analysis of the role of the state in a particular society and an empirical examination of the historical development of specific social conditions. In my approach, "What is the state?" centers largely on the classic debate about the relationship between the state and class interests. "Why does it exist?" refers to the objectives inherent in the exercise of power. "How does it rule?" treats the means by which the state achieves its political domination. It is noteworthy that late-twentieth-century literature on the state tends to eschew the first two questions, moving directly to the third, "How do states rule?" In general, scholars examine fundamental issues—such as how states organize consent, suppress opposition, and protect sovereignty—without addressing the prior issues, namely, the class nature of the state and its objectives of rule. I propose that this approach leaves many substantive issues about the state unresolved.

This essay analyzes changing state policy in a variety of countries over a long period of time; it treats states of different kinds, with different objectives, and different methods of rule. In response to the question "What is the state?" I propose that despite their heterogeneity and under ordinary conditions, these Latin American states ruled *in* the interests of a portion of the society's upper classes *through* the general interest of the populace—insofar as that was possible. By this I mean that except under extraordinary circumstances, states ruled in the class interests of an elite, but with an ideology that rule was in the wider interests of a broader portion of society.

In this interpretation, class rule does not imply that the exercise of power at all times directly promoted the well-being of the dominant classes nor that those states should be understood simply as a tool wielded by economic elites to achieve their aims or to impose their will. Rather, insofar as those states presented themselves as governing in the common good, politics involved the construction of consent alongside the imposition of authority. It is a truism that subaltern classes always endeavor to exert pressure on the state, but only in unusual historical conjunctures, and even then only briefly, have exploited classes exercised state power. I suggest, therefore, that it is useful to think of the state as operating within a gravitational field in which the pull of the exploiting classes is considerable and the pull of the exploited classes considerably less. Or, as one historian has written, the state's many activities take place within the *field of force* of the dominant classes.[11]

Turning to question two—"Why does the state exist?"—in all but extraordinary circumstances, the primary objective of rule is to enable the exploiting classes to appropriate labor and resources from the subordinate classes. How this appropriation is achieved depends upon the mode of production or the way economics, politics, and social life are organized. Finally, "how rule is accomplished" is the story of how exploiting classes, under unique historical and social conditions, establish and perpetuate their rule. In contrast to most capitalist states, premodern states in the Latin America of the long nineteenth century did relatively little to camouflage their class character.[12] To the extent that politicians masqueraded as ruling in the common interest, they portrayed themselves as benevolent *patrones* who governed for the good of their subordinates. In the last twenty years, scholars have come to recognize that the exercise of state power involves the politics not only of class, but also of race and gender. Therefore, the answers to these three questions about the state—What is it? Why does it exist? and How does it accomplish rule?—rest on an analysis of changing class, race, and gender relations in society.

Recently, historians writing about state formation in Latin America have been influenced by a neo-Marxian tradition, particularly by Philip Corrigan and Derek Sayer.[13] Their book, *The Great Arch: English State Formation as Cultural Revolution,* argues that states endeavor to create a political culture that naturalizes one form of social domination. Utilizing coercion and constructing consent, states gradually make it appear that one historically specific way of organizing society is the only "natural" way. In this approach, the state—the organized power of the ruling classes—normalizes particular social relations and identities, and destroys others. As Corrigan and Sayer emphasize, states play a critical role in transforming the way ruling classes appropriate labor (or the products of labor) from exploited classes. Also, states frequently take the lead in transforming social relations, consciousness, and culture more generally. This understanding of state making is particularly relevant to gender. With its array of governmental, juridical, cultural, and overtly coercive institutions, state politics normalizes a variety of gender relations. Acceptable and unacceptable ways of being female and male may vary, depending on class and race. However, states establish a quasi-official gender regime by regulating as many aspects of life as they can reach, including sexual practices, prostitution, vagrancy, contraception, abortion, marriage, and the family. Because states are part of and act within particular societies, theories of the state in the abstract are of limited analytic value. Therefore, before examining the ways that states altered constructions of gender in the long nineteenth century, I turn to a very brief characterization of those states and societies.

This chapter treats an era that largely predated the rise of capitalism in Latin America. By capitalist, I mean a society permeated by the market and organized around relations of free wage labor. In the nineteenth century, politics and economics in most of Latin America were based largely on patronage and often involved the relatively undisguised use of force. Toward the end of the era, capitalist relations began to assume a certain importance in some of the countries, notably Argentina. But capitalism had yet to revolutionize most Latin American societies in the sense that economic and political life, as well as consciousness, still tended to be dominated by personal as opposed to market relations.

Politics in colonial Spanish and Portuguese America was based on the ideology that the legitimacy of the state derived from God. Nevertheless, state power ultimately derived from the state's capacity to impose its rule with violence. The colonial state perpetuated a hierarchical social order differentiated primarily by gender, race, and official status. Within the limits of the autocratic state, consent of the governed was fostered by a patriarchal system in which senior males exercised authority in the home, the community, and the polity.

Liberal states came to power in most Latin American countries in the middle of the nineteenth century and ran the gamut from a more radical liberalism in Mexico to a constrained version under the empire in Brazil. To a greater or lesser extent, liberals advocated free trade, private property, and anticlericalism. In line with most of their counterparts in Europe and the United States, Latin American liberals promoted freedom of property, not freedom of persons. Consequently, liberals in power in Latin America sought to reduce corporate control over land by the church and Indian Communities in order to foster private property in land. At the same time, liberal states advocated and often directly organized unfree labor systems— debt peonage, state labor drafts, and slavery. Their promotion of forced labor rested on two pillars: first, the ideology that Indians, mulattos, blacks, and peasants in general were primitives who had to be forced out of their natural laziness into the world of work; second, the material reality that, in the absence of a market in labor power, the landed elites had to use overt violence to recruit and discipline a labor force if they were going to enrich themselves from export agriculture.

Rejecting the old ideology of divine right and hereditary privilege, liberals asserted that the right to rule derived from the social superiority of elite males. They believed it was the natural right of men with wealth or professional status to exercise political authority.[14] This belief marked a change from, but not a radical break with, the patriarchal principles of the late colony, which remained embedded in liberal thought. Consequently, the ideology and practices of patriarchalism continued to underpin the social hierarchy. Senior men governed females and younger males in their household, a system that sustained the paternalist ideologies of the men who governed the nation and community. In line with these practices, liberal states established a polity based on restricted representation. In most countries, full political participation was the purview of males with money or a profession. Other members of society had limited political rights; in particular, they did not have the right to vote. For the majority of the population, exclusion from the political sphere mirrored their lack of freedom in the economic sphere. Liberals represented this exclusion as government for the people, so consent of the governed was fostered by a paternalist ideology underpinned by the state's capacity to impose its rule with force.

Throughout the region, except in Brazil and Cuba, there was an interregnum of early republics between the late colonial and liberal states. These states were unstable regimes, struggling to rule not-yet-existing nations. More than anything else, they were bridges between the fall of empire and the rise of liberal states across the region.

Part Two: Late Colony: the Myth of Women without Rights

Mature colonial society was a corporate patriarchy, divided along the lines of estate, race, and gender.[15] In Spanish America, the social order was officially segmented into three strata: republic of the Indians, republic of the Spaniards, and *castas*. The category *casta* usually included all people of mixed race: called *mestizo* if they were of Spanish-Indian heritage, and *negro* or *mulatto* if of African ancestry. Each strata was further subdivided by sex. Portuguese America had many more racial categories, all subdivided by sex. The Spanish and Portuguese Crowns codified the privileges and obligations of subjects in each group. These elaborate systems of race-gender segregation were spelled out in decrees that detailed which peoples could occupy positions in the church, the guilds, and the professions, which paid tribute and had labor obligations, and even which could wear jewelry and imported cloth.

As María Eugenia Chaves describes in her chapter in this volume, in practice, women's privileges and obligations, notwithstanding the text of decrees, were conditional upon their honor. Chaves develops her argument through an examination of a trial in late-eighteenth-century Guayaquil, in which a female slave challenged her slave status by arguing that she was publicly recognized to be a woman of honorable morals. Drawing on the text of a lengthy court case, Chaves demonstrates how the Spanish colonial state naturalized racially differentiated norms of femininity. Her essay explores the parallels between the upper-class ideology that slaves were sexually licentious by nature and the quasi-official classification of all slaves as people without honor.

It is worth noting that in the U.S. South before the Civil War, honor also resided in the public sphere. As Patricia J. Williams argues, "character was a central ingredient in proving racial identity during the nineteenth century [in the South]."[16] In exploring the "litigation of whiteness," she shows that along with skin color, reputation and "white conduct and character" were all essential to the "performing" of whiteness.

Returning to Ibero-America, the patriarchal character of colonial society was codified in a succession of royal proclamations that dated from the time of Conquest.[17] These decrees granted fathers and husbands legal authority in their households and established a regulatory framework that restricted and protected women and children. Evidence of the naturalization of patriarchal authority in those societies is the absence of religious or philosophical disputation regarding women's subordination. In contrast to the celebrated Las Casas–Sepúlveda debates over the relative merits of Indian versus African slavery, there was no public justification of female subordination. In Ibero-America, men's gender privileges and obligations were regarded as natural law. It was taken to be self-evident that women were not equal to men. Therefore, senior males' authority derived from their "natural-born" superiority to women.

State theory in the colonial era rested on the principle that a well-ordered society was composed of well-ruled families. Such families were governed by patriarchs who exercised power, demanded obedience, provided maintenance, and guaranteed protection.[18] Colonial officials drew on legal and cultural norms of patriarchal authority to lend legitimacy to the authority of the state. Their political discourse was impregnated with analogies between the king and the family father. In this model of government, the Crown was like the benevolent father who ruled over and protected his family. Like all good fathers, he rewarded his children when they behaved well and punished them when they behaved badly.

Male prerogatives in colonial society were pervasive. Nevertheless, the extent of women's legal subordination has been greatly exaggerated. Frequently, it has been argued that the colonial state accorded women few rights and denied them juridical personhood.[19] This is a myth: the Ibero-American colonial state did not deny women a legal existence. Relative to most contemporary states, and in particular contrast to the Anglo-Saxon legal tradition, where until the late nineteenth century women *were* virtually denied juridical personhood, the Spanish and Portuguese Crowns granted women extensive privileges. Women could sign contracts, ratify official documents, make wills, and appear in court. In the Anglo-Saxon world, with its tradition of primogeniture and entail, it was rare for women to own and control landed property. By contrast, in the Ibero-American world, women of the propertied classes were guaranteed an equal share of their parents' wealth, including land, by mandatory partible inheritance laws. Therefore, one of the salient ways in which the late colonial state in Latin America constructed gender was to guarantee to women property rights and an equal share of their family's fortune. It is noteworthy that female property ownership may well explain, in part, the high proportion of female household heads in Ibero-America, relative to the number in Europe and the United States in the eighteenth and nineteenth centuries. My chapter in the second part of this volume explores this issue and its ramifications in the case of Nicaragua.

Of course, like all myths, the myth of the colonial woman without rights contains certain truths. Although less sexist than most contemporary systems of jurisprudence, the Ibero-American legal tradition profoundly circumscribed women's rights. First, only widows and unmarried adult females (if legally emancipated by fathers) exercised rights of contract and property. Married women and minors were subject to direct patriarchal control and forfeited their juridical persona, including administration of property, to their father or husband.[20] Second, women were not permitted to govern another person. Unlike men, who exercised patriarchal authority (*patria potestad*) over their wives and children, women had absolutely no legal authority over their children.[21] This contrast between female status vis-à-vis property and children had far-reaching implications, notably because few people (male or female) were property owners in this era, but many women headed households.[22]

In the late eighteenth century, when internal rebellion and external aggression were undermining the stability of the Spanish colonial state, the politics of gender acquired a new significance. As Chaves argues, toward the end of the colonial era, the official racial hierarchy was falling apart. First, miscegenation made it increasingly difficult to maintain separate racial groupings. Second, rich mestizos and mulattos often purchased racial mobility, or "whitening." These changes tended to blur race- and gender-based social distinctions. In their efforts to shore up the old social order, the Portuguese and Spanish colonial governments enacted laws in the 1770s that strengthened parents' rights to veto their children's choice of marriage partner.[23] Although at first glance these laws might seem of marginal significance, they were important signals of the states' attempts to reinforce more absolutist understandings of patriarchal authority in the home and in the body politic, as a number of historians have argued.[24]

In contrast to canon law, which before the 1770s had regulated marriage choice and which protected men's and women's freedom to select their spouse, the new secular laws expanded parents' rights to intervene if their child's proposed consort was of inferior social or racial status. It is significant that at a moment when the Crown sought to legitimate its rule, the state appropriated authority from the church. By circumscribing church powers in an area so economically important and so sacred as the regulation of marriage partners, the state moved to reinforce its political domination.[25]

In addition to treating the symbolic effects of this matrimonial law reform, historians have tracked its practical consequences.[26] Before the state claimed for itself the power to regulate choice of marriage partner, disputes between parents and children were argued in church courts. There, ecclesiastical judges were guided by the sacramental nature of marriage, which upheld the principle of free will regarding choice of marriage partner.[27] In other words, religious doctrine and practice had tended to restrict the authority of the family patriarch. However, following the reform, these disputes came under the jurisdiction of state courts, which sustained the father's authority to overrule—and to rule over—his children. This shift brings to the fore an important conceptual issue: secularization and its gendered effects. Reform of marital law was an early indicator of a trend that became increasingly apparent over the course of the nineteenth century: the transition from ecclesiastical to secular governance tended to strengthen patriarchal authority.

In Spanish America, the state's attempts to resurrect social practices associated with so-called traditional values collided with modernizing policies called forth by pressures for change. As a number of historians have noted, the late colonial state asserted a more absolutist model of patriarchal privilege at the same time as it dismantled certain exclusionary practices that sustained the patriarchal order.[28] Near its end, the colonial powers expanded educational and economic opportunities for females. In both areas, the entry of women into the male domain came about in response to a combination of enlightenment ideas and state efforts to promote economic growth. The Bourbon state in Spanish America encouraged basic education for women so they could more effectively moralize and educate their children. As William E. French argues, "Motherhood became a civic responsibility that only enlightened women could fulfil."[29] At the same time, the state overturned laws that barred women from joining artisan guilds.[30] Though the immediate impact of these reforms was limited, as few females enrolled in schools or joined guilds, they had a wider significance. The erosion of barriers to female education and employment laid the basis for women's autonomy from direct patriarchal authority.

Part Three: Exclusionary Republics

Following independence, the state virtually disappeared in Spanish America. The exceptions were few, notably Chile and Costa Rica.[31] In the rest of the region, elites fought among themselves not so much to control the state, which existed in name only, but to accumulate sufficient power to construct one. It is frequently noted that in periods of upheaval, politicians link appeals for order with calls for a return to patriarchal values. Paradoxically, during Spanish America's independence wars, both royalists and republicans claimed for themselves the patriarchal tradition. Rebecca Earle's chapter on the independence era in Colombia illustrates the ways in which royalists stressed the absolute authority of the king, and republicans emphasized the contingent nature of the Crown's patriarchal authority. Steve J. Stern's paradigm of contested patriarchal models, absolutist versus contingent, is appropriate here.[32] In a classic formulation of the contingent nature of patriarchal privilege, Simón Bolívar declared that because the king had violated his familial duties and obligations, the population had the right to rebel. In a more absolutist vein, royalists demanded obedience to the king and called on the population to "honor thy father."

After independence was won or, as in some places, granted by default, republicans accommodated their patriarchal discourse to the new situation. Leaders of the early republics, switching to an absolutist model of patriarchal rights, assumed the mantle of the benevolent father who de-manded obedience and respect from his children. Earle describes how the political elite in Colombia demobilized the female population, which had been drawn into active participation on both sides in the wars.[33] Following independence, considerable gender disorder remained as women's pres-ence continued to be felt in spheres regarded as exclusively male.[34] Politi-cians moved swiftly to make it clear that they would not tolerate female activities of this nature. They urged women to return home where they belonged and sought to marginalize them from the public sphere, sym-bolically as well as literally. In some regions, demographic change imposed a particular urgency on elite intentions to fortify patriarchal authority and remove women from the public domain. As a legacy of war, the population was overwhelmingly female in some of the new republics. For instance, in Argentina, females outnumbered males in the decades after independence by a ratio of approximately three to two, and the balance between the sexes was not restored until the middle of the century.[35]

The process by which political authority was reestablished in the half century following independence was deeply gendered. The new countries of Latin America remained highly unstable, debilitated by coups, intra-elite wars, popular rebellions, and banditry. As the corporate social order of the colonial era was gradually dismantled, the family became the bulwark of the new society.[36] Recognizing that the state was too weak to rule effec-tively, some politicians took comfort in the idea that elite family networks would serve as the glue to hold society together.[37] They advocated a politi-cal model wherein male elders represented both the family to the state and the state inside the family. With this in mind, politicians sought to enhance the powers of the family patriarch and to link their own claims to political authority with the traditional prerogatives of the family father.[38] The 1853 inaugural address of Nicaragua's supreme director, Fruto Chamorro, is emblematic of this political philosophy: "I consider myself as a loving but rigid father of the family [who] always seeks the welfare of his children. . . . I will maintain the peace, but like a good father of the family I will punish the wayward son who disturbs it."[39]

In the United States and Western Europe, politicians influenced by the Enlightenment advocated a fraternal contract that extended political rights exclusively to propertied males. They called this the "Liberal Contract," but Carole Pateman calls it the "sexual contract" because political rights were synonymous with patriarchal rights over women.[40] This sexual contract was spelled out in some of Latin America's first constitutions. In Mexico and Central America, for example, men became citizens at a younger age if they were married (provided, of course, they fulfilled the property requirement) than if they were single.[41] In a similar vein, citizenship could be suspended if a man showed ingratitude toward his father.[42] Such conditions underlined the importance Latin America's founding fathers accorded patriarchal authority in the home. As well as institutionalizing family patriarchy, the constitutions codified the public authority of elite patriarchs *cum* fathers. In this way, early republics were polities of propertied males who governed their subordinates, male and female, in and beyond the confines of their families.

Benedict Anderson argues that the transition from premodern sacred communities and dynastic realms to the imagined community of modern nation-states required new symbols to represent the nation and new ideologies to legitimate and support new forms of state power.[43] Such new symbols and ideologies were not the predominant characteristic of early Latin American nationalism, however. The imagined communities of the young republics largely reworked old symbols and traditional ideologies. In their search for stability, Latin America's republican leaders attempted to naturalize the patriarchalism they inherited. As a consequence, family patriarchy possibly acquired a greater political significance in the new society than it had had in the old.

Reforms in education and employment countered somewhat the trend toward state support of patriarchal absolutism with a protodevelopmentalist mentality; Mexican politicians made education obligatory for girls and boys between the ages of seven and fifteen. By the 1840s, the number of females and males enrolled in schools in Mexico City was roughly equal. Though females were denied access to secondary schooling, primary education opened up certain vocational opportunities for them, which in turn loosened the strictures of patriarchal control.[44] Such measures were a continuation of policies initiated by the colonial state and demonstrated a commitment by the region's new leaders to the principle of basic education for females.

Part Four: Gendered Liberalism

Latin America's liberal states ushered in two great social transformations: the large-scale privatization of land and the secularization of society. These reforms—or in the case of women, we might say "counterreforms"— radically altered the regulatory frameworks that governed gender relations. Laws promoting the rise of private property in land had largely negative implications for women because they were accompanied by provisions that abrogated much of the legal protection women had enjoyed "from time immemorial" to their share of family property. Secularization tended to reinforce wives' subordination to patriarchal authority. As states reworked the juridical frameworks that restricted and protected women, reforms tended to weaken women's historic rights to property and the church's official protection of sexual equality within marriage. At the same time, however, governments passed laws that strengthened women's personal rights, especially to control male violence. State regulation of gender followed similar trends across the continent; nevertheless, there were some significant differences in national experiences.

After independence in most of Spanish America, landowners, mineowners, and merchants were more preoccupied with fighting each other than with figuring out ways to appropriate the labor of the poor.[45] Once order was restored, around midcentury, elites sought to forge a state that above all would enable them to acquire land and labor to produce coffee, nitrates, metals, beef, and other products for export. Although ideological differences between liberals and conservatives have been exaggerated, liberals did tend to be more aggressive than their political rivals in dismantling corporate privileges inherited from the colonial era, privileges that they believed inhibited economic growth. Consequently, liberals viewed the church and the Indian Communities, where they existed, as prime targets for reform.[46] To this end, under the auspices of liberal politicians, the state introduced laws that subverted corporate land rights and vastly expanded private property in land.[47]

The rise of private property in land revolutionized the social order in every Latin American country in the nineteenth century. However, contrary to conventional wisdom, I maintain that rather than unleashing capitalism, the rise of private property in land retarded it in many countries.

With privatization, many small and medium peasants across the continent (with Brazil and the Argentine state the great exceptions) acquired some security of tenure and title to land.[48] This new form of *landedness* impeded the expansion of exports, liberals' primary goal. Exporters found it hard to appropriate labor from landed peasants, and peasant property inhibited the spread of a market in land. To resolve these difficulties, liberals in government in almost every country institutionalized forced labor regimes. Consequently, even more so than their counterparts in Western Europe and the United States, Latin America's liberals were obsessed with protecting the rights of property, while turning a blind eye to the rights of "man"—and woman.

The new property regime in Latin America had important implications for gender relations. Yet, little attention was paid to family law in the decades following independence for two reasons: first, politicians believed that patriarchal prerogatives imparted stability to a social order under threat; second, the state was too weak to enact new codes of law. Consequently, elaboration of civil and criminal codes, a central aspect of state regulation of gender, was postponed throughout Latin America until nation-states were stronger in the second half of the nineteenth century.

When jurists finally turned their attention to drafting new laws and legal codes for postcolonial society, several issues high on their agenda had major implications for gender—including property rights, inheritance rights, and parental authority. After independence, the first wave of family law reform reduced patriarchal authority over children.[49] In Mexico, Argentina, Brazil, and most other countries, changes to the civil codes released unmarried adults from parental authority and lowered the age of majority. These measures reduced the jurisdiction of male elders within the family and expanded the freedom of adult children, female and male, in personal and financial matters. However, jurists in almost all Latin American countries (e.g., Mexico, Chile, Argentina, Brazil, and Central America) rejected proposals to reduce patriarchal authority over married women. Consequently, wives were excluded from the general expansion in personal rights. As Silvia Arrom suggests, this exclusion in effect increased married women's relative subordination to their husbands.[50]

Justifying his opposition to the emancipation of wives, a Mexican jurist declared that wives should "recognize the authority of their consorts as heads of family, in order to maintain the order and tranquillity of families, on which the State in large part depends." And as another Mexican politician explained, if wives were emancipated from their husbands' authority, it would "risk the continued mutiny of the population against the established authority, and undermine the stability of the Mexican state."[51] Apparently these absolutist interpretations of patriarchal right enjoyed widespread popular support, at least among men. Drawing on a number of legal cases, Arrom found that most men believed their wives should remain subordinated to their authority.[52]

With the rise of private property in land, parents' legal obligation upon their death to divide property equally among their legitimate children, or mandatory partible inheritance, was abolished in Mexico, Central America, and other countries of the region. This reform had negative implications for women. From the proverbial "time immemorial," inheritance laws in the Spanish and Portuguese empires had required parents to distribute property and wealth equally to sons and daughters. These laws were in marked contrast to the Anglo-Saxon property regime in which primogeniture favored eldest sons. But the commission drafting the Mexican Civil Code of 1884, which ended obligatory partible inheritance, apparently was inspired by English law. In a speech justifying the reform of inheritance law, one jurist extolled England, "that great nation . . . that is today the most free and perhaps the most civilized in the world."[53] One may infer that he was voicing admiration for the Anglo-Saxon common law tradition in which the eldest son generally inherited landed property. This example suggests that some Mexican lawmakers believed subdivision of property contributed to economic backwardness. Perhaps they were right; nevertheless, the abolition of mandatory partible inheritance was detrimental to women. With new laws promoting privatization of land, which transformed property relations in all social strata, including the peasantry, the elimination of the guarantee that women receive an equal portion of their parents' estate, no matter how grand or humble it might be, worked to undermine women's economic security. In this context, it is particularly significant that mandatory partible inheritance remained in effect in Brazil, Argentina, and Uruguay until the middle of the twentieth century.[54] These contrasting paths suggest the need for cross-country comparisons on the effects of inheritance reform on female-male property ownership and on gender relations more widely.

In the second half of the nineteenth century, states made additional changes to family and property law that undermined women's rights to the family fortune, such as it might be. First, there was the end of the obligatory dowry; second, the abolition of the requirement that the property of married couples be jointly owned. The second reform allowed both men and women to exclude their spouse from sharing ownership. Although the first reform was characteristic of all Latin America,[55] the second pertained only to Mexico and Central America.[56] Muriel Nazzari has studied the effects of the "disappearance of the dowry" among families of the São Paulo elite. However, more research is needed before we will be able to discern regional trends in the practical consequences of these reforms or counterreforms.

Overall, the patriarchal inheritance system, which promoted gender parity in property ownership, was part of an ancien régime that liberal politicians sought to sweep away in their quest for "Order and Progress." Just as they regarded church and community property as impediments to the free market, so it seems they regarded the legal protection women enjoyed to land and wealth. In the eyes of more radical liberals, such as those in Mexico, these particular impediments had to be swept aside to make way for the revolutionary transformations that the market would bring.

The legal reform of property rights points to a widening of gender inequalities, particularly in Mexico. However, more research is needed to specify the long-term gendered consequences of liberal family and property laws in different regional and national contexts. In this regard, it is important to remember that the category *women*—insofar as it does not differentiate women according to status, class, ethnicity, and race—is of limited analytical value in tracking gender changes within the social order. For one, the effect of legal changes was different and often contradictory for single, widowed, and married women. Second, class, ethnicity, and race conditioned how women were affected by the law. Finally, the disjuncture between state policy and social practices also comes into play. For instance, where compulsory partible inheritance and community property were abolished in law, there is evidence that in practice they remained the norm.[57]

Research on the effects of liberal reforms on women's access to land points to the diversity of local, regional, and national experiences across Latin America. It shows that it is essential, for instance, to distinguish between indigenous women who lived in communities where communal property was dismembered and women who had for centuries been part of the private property sector. It is noteworthy that among indigenous regions there is evidence of a heterogeneity of experiences. Florencia Mallon's analysis of the sexual differentiation of land privatization in Puebla, Mexico, suggests that law reform had negative consequences for women. None of the new land titles distributed in the 1860s went to women; they obtained access to land only by virtue of their ties to men, or as wives and mothers.[58] Although Mallon's conclusion is supported by another study from Mexico,[59] those experiences contrast with other cases where land privatization dismantled barriers to Indian women's acquisition of land.[60] We might conclude, tentatively, that although land privatization reduced men's common property rights, its effect on women was more contradictory. Where it extended the rule of Hispanic laws and practices, such as in the former Indian communities, liberal agrarian reforms may have expanded poor women's opportunities to own and control land.

Liberal reforms to property and family law were not all of a piece. However, it would seem that change moved in the direction of expanding gender inequalities.[61] Reform to inheritance law had negative implications for gender parity insofar as it reduced protective measures for women. In contrast, what I call the "ladinoization of gender" in Nicaragua may have benefited indigenous women in that it opened the way for them to acquire rights to property, a way previously blocked by customary practices in Indian communities.

Part Five: Secularization of Marriage

The second great transformation effected by liberal states was the secularization of society. In Latin America, the majority of incipient nation-states sought to legitimate their authority by wresting power from the church. In part this battle was played out in the realm of gender. Governments appropriated for themselves powers previously wielded by the Catholic Church—the regulation of marriage, annulment, sexuality, and legitimacy of birth. Insofar as the state claimed for itself the authority to regulate so central and traditionally sacred areas of life, it was a bold move.

Lewis Namier warned against imagining the past in terms of our own experience.[62] This caveat is particularly relevant for studying the historical construction of gender. For instance, it is often argued that the Catholic Church has always undermined gender equality. The conclusion scholars draw from this interpretation is that secularization has always modernized the gender order.[63] Neither the former nor the latter propositions are entirely true in the case of Latin America. Secularization in Latin America had contradictory gendered effects over the course of the long nineteenth century.[64] To the extent that Catholicism naturalized the notion that motherhood was the sole purpose of women's lives, it played a reactionary role. However, Catholic doctrine held that marriage was a sacred union of equals; to the extent that the church put into practice this article of faith, secularization thus tended to expand inequalities between men and women, particularly within marriage.

There is increasing evidence that state regulation of marriage and sexuality reinforced patriarchal authority over wives in the nineteenth century. Analyzing changes in the policing of married life in Costa Rica, Eugenia Rodríguez argues that after independence in 1821, when the state assumed authority over marriage, secular courts attempted to modernize, not to reduce, patriarchal power. Drawing on legal cases, she highlights how courts played a role in civilizing husbands' behavior toward wives. A similar point is made by Donna J. Guy, who analyzes court cases in Argentina later in the century.

The particular "liberal" combination of privatization and secularization had negative repercussions for many women. In the 1770s, royal decrees strengthened patriarchal control over family fortunes; one hundred years later, in the 1870s, the state again intervened to protect patriarchal control over children and money. With the rise of private property, the question of heirs became relevant to broader sectors of society. Consequently, although colonial laws had regulated the identification of legitimate heirs, civil codes drafted by liberal states reinforced a husband's control over his wife's body for inheritance purposes. For instance, the codes spelled out that husbands could appoint their own "representatives" to witness their wives giving birth, and in cases of marital separation husbands were empowered to place estranged wives under the protection of an honorable family for ten months. The objective of both measures was undoubtedly to assist men in identifying their offspring.[65]

Perhaps the clearest contrast between religious and secular regulation of marriage concerned adultery. In Catholic doctrine, adultery by husbands and wives is equally sinful, and there is evidence that ecclesiastical courts in Latin America tended to judge male and female adulterers similarly.[66] That changed after the regulation of marriage and adultery passed from the church to the state. In the nineteenth century, Latin America's civil codes virtually legalized adultery for males and made it a capital offence for females. In Mexico, Argentina, and Nicaragua, for instance, a husband's infidelity was neither criminalized nor considered grounds for divorce unless it took place in the marriage bed or created a public scandal.[67] This legal tolerance did not extend to wives; if a husband could prove that his wife had sex with another man, he enjoyed impunity within the law to kill her. In practice, this impunity was often extended to husbands whose wives were considered to be promiscuous in the "public's opinion." In other words, regarding sexual mores, secularization tended to override the church-based single standard with a double standard, although perhaps only to codify existing customs and attitudes.[68] It is significant that male adultery remained legal and female adultery remained criminal in most countries of the region well into the twentieth century.[69]

Secularization did not create a blanket system of heightened gendered oppression. Late-nineteenth-century legal reforms benefited women in several ways. Over the course of the long nineteenth century, women's legal authority over their children increased slowly, if unevenly. In the late colony, widows and single mothers were legally responsible to provide for and protect their children, but had no legal authority over them. By the close of the nineteenth century, in most countries all *except* married women had the right to govern their children.[70] Despite its narrow reach, this reform was a watershed in Latin America. It marked the first time women were legally permitted to exercise authority over another person. It is significant, however, that wives were not granted parental authority over their children until after the turn of the twentieth century when women's organizations fought for reform of patria potestad.

Liberal states advanced the cause of women in a number of other ways, including increased intervention in the domestic sphere to control male violence. Three chapters in this volume examine the implementation of laws designed to protect women and children from abuse. Rodríguez describes how courts in Costa Rica tended to punish husbands who physically abused their wives. She goes on to argue that the courts attempted to impose on all sectors of society an upper-class marriage ideal that normalized the roles of male breadwinner and female homemaker. This differentiation of gender roles within the family was new to the lower classes. The upper-class family model was detrimental to the poorer sectors of society, especially because it delegitimated a gamut of women's traditional economic activities outside the home. Rodríguez concludes that in the end, the expansion of judicial regulation of marriage that accompanied the consolidation of the liberal state had contradictory consequences for men and women.

The modernization of patriarchal power over wives is one of the leitmotifs of this collection, treated explicitly in chapters about the nineteenth century by Eugenia Rodríguez and Donna J. Guy.[71] Turning to the twentieth century, Mary Kay Vaughn analyzes how the postrevolutionary state in Mexico attempted to remake the peasant family in the interests of nation building and development. Ann Varley examines another aspect of modernization of patriarchy in Mexico. Drawing on Ana María Alonso, she argues that the state attempted to replace violence as a source of authority in the domestic sphere with more "modern" and reasoned notions of patriarchal power.

Charting the history of state regulation of fatherhood in Argentina, Guy shows that just as the state was empowered to protect patriarchal authority by granting men rights and privileges, it could also rescind those powers if a judge decided that a father had not fulfilled his paternal obligations. Through an examination of court cases, mostly for the later nineteenth century, she describes how the Argentine state weakened the absolute authority of the family patriarch. Notwithstanding men's contention that the state had no right to interfere in private family matters, courts abrogated the patria potestad of negligent and violent fathers. Guy found, however, that even when judges ruled against abusive fathers, they did so halfheartedly, apparently loath to diminish patriarchal authority. Her research shows that courts tended to take the word of fathers over mothers, with the overall effect of reinforcing men's patriarchal authority. In support of this view, she demonstrates that even in sentencing abusive fathers and husbands, judges often let them off with warnings or light punishments.

Notwithstanding the limits of state intervention in Latin America with regard to gender relations in the home, Guy argues that state powers to curb the authority of the patriarch within the family was and is a characteristic that distinguishes Latin America from other parts of the so-called

Third World. As she points out, the contrast between Latin America and the Middle East is particularly striking, where male power in the home has been less encumbered by the state. Guy underlines an important issue that merits comparative research to discern the causes and consequences of these contrasting models of state action regarding gender.

Throughout Latin America, secularization opened the way for radical measures on the issue of divorce. In Mexico, where marriage was removed from church authority in 1859, the Civil Code of 1884 permitted marital separation on the grounds of mutual incompatibility. This change was a milestone because the law upheld the principle that the rights and happiness of individuals—women and men—were more important than preservation of the family. Although it is important to remember that in the nineteenth century the Mexican state did not go all the way toward legalizing divorce, as some lawyers and legislators proposed, its steps in this direction, hesitant though they might seem, were remarkable.[72] Finally, and also on the positive side, in the late nineteenth century, secularization spawned the expansion of nonreligious education, much of it vocational in nature. This expansion was emancipatory, particularly for women who over the next decades would enter the paid labor force in increasing numbers.[73]

Part Six: The Long Century's End

The nineteenth century was long for women. Organizations of and for women emerged only toward the end of the century in Latin America. Prior to the birth of protofeminist associations, state policy was rarely framed in response to female mobilization. The lack of female voices in legal debates may explain why the rise of private property in Latin America was associated with a decline in protective measures that historically had guaranteed women a fair share of their family's wealth.

In the first decades of the twentieth century, female protagonists appeared on the political stage, calling for changes in state policy toward women.[74] In increasing numbers, women directly confronted the state—demanding the vote, improved working conditions, and changes to family and property law. This confrontation marked a watershed. Exceedingly slowly and very unevenly, Latin American states dismantled some of the legal and institutional foundations of patriarchal authority. The process dragged on for another century and continues to unfold with the turn of the millennium.

Historians—including historians who study gender—have tended to present the past as a narrative of progressive, sometimes linear change. Women's history is often imbued with a deeply teleological current, one that perpetuates the idea that over time gender inequalities have been and will be incrementally dismantled. However often we remind ourselves that history is not linear, the idea retains a certain power. The long nineteenth century in Latin America is generally viewed as an era of progressive modernization of gender relations, characterized by slow but steady advances in state policy toward women. Although elements of this interpretation are valid, this essay suggests that future research may reveal that state action over the long nineteenth century hardened patriarchal authority in important areas of life.[75] Such findings would lend weight to the view that it was the rise of organizations of and for women—feminist organizations—around the turn of the twentieth century that pushed states to move more consistently in the direction of dismantling patriarchal privileges.

Notes

To the extent this essay successfully balances the general with the particular in its interpretation of regional trends in state-gender relations, it is because a number of scholars have shared generously of their time and expertise. In addition to the contributors to this volume, I thank Silvia Arrom, Asunción Lavrin, Susan Besse, Carmen Ramos Escandón, Muriel Nazzari, Robbie Gray, Elizabeth Kuznesof, and the anonymous reviewers. The essay has also benefited from discussions with John Weeks, Steven Topik, Lowell Gudmundson, and Anwar Shaikh.

1 Joan W. Scott, "Gender: A Useful Category of Historical Analysis," *American Historical Review* 91, no. 5 (December 1986): 1053–75.

2 For recent periodizations of the Latin American state, see Menno Vellinga, ed., *The Changing Role of the State in Latin America* (Boulder, Colo.: Westview, 1998)—in particular, chapters by Vellinga and Smith.

3 It is noteworthy that in the excellent collection edited by Vellinga, *Changing Role of the State,* with thirteen essays on the state in Latin America, none is about gender and the state. Joe Foweraker's chapter, "Social Movements and Citizenship Rights in Latin America" (285–88), is the only contribution that addresses gender issues at all. This absence is all the more notable because, as Sarah

Radcliffe argues, although in the 1980s and 1990s, Latin American states have significantly "rolled back," in policies affecting women they have "rolled forward." Sarah A. Radcliffe, "Latina Labour: Restructuring of Work and Renegotiations of Gender Relations in contemporary Latin America," *Environment and Planning* 31, no. 2 (1999): 196–208.

4 R. W. Connell, "The State, Gender, and Sexual Politics: Theory and Appraisal," in *Power / Gender: Social Relations in Theory and Practice,* ed. H. Lorraine Radtke and Hendrikus J. Stam (London and Thousand Oaks, Calif.: Sage, 1994), 136–73, and *Gender and Power: Society, the Person, and Sexual Politics* (Oxford: Polity, 1987); Shirin M. Rai and Geraldine Lievesley, eds., *Women and the State: International Perspectives* (London: Taylor and Francis, 1996).

5 Joan Scott, "Women in History: The Modern Period," *Past and Present* 101 (1983): 141–57; Elizabeth Fox-Genovese, "Placing Women's History in History," *New Left Review* 133 (1982): 5–29.

6 Joan Kelly-Gadol, "Did Women Have a Renaissance?" in *Becoming Visible: Women in European History,* ed. Renate Bridenthal and Claudia Koonz (Boston: Houghton and Mifflin, 1977), 137–64.

7 Carmen Ramos Escandón analyzes this question with regard to Mexico in "Reading Gender in History," in *Gender Politics in Latin America: Debates in Theory and Practice,* Elizabeth Dore, ed. (New York: Monthly Review, 1997), 149–60.

8 For Latin American historians, the long nineteenth century generally begins with the Bourbon Reforms in the 1760s and ends with the Great Depression in 1930. For the purposes of this analysis of gender and state making, the long nineteenth century refers to the era from 1760 to 1900.

9 This theme runs through the volume. See, in particular, chapters by Rodríguez, Chaves, Dore, Guy, Rosemblatt, Gotkowitz, and Vaughan.

10 In *Foundational Fictions: The National Romances of Latin America* (Berkeley: University of California Press, 1991), Doris Sommer demonstrates how gendered symbols and ideologies were reworked in the construction of the political legitimacy of the white (European) male republican elite in Latin America. For analysis of how gendered ideals are represented in official ceremonies, see Gotkowitz in this volume, and Marjorie Becker, "Torching La Purísima, Dancing at the Alter: The Construction of Revolutionary Hegemony in Michoacán, 1934–1940," in *Everyday Forms of State Formation: Revolution and Negotiation of Rule in Modern Mexico,* ed. Gilbert Joseph and Daniel Nugent (Durham, N.C.: Duke University Press, 1994), 247–64.

11 The term *field of force* is from William Roseberry, "An Introduction," in *Coffee, Society, and Power in Latin America,* ed. William Roseberry, Lowell Gudmundson, and Mario Samper Kutschbach (Baltimore: Johns Hopkins University Press, 1995), 1–33. Anwar Shaikh suggested the gravitational field analogy.

12 For my interpretation of the noncapitalist nature of some Latin American countries in the nineteenth century, see Elizabeth Dore, "Land Privatization and the Differentiation of the Peasantry: Nicaragua's Coffee Revolution, 1850–

1920," *Journal of Historical Sociology* 8, no. 3 (September 1995): 303–26, and my work in progress, "The Myth of Modernity: Nicaragua, 1840–1979."

13 Philip Corrigan and Derek Sayer, *The Great Arch: English State Formation as Cultural Revolution* (Oxford and New York: Basil Blackwell, 1985). For application to Latin America, see Joseph and Nugent, eds., *Everyday Forms.*

14 Florencia E. Mallon analyzes an alternative "popular liberalism" in *Peasant and Nation: The Making of Postcolonial Mexico and Peru* (Berkeley: University of California Press, 1995).

15 Silvia Marina Arrom was the first to use the term *corporate patriarchy. The Women of Mexico City, 1790–1857* (Stanford: Stanford University Press, 1985), 76.

16 Patricia J. Williams, "The Contentiousness of Their Character," *The Nation* 268, no. 1 (4 January 1999), 10. Her argument is drawn from Ariela Gross, "Litigating Whiteness," *Yale Law Journal* 108 (1998): 109–89.

17 Colonial law was based on the Siete Partidas, the Leyes de Toro, and the Council of Trent, which date from the fifteenth and sixteenth centuries.

18 Arrom, *Women of Mexico City,* 95 ff.; and Patricia Seed, *To Love, Honor, and Obey in Colonial Mexico* (Stanford: Stanford University Press, 1988), 61–108.

19 This view is presented in a number of studies, including Jean Franco, *Plotting Women: Gender and Representation in Mexico* (New York: Columbia University Press, 1990).

20 The question of the proportion of women subject to direct patriarchal control is open to debate. As Arrom shows, the census of 1811 for Mexico City lists as married only 44 percent of women age twenty-five or over—a minority. The rest were listed as single or widowed. The majority would have exercised rights to property and wealth. See, *Women of Mexico City,* chap. 3.

21 Asunción Lavrin includes qualifiers in her remarks about women's exercise of patria potestad in the late colonial era. "Women in Spanish American Colonial Society," in *Cambridge History of Latin America,* 11 vols., ed. Leslie Bethell (Cambridge: Cambridge University Press, 1984), 2:327.

22 The consensus in Latin American family history is that in the late eighteenth and nineteenth centuries a large number of households across the region were headed by women. For a summary and critique of Latin American family history, see Elizabeth Dore, "The Holy Family: Imagined Households in Latin American History," in Dore, ed., *Gender Politics in Latin America,* 101–17. Also, K. Lynn Stoner, "Directions in Latin American Women's History, 1977–1985," *Latin American Research Review* 22, no. 2 (1987): 101–34; Elizabeth Anne Kuznesof, "The History of the Family in Latin America: A Critique of Recent Work," *Latin American Research Review* 24, no. 2 (1989): 168–86; and the special issue of the *Journal of Family History* 16, no. 3 (1991).

23 In the Spanish Empire, these changes were decreed in Royal Pragmaticas. In Mexico, the Pragmatica became law in 1776, and 1778 in Argentina. Portugal passed a similar law in 1775. For analysis of its effects in Brazil, see Muriel

Nazzari, *The Disappearance of the Dowry: Families and Social Change in São Paulo* (Stanford: Stanford University Press, 1991), 130–32 and n. 24.

24 Lavrin, "Women in Spanish American Colonial Society," 321–55; John Tutino, "Power, Class, and Family: Men and Women in the Mexican Elite, 1750–1810," *The Americas* 39, no. 3 (1983): 359–82; Seed, *To Love, Honor, and Obey;* Arrom, *Women of Mexico City,* 11, 62, 77.

25 A caveat is in order. Insofar as the decree was enacted throughout the Spanish Empire, emphasis on the particular vulnerability of the colonial state might be a mistake.

26 Seed, *To Love, Honor, and Obey,* 227–41; Susan M. Socolow, "Acceptable Partners: Marriage Choice in Colonial Argentina, 1780–1810," in *Sexuality and Marriage in Colonial Latin America,* ed. Asunción Lavrin (Lincoln and London: University of Nebraska Press, 1989), 209–36; Verena Martínez-Alier, *Marriage, Class, and Colour in Nineteenth Century Cuba: A Study of Racial Attitudes and Sexual Values in a Slave Society,* 2d ed. (Ann Arbor: University of Michigan Press, 1989).

27 Seed, *To Love, Honor, and Obey,* 5.

28 Lavrin, "Women in Spanish American Colonial Society"; Arrom, *Women of Mexico City,* chap. 2.

29 William E. French, "Prostitutes and Guardian Angels: Women, Work, and the Family in Porfirian Mexico," *Hispanic American Historical Review* 72, no. 4 (1992), 532.

30 María de la Luz Parcero, *Condiciones de la mujer en México durante el Siglo XIX* (Mexico City: Instituto Nacional de Anthropologia e Historia, 1992), 54, 70; Arrom, *Women of Mexico City,* 18.

31 For the Costa Rican case, see Iván Molina Jiménez, *Historia de Costa Rica* (San José: Editorial Universidad de Costa Rica, 1998).

32 Steve J. Stern, *The Secret History of Gender: Women, Men, and Power in Late Colonial Mexico* (Chapel Hill and London: University of North Carolina Press, 1995), 20 ff.

33 These were the first examples in Latin America of the mobilization of women into sex-segregated organizations, other than for religious purposes. Arrom, *Women of Mexico City,* 11.

34 Francine Masiello, "Women, State, and Family in Latin American Literature of the 1920s," in Seminar on Feminism and Culture in Latin America, *Women, Culture, and Politics in Latin America* (Berkeley and Oxford: University of California Press, 1990), 27–47.

35 Mark Szuchman, *Order, Family, and Community in Buenos Aires, 1810–1860* (Stanford: Stanford University Press, 1988), 190.

36 Ibid., 225–30; Masiello, "Women, State, and Family," 33; Arrom, *Women of Mexico City,* 77; E. Bradford Burns, *Patriarch and Folk: The Emergence of Nicaragua, 1789–1858* (Cambridge, Mass.: Harvard University Press, 1991), 76.

37 Stoner, "Directions in Latin American Women's History," 101–34; Diana A. Balmori and Stuart Voss, *Notable Family Networks in Latin America* (Chicago: Univer-

sity of Chicago Press, 1984); Larissa Lomnitz and Marisol Pérez Lizaur, "The History of a Mexican Urban Family," *Journal of Family History* 3, no. 4 (winter 1978): 392–409; Linda Lewin, "Some Historical Implications of Kinship Organizations for Family-Based Politics in the Brazilian Northeast," *Comparative Studies in Society and History* 21, no. 2 (1979): 262–92; Elizabeth Kuznesof, "A familia na sociedade brasileira: Parentesco, clientelismo, y estructura social, São Paulo, 1700–1980," *Revista Brasileira de Historia,* ANPUH 9, no. 17 (September 1988–February 1989): 37–63. For a comparative perspective, see Sarah Handley's argument that propertied dynasties were the mainstay of the French state; "Social Sites of Political Practice in France: Lawsuits, Civil Rights, and the Separation of Powers in Domestic and State Government, 1500–1800," *American Historical Review* 102, no. 1 (1997): 27–52.

38 Szuchman, *Order, Family, and Community,* 225–35; Masiello, "Women, State, and Family," 27–47. Sandra McGee Deutsch argues that this model continued well into the twentieth century. See "Gender and Sociopolitical Change in Twentieth-Century Latin America," *Hispanic American Historical Review* 71, no. 2 (1991): 259–306.

39 Burns, *Patriarch and Folk,* 80. Chamorro's inaugural address was first published in *La Gaceta Oficial de Nicaragua* (Granada), 4 October 1853.

40 Carole Pateman, *The Sexual Contract* (Cambridge: Polity, 1988).

41 Burns, writing on the Nicaraguan Constitution of 1838, *Patriarch and Folk,* 78; Donna J. Guy, *Sex and Danger in Buenos Aires: Prostitution, Family, and Nation in Argentina* (Lincoln: University of Nebraska Press, 1991).

42 Burns, *Patriarch and Folk,* 80.

43 Benedict Anderson, *Imagined Communities: Reflections on the Origin and Spread of Nationalism* (London: Verso, 1983), 6, 131.

44 Francoise Carner, "Estereotipos femininos en el siglo XIX," in *Presencia y transparencia: La mujer en la historia de Mexico,* ed. Carmen Ramos Escandón (Mexico City: El Colegio de Mexico, 1987), 95–110; Arrom, *Women of Mexico City,* 21–27; Parcero, *Condiciones de la mujer,* 70; Lavrin, "Women in Spanish American Colonial Society," 345.

45 E. Bradford Burns, *The Poverty of Progress: Latin America in the Nineteenth Century* (New York: Norton, 1986).

46 Whereas Brazil had liberal and conservative governments, the Portuguese had never granted communal land rights to Indians. Consequently, in Brazil there was no process of privatizing corporate lands of Indian Communities.

47 Robert G. Williams, *States and Social Evolution: Coffee and the Rise of National Governments in Central America* (Chapel Hill: University of North Carolina Press, 1994). Dore, "Land Privatization and the Differentiation of the Peasantry."

48 David McCreery, *Rural Guatemala, 1760–1940* (Stanford: Stanford University Press, 1994); Alan Knight, *The Mexican Revolution* 2 vols. (Cambridge: Cambridge University Press, 1986), vol. 1.

49 This discussion of changes to family law is based on Arrom, *Women of Mexico*

City, 55–96; Silvia Marina Arrom, "Changes in Mexican Family Law in the Nineteenth Century: The Civil Codes of 1870 and 1884," *Journal of Family History* 10, no. 3 (fall 1985): 376–91; and Donna Guy, "Lower Class Families, Women, and the Law in Nineteenth Century Argentina," *Journal of Family History* 10, no. 3 (fall 1985): 318–31.

50 Arrom, *Women of Mexico City,* 93–96.

51 Arrom, "Changes in Mexican Family Law," 92.

52 Arrom, *Women of Mexico City,* 231.

53 Arrom, "Changes in Mexican Family Law," 96–97.

54 For Brazil, see Muriel Nazzari, "Widows as Obstacles to Business: British Objections to Brazilian Marriage and Inheritance Laws," *Comparative Studies in Society and History* 37, no. 4 (October 1995): 781–802. For the Southern Cone, see Asunción Lavrin, *Women, Feminism, and Social Change in Argentina, Chile, and Uruguay, 1890–1940* (Lincoln: University of Nebraska Press, 1995), chap. 6.

55 On dowries in Brazil, see Nazzari, *Disappearance of the Dowry* and "Widows as Obstacles"; also, Alida Metcalf, *Family and Frontier in Colonial Brazil* (Berkeley: University of California Press, 1992). For Mexico, see Asunción Lavrin and Edith Couturier, "Dowries and Wills: A View of Women's Socio-Economic Role in Colonial Guadalajara and Puebla, 1640–1790," *Hispanic American Historical Review* 59, no. 2 (1979): 280–304.

56 Arrom, "Changes in Mexican Family Law," 95.

57 Correspondence with Silvia Arrom, October 1996.

58 Florencia Mallon, "Exploring the Origins of Democratic Patriarchy in Mexico: Gender and Popular Resistance in the Puebla Highlands, 1850–1876," in *Creating Spaces, Shaping Transitions: Women of the Mexican Countryside, 1850–1996,* ed. Heather Fowler-Salamini and Mary Kay Vaughan (Tucson: University of Arizona Press, 1994), 3–26.

59 Deborah Kanter, "Native Female Land-Tenure and Its Decline in Mexico, 1750–1900," *Ethnohistory* 42, no. 2 (1995): 607–16.

60 See my chapter on Nicaragua in this volume. Also, Daniel Nugent and Ana María Alonso, "Multiple Selective Traditions in Agrarian Reform and Agrarian Struggle: Popular Culture and State Formation in the Ejido of Namiquipa, Chihuahua," in Joseph and Nugent, eds., *Everyday Forms of State Formation,* 209–46; Heather Fowler-Salamini, "Gender, Work, and Coffee in Cordoba, Veracruz, 1850–1910," and Francine R. Chassen-Lopez, "Cheaper Than Machines: Women and Agriculture in Porfirian Oaxaca, 1880–1911," both in Fowler-Salamini and Vaughan, eds., *Women of the Mexican Countryside,* 27–73.

61 This argument is to an extent consistent with, but not the same as, Frederick Engels, *The Origin of the Family, Private Property, and the State* (London: Lawrence and Wishart, 1973).

62 "One would expect people to remember the past and imagine the future. But in fact when discoursing or writing about history, they imagine it in terms of their own experience, and when trying to gauge the future, they cite supposed analo-

gies from the past: till, by a double process of repitition, they imagine the past and remember the future." Lewis Namier, *Conflicts: Studies in Contemporary History* (London: Macmillan, 1942), 4.

63 For the former, see Marta Lamas, "Scenes from a Mexican Battlefield," *NACLA: Report on the Americas* 31, no. 4 (January–February 1998): 17–22; for a critique of the latter view, see Deniz Kandiyoti, "End of Empire: Islam, Nationalism, and Women in Turkey," in *Women, Islam and the State*, ed. Deniz Kandiyoti (London: Macmillan, 1991), 22–47.

64 Lyndal Roper makes a similar argument for the effects of the Reformation in Western Europe; see *Oedipus and the Devil: Witchcraft, Sexuality, and Religion in Early Modern Europe* (London: Routledge, 1994).

65 Dore, "The Holy Family," 108–11.

66 Martinez-Alier, *Marriage, Class, and Colour.*

67 Arrom, "Changes in Mexican Family Law," 94; Dore, "The Holy Family," 111; Guy, "Lower Class Families," 318–31.

68 Silvia Arrom makes the same argument in "Changes in Mexican Family Law," 305–17.

69 Lavrin, *Women, Feminism, and Social Change*, chaps. 4, 5, 6.

70 For the case of Mexico, see Arrom, "Changes in Mexican Family Law," 91.

71 The modernization of patriarchy in Brazil is analyzed by Susan K. Besse, *Restructuring Patriarchy: The Modernization of Gender Inequality in Brazil, 1914–1940* (Chapel Hill: University of North Carolina Press, 1996).

72 Lavrin, *Women, Feminism, and Social Change*, chap. 7; Arrom, "Changes in Mexican Family Law."

73 Mary K. Vaughan, "Women, Class, and Education in Mexico, 1880–1928," *Latin American Perspectives* 4, nos. 1–2 (winter–spring 1977): 135–52.

74 The first women's organizations were founded in Brazil and Argentina. Lavrin, introduction to *Women, Feminism, and Social Change*; K. Lynn Stoner, *From the House to the Street: The Cuban Woman's Movement for Legal Reform, 1898–1940* (Durham, N.C., and London: Duke University Press, 1991); Besse, *Restructuring Patriarchy*; and June E. Hahner, "The Nineteenth Century Feminist Press and Women's Rights in Brazil," in *Latin American Women: Historical Perspectives*, ed. Asunción Lavrin (Westport, Conn., and London: Greenwood, 1978), 254–85.

75 This interpretation is shared by Arrom, "Mexican Women: Historical Perspectives," lecture delivered at Brandeis University, 23 October 1991; and Lavrin, *Women, Feminism, and Social Change*, chap. 6.

Maxine Molyneux

Twentieth-Century

State Formations in Latin America

Recent feminist historiography has begun to document changes in women's social and legal position over the course of the twentieth century in Latin America.[1] It has emphasized the contribution of women's movements to this process, uncovering what had indeed been a hidden history of female activism. If this activism helped to propel such momentous changes in gender relations, it was more often than not directed at states; women's movements lobbied their governments for change, sometimes opposing policies and sometimes entering into opposition to military rule. Governments varied in their responses and in their policies with respect to gender relations, but gender issues became an integral part of their policies and programs.

The turn to democracy in the mid-1980s in Latin America brought the state under scrutiny as a focus of feminist politics and policy. At the same time, scholars began to investigate the role that states have played and continue to play in the ordering of social life, whether directly through legislation or indirectly through social and economic policy. Yet the state, as an object of theory and empirical investigation, was not a major theoretical concern within Latin American feminism, as it was in Europe and the United States. Different historical circumstances produced distinct analytic concerns. In the latter, feminist political theorists were interrogating the history of Western liberalism and critiquing the shortcomings of liberal democracy; in Latin America, much of which was in the grip of military dictatorships, social movements constituted the main political dynamic and the locus of scholarly attention.[2]

The extensive scholarship on the state in twentieth-century Latin America did not deploy gender as a category of analysis.[3] This neglect was in part a reflection of the normative bias of male-dominated disciplines, but it was also an effect of the theoretical approaches to the state that predominated from the mid-1970s. Political theorists were concerned with identifying the specificity of state forms in relation to institutional arrangements or capitalist economies, and under the influence of structural Marxism, a body of work on the variant forms of the capitalist state emerged. This work included discussion of the exceptionalist authoritarian regimes of Southern Europe, which suggested parallels with the military regimes that came to power in many Latin American countries from the mid-1960s.[4] Latin American scholars contributed to this work, taking up a theme long present in regional debates on the state: its autonomy from class forces. An extensive literature sought to understand the specific nature of what came to be called, following Guillermo O'Donnell, the "bureaucratic-authoritarian" state, a nomenclature that reflected both the accelerated expansion of the state bureaucracies that took place in Latin America during this period and the ascendancy of a more technocratic, less ideological ruling group. These states were identified as having inaugurated a new regime of capital accumulation, one that broke with the prevailing Cepalista[5] consensus and redirected Latin American economies toward the global market, while brutally suppressing populist institutions, expectations, and aspirations.[6]

Meanwhile, in a parallel but unconnected project, feminist theorizing in Latin America, in common with that elsewhere, was initially more concerned with providing a gendered account of capitalist development than with issues of state power.[7] It took the economic crisis of the 1980s to bring these gendered analyses of the economy into mainstream policy debates over the human costs of adjustment. As in the economic domain, so in the political: the central feminist insight was that the private or reproductive sphere, the social terrain upon which gender divisions and inequalities are constituted, lies at the interface between state and civil society. If, in Latin America, the 1980s was therefore a decade in which gender analysis revolutionized development policy debates, it was also one in which the state was reconceptualized. The turn to democracy in the latter half of the 1980s occurred at a time when the impact of new trends in social theory opened up the terrain of state-society relations to fuller exploration. There were many tributary elements in this shift: the demise of structuralist Marxism, the influence of Gramsci's theory of hegemony, and French poststructuralism were all significant, but so too was the work of neo-Weberians within the field of historical sociology.[8] A proposition common to several of these approaches—that a crucial dimension of state power is implicated in the articulation or reproduction of social relations—was interpreted to include a broader focus than class relations, embracing gendered and racialized formations along with their cultural and institutional modalities. Political theorists in effect began to rehabilitate "the social" as an object of analysis;[9] in so doing they encountered a flourishing field of scholarship in the fields of sociology and history that suggested that gender was an important element in and cast new light on the sociopolitical dimensions of institutionalized power.

While theoretical developments within the field of politics and power are necessarily diverse, two contrasting but sometimes overlapping fields of study have made their mark on the more recent Latin American literature on gender and politics. The first is citizenship studies, influenced by the rediscovery of T. H. Marshall's pioneering work.[10] This interest in citizenship was reawakened in the 1980s when political sociologists were engaged in elaborating comparative and historical approaches to state formation. The work of Bryan Turner, Michael Mann, Philip Corrigan and Derek Sayer, among others, critiqued and developed Marshall's analysis for, among other things, its "stagism" and its lack of comparative reach. Turner, on the basis of historical and regional studies, argued that the evolution of the different elements of citizenship (civil, political, social) was a contingent and variable process and one, moreover, that was in constant flux. This opened the way for international comparisons of the evolution of citizenship and of its variable meanings and modalities.[11]

Citizenship studies have since focused attention on the processes of inclusion and exclusion within nation states. As citizenship cannot be understood in abstraction from the social domain, it has provided a framework for problematizing the changing relations between state and society. As the legal and cultural foundation of the relation between state and society, citizenship specifies the basis of social membership and of the social contract that it implies. In postauthoritarian Latin America,[12] citizenship has become the currency of much political and development work, and has provided a framework for interpreting the history of Latin American state evolution. In the 1990s, citizenship studies have begun to engage with the more recent changes that have attended globalization and the ascendancy of neoliberal policies in the region.[13]

The recuperation of citizenship has had a specific gender focus. In deconstructing the assumptions underlying liberal theory, the work of feminist theorists, notably that of Carole Pateman and Jean Bethke Elshstain, has exposed the masculinist bias that inhered in its conception of politics and citizenship.[14] The liberal construct of the individual has been shown to be an abstraction postulated upon a masculine ideal and associated with public life, whereas relations between the sexes and the work within the private sphere were naturalized, as was women's subordination within marriage. The sexual contract underlying the civil contract of liberal polities has since been the subject of extensive feminist inquiry, one paralleled by the efforts of women's movements to redefine the terms of women's inscription into citizenship on more favorable terms. In Latin America, as the chapters in this volume show, struggles for citizenship have animated women's movements throughout the course of the twentieth century. They have posed and reposed the unresolved question of how citizenship can be reformulated to encompass gender difference without at the same time signifying inequality.

The other significant development in the field of Latin American studies, which has engaged gender relations, has been the shift away from state-centered analyses toward society-centered analyses of power and authority. This development, inspired above all by Foucault's work, has greatly enriched understanding of the multiple processes within the family, community, civil society, and cultural practices that work to normalize patterns of authority, privilege, and marginalization. It has brought the social relations of power into sharper focus and has provided a fertile terrain for gender analysis. However, the focus on the social and decentered dimensions of power not only has entailed a shift away from the state, but has in many cases led to its being excluded from the analysis altogether. Yet, if the state is not the sole repository of power, it nonetheless remains a major site in which power is concentrated and legitimized. The effects of that power and its limits remain necessary elements in analyzing the social domain.

Theorizing States

Over the course of the twentieth century, states appear to have become less authoritarian and less patriarchal. At the same time, they have also come to play what some have seen as an increasingly significant role in the ordering of social and economic life. Although not always exercising power directly, the modern state nonetheless enjoys considerable, if varying, capacities to influence society both coercively and consensually—through law, social welfare, and economic and social policy, as well as through attempts to regulate the norms of public culture. If states are not to be conceived in simple terms as instruments in the realization of some defined class, elite, or sectoral interest, they are nonetheless purposive agencies. State power is wielded by and subjected to the influence of agents, usually ones with economic power and interests. Dominant social forces seek the maximization of their interests within a determinate social and economic order, and they formulate their own goals in terms of certain principles of rule.

States can be defined as a set of coercive and administrative institutions that have as their object the exercise of various forms of power. They claim control over territory and rule through a combination of coercion and consent, marshaling sometimes formidable economic and social resources in the pursuit of what their rulers define as societal goals, and developing their policies in conformity with these goals. While there is clearly a close relationship between states and governments, states include but are not coterminous with the institutions of the body politic; modern states comprise a coercive apparatus for securing public order and international security; an administrative apparatus of public service that more often than not includes education, health, and welfare systems; an array of departments involved in economic and fiscal policy; a political apparatus of national and local government; and a juridical complex of laws and courts.

As part of their self-legitimation and their attempt to establish hegemony, states generate and disseminate accounts of the national interest, seeking to define the boundaries and meaning of nationhood and citizenship, while presiding over an extensive system of law that regulates economic and social life. They therefore act in many domains—economic, international, and social—through a plurality of institutions and noninstitutional arenas, as well as interacting with other sources of social power. If states represent a concentration of institutional power, its exercise is both direct and indirect. States also govern "at a distance"—through society by means of diffuse, often invisible mechanisms of rule. Even with the shift toward the shrinking state of neoliberalism and the ebbing of state power through globalization, states retain significant force and a not inconsiderable influence in shaping the contours and fortunes of societies.

Yet states are far from constituting the all-powerful monoliths they are sometimes assumed to be. Recent work on the state has tended to emphasize the limits of state power and of its social effects. Three elements in this reconceptualization are important to signal here because they are pertinent to the analysis of state-gender relations. The first is that the state is conceived as an arena of struggle in which policy outcomes are more contingent and unpredictable, sometimes irrational or suboptimal, than might be supposed. Second, the transformative power of the state is limited, both at its point of origin and in its effects. States can be weak, ineffective, neglectful, corrupt. Third, states do not stand "above society" in a simple hierarchy of determinacy; instead, state-society relations are involved in a reciprocal (if usually unequal) causality or synergy.[15]

What this implies is that the powers of the state are limited both in their effective reach and capacity and because they encounter resistance of various kinds, whether from political or civil society. Thus, the power states have to affect social relations is neither absolute nor monolithic, nor is the exercise of power a zero-sum game. With its varied institutions and social relations, society is also a site of power and resistance. It follows that it is erroneous to assume that states can simply transform social relations or that they can always realize their policy intentions. Moreover, as many instances show, policies and state intervention can have consequences quite different from those aimed for, thus confounding simple causal models of state-society relations that see social relations as an effect of the state. If the state cannot be conceived in any simple sense as merely *acting upon* society, this is also because states and society are deeply entwined. While states necessarily exert some influence over society, they are also permeated *by* it through the absorption of prevailing discourses, practices, and social relations.

State-Gender Relations

The pervasiveness of state power and its social character mean that gender relations are necessarily imbricated in a whole range of state policies and in their effects. Gender is a fundamental category of social organization and a major means by which social relations and inequality are structured. Just as states operate within societies deeply marked by class and racial divisions, so too do they operate within societies structured by gender relations. States therefore are saturated by gender in that they both influence gender relations and are influenced by them. The colonial state in Latin America was explicitly concerned to preserve and reproduce gender and ethnic inequalities as part of the system of rule. This was to a considerable degree premised on notions of patriarchal right, a metaphor absorbed into the system of rule itself. Postcolonial states, by adopting the Napoleonic Code, did little to alter this legacy in the domain of the family. The birth of liberalism may have signaled a displacement of patriarchal rule by contractarianism in the public sphere, but patriarchal authority continued to prevail in the domestic and public spheres until challenged by the combined assaults of modernity and the mobilization of women within protest movements from the later nineteenth century onward.

If the twentieth century has seen moves toward gender justice in Latin America as in many other parts of the world, the presumptions of public policy imply continuities in the hierarchical ordering of gender relations. As institutions affected by and in turn affecting gender relations, states cannot be conceived of as neutral arbiters. Gender relations are founded on an inequality of status and means, which states have largely served to perpetuate and enforce. Whether through intention, through the effects of policies, or through an indifference and inaction that maintain the power relations enshrined by the status quo, states are implicated in the ordering of gender relations in the societies over which they preside.

This raises the question of how to characterize gender-state relations, an issue that remains contested within feminist theory. Some approaches have seen the state as an instrument of patriarchal power and masculine interests,[16] whereas others treat it as a more fragmented or even contradictory entity. In the latter view, the state is a site of struggle in which competing interests vie for power, and the outcome is unpredictable. It does not exclude the possibility of some gains for the disadvantaged, among whom women tend to predominate.[17] In other words, while states are not neutral with respect to gender, neither are they impermeable bastions of masculine power.

Whether framed in terms of gender or class interests, state policies and judicial forms are not usefully understood as unified expressions of some clear intentionality. Certainly, there are authoritarian state forms that seek to impose such uniformity in the pursuit of the national interest or the ideal society. However, the projects of liberal states appear less ideological and less cohesive if only because their form of rule presupposes a degree of pluralism in the political field and the necessary correlates of such pluralism—bargaining, competition, and compromise.[18] In modern democratic states, policies may evolve in different departments or be pursued by different lobbies that deploy different strategic resources (discursive, political, economic). This means that there may be considerable variation in the policies pursued and that some may even conflict with others.

States have served at times to undermine patriarchal relations and redress gender inequalities. As purveyors of new rights for women and as vehicles of social policy, states have acted in certain ways to equalize the gender order and to remove some of the more striking forms of injustice. That they may have done so for instrumental "reasons of state," in furtherance of something defined as the national interest rather than for the disinterested pursuit of social justice is a matter for scholarly inquiry and debate; the point remains that states have positioned themselves in a variety of different ways in relation to gender inequality, sometimes developing policies to alleviate or eliminate it in certain domains. No essential relation can therefore be established between states and the perpetuation of gender inequality. Sometimes states have been in advance of society in the pursuit of more equitable arrangements between the sexes; sometimes they have sought to reverse the advances toward equality pursued by their predecessors. State-gender relations must therefore be understood as variable and contingent because they depend on many factors, including broader considerations of policy and rulers' political calculations of their interests.

Although a gendered analysis of the state must therefore be historical and contextual, it must also be able to find ways of conceptualizing the significant differences between states and their social and political projects. Different political principles, rationalities, and forms of legitimation prescribe different programs, rhetorics, and policies. Such differences have been the basis of attempts to provide a periodization of state forms in Latin America and elsewhere, and it is interesting to consider whether a gendered periodization would conform or subvert the terms on which conventional accounts rest. Many difficulties confront any task of periodization;

noting only two may be sufficient to ensure caution in such an undertaking. First, few if any states have clearly delimited "projects." It may be possible to identify the specific elements that distinguish the projects of certain socialist or populist states, but the projects of liberal states appear more elusive or more diverse, bound up as they often are with more pragmatic, less openly prosecuted, ideological goals. Secondly, state forms often evolve over time, and only rarely are fundamental changes in direction and project clearly visible from the outset. Moreover, in any transformation the discrete but combined elements involved are often subject to different rhythms and dynamics of change. With the exception of clear conjunctural ruptures such as those represented by revolutions, the periodization of state forms, if not an impossibility, is a formidable task, particularly so from a gendered perspective; this is because continuities in laws, policies, and official discourses from one regime to the next can be as significant for gender relations as the changes.

These difficulties as well as the potentiality for further work in this area are illustrated by the chapters on the twentieth century in this volume. From a variety of perspectives, they analyze markedly different societies and political histories, serving as important reminders of how contingent is the process of state formation and how varied and changing is the policy environment in which governments legislate. Yet for all their diversity, there were striking continuities across states in matters of public policy, an outcome of their participation in the broader international and regional debates that have influenced the evolution of state-gender relations. Scholarship on twentieth-century Latin America has identified a core of five broad categories of state formation: in their ideal typical forms, these are the liberal or oligarchic state, the corporatist-populist state, the bureaucratic-authoritarian state, the socialist state, and the democratic neoliberal state.[19] Although, as we have noted, gender barely figured in the considerable literature on these state forms, recent work has shown that each has had implications for the gender order, and each has rested on assumptions that were themselves gendered. While the task of providing a gendered analysis of Latin American state forms is at an early stage, the outline of such an analysis of some of the main twentieth-century Latin American state formations and state projects is sketched below in order to contextualize the chapters that make up the second part of this volume.[20]

Early-Twentieth-Century Liberalism

In the conventional periodizations of Latin American history, the early decades of the twentieth century, up to the world financial crisis of 1929, are characterized by the continuation of the liberal project begun in the mid- to late nineteenth century. For all its variations, this project was premised on limited enfranchisement and a more or less laissez-faire economic policy.[21] Latin American governments remained for the most part dominated by liberal oligarchies or their proxies, who maintained an active commitment to the integration of their countries into the world economy. They pursued policies that aimed to modernize their societies and economies along broadly Western lines through attracting infrastructural investment and through "civilizing" the population by means of a secular educational system. A widespread if elitist enthusiasm for progress and, as the century advanced, for the application of science and rationality to the modernizing project were essential features of the liberal period and went along with an increasing administrative and legal rationalization of social life.

The apparent continuity in the liberal project was, however, disrupted by some important developments. The early decades of the century saw growing tensions resulting from economic development, rapid social change, and, in some countries, large-scale immigration. Discontent with the exclusionary rule of the agrarian elites grew as new social classes emerged to demand political rights, while opposition parties emerged and vied for power. Organized labor, professional classes, and women's movements placed new demands on their governments for reform, ones that sought to challenge and in some ways redefine the relationship between state and society.

The first three decades of the twentieth century were therefore ones of considerable social change, none more convulsive than the Mexican Revolution, which sent shock waves through the subcontinent. The eruption of the revolution in 1910 and the bloody turmoil that ensued in the following decades dramatically symbolized the fate of the old order in Mexico, with a finality that was at once terrifying and inspirational. For many Latin American rulers and intellectuals, the revolution represented a necessary rebirth of Latin American nationhood, but one that should be achieved without bloodshed, if possible, and without the dangerous radicalism of the revolutionary years. This cataclysmic event, coinciding with the economic consequences of the First World War, gave to questions of national development and identity in Latin America a new urgency and significance.

Although they participated in a Western cosmopolitan cultural world, Latin America's liberal elites were aware that they presided over economies and societies that were unevenly developed economically as well as socially and culturally diverse. Questions of nationhood and modernity were debated within a broad consensus that considered Latin America's progress to be burdened by an archaic and heterogeneous society on which an incomplete modernity was being progressively superimposed.[22] Strategies of state formation were premised on the inclusion of some and the exclusion of others in the nation; the varying fates of the nation's "others"—whether indigenous, black, or immigrant—form an integral part of the history of Latin American state formation, although less well analyzed are the gendered aspects of their incorporation and exclusion.[23] Whichever strategy was deployed—inclusion of Amerindians in Mexico after the revolution or violent exclusion through annihilation in military campaigns, as in Argentina in the 1880s—the concern of Latin American statesmen was how to achieve a prosperous modernity while maintaining a firm grip on public order. What kind of state and what policies were appropriate for the realization of these aims were matters of considerable dispute and some experimentation; they remained so throughout the twentieth century.

In the all-male and virtually all-white composition of their parliaments, the liberal states that presided over Latin America's early-twentieth-century development reflected a social reality in the distribution of power that was only slowly changing. Yet as a result of the expansion in educational and employment opportunities, urban women of all classes had gained some material autonomy.[24] By the 1910s they had become a presence in public life as workers, shop assistants, professionals, and traders. But if they married, they were still treated as minors in law. In most countries where the Napoleonic Code was the basis of legislation, they had virtually no rights in the family; if employed, they were required to hand over their earnings to their husbands and enjoyed no automatic rights to marital property. They were not allowed to testify in court or hold public office, and they enjoyed no authority over or claim to their children under the rulings of *patria potestad* (parental authority). Women were regarded as lacking in rationality, as too weak and impulsive to be treated as the equals of men. They were therefore regarded as "outside citizenship" and as such in need of protection, like children. In the words of a Uruguayan legislator, women were treated as inferior beings, as entities without rights, as little more than domestic animals.[25] Moreover, in Latin America, as in some other parts of the world, full female suffrage was in the main granted only after the outbreak of World War II.[26] Thus, a century after independence, the rights of political citizenship could be claimed only by men, and in the majority of Latin American states, only by those with property, literacy, or national service to their credit.

It is not surprising, then, that this period was marked by the political ascendance of Latin American feminism. As a current of thought and as a social movement, feminism had emerged in Argentina, Mexico, Brazil, Peru, Costa Rica, and Chile in the late nineteenth century, borne by immigrants from Europe and fueled by conditions in the former colonies. By the first decades of the twentieth century, socialist, anarchist, and liberal feminist organizations were active across a diverse range of countries. Both middle- and working-class women—exasperated by the continuing injustices they suffered in the law, the workplace, and the family—demanded changes consonant with their absorption into education and employment.[27] The first International Women's Congress held in Argentina in 1910 showed not only that women demanded juridical equality and (even though less enthusiastically) suffrage, but that they also had expectations of the state in the areas of social rights—particularly education, health, and welfare.[28] These were becoming sites of female activism and employment, and were set to expand considerably in the decades to come.

Feminism evolved within a cultural context that was in many ways inimical to gender equality. Ideas of gender difference were strongly rooted in Catholicism, which gave symbolic meaning to maternalist constructions of femininity and underpinned the idea of separate spheres for men and women. Although the secular and modernist orientation of progressive liberals led them to support some improvement in women's rights and to oppose church authority in matters of marriage, they held to contemporary scientific explanations of gender roles as rooted in biological difference.[29] These ideas were part of the common currency of the age and influenced the way in which the issue of difference was played out with respect to women's rights, social policy, and political participation.

Yet as historians of Latin American feminism have shown, and as several of the chapters in this volume argue, women learned not so much to challenge as to deploy the language of difference in ways that destabilized the traditional binaries that served to disqualify them from full citizenship. They used ideas of domestic and maternal virtues as a basis for activism and to create ties of female solidarity. As their forebears had done a century before in the republican wars, they took these "feminine virtues" out of the home and into the public space, and demanded that they be recognized as a service to the nation. Ideas of women's moral superiority and altruism were used by advocates of female suffrage to call for a remoralization of the political sphere through the entry of women into this hitherto masculine domain.[30] Women therefore accepted the principle of sex difference, but they did not accept it as a basis for unjustified discrimination. Leaders of women's movements challenged their treatment in the law and contested the terms of their social and political exclusion, but they did so in ways that acknowledged the special significance of their role in the family. Indeed, Latin American feminists highlighted gender differences and framed their demands for citizenship in terms of their maternal "social function" and superior morality, which they would deploy in the service of society.[31] This civic maternalism remained a significant element in women's bid for citizenship and was a theme that, with variations, traversed the different state forms that emerged in Latin America in the course of the twentieth century. It was deployed by feminists and by states alike, albeit to serve different ends.

How successful was first-wave feminism in Latin America in challenging the patriarchal exclusion of liberalism? One reading of this period stresses the continuity in patriarchal privilege and male control over women that prevailed in law and public life more generally. Nineteenth-century discourses about the frailty of the family were repeatedly reinvoked by conservatives in debates about the destabilizing effects of modernity. Family unity under male guardianship was linked to ideas of national health, a theme reworked within different political contexts to justify continuing patriarchal privilege and authority. But the policies of liberal states increasingly pulled in opposite directions. On the one hand, they promoted female education and reluctantly tolerated women's employment because it was necessary to the national development effort; on the other hand, they kept legal codes that placed women firmly under the tutelary control of fathers and husbands, and introduced protective legislation that restricted women's role in the workplace. The very fact that social relations were changing so dramatically may have worked for their preservation. There were exceptions, of course. In some cases—such as Uruguay, Argentina, and Mexico—radical liberal and socialist ideas were influential in framing reforms. New codes were introduced that redefined the terms of paternal authority in the home and gave women some new rights and recognition in the public sphere of education and employment.

Modernity was both welcomed and feared—unleashing, as it did, new forces into the society, including monstrous regiments of apparently unattached and uncontrolled women. By the 1920s and 1930s, public debate about women's place in society reflected more general anxieties about social disintegration and national uncertainty, which were in turn a product of troubled attitudes toward women's rapidly changing place in the new nation-states. Working women and "free" women violated understandings of women's proper place in society. In confrontations with authority that unsettled prevailing views of women as compliant and passive subordinates, women workers engaged in strikes and participated in demonstrations in pursuit of their demands for better pay and conditions. More disturbing still were those women who were able to engage in commercial sex, a potent signifier of transgressive female behavior. The "new women" and their "free" sexuality threatened family life, the bedrock of the nation.[32] The regulation of women, the female body, and sexuality were thus inscribed in the processes of state making.

Although feminists continued to press their case in what should have been a more favorable social context, their victories were uneven. The prolonged debate on reforming civil codes and the patriarchal premises of patria potestad had begun in the Southern Cone as early as the 1880s, and the Brazilian Congress had debated divorce in 1881. Pressure for reform in women's legal and constitutional status came from three directions: liberal, male-dominated political parties; autonomous women's organizations and movements; and, from the second decade of the twentieth century onward, some populist movements that began to take an interest in feminist demands. Yet prior to 1930 only a few states moved toward juridical equality between the sexes in the family by reforming the civil codes, Argentina in 1926 and Mexico in 1928 among them, and even they delayed female suffrage until after the Second World War. Women may have had increasing access to the public realm of work, even gaining entry into the professions, but they continued to be regarded as trespassers on a terrain that did not belong to them. For all that liberal states had responded to some of the pressures for change induced by modernity, they remained for the most part resilient if ambivalent guarantors of masculine authority and privilege.

Such generalizations, however, must be tempered by the recognition of considerable diversity in the matter of women's rights. Liberal governments were not patriarchal monoliths, and women were not the passive objects of their policies. As women became more autonomous, more articulate, and less accepting of the authority of husbands and fathers, reformers (both socialist and liberal modernizers) sought to bring legal provisions in line with the new reality. The patriarchal basis of law was seen by at least some elements within the liberal elites as out of step with the modern world that Latin America sought to join. As the cases of Uruguay, Mexico, Cuba, and Brazil show, this was a period in which male allies could be essential in securing some improvement in women's rights.[33] Yet, women's agency played its part in shaping the direction of policy as it did in changing gender relations.[34] Women persisted in making demands of the state, and their active pursuit of reform made them participants in that process as well as objects of law and policy.

Women were therefore not excluded from the liberal project, and as time progressed, they became a more visible part of it. If this was evident in the area of employment, which drew increasing numbers of women into economic life, it was also apparent in the expanding arena of social reform. From the first decades of the century, state activity increased in the domain of social regulation—one of several significant developments in the state that both affected the gender order and testified to the changes already taking place within it. Latin American governments entertained positivist notions of the perfectibility of society through a measure of state intervention. They increasingly recognized that a modern social order depended upon social integration and that states had some responsibility toward the people they governed—if only to eliminate some of the conditions that caused discontent. Radicalism of the kind represented by the Mexican Revolution or by socialists and anarchists was ruled out as dangerous and inappropriate. Instead, improving the "race" in order to secure the conditions for development and to head off threats of disorder became the leitmotif of the social reform and eugenics movements. As these ideas gathered strength in Europe and the United States in the 1920s and 1930s, they also found adherents in parts of Latin America among the growing class of professionals who had an increasingly influential role in the legislature. The promoters of social hygiene and of the science of *puericultura* or child development energetically supported policy and legal changes, and in some ways prepared the way for the social legislation and policies of the populist states that followed.

Philanthropic welfarism had existed in Latin America from the colonial period, but it had been small scale and more often than not church based. This pattern of provision continued until the 1940s, but it was paralleled in the more developed states by an incremental assumption of social responsibility by governments. During the period from 1900 to 1940, the embryonic elements of the Latin American social state began to form. Women were active participants in the development and practice of public welfare and social reform. They had long participated in the administration and dispensation of charitable activities, an involvement regarded as a natural extension of women's family roles and deemed suitable for women's special attributes and concerns—even by the church, which otherwise opposed women working outside the home. In the countries of the Southern Cone and in Mexico, the later 1920s and the 1930s saw the creation of professional bodies dedicated to social work and the absorption of thousands of women into their ranks. As Laura Gotkowitz notes with regard to the Bolivian case, and Mary Kay Vaughan with regard to the Mexican, women found an important niche within the emerging structures and practices of state welfarism. Women's work and their lobbying in this area were important in the development of welfare provision and social legislation.[35]

The entry of science and rationality into the service of the state opened up this fertile field for female activism. Women in paid and voluntary capacities mobilized around the social hygiene and eugenics movements, which promoted ideas of social modernity as a sine qua non of economic development. Feminist campaigners eager to bring the family under the reformers' gaze joined in the assault on archaic family practices, seen as founded on ignorance and as leading to degeneracy and the debilitation of the race. Increasingly during the 1920s, women participated in the work of "social hygiene" in large numbers: they assisted as volunteers and professionals in programs concerned with child and maternal health and poverty alleviation, and in campaigns to restore the family to the center of a stable national community. The class divide in this work was evident, with professional and elite women engaged in efforts to redeem from "degradation" the families of the poor and the women within them.

At the same time, women were also becoming the objects of state regulation, again partly through their own efforts and demands. Alongside or within socialist movements, women pressed for the regulation of their working hours in order to protect themselves from overexploitation and to safeguard their "maternal functions." As early as 1906, bills were proposed in Uruguay to give rights to maternity leave, and legislation to restrict women's working hours was first introduced in Argentina in 1905.[36] Paternalist sentiments were aroused by such claims, and women were grouped, along with children, as those who required protection because they lacked citizenship. Most Latin American countries followed Uruguay's lead and passed laws to reduce women's working hours, sometimes arguing that such a reduction was necessary to safeguard their reproductive capacities and at other times that their moral virtue was at risk.[37]

But it was in the 1930s that motherhood came under scrutiny as an object of knowledge and target of intervention, with numerous legal measures being passed—including children's codes and maternity and family acts. As "maternal eugenics" gained in support,[38] efforts intensified to have women's reproductive functions protected in law and their child-rearing methods improved. So it was that in 1934 women workers acquired rights to maternity leave (seventy-five days in toto), maternity pay, and free midwifery. In 1937, mother and childcare protection centers were established. Mothers, actual and potential, were also to be protected from sexually transmitted disease. An enthusiasm for prenuptial certificates to detect disease before marriage was an issue on which feminists and congressmen coincided. Here, it was men's sexuality and prerogatives that were the focus of bureaucratic interest and regulation; many women supported these initiatives as necessary to protect wives from disease resulting from men's philandering, double standards, and sexual mores.

In the Southern Cone, a growing concern with demography, a product of declining birth rates and the end of the large immigration flows to Latin America, brought motherhood into alignment with discourses of national duty.[39] If motherhood had been seen in the 1916 bid for suffrage in Argentina as the female equivalent to military service for men, in the 1930s a similar argument was deployed by governments where state legislators were growing anxious about demographic trends. Women were increasingly urged to be mindful of their national duty to provide the future generation as maternity and fertility became crucial resources for the nation justifying further state regulation of women's bodies.[40] In some cases, women became the objects of authoritarian and patriarchal forms of state intervention; in Chile and Mexico, abandoning the home became a particular female crime, and in 1931 the Chilean government approved a Sanitary Code—which protected mothers' milk from commercialization—and ruled against wet nursing, stipulating that mothers were obliged to nurse for five months after the birth of a baby. These claims over women's bodies made on behalf of the nation were asserted in a context where first-wave liberal and socialist women's movements were losing their impetus and being overtaken by a new dynamic and a new constellation of state forms.

The tension that characterized the modernizing project of liberalism with regard to women was never resolved. Reform bills were formulated that conferred new rights on married women, but were resisted, diluted, or not passed at all in Congress. In this sense, for all that liberal states sought to secure the nation's passage into the modern world, they wished to do so while retaining a firm grip on the family and on women, none firmer than that conferred by the patriarchal status quo. Legal reforms there were, but ones that did not tinker too radically with the system of patriarchal right.

The Mexican Revolution:
The Birth of Corporatist Populism

The first alternative state form to the liberal variant to appear in twentieth-century Latin America was that which was born out of the Mexican Revolution. Initiated by urban middle- and upper-class men, the revolution soon acquired a popular cast as the rural poor took up arms to demand bread and land. By 1917, the year of the promulgation of a new constitution, the radicalism of the revolution was enshrined in a secular, nationalist project of modernization exemplified by its commitment to a program of radical land reform that aimed simultaneously to destroy the agrarian landowning classes and to deal a blow to the Catholic Church. It would take more than a decade after the turmoil to create a new state and to implement the reforms, but what evolved under Lázaro Cárdenas (1934–40) was a state very different from the liberal conservatism that had preceded it. Its corporatist structures, populist rhetoric, and nationalist economic measures foreshadowed political developments elsewhere in Latin America in the 1940s.

For all its radical promise, as Mary Kay Vaughan and Ann Varley show in this volume, the Mexican Revolution, like those of France and Russia, was a masculine affair. Despite the years of social upheaval, the involvement of women as soldiers and activists in its fortunes, and the spirited feminist campaigns, the gender order proved remarkably resilient to change. Yet legal reforms granting women new rights in the family were introduced in 1917 through the Constitution and related legislation.[41] In a bold move, matching Uruguay's law of 1907,[42] divorce was legalized, and wives acquired the right to draw up contracts and gained equal custody over children.[43] Yet the same legislation barred them from engaging in a business or profession without their husband's consent. Articles 34 and 35 of the Constitution stipulated that suffrage, citizenship, and the holding of public office were male prerogatives. Feminist demands for female enfranchisement were rejected in 1917 on the grounds that in Mexico women had not achieved the break with the family required by progress toward civilization; their interests remained entwined with those of their male kin, and thus they should not feel the need to participate in public affairs.[44] Feminists had to struggle another decade before they secured further reform of the Civil Code eventually achieved in 1928. Even with these reforms, not only did great inequalities remain in law, but the lives of millions of women in Mexico lay outside its scope and remained subject to a de facto patriarchal order.[45] Postrevolutionary administrations remained both ambivalent and instrumental in their response to feminist demands.

Revolutions tend to result in stronger, more centralized states, and once the new Mexican state was consolidated, the priorities of national development returned. The revolutionary government assigned to the state the responsibility for securing progress through economic and social modernization. Faced with what was seen as an untransformed traditional society in the rural areas, Mexico's postrevolutionary governments brought in policies designed to modernize social relations. From the nineteenth century onward, liberals and socialists alike had argued that family reform and women's emancipation from patriarchal absolutism were an integral part of modernization and a necessary concomitant of economic growth.[46] Mexico was one of several modernizing nationalist states that in the 1920s and 1930s adopted policies designed to erode the traditional gender order and to free women from patriarchal absolutism. Through legislation, education, and policies to provide female employment, Mexico's revolutionary leadership sought to promote the transformation of the "backward" rural economies. Gender relations therefore became a matter of state concern as a result of development imperatives rather than the desire to promote women's emancipation. As Vaughan argues, rural development policy in Mexico sought to destroy premodern networks of power in order to replace them with modern commercial networks.[47] This effort at nation building aimed to accomplish three things in the area of gender relations: to refashion male productive practices and sociability, and so to foster an orientation toward state and market, away from local networks; to place children under state tutelage through education to ensure patriotic development; and to rationalize the domestic sphere and reproductive work through the propagation of modern "scientific" notions of human development. As elsewhere in Latin America in the 1930s, an enthusiasm for the application of science to social regulation underpinned efforts to modernize the family through the technologies of reproduction, health care, and puericultura or child development.

Meanwhile, state formation proceeded along corporatist lines under the control of the ruling Partido Nacional Revolucionario (PNR) (later the Partido Revolucionario Institucional [PRI]). State structures created a privileged channel for state authority over civil society, and organized interests were represented within four vertically organized sectoral associations. Women's sections were formed within recognized organizations—the National Peasant Confederation (CNC), the Confederation of Mexican Workers (CTM), and the National Confederation of Popular Organizations (CNOP)—and Acción Femenina, a party-controlled organization, was established under Cárdenas.[48] The 1930s saw considerable mobilization of women in pursuit of reform; in 1935, a women's association called Frente Único pro Derechos de la Mujer (United Front for Women's Rights) (FUPDM) became a broad coalition representing eighty-eight organizations with a membership of fifty thousand. By the 1940s, however, its demands for suffrage and for further reform in women's rights were supplanted by a program of social welfare. Between 1940 and 1946 in response to Mexico's entry into the war on the side of the Allied powers, it became the Committee for the Defense of the Nation and lost much of its former dynamism.[49]

Women were therefore accorded some rights and recognition by Mexico's postrevolutionary governments, and they were mobilized into the service of the state in the domains of public welfare and party work. But as in other postrevolutionary states, independent feminist organizations found decreasing space in which to operate. Faced with strong antifeminist and pro-church sentiments on the part of many women, the ruling party put reasons of state before principle—a policy nowhere more evident than in the matter of women's political rights. Demands for female suffrage at the national level were repeatedly rejected on the grounds that women's innate religiosity, "fanaticism," and conservatism might threaten the interests of the revolutionary state. Although women could vote in some regions at the municipal level from 1922, it was only under Miguel Alemán's administration (1946–52) that they acquired the right to vote *and* to stand in all municipal elections. The grounds on which this concession was granted were the same as they had been twenty years before: local concerns were more appropriate to women's interests. As Alemán expressed it, "the municipal organization is the one that cares most about the interests of the family and must pay most attention to the needs of the family and of children."[50] Feminist campaigning eventually, in 1953, gained Mexican women the right to vote and to stand in national elections. Moreover, as Varley shows, not until 1974 was the clause making wives responsible for household work and management repealed. Gender roles, rights, and duties remained inscribed in laws that upheld the normative order within the home. Yet Varley's analysis of the judicial interpretations of the civil codes nonetheless shows that these definitions shifted over the course of the century, placing limits not only on men's authority over their wives, but endowing women with the right to a family home free from the presence and domination of in-laws. In uncovering the assumptions behind the application of the codes, specifically the clause concerning "abandonment of the marital home," Varley reveals significant shifts over time in the "patriarchal bargain" struck on marriage, concluding that although male authority was preserved, the terms of its legal rationalization were modernized.

Corporatism and Populism: A New Ethos of Authority

The period between 1930 and 1950 is identified in Latin America with corporatist state formations and populist governments.[51] It was significant in that it marked the mobilization of mass popular support and the extension of the franchise to include literate men and women. The states that emerged in the aftermath of liberalism were cast as the radical antagonists of their oligarchic predecessors. Where liberalism was elitist, outward oriented, and exclusionary, the new governments presented themselves as plebeian, nationalist, and inclusionary, and advocated an inward-directed economy based on import substitution industrialization. Liberal democratic ideas were not forsaken by either populist or socialist governments, but were applied selectively, persisting most evidently in the importance accorded to electoral processes that brought these radical popular governments to power with significant majorities. This climate of political mobilization had important consequences for women's political rights, for it contributed to the accumulating pressures on governments both internal and international to extend suffrage to women. Even conservative parties found themselves mobilizing women and supporting bills for their enfranchisement, although the acquisition of formal political rights did not always lead to their being permitted to practice.

The collapse of the world economy in 1929 inaugurated an epoch in which states virtually everywhere acquired an expanded role in economic and social regulation, one that would endure for almost half a century. Latin America was no exception. The contraction of export markets in the world crisis placed Latin American liberalism under considerable strain, putting in question its economic rationale, while the popular challenge to its political exclusivity grew. Whereas in the United States and parts of Europe the 1930s signaled a broader acceptance of the idea of public welfare, in Latin America the states that had evolved by the end of the Second World War drew on ideas of nationalism, corporatism,[52] and populism, thus giving a distinctive, regional cast to modalities of state regulation and political inclusion.

The states of Cárdenas, Getúlio Vargas, and Juan Perón represent variant forms of the populist corporatism that marks this period of Latin American political history. Although a self-confident populist project was forged in Latin America in the 1940s, the elements of that project were already present in the continent's political evolution, not only in the Mexican Revolution, but in the populist parties of Argentina and Peru that had come to prominence in the second and third decades of the century respectively. By the late 1930s, populist parties had come to power in several other Latin American countries with a promise to remake their societies, build up their industrial strength, and incorporate the masses into political life. In ap-

parent contrast, socialist parties in Chile and Cuba led coalition governments; yet for all their distinctiveness, these governments too shared in the
broader regional and international zeitgeist that expressed societal goals in
terms of attaining national economic development and greater social justice. Although they were not state-corporatist regimes *strictu senso,* they
sought ways of achieving the incorporation of the working class in social
pacts.[53] As Karin Rosemblatt argues in this volume, the Chilean popular-
front coalitions—which won elections in 1932, 1942, and 1946—shared in a
widespread concern to head off the threat of social disorder. Like their
corporatist and populist counterparts, they promoted the ideal of a unified
nation based on organicist ideas of social inclusion and class harmony.

This concept of the good society underpinned the bargains that governments of different types struck with key sections of organized labor, establishing a vertical system of control and co-option through an expanded
state apparatus. In the 1940s, corporatist ideas found favor with elites who
supported reform and modernization, but who were concerned to address
what they saw as the twin menace of class conflict and communism. For
many statesmen of the time, the priority was to forge a national project
that would meet the challenge of more radical alternatives by securing an
inclusionary model of national development. But corporatism, even in its
weaker and less ideological forms, was premised on gendered assumptions.
Corporatist bargaining established a political bond between the worker
and the party, ensuring the loyalty of the more effective sectors of organized labor. Male-dominated trade unions were the principal beneficiaries
of corporatist social contracts that enrolled men in the service of the state
as workers and patriots, their compliance secured through negotiated pacts
over wages, working conditions, and social security. Even where women
had acquired a significant presence in the workforce, they labored in poorly
paid, less organized sectors. Not only were they marginal to the contrac-
tual negotiations of the corporatist state, but they also occupied an ambiguous place in populist rhetoric. While state propaganda celebrated the
hombría (manliness) of the nation's workers, the very fact that women
worked at all was regarded by many congressmen in the 1940s as a symp-
tom of the nation's backwardness rather than as a sign of progress, as
socialists once proclaimed.[54] In Argentina at this time, working women
were regarded as unfortunates to be pitied and protected by the state and
by their husbands.[55] Optimally, they should be able to withdraw from the

workforce altogether, a move that would be enabled by the restitution of a family wage. This historic demand of organized labor was premised on female dependency and the presence in the family of the full-time housewife and mother. Yet as Rosemblatt shows in the case of Chile, the state, trades unions, and oppositional parties also shared a concern to discipline and domesticate men. In being elevated to his "appropriate" place of authority, the paterfamilias was required to discharge that authority with responsibility and self-discipline. The sober, hardworking father was the natural complement to the dependent housewife-mother. The worker's family was now an object of concern to be regulated not only through the external agencies of the state (social workers, social hygienists, and the like), but through new norms of appropriate conduct. Performance at work and conduct at home unified the public and private worlds as sites of intervention.

Corporatist bargaining did, however, secure the passage of numerous welfare measures, many of which had been promoted by eugenicists and other reformers in previous decades but had not been approved or, if approved, had lain dormant on the statute books. Drawing on earlier arguments for social inclusion and class harmony, populist governments sought to establish a more extensive system of welfare, albeit one that was only selectively inclusive and that reproduced the clientilistic structure of corporatist favoritism. Yet although the client-citizens of the new states, both male and female, enjoyed an expansion of their social rights, these redistributive measures had a paternalist character because they assumed the interests of male wage earners as principal beneficiaries; women qualified for benefits chiefly as the dependents of men. The apparent exception was the unmarried mother, whose cause some populist states made their own. Lone mothers became a symbol of the compassionate, protective, and paternal nature of populist regimes, which arranged for the state to replace the husband in providing dignity and sustenance. In what was largely an urban system of welfare, rural and indigenous women were often excluded from these and other entitlements and were more often than not denied rights to property in land. The latter, through law or custom, remained a male prerogative, thus revealing the bias as well as the limits of populist policies.[56]

Whether populist, liberal, or socialist-led popular fronts, states in this period continued to support—through rhetoric, policy, and law—traditional family values based on notions of female dependency, service, and subordination. The personalist regimes of Perón and Vargas in the era of high populism used familial and patriarchal symbolism as metaphors of state rule. In Argentina, Perón was hailed as the father of the nation, although initially he cast himself as the leader of a fraternal republic: he, like Vargas in Brazil, had rebelled against the old fathers, the hated oligarchs, and could claim to be revolutionary in attacking the ancien régime, celebrating demotic values and championing social justice. Populist regimes of whatever stripe were a combination of authoritarian and democratic appeals. They were democratic in their inclusionary rhetoric and policies,[57] and some, like Perón, consolidated their rule through elections. But populism was also authoritarian in its appeal and in its practice. Strong government and fascist ideas were admired, and a role for the military in politics was taken for granted. The organization of power was clearly vertical and gendered, and the state did not hesitate to intervene in recalcitrant or uncooperative trade unions.

Yet for all their invocation of a traditional gender order, populist states were innovative in several respects, not least in their creation of a female constituency. Although they did the business of politics with men, they sought to mobilize women, and they made direct appeals to women as political subjects. Laura Gotkowitz shows in her chapter on Bolivia how a military populist regime incorporated women into its project both symbolically through discourses of heroic maternalism and legally through changes that expanded maternity rights and political rights. The 1945 Constitution gave literate women the right to vote, albeit only in municipal elections. Through an analysis of the changing signification of a public statue commemorating an episode when mestizo and indigenous women rallied to the republican cause, Gotkowitz shows how the populist military government converted the statue into a sign of its commitment to the people. Thus, gender and ethnicity were imbricated in changing definitions of the nation in which poor, mestizo women were promoted as the sign of national virtue and devotion.

So often ignored in political rhetoric, women at last figured under populist regimes as addressees in the discourses of populist leaders. This phenomenon was nowhere clearer than in Argentina, which, uniquely in Latin America, saw the rise of a woman to the apex of political power. In Eva Perón, the government acquired a formidable accomplice. She redefined the terms of women's citizenship so as to include women as participants in the political process, while at the same time inscribing the meaning of female political incorporation within the familiar terms of femininity.[58] As Jo Fisher argues, despite Eva's controversial role in Argentina's political life, she can be credited with having included working-class women in the efforts to refashion the Argentine nation. Yet the terms of this appeal positioned them as the loyal supporters of their Peronist men; women were given the vote not in order to advance their own interests as women, but in order to render their support to the Peronist party. Peronism therefore mobilized women but made it clear that the gender order would be maintained. Eva's discourse invoked older arguments about women's special feminine attributes in an effort to direct them into the service of the state. She spoke of the need to moralize political life through women's participation—referring to her own role in politics as the heart, whereas Perón, in a predictable binary, was the head. Although feminists of the first wave had deployed a similar language and argument, these were now summoned in the service of the state.

The potent appeal of Peronism endured long beyond its period in power and included a broad base of female support. Fisher shows that it was sustained in large part by women at the lower levels of the class pyramid who identified with Evita's symbolic appeal to wifely virtues, femininity, and motherhood. Fifty years later, that appeal persisted in a working-class housewives' association that claimed a membership of half a million. Eva had sought to dignify housework and motherhood, and in the struggle of the Sindicato de Amas de Casa (SACRA)—Housewives' Union—to recognize this dimension of women's work and political identity, her memory and her vision of a dignified role for women in the home lived on.

Although the state-centered projects of populism and corporatism mobilized many women, they nonetheless sought to guarantee a stable reproduction of gender difference through maintaining sex-typed educational curricula, different employment opportunities, fixed family responsibilities, and standards of sexual behavior. Some populist states sought to incorporate loyal female supporters into their power structures so long as they did not challenge policy, and feminist movements and ideas were marginalized when not openly opposed. But in the course of the evolution of these states, women gained formal political rights and some measure of social welfare by virtue of marriage, employment, or motherhood. They would have to wait for feminism's second wave and for the growth of an international women's movement to provide a fresh impulsion to their historic demands.

State Socialism: The Case of Cuba

Socialist ideas represented a continuity with, but a deepening of, the radical antiliberal tradition in Latin America. Socialism offered an alternative to both liberalism and capitalism, one that would simultaneously secure the goals of national development and social justice. Unique among the radical ideologies that traversed Latin America, socialism professed the full equality of men and women, and in identifying the family as a major site of inequality, it proposed to remove the basis of the traditional gender order by giving women new rights and the means to achieve economic autonomy through employment.

The influence of socialist ideas can be traced in the evolution of Latin American legal reform from the early twentieth century. Socialists in Argentina and Uruguay had supported radical changes in the law to give women political rights and to end their "double exploitation"—in the workplace and in the family, where they were subject to "mistreatment by husbands and fathers."[59] But as a state form, socialism was realized in only one country in the subcontinent. Of the two self-proclaimed socialist revolutions in Latin America, those of Cuba and Nicaragua, the former was alone in establishing a planned economy and a state premised on the idea of the "dictatorship of the proletariat." Similar in its institutional arrangements to the states of the Soviet bloc, but with a leader who was both charismatic and, unlike those of Eastern Europe, widely perceived as the bearer of a legitimate authority, Cuban state socialism came into being as a result of a popular, nationalist revolution.

What was the gender order of socialism? In its ideal self-representation and in its constitutional commitments, socialism was founded on principles of equality and social justice. It opposed traditional forms of patriarchy and sought to modernize social relations as part of its development strategy and its embrace of modernity in general. Women were to be emancipated from the oppression they suffered under previous states and economic arrangements, and they were to be mobilized into the service of the state as paid and voluntary workers, political activists, and mothers. The Cuban Constitution, like its counterparts elsewhere, promised to respect and protect women's maternal functions, while pledging the state to assist in the rearing of children so that women could effectively perform their two roles: as mothers and as worker-citizens.

The Cuban Revolution occurred before feminism's second wave, and in contrast to Nicaragua, its leadership never openly embraced feminist ideas. It never spawned, nor would it have tolerated, the kind of loyal feminist opposition that, in Nicaragua's more pluralized political context, was able to achieve a feminist input into state policies and law. In Cuba, as I argue in my chapter in part 2, the women's organization—the Federación de Mujeres Cubanas (FMC)—was closely identified with the apparatus of rule as embodied in the party and the state. If women's emancipation meant modernizing the family and providing employment and social entitlements, it did not necessarily mean equal representation within the state. Meanwhile, the burden of daily life associated with a shortage economy largely fell on women. Their efforts on behalf of household reproduction was acknowledged by the FMC to have disqualified them from taking a fuller role in political life. Thus, although Cuban socialism promoted equality in the law, achieved a greater incorporation of women in the public sphere, and alone of Latin American states ensured the reproductive rights of women, it did less to resolve the persistent gender inequalities in social life. Women remained second-class citizens even in the state with the greatest commitment to gender equality and with the fewest legal impediments to achieving it.

Military Rule and State Terror

The wave of dictatorships that swept across much of Latin America between 1964 and 1976, signaled the beginning of the end of the project of state-centered development put in place after the crisis of the 1930s. Although the period of classical populism ended with the demise of its leaders, elements of its economic project—modernized through the ideas of the Economic Commission for Latin America (ECLA)—continued for some time afterward in the policies of inward-directed growth and import substitution industrialization. At the same time, corporatist bargaining structures and a commitment to maintain employment levels and welfare systems extended the "co-optative democracy" associated with the populist era for a further quarter century.

Much has been written on the combined domestic and international factors that precipitated this state form into terminal crisis. Accumulating economic problems and growing social turmoil were greatly exacerbated by the successive rises in oil prices after 1973, providing the military elite with the excuse to intervene. The subsequent and unexpectedly ferocious repression that these dictatorships presided over in more than a dozen Latin American countries was confirmation for many scholars of the underlying fragility of Latin American democracies.

Feminist analyses of the military dictatorships has produced an extensive literature focusing on three main issues: the significance of military rule as a gendered regime of domination; the gendered forms of resistance to the military; and the gendered effects of the macroeconomic policies adopted under the guidance of the International Monetary Fund (IMF) and the World Bank. Of the three, it was the first that engaged most directly with the state. Gendered analyses of the dictatorships take as their starting point the way in which the military sought to legitimize its rule by claiming to act in the interests of national security in its efforts to reestablish order and end the political and economic chaos that prevailed.[60] The rhetoric of the military was gendered in ways that have been seen as an invocation of historical forms of Latin American nationalism. From the earliest times, visions of nationhood have invested states with gendered virtues—sometimes masculine as in heroism and glory, sometimes feminine with the beloved land invested with the qualities of maternal fecundity or subjected to violation through foreign rule. In Diane Taylor's analysis of military rhetoric, the *patria* was constructed in the masculinist imaginary as feminine, a beloved mother(land) despoiled by enemies who had to be subdued in order to recover a pure and glorious nationhood. These images placed a heroic, virile military in opposition to an unruly other located in the feminine position as chaotic and subversive, in need of subjugation and discipline.[61] If in the nineteenth century the enemy was defined as the indigenous peoples who were "threatening civilization," in the 1970s it was "subversives" who were charged with threatening not only the state but the nation's very way of life.[62] Feminists were considered to be among the subversives and were targeted as such.

Analyses such as those by Ximena Bunster Burotto, Diane Taylor, and Nancy Hollander have stressed how gender suffused the apparatus and repertoire of terror deployed by the military.[63] The widespread use of torture against prisoners was both eroticized and sexualized. Women were routinely raped and otherwise sexually abused in ways that expressed a sadistic misogyny.[64] Men too were raped in "mechanical acts of sodomy which reconstituted their bodies as homosexuals, and later as passive, broken, 'females' in ordeals of agony and humiliation."[65] Thus, even in torture, the gender hierarchy was reproduced.

Among the grotesque rationalizations for the repression advanced by military regimes was the claim to be "destroying in order to build." The society had become rotten and at its core was a failure of basic values and institutions. The family, above all, had failed in its duty to raise good, upright, and obedient citizens. By implication, the new society that the military promised to create was one that would restore authority through a return to a patriarchal order founded on a retraditionalized, privatized family. Women would be disciplined and their rights curtailed. In Chile, legislation restricting women's reproductive rights—tightened laws on abortion and the banning of the distribution of contraceptives through state agencies—was one aspect of the gendered politics of the military.[66] One of General Augusto Pinochet's last pieces of legislation was to change the Constitution to enshrine the principle of protecting life, thus ensuring that changes to the abortion law sought by women's movements would be thwarted.

The state discourse on motherhood that emerged during the years of the dictatorships thus elevated motherhood and family values as the sine qua non of a healthy nation, at the very moment when family life was being destroyed by state terror and undermined by the austerity policies.[67] This hypocrisy was seized on by the groups of mothers of the disappeared, whose challenge to military rule in several countries was framed in terms of a maternal imperative to recover their lost children.[68] The mothers constituted one of the most visible and potent challenges to military rule and yet formed a group that in other respects remained powerless. The status of motherhood conferred a degree of protection from annihilation. The demands of the Madres de la Plaza de Mayo had a moral force that gave their movement an impact quite disproportionate to its size and formal influence. This gross asymmetry in power relations and the opposing of the dehumanized "rational" goals of the military with the values of sentiment and self-sacrifice[69] provided symbolic confirmation of the power relations that governed state and gender.[70]

If the motherist movements represented one response to the state violence of the military regimes, they did so in a context in which women's political presence was growing both at the popular level and through the spread of feminist movements. Second-wave feminism in Latin America was born in the 1970s and received support from the international women's movement, whose presence grew steadily at the United Nations Conferences for the Decade for Women (1975–85). The regional activities stimulated by the Decade for Women drew national movements into closer alignment and cooperation, while the greater visibility accorded to women's issues put pressure on Latin American governments to improve their record on women's rights and equality.[71] Some of the first women's secretariats were established within Latin American states after the conference in Mexico that inaugurated the decade in 1975. A parallel process was the growth of popular women's movements as a result of efforts to meet basic needs in the context of acute shortage and economic deprivation. These varied movements contributed to the eventual demise of the military[72] and were to play an important part in the restoration of democracy to the region.[73]

Military rule was associated with another historic shift in Latin American state forms, for during the years of dictatorship and bloody repression, a new political economy was being forged, and previous understandings of the role of the state in economic and social life were being radically revised. Latin America in effect underwent a political and economic transition, with the resultant turn to what is popularly termed *neoliberalism*. It was not alone in undergoing this shift, and the policies it was associated with reflected a global trend, one that was most dramatically evidenced in the regimes that followed the collapse of communism in the Soviet bloc. Whether described in terms of the end of the developmental state or of the rise of neoliberalism, there occurred a more generalized, international shift away from the weakening consensus about the role of the state in the economy and in the domain of social welfare.

The elements of these policies, initially contained in structural adjustment packages, signaled a more general move toward a greater role for market mechanisms in the ordering of social and economic life, and announced the birth of a new economic model.[74] Although there was considerable variation in their timing, application, and outcome in Latin America, the policies adopted from the mid-1970s shared a common set of assumptions. They sought to reduce the state's role in the economy and in the delivery of social welfare, and promoted an intensified integration in the regional and global economies.

What impact did these changes have on gender relations? An extensive body of work has argued that the burden of restructuring fell disproportionately on poor women.[75] Already disadvantaged within the division of labor in terms of economic security and reward, a large proportion of women in white collar and light industry jobs joined the ranks of the unemployed and indigent, while others entered poorly paid casual work or eked out a living in the informal sector. At the same time, the rise in the burden of care and the pressures of economic survival were reflected in rising female morbidity rates. Feminist economists have provided a radical critique of the premises of macroeconomic policies and of their gendered effects.[76] In questioning the fundamental categories of mainstream economic thought and the unequal value it assigns to productive and reproductive work, a further dimension of state complicity in maintaining and reproducing gender inequalities has been revealed. Moreover, the devolution of some aspects of the state's former responsibilities to the market and to civil society—the community, nongovernmental organizations (NGOS), the private sector, and the family—represented a shift in the terms of prevailing understandings of the obligations of the state to its citizenry. A new social contract was evolving and, along with it, new relations between states and societies, one premised on an expanded role for women's work, both paid and unpaid.

Redemocratization and Neoliberalism

The collapse of military rule in the 1980s and the return of civilian governments to power were accompanied by a deepening of the restructuring process, but in the context of a greater commitment to social justice and "good governance." This was the paradox of the 1990s that women's movements confronted: if the economic reforms had met with mixed results, in the political realm there were some positive developments. Partly under the influence of the international women's movement, partly due to the greater self-confidence and organizational strength of national women's movements, and partly in an effort to present a modern face to the world, newly elected democratic governments recognized women as a constituency that required representation in the state. Some, like Chile's Concertación government (1990), acknowledged the "social debt" that had been incurred as a result of decades of adjustment, one to which women had a special claim. In Argentina, Raúl Alfonsín incorporated women's demands for the liberalization of divorce and the reform of patria potestad in his electoral campaign of 1983. Government machinery was reformed to allow women's issues some representation, sometimes within ministries, sometimes in offices attached to the presidential office. Women's offices or secretariats, if they did not already exist, were established in virtually all Latin American states to assist in policy formulation and implementation. Laws requiring parties to have a minimum number of female candidates were adopted in ten countries, including Argentina 1991,[77] Brazil 1997, Bolivia 1997, Paraguay 1996, Venezuela 1998, Ecuador 1997, Peru 1997, and were proposed in others. Meanwhile legal reforms gave women new rights or restored and extended ones that had been removed by military regimes.

Yet for women's movements, the issue of whether and how to deal with the state—to work in or against it—remained a divisive one.[78] The principle of autonomy had a special resonance in Latin America, where female activism was often oppositional in conditions of political repression, and many feminists critiqued the masculinist favoritism, sexism, and authoritarianism of political parties and organizations. These experiences had helped to foster a critical view of prevailing organizational forms and a desire to develop a new way of doing politics associated with principles of autonomy, internal democracy, and egalitarianism. With the return of democratic governments and political parties, women's movements were faced with the question of how they should position themselves in relation to political society and whether they should retain their place in the political division of labor, as activists within civil society, a position that gained in strength with the growth of NGO activity as an important site of female activism.[79]

Two contrasting cases of how women's movements engaged with post-authoritarian states are discussed in the chapters by Jo Fisher and Fiona Macaulay. Fisher's study of the Argentine Housewives' Union (SACRA) in Argentina examines its demands for official recognition in the light of its

identification with Peronism and support for the Carlos Menem government after 1989. A working-class women's movement that had little time
for what it saw as middle-class feminism, SACRA identified with the historical project of Peronist corporatism and Eva's appeal on behalf of a dignified role for women in the home. In this sense, SACRA was committed to a
politics of difference, based on a revaluation of domestic work that entitled
women to state recognition, wages, and social security. It succeeded in
achieving some of its demands under the Menem administration, with
which it developed a special relationship. Fisher suggests that this relationship eventuated in SACRA supporting Menem's antiabortion stance at the
International Women's Conference at Beijing, thus further dividing it from
other feminist organizations.

Macaulay's chapter examines the contrasting case of a feminist lobbying
organization in Brazil. Largely comprising professional women, the Centro
Feminista de Estudos e Assessoria (CFEMEA) chose to operate according to
principles of autonomy, while directing its energies to the achievement of
legal reform. It eschewed special links with political parties, and while it
engaged with government and parties on public policy and legal issues, it
maintained its independence from the state. Unlike women's secretariats,
such as the Servicio Nacional de la Mujer (SERNAM) in Chile,[80] it had no
role or representation in the state itself. As Macaulay argues, this enabled
it to play a mediating role between women's movements and the state,
and allowed it to draw on the collaboration of women from a range of
political parties. It thus bridged a classic dichotomy that pits autonomy
against integration as the two options for women's movements in relation
to the state.

The effectiveness of all such interventions is, however, contingent on
more than securing "woman's spaces" within the political arena. In the first
place, it depends on the nature of the state and government—contingencies
that remain critically important in determining the success of claims on
the state for resources and policy changes. The degree of commitment to
democracy more generally, the sympathy governments express toward
women's issues, and the general direction of policy depend crucially on the
party in power—on its political ideology and hence its openness to wom-
en's representation and gender issues. Secondly, the allocation of institutional space within the state is not a sufficient condition for meaningful
change; women's secretariats or advocates need political muscle to keep

their demands on the agenda and to push for their realization. As much of the literature has argued, beyond issues of resources, allies, and institutional authority, the success of those *in* government has always depended on strong linkages with those outside it—that is, in movements or organizations within civil society.

Conclusions

With these developments, the twentieth century has closed on significant if fragile gains for women in the domain of the state.[81] For most of the century, women were kept out of political power, but as the chapters in this volume show, they were increasingly if selectively incorporated into the successive projects of states. As symbols of nationhood or public virtue, as subjects and objects of policy, and as the targets of political appeals, women became of increasing significance to governments as the century progressed. Modernity, as envisioned by Latin American elites, was itself premised on the selective incorporation of women into public life. Gender relations more broadly were also the subject of government concern and legislation, often constituting a site of struggle between conflicting views of the effects of modernity. The fates of family and nation were bound up with issues of women's roles and emancipation from male tutelage; women could not forever be denied citizenship rights, even if they acquired them on terms initially different from men's.

Women not only figured in the various debates over the direction of politics and policy, but were active participants in them. Although women's organizations lacked the institutional power to determine policy, they were often able to influence its character and content. Women's agency was a significant factor in the balance of forces that influenced gender relations in the region, but we should be careful to remember how dependent it was on favorable contexts and political alliances as well as how diverse in character and politics it was.[82] The history of feminism has received more scholarly attention than has antifeminism, but both have generated much passion and female activism. Not all women activists were feminists, and some actively opposed feminist demands; but equally, not all feminists were from the privileged sectors of society, even though more often than not they are the ones who are remembered through their writings. The very meaning of feminism has itself been contested, redefined, and pluralized over the course of the century. As women's movements have developed and changed, they have seen the greater participation of women from the popular classes, including those previously marginalized and silenced through racialized forms of exclusion. The extension of meaningful citizenship to these new claimants within the political arena is one of the most significant challenges faced by the postauthoritarian democracies and by those committed to deepening and extending its scope in Latin America.

A review of the changes in gender-state relations in Latin America over the course of the twentieth century shows that female activism ensured that some account was taken of women's interests. Yet concessions from governments were piecemeal, usually minimal, and the arenas of decision-making power remained largely impermeable to female accession until the century's close. More generally, the social organization of power, not only in the state but in much of civil society, retained a predominantly masculine character. For all the variability of Latin American state forms and the diversity of gender-state relations, no state, even the most apparently radical, achieved anything approaching gender equality in the political sphere. In the exercise of political power, twentieth-century states acted in the main to retain a masculine bias in the organization of the societies over which they presided. Even with the greater representation of women's interests in postauthoritarian governments, it remains the case that "government is conducted as if men's interests were the only ones that mattered."[83] Yet over the century, traditional masculine privileges were slowly if incompletely eroded as the material, cultural, and juridical foundations of patriarchy were significantly weakened; patriarchy may have been merely modernized, but in the process it was deprived of some of its former supports and potency. What impact this had on the varying constructions of masculinity and legal understandings of it is an essential if underresearched area of analysis. But as the work in this volume shows, shifting definitions of paternal duty and authority were indicative of the changing relations between gender and state. These changes were propelled by broader societal developments, notably in the realm of work, which acted to destabilize the balance of power within the family, albeit within persistent relations of inequality.

Viewed comparatively, Latin America was occasionally ahead or not far behind its northern counterparts in the matter of women's political and social rights. However, family reform proceeded unevenly, and masculine prerogatives prevailed uncontested in matters of sexuality. Even when laws did change, social relations and attitudes did not or did so only slowly. It may have been a capital offense for husbands to murder their wives in Latin America in the nineteenth century, but even a decade ago, courts could be sympathetic to murderous husbands who were seen as acting to defend their honor or as being justly provoked by the sexual insubordination of their wives. In public as in private life, the double standard in sexual morality retained its force. Similarly, domestic violence and rape, long the subjects of legal regulation, became objects of sustained campaigns for reform only in recent decades, not just in Latin America but elsewhere in the world.[84] The Brazilian Constitution of 1988 is one of the few in the world to declare a state interest in the curtailing of domestic violence, a clause that would not be there but for the concerted actions of the Brazilian women's movement. Six years later, in 1994, the Organization of American States approved the Inter-American Convention for preventing, sanctioning, and eradicating violence against women. Meanwhile, states and the Catholic Church have been reluctant to relinquish their power over women's bodies. Little progress has been made in the matter of reproductive rights, which have not been recognized as such in the organic laws of any Latin American country. Abortion is still illegal and subject to penal sanctions in Latin America (with the exception of Cuba), and contraception is still frowned upon by the church. In the 1990s, divorce, too, remained subject to restriction in the majority of Latin American countries and illegal in Chile.[85]

Gender ideologies, identities, and interests have remained strongly differentiated in Latin America, and the identification of women with the family retains considerable force as a political and cultural trope. With few exceptions, Latin American states and women's movements never embraced "equality feminism" with much enthusiasm, and even revolutionary Cuba showed ambivalence in this regard. As we have seen, gender ideologies sometimes worked to women's advantage, but more often than not they were turned against them. The individuation of women's rights *from* the family did not occur as early or as radically as it did in parts of Europe and the United States. Whether this was one reason for the region's relatively slow advance in matters of women's rights *in* the family is a matter for future enquiry and debate. For contemporary feminists well versed in the arguments over "difference," Latin America's state-gender relations may provide some salutary lessons. The attempts by Latin American feminists to speak in a different voice and to reconcile rights, social justice, and motherhood with national interests may have ceded too much ground to defenders of masculine privilege.[86] The eventual reform of the civil codes, for which first-wave feminists had struggled so long, was often justified by legislators as giving mothers the rights they needed to better perform their role in the family. Women were granted control over their earnings and property for the sake of their children[87] in the same way that women workers defended their right to work.[88]

These ambiguities in Latin America reflected tensions common to all contemporary societies. From the time of the industrial revolution, the division of labor between work and care has been expressed in an unresolved tension between the organization of work and social needs.[89] It has also defined different forms of social participation for men and women and different gender identities. In Latin America, women were assigned the values of altruism, affectivity, and moral virtue—values reflected in the assumptions that governed public policy throughout the century. Although these gendered ontologies expressed fundamental inequalities in the organization of society and the meanings of citizenship, most women continued to identify with them and framed their priorities accordingly. If policies based on gender difference served to deepen gender inequalities, they could still gain the support of many women. These tensions have run through women's movements across Latin America and have reappeared in the new arenas of policymaking within the state. In most cases, state agencies pursue an agenda to promote women's interests through egalitarian initiatives, but at the same time they declare their aim to "promote and protect the family," as if the former were coincident with the latter.[90] In Latin America, as elsewhere, much depends on the continuing efforts to secure more democratic states and socially just societies, a project still far from realized.

As the chapters in this volume show, Latin American states have intervened to varying degrees in the "social organization of the relations between the sexes,"[91] but it is a moot question whether the era of interventionist pretensions is waning or gathering a new, if dispersed, strength. The populist regimes have been described as resulting in an avalanche of social and labor legislation,[92] but much of that legislation presumed a traditional gender order. Most of the military dictatorships took measures to retraditionalize the family, some going so far as to restrict family planning and divorce. The new democracies returned the situation to the status quo ante and, with or without support from women's movements, introduced new rights for women in political life and in the workplace—from equal pay to protection from sexual harassment. The 1990s may have seen the redefinition of the role of the state and some diminution in its former responsibilities within the realm of welfare and economic management, but in the area of law it saw considerable and in some cases unparalleled activity concerning gender relations, sometimes of a strikingly contradictory character.[93] While gender became once again a sign of Latin American modernity as the new democracies struggled to overcome the stigma of a terrible past, right-wing parties were also able to mobilize support for conservative and at times explicitly antifeminist agendas.

The regulation of gender relations by external authorities has been a feature of all social life, but what is of interest in the twentieth century is the degree to which earlier modes of regulation changed and whether these changes delivered greater freedom for the female sex. As institutionalized forms of patriarchy waned, states assumed greater authority in underwriting the gender order. But as states progressively relinquish their interventionist pretensions in the new era of liberal governance, how will gender relations be affected? Will we see subtle shifts in the balance between state and market in the regulation of gender relations, as the more manifest powers of the state give way to the more subtle and insidious disciplines of the market? Or will states, in an excess of bureaucratic zeal, continue their intervention into the most intimate realms of human relations, and will they do so with or without the blessing of feminism?

In gender matters, as in all areas of political and social life, there are no simple judgments, no condition that is unassailable or immune to redefinition. The rights that Latin American women have won over the past two centuries reflect not so much a steady advance toward some goal of full emancipation as the outcome of conflicts with the state and with society in which partial, precarious, and sometimes unwanted freedoms have been won, and in which the goals of these movements have been reformulated. This will necessarily remain the case. It is, therefore, in that broader context—international, political, and social—that women in Latin America will continue to pursue and define their goals. If these chapters on the past two centuries provide a retrospective insight on these struggles, they may also serve, in small degree, as a prelude to the aspirations of women in the decades to come.

Notes

1   See inter alia: A. Lavrin, *Women, Feminism, and Social Change in Argentina, Chile, and Uruguay, 1890–1940* (Lincoln: University of Nebraska Press, 1996); Eugenia Rodríguez, ed., *Entre silencios y voces: Género e historia en América Central (1750–1990)* (San José: Centro Nacional para el Desarrollo de la Mujer y la Familia, 1997); Maritza Villavicencio, *Del silencio a la palabra: Mujeres peruanas en los siglos XIX–XX* (Lima: Ediciones Flora Tristán, Centro de la Mujer Peruana, 1992); June Hahner, *Emancipating the Female Sex: The Struggle for Women's Rights in Brazil, 1850–1940* (Durham, N.C.: Duke University Press, 1990); C. Lynne Stoner, *From the House to the Streets: The Cuban Women's Movement for Legal Reform* (Durham, N.C.: Duke University Press, 1988); F. Miller, *Latin American Women and the Search for Social Justice* (Hanover: University Press of New England, 1991); Sonia Alvarez, *Engendering Democracy in Brazil* (Princeton, N.J.: Princeton University Press, 1990); Line Bareiro and Clyde Soto, eds., *Ciudadanas: Una memoria inconstante* (Caracas: Centro de Documentación y Estudios, Nueva Sociedad, 1997; Susan K. Besse, *Restructuring Patriarchy: The Modernization of Gender Inequality in Brazil, 1914–1940* (Chapel Hill and London: University of North Carolina Press, 1996); Maria del Carmen Feijoó, *Las Feministas* (Buenos Aires: Centro Editor de America Latina, 1982); Carmen Ramos et al., eds., *Presencia y transparencia: La mujer en la historia de México* (Mexico City: El Colegio de México, 1987). For a detailed analysis of state policies and ideology in fields that directly affected women, see Susana Novick, *Politica y población: Argentina 1870–1989*, 2 vols. (Buenos Aires: Biblioteca Politica, 1992) and *Mujer, estado, y políticas sociales* (Buenos Aires: Biblioteca Política, 1993).

2   The study of gender and the state in the developing countries was in general an area that attracted little scholarship. For exceptions, see Sue Ellen Charlton, J. Everett, and K. Staudt, eds., *Women, the State, and Development* (Albany, N.Y.: SUNY, 1989); and Shirin M. Rai and Geraldine Lievesley, eds., *Women and the State: International Perspectives* (London: Taylor and Francis, 1996).

3   This feature was widely shared in the literature on the state. See general critiques by S. Franzway et al., *Staking a Claim: Feminism, Bureaucracy, and the State* (Cambridge: Polity, 1989), and by Sylvia Walby, *Theorising Patriarchy* (Cambridge: Polity, 1989). Jane Jaquette has noted the absence of engagement with gender in the Latin American literature on politics and the state in "Rewriting the Scripts: Gender in the Comparative Study of Latin American Politics," in *Latin America in Comparative Perspective*, ed. P. Smith (Boulder, Colo.: Westview, 1995), 128. In *State Theory: Putting Capitalist States in their Place* (Philadelphia:

Pennsylvania University Press, 1990), Bob Jessop notes that one of his main "errors and omissions" (13) was his lack of engagement with feminist theory.

4 The work of Nicos Poulantzas was influential in this debate, especially his theory of capitalist exceptionalism elaborated in *Fascisme et dictature* (Paris: Maspero, 1970). Latin American work on the state was also increasingly influenced by Juan Linz's analysis of authoritarianism and transitions from authoritarian regimes. On the latter, see Scott Mainwaring and Arturo Valenzuela, eds., *Politics, Society, and Democracy: Latin America* (Boulder, Colo.: Westview, 1998).

5 *Cepalista* refers to the policies of the Economic Commission of Latin America (Comisión Económica de América Latina), an agency of the UN that was under the direction of Raúl Prebisch.

6 Guillermo O'Donnell, *Modernization and Bureaucratic-Authoritarianism: Studies in South American Politics* (Berkeley and Los Angeles: University of California Press, 1973).

7 For early treatments of the state, see Elsa Cheney's classic, *Supermadre: Women in Politics in Latin America* (Austin: Institute of Latin American Studies, 1979), and Silvia Rodríguez Villamil and Graciela Sapriza, *Mujer, estado, y Política en el Uruguay del siglo XX* (Montevideo: Banda Oriental, 1984), which analyzes state policies in Uruguay in five areas: women's civil and political rights, participation in education, protection as mothers, labor law, and social security.

8 Michael Mann and Theda Skocpol have both engaged with the social dimensions of state power, and Skocpol has made an important contribution to the study of gender-state relations in her 1992 volume. See Michael Mann, *The Sources of Social Power*, vols. 1 and 2 (Cambridge: Cambridge University Press, 1986 and 1993); Theda Skocpol, *States and Social Revolution* (Cambridge: Cambridge University Press, 1978), and *Protecting Soldiers and Mothers: The Political Origins of Social Policy in the United States* (Cambridge, Mass., and London: Harvard University Press, 1992).

9 See Norbert Lechner, *Los patios interiores de la democracia: Subjectividad y política* (Santiago de Chile: Fondo de Cultura Económica, 1988), on the importance of including the social realm in the analysis of states. An example of the shifting terms of the Latin American debate on the state is Norberto Lechner, ed., *Estado y política en América Latina* (Mexico City and Madrid: Siglo XXI, 1983).

10 T. H. Marshall, *Citizenship and Social Class and Other Essays* (Cambridge: Cambridge University Press, 1950), and *Class, Citizenship, and Social Development* (New York: Doubleday, 1964).

11 Bryan S. Turner, *Citizenship and Capitalism: The Debate over Reformism* (London: Allen and Unwin, 1986).

12 *Postauthoritarian* is used as a shorthand term to refer to the governments elected to power following the fall of the military dictatorships in the 1980s. It is not meant to imply that the democratically elected governments were devoid of authoritarian characteristics.

13 For applications of a citizenship perspective, see inter alia, Elizabeth Jelin, ed., *Ciudadanía e identidad: Las mujeres en los movimientos sociales latinoamericanos* (Geneva: UNRISD, 1987); Elizabeth Jelin and Eric Hershberg, *Constructing Democracy in Latin America* (Boulder, Colo.: Westview, 1996); Eugenia Hola and Ana María Portugal, eds., *La Ciudadanía: A Debate* (Santiago de Chile: Isis International, 1997); Line Bareiro and Clyde Soto, eds., *Ciudadanas: Una memoria inconstante* (Caracas: Centro de Documentación y Estudios, CDE Editorial, Nueva Sociedad, 1997); Bérengère Marques-Pereira and A. Carrier, eds., *La Citoyenneté sociale des femmes au Brésil* (Brussels: CELA-IS, 1996). There is also an extensive bibliography on human rights: see, for example, Ximena Bunster and Regina Rodríguez, eds., *La mujer ausente: Derechos humanos en el mundo* (Santiago de Chile: Isis International, 1991); Elizabeth Jelin et al., eds., *Vida cotidiana y control institucional en la Argentina de los '90* (Buenos Aires: Nuevohacer, 1996).

14 Jean Bethke Elshtain, *Public Man, Private Woman* (Princeton, N.J.: Princeton University Press, 1981), and Carol Pateman, *The Sexual Contract* (Cambridge: Polity, 1988). Important contributions have also been made by Anne Phillips, *Democracy and Difference* (Cambridge: Polity, 1993) and *Engendering Democracy* (Cambridge: Polity, 1991); Ann Sassoon, *Women and the State: Boundaries of the Public and Private* (London and New York: Routledge, 1987); Nira Yuval-Davis and Floya Anthius, eds., *Women-Nation-State* (Basingstoke: Macmillan, 1989); and Nira Yuval-Davis, *Gender and Nation* (London: Sage, 1997).

15 A substantial literature exists on Latin America's "weak states," with their resulting inability to resist permeation by special interests, let alone fulfill their responsibilities.

16 See Catharine A. MacKinnon, "Feminism, Marxism, Method, and the State: An Agenda for Theory," *Signs* 7, no. 3 (1982): 515–44, and Maria Mies, *Patriarchy and Accumulation on a World Scale* (London: Zed Press, 1986), for contrasting examples of this approach.

17 For states as sites of struggle, see Barry Hindess, "Power, Interests, and the Outcome of Struggle," *Sociology* 16, no. 4:2 (1982): 498–511; R. Pringle and Sophie Watson, "Women's Interests and the Post-Structuralist State," in *Destabilising Theory*, ed. Michèle Barrett and Ann Phillips (Cambridge: Polity, 1992), 53–73; Sophie Watson, ed., *Playing the State* (London: Verso, 1990); Rai and Lievesley, eds. *Women and the State;* Sonia Alvarez, *Engendering Democracy in Brazil,* is closer to this perspective in seeing state practices and policies in contingent rather than essentialist terms.

18 This is not to imply that liberalism lacks ideology: one has only to think of the energetic cultivation of nationalist identification in the United States to underscore this point. See R. N. Bellah's "Civil Religion in America," *Daedalus* 96 (1967): 1–21, and *Beyond Belief: Essays on Religion in a Post Traditional World* (New York: Harper and Row, 1970).

19 This is not an exhaustive list of Latin American state forms, and within each of the five listed here, there are subcategories.

20 This sketch is intended to be merely suggestive with no pretensions to be exhaustive. In taking the standard periodizations, it cannot, of necessity, reflect the rich diversity of Latin American state forms and societies or deal with the reasons why states differed in their policies toward gender issues. This historical and analytic work is essential, necessary, and ongoing in Latin America.

21 "More or less" because as Peter Smith in *Latin America in Comparative Perspective: New Approaches to Methods and Analysis* (Boulder, Colo.: Westview, 1995) and others have argued, Latin American liberal states were never completely noninterventionist.

22 These visions of nationhood invested states with masculine virtues of heroism and glory or with feminine qualities of maternal fecundity. See Yuval-Davis, *Gender and Nation,* and Yuval-Davis and Anthius, eds., *Women-Nation-State.*

23 See Jean Franco, *Plotting Women: Gender and Representation in Mexico* (New York: Columbia University Press, 1988); Sarah Radcliffe and Sally Westwood, *Remaking the Nation* (London: Routledge, 1996); Francine Masiello, "Women, State, and Family in Latin American Literature of the 1920s," in *Women, Culture, and Politics in Latin America,* ed. the Seminar on Feminism and Culture in Latin America (Berkeley and Los Angeles: University of California Press, 1990), 27–47.

24 Girls were included in the liberal project of expanding education, but were initially admitted only to primary schools. Secondary- and tertiary-level education remained male prerogatives, and the latter only slowly bowed to pressure to admit women.

25 This was how Senator Miranda saw it in 1914, a period of intense debate in Uruguay over women's rights. Villamil and Sapriza, *Mujer, estado, y política,* 72.

26 When the Second World War broke out, only four countries had enacted legislation allowing women to vote in national elections (Ecuador 1929, Brazil 1932, Uruguay 1932, and Cuba 1934, El Salvador following suit in 1939).

27 Although first-wave feminism is largely associated with the activism of professional and elite women, it was a broader social movement, including working-class women. See inter alia, Maria del Carmen Feijoó, "Las trabajadoras porteñas a comienzos del siglo XX," in *Mundo urbano y cultura popular,* ed. Diego Armus (Buenos Aires: Sudamericana, 1990); Joel Wolfe, *São Paulo and the Rise of Brazil's Industrial Working Class, 1900–1955* (Durham, N.C., and London: Duke University Press, 1993); Maxine Molyneux, "No God! No Boss! No Husband! Anarchist Feminism in 19th Century Argentina," *Latin American Perspectives* 13, no. 1 (1986): 119–46.

28 This was the Congreso Internacional Femenino, in which "Femenino" here is best translated as "Women's" rather than "Feminine," which carries a different meaning in English.

29 As *El Día,* the newspaper of the pro-suffrage Partido Colorado in Uruguay, stated in 1914, "la mujer sea más indicada que el hombre para ciertas labores." Cited in Villamil and Sapriza, *Mujer, estado, y política,* 61.

30 See reformist Carlos Vaz Ferreira's lectures delivered from 1916 onward for

contemporary arguments concerning women's capacities, in *Sobre feminismo* (Buenos Aires: Editorial Losada, 1945).

31 Miller (*Latin American Women*); Lavrin (*Women, Feminism, and Social Change*); Hahner (*Emancipating the Female Sex*) all make this important point.

32 Prostitution became a significant urban phenomenon in much of Latin America in the early decades of the century. Attempts were made to regulate and at times suppress the activities of prostitutes in accordance with prevailing concerns with social hygiene and social order. Immigrant women in particular excited much general unease; apparently unattached and unchaperoned, they became the object of prurient speculation and were blamed for the rise in prostitution, even though it had increased in countries where immigration was minimal. See Donna Guy, *Sex and Danger: Prostitution, Family, and Nation in Argentina* (Lincoln and London: University of Nebraska Press, 1990).

33 Here socialist parties were especially important. On Argentina, for example, see Maria del Carmen Feijoó, "Las luchas feministas," *Todo Es Historia* (Buenos Aires) 11, no. 128 (January 1978): 6–23.

34 Theda Skocpol's account of the role of female agency and of civic maternalism in the formulation of social policy in the United States has been important in shifting the interpretative balance from a patriarchy analysis to one that stresses politics and agency. See *Protecting Soldiers and Mothers*. See Vallamil and Sapriza, *Mujer, estado, y política,* for the view that women's activism in Uruguay was a relatively minor factor in the process of securing gender equality because the radical-liberal project of Jose Batlle y Ordonez's (1903–7, 1911–15) Colorado Party took the lead.

35 Lavrin makes this important point in *Women, Feminism, and Social Change,* passim.

36 Bismarkian legislation was an influence here.

37 Women workers were considered morally at risk from the masculine environment of the workplace. See Daniel James, "Poetry, Factory Labor, and Female Sexuality in Peronist Argentina," *Journal of Latin American Cultural Studies* 6, no. 2 (1997): 131–52; also, John D. French and D. James, *The Gendered Worlds of Latin American Women Workers* (Durham, N.C., and London: Duke University Press, 1997).

38 This is Nancy Stepan's term; see *The Hour of Eugenics* (Ithaca: Cornell University Press, 1991).

39 There is a large literature on the link between demographic trends and social policy. See, for example, Colin Lewis, "Economic Restructuring and Labour Scarcity: Labour in the 1920s," in *Essays in Argentine Labour History 1870–1930,* ed. Jeremy Adelman (London and Oxford: Macmillan, 1992), 177–98, and Novick, *Mujer, estado, y políticas sociales.*

40 Stepan, *Hour of Eugenics.*

41 On feminism in Mexico, see inter alia: Ramos et al., eds. *Presencia y transparencia;* Diane Mitsch Bush and Stephen Mumme, "Gender and the Mexican Revo-

lution: The Intersection of Family, State, and Church," in *Women and Revolution in Africa, Asia and the New World,* ed. Mary Ann Tétrault (Columbia: University of North Carolina, 1994), 343–66; Anna María Fernández Poncela, ed., *Participación política: Las mujeres en México al final del milenio* (Mexico City: Colegio de México, 1995); Ana Lau and Carmen Ramos, eds., *Mujeres y revolución 1900–1917* (Mexico City: INHERM / INAH, 1993); Esperanza Tuñon, *Mujeres que se organizen* (Mexico City: Porrua, 1992). Sandra Mcgee Deutsch's review essay is also an excellent resource: "Gender and Sociopolitical Change in Twentieth-Century Latin America," *Hispanic American Historical Review,* 71, no. 2 (1991): 251–309.

42 Uruguay's amended divorce law of 1913 was one of the most advanced in the world and allowed for divorce by the sole will of the woman ("por la sola voluntad de la mujer"). Lavrin, *Women, Feminism, and Social Change,* 321.

43 The new divorce law reflected the aspirations of the anticlerical revolutionary elite anxious to wrest power from the church and was not popular among the mass of Mexican women.

44 "[L]a actividad de la mujer no ha salido del circulo del hogar doméstico, ni sus intereses se han desvinculado de los miembros masculinos de la familia, no ha llegado . . . romperse la unidad de la familia, como llega a suceder con el avance de la civilización, las mujeres no sienten pues la necesidad de participar en los asuntos públicos." *Diario de los Debates del Congreso Constiuyente, 1916–1917* (Mexico, 1960), 1–829. Cited in Enriqueta Tuñon, "La lucha política de la mujer mexicana por el derecho al sufragio y sus repercusiones," in Ramos et al., eds., *Presencia y transparencia,* 184.

45 Anna Macías, *Against All Odds: The Feminist Movement in Mexico to 1940* (Westport, Conn.: Greenwood, 1982).

46 See my "Family Reform in Socialist States: The Hidden Agenda," *Feminist Review* 21 (winter 1985): 47–64.

47 See also Mary Kay Vaughan, *Cultural Politics in Revolution: Peasants, Teachers, and Schools in Mexico 1930–1940* (Tucson: University of Arizona Press, 1997).

48 Acción Femenina's goals were to incorporate women into political life; promote equal rights for women to develop their faculties to the extent of their capabilities; to campaign against alcoholism, illiteracy, and religious fanaticism; and to attain equal rights for women in the civil, social, economic, and political arenas of Mexico. Shirlene A. Soto, *Emergence of the Modern Mexican Woman: Her Participation in Revolution and Struggle for Equality 1910–1940* (Denver: Arden, 1990), 123.

49 Carmen Ramos Escandón, "Women and Power in Mexico: The Forgotten Heritage," *Women's Participation in Mexican Political Life,* ed. Victoria E. Rodríguez (Boulder, Colo.: Westview, 1998), 87–102.

50 Quoted in Escandón, "Women and Power in Mexico," 100.

51 Although 1930 can be taken as a key moment in Latin American and world history, there were no neat ruptures in state forms. But the 1930s deserve more attention as a period of significant legislative and social change.

52 As Menno Vellinga states, "Purely corporatist systems never emerged, and, in practice, corporatist elements were combined with those originating in other traditions, including liberal-democratic ones." *The Changing Role of the State in Latin America* (Boulder, Colo.: Westview, 1998), 8.

53 Variant forms of corporatism have been acknowledged following Phillippe Schmitter's distinction between state corporatism and social corporatism. "Still the Century of Corporatism?" *Review of Politics* 36 (1974): 85–131.

54 There were of course divisions on this issue within socialism. Some joined conservatives in pitying the working woman and seeing her as a victim of capitalism, although it was usually acknowledged within socialist discourses that women were the victims of both capitalism and patriarchy.

55 James, "Poetry, Factory Labour, and Female Sexuality."

56 See Christopher Abel and Colin Lewis, eds., *Welfare, Poverty, and Development in Latin America* (London and Oxford: Macmillan, 1993).

57 See Ernesto Laclau, *Politics and Ideology in Marxist Theory* (London: Verso, 1977), for an influential variant of this view.

58 For different interpretations of the significance of Eva Perón, see inter alia: Susana Bianchi and Norma Sanchís, *El Partido Perónista Femenino* (Buenos Aires: Centro Editor de América Latina, 1988); Nicholas Fraser and Marysa Navarro, *Eva Perón* (London: André Deutsch, 1980); Alicia Dujovne Ortiz, *Eva Perón: La Biografía* (Buenos Aires: Aguilar, 1995).

59 *El Socialista* (Uruguay), 9 January 1907. Cited in Villamil and Sapriza, *Mujer, estado, y política.*

60 María del Carmen Feijoó with Marcela María Alejandra Nari, "Women and Democracy in Argentina," in Jane Jaquette, ed., *The Women's Movement in Latin America,* 2d ed. (Boulder, Colo.: Westview, 1994), 66–109. M. J. Schirmer, "Those Who Die for Life Cannot Be Called Dead: Women and the Human Rights Protest in Latin America," *Feminist Review* 32 (summer 1989): 3–29; Jennifer Schirmer, "The Seeking of Truth and the Gendering of Consciousness," in *VIVA: Women and Popular Protest in Latin America,* ed. Sarah Radcliffe and Sallie Westwood (London: Routledge, 1993), 30–64.

61 Diane Taylor, *Disappearing Acts* (Durham, N.C.: Duke University Press, 1997).

62 It was common for military dictatorships to police the dress and deportment of men and women in conformity with what were considered the appropriate values for the nation.

63 Ximena Bunster Burroto, "Surviving beyond Fear: Women and Torture in Latin America," in *Women and Change in Latin America: New Directions in Sex and Class,* ed. June Nash and Helen Safa (New York: Bergin and Garvey, 1986); Bunster and Rodriguez, eds., *La mujer ausente; The Report of the Argentine National Commission on the Disappeared, Nunca Más* (New York: Farrar Straus Giroux, 1986); and Nancy Caro Hollander, "The Gendering of Human Rights: Women and the Latin American Terrorist State," *Feminist Studies* 22, no. 1 (spring 1996): 41–80.

64 Hollander, "Gendering of Human Rights."

65 Taylor, *Disappearing Acts,* 157.

66 This was de facto the case in Argentina, too, although it was under the second Peronist government (1973–76) that contraception was restricted and placed under state control. Jo Fisher, *Mothers of the Disappeared* (London: Zed Books, 1989).

67 The number of female-headed households increased during the "lost decade."

68 In Guatemala and El Salvador, the mothers groups were also at the forefront of protests at atrocities practiced by the military against indigenous people. See Lynn Stephen, *Women and Social Movements in Latin America: Power from Below* (Austin: University of Texas Press, 1997).

69 Jane Jaquette, ed., *The Women's Movement in Latin America,* 2d ed. (Boulder, Colo.: Westview, 1994).

70 María del Carmen Feijoó ("Women and Democracy," in Jaquette, ed. *Women's Movement in Latin America*), sees this as limiting the political development of the mothers and as promoting ideals of womanhood that were serving to undermine rather than fortify feminist claims for equality. She acknowledges that in some ways these motherist movements challenged or at least redefined what it meant to be a mother. The Mothers evoked age-old images of the eternal feminine, one in which suffering and strength combined, yet they forced a public recognition of the reality of motherhood and defined and transformed what was private into a matter of collective public protest. Motherhood itself was made the basis of an ethical critique of society and its values. It was transformed from a passive, family-centered identification into a concern for humanizing and democratizing society. This transgression, this movement from the private space to the political arena, in Argentina earned them the dictatorship's dismissive epithet "las locas."

71 For accounts of this greater regional contact and cooperation, and for discussions of the regional *encuentros,* see the essays by Gina Vargas and by Nancy Saporta Sternbach et al. in *Mujeres y participación política,* ed. Magdalena León (Bogotá: TM Editores, 1994).

72 A large literature on women's movements and their contribution to ending military rule exists. See, for example, Alvarez, *Engendering Democracy in Brazil;* Jaquette, *Women's Movement in Latin America;* Miller, *Latin American Women;* Georgina Waylen, *Gender in Third World Politics* (Buckingham: Open University Press, 1996); Elizabeth Jelin, ed., *Women and Social Change in Latin America* (London: Zed and UNRISD, 1990); Jo Fisher, *Out of the Shadows: Women, Resistance and Politics in South America* (London: Latin American Bureau, 1993); Teresa Valdés and Marisa Weinstein, *Mujeres que sueñan: Las organizaciones de pobladoras en Chile: 1973–1989* (Santiago: FLACSO, 1993). Geertje Lycklama à Nijeholt, Virginia Vargas, and Saskia Wieringa, eds., *Women's Movements and Public Policy in Europe, Latin America, and the Caribbean* (New York and London: Garland, 1998).

73 Women's movements at this time were important in at least two respects: in developing the associational life of civil society and in bringing issues of "private" concern—such as violence in the family—to the public realm.

74 The term *new economic model* is defined in Victor Bulmer-Thomas, ed., *The New Economic Model in Latin America* (London: ILAS / Macmillan, 1996).

75 For work on this issue, see Isobella Bakker, ed., *The Strategic Silence: Gender and Economic Policy* (London: Zed, 1994).

76 See especially the pioneering work of Diane Elson, *Male Bias in the Development Process* (Manchester: Manchester University Press, 1991), and "Gender Awareness in Modelling Structural Adjustment," *World Development* 23, no. 11 (1995): 1851–68. For discussion of Latin America, see María Rosa Renzi and Sonia Agurto, *La esperanza tiene nombre de mujer: La economía nicaraguense desde una perspectiva de género* (Managua: FIDEG, 1997); Gonzalez de la Rocha, "Crisis, economía doméstica y trabajo feminino en Guadalajara," in *Trabajo poder y sexualidad*, ed. O. de Oliveira (Mexico City: PIEM, 1991), 159–85.

77 Argentina took the step of incorporating the quota principle into the electoral code. The Quota Law (Ley de Cupos) required all political parties to have a minimum of 30 percent female candidates on electoral slates. Women's representation in Congress has consequently soared from 5 percent in 1991 to 28 percent in 1995.

78 This issue was the subject of acrimonious division in the 1996 Encuentro in Chile. For a discussion of the general issues in the regional context, see inter alia: León, ed., *Mujeres y Participación Política;* Julieta Kirkwood, *Ser política en Chile: Los nudos de la sabiduria feminista* (Santiago: Editorial Cuarto Propio, 1990); Nijeholt, Vargas, and Wieringa, eds., *Women's Movements and Public Policy in Europe;* Poncela, ed., *Participación política;* Rodríguez, ed., *Women's Participation in Mexican Political Life.*

79 Sonia Alvarez notes this development as marking a new phase in the Latin American women's movement. See "Advocating Feminism: The Latin American Feminist NGO 'Boom,'" Schomburg-Moreno Lecture, Mount Holyoke College, March 1998.

80 The Servicio Nacional de la Mujer was set up in 1991 and had as its head a ministerial appointment. See Natacha Molina, "Women's Struggle for Equality and Citizenship in Chile," in Lycklama à Nijeholt, Vargas, and Wieringa, eds., *Women's Movements,* 127–41.

81 In the 1990s, women's representation in the Chambers of Deputies was as follows: (percent of women) Argentina 27.6 percent, 1997; Brazil 6.6 percent, 1994; Chile 10.8 percent, 1997; Colombia 11 percent, 1994; Costa Rica 19.3 percent, 1998; Cuba 27.6 percent, 1998; Dominican Republic 11.7 percent, 1994; Ecuador 5.2 percent, 1994; El Salvador 16.7 percent, 1997; Mexico 17.4 percent, 1997; Peru 10.8 percent, 1995; Uruguay 7.1 percent, 1994. The average for all Latin American countries: 12 percent. Female representation in senates was lower, with a mean

of 7.6 percent. Data compiled by Nikki Craske from Interparliamentary Union sources. *Women and Politics in Latin America* (Cambridge: Polity, 1999).

82 This question of women's diverse interests and the different kinds of women's movements which can be identified is examined in my "Analysing Women's Movements," in *Feminist Visions of Development: Gender Analysis and Policy,* ed. R. Pearson and C. Jackson (London and New York: Routledge, 1998), 65–88.

83 Watson, ed., *Playing the State* develops this point. Introduction, 3–20, passim.

84 Although Thomas Miller Klubrock has shown that whether domestic violence was taken to the courts was a matter contingent on the interests it served and on women's ability to prosecute their case. See "Morality and Good Habits," in French and James, eds., *Gendered Worlds,* 232–63.

85 See Teresa Valdés and Enrique Gomáriz, *Mujeres latinoamericanas en cifras: Tomo comparativo* (Santiago: FLACSO, 1995).

86 Lavrin (*Women, Feminism, and Social Change*) suggests that this was the case in the Southern Cone in the period up until the 1940s.

87 Ibid.

88 See Zaida Lobato, "Women Workers in the 'Cathedrals of Corned Beef': Structure and Subjectivity in the Argentine Meatpacking Industry," in James and French, eds., *Gendered Worlds,* 54–71.

89 Sassoon, *Women and the State.*

90 Only relatively recently have attempts been made to overcome the "false dichotomies" and the classic binaries of the past—in ways that surpass the terms of the old debates about equality and difference—in an effort to reconceptualize gender relations, rights, and justice.

91 Joan Scott's term; see "Gender: A Useful Category of Historical Analysis," *American Historical Review* 91, no. 5 (1986): 1067–70.

92 French and James, eds., *Gendered Worlds,* introduction, 10.

93 Menem's presidency can be seen as an example of this volatility.

II

Case Studies

Eugenia Rodríguez S.

Civilizing Domestic Life in the Central

Valley of Costa Rica, 1750–1850

The objective of this chapter is to explore changes in ideals of and attitudes toward marriage relationships, gender roles, and domestic violence in the Central Valley of Costa Rica between 1750 and 1850. I examine some historical myths about marriage: first, that domestic violence was unknown in Costa Rican society; second, that it was a practice exclusive of popular sectors; and third, that wives were passive victims of patriarchal dominance, incapable of resisting and impugning male dominance.[1] These myths are evident in the chronicles written by Moritz Wagner and Carl Scherzer, two German scientists who visited Costa Rica in 1853. They observed that

> happy marriages, according to our German concept, are perhaps as rare in Costa Rica as the unhappy ones. . . . That repeated enchantment, the languishing of love, those tender looks and kisses that characterize a honeymoon in Germany, and that seem so natural to the newlyweds, as they seem annoying to the unmarried eyewitness, do not exist here. There is no expression equivalent to "weeks of tinsel" or "months of honey;" neither does any drowsyness follow the drunkenness; once past the loving ecstasy the spouses do not fight, nor do they beat each other. Relationships that so calmly began continue developing quite regularly for the rest of their life. Mutual rights are respected.[2]

The Central Valley was the most important region between 1750 and 1850, with 80 percent of the total population (61,714 inhabitants in 1843–44).[3] Besides, it had a specific ethnic and cultural identity born out of the predominance of Catholicism and a population of mestizos, a racial and cultural mix of Indians and Europeans. Its population also included Indian and black minorities, located mainly in marginal areas. Toward the end of the eighteenth century, the Central Valley experienced an increase in marriage rates, which was associated with a decrease in illegitimacy, a tendency that intensified during the nineteenth century. Illegitimacy decreased from 40 percent at the end of the eighteenth century to 20 percent and 10 percent in the nineteenth century. The nineteenth-century marriage pattern in the Central Valley closely resembled the Western European experience.[4]

Study of the 1750–1850 period is important because it reveals the long-range impact of mechanisms used by the state and the community to regulate domestic morality and to legitimize and normalize a particular gender order. In particular, it highlights changes and continuities in the ideals of, perceptions of, and attitudes toward marriage, conjugal relationships, and domestic violence. Around 1750, the Central Valley saw the beginning of economic and demographic growth based on the spontaneous agricultural colonization of a free, mestizo peasantry. At the same time, commercial and crafts activities expanded, and foreign commerce developed. These developments were limited, however, because Costa Rica was a marginal province of the Kingdom of Guatemala. Therefore, the most dramatic socioeconomic changes occurred after independence in 1821.

The 1821–50 period can be considered an initial stage in the development of agrarian capitalism. In fact, this phase was characterized by growth in the production of agricultural exports—mainly coffee—as well as expansion of credit, international trade, and new technologies that industrialized coffee production. This growth generated a market of land and labor, which contributed to the initial settlement of the northwestern area of the Central Valley. The rise of agrarian capitalism transformed towns, changed the division of labor within the family, and stimulated the rise of paid labor, among other things.[5]

The process of liberal state formation in the 1821–70 period was characterized by constant struggles between competing merchant clans who, between 1840 and 1870, intermittently deposed one another through barracks coups in order to get access to power.[6] However, like Chile and Brazil, Costa Rica did not experience long-lasting institutional ruptures and bloody civil wars.[7] After 1870, the transformation of politics began under the dictatorship of General Tomás Guardia (1870–82) and his successors, Próspero Fernández (1882–85) and Bernardo Soto (1885–89). According to Iván Molina and Steven Palmer, these two decades, in particular, saw a great expansion of public administration and the rise of a group of politicians and intellectuals who had a clear plan of liberal reforms:

> Like similar efforts throughout Latin America at this time, Costa Rica's reforms were intended to strengthen political authority, favor the expansion of capitalist agriculture, and "civilize" the lower classes. New civil and penal codes were enacted, and police and administrative posts were multiplied throughout the country. . . . Perhaps of most importance, a centralized, secular, and free system of primary education was created (and made mandatory) to instruct the uncouth artisans, laborers and peasants . . . in new skills and new values. With messianic zeal, the priests of progress—lawyers, physicians, teachers and journalists—began to spread the modern values of patriotism, capitalism, science, hygiene and racial purity.[8]

Following Philip Corrigan and Derek Sayer's argument, Elizabeth Dore states that with "an array of governmental, juridical, cultural, and coercive institutions, state politics normalizes a variety of gender relations."[9] The main thesis of this chapter is that the century from 1750 to 1850 saw a rise in the ideal of the upper-class family, consisting of the male self-sufficient breadwinner and the dependent homemaking wife subjected to domestic space. In tandem, there developed a heightened appreciation of the ideal of marital relations as intimate, harmonious, and affectionate. The development of the civil judicial apparatus played a key role in these changes, by means of the centralization of the state. This expansion of the judicial apparatus stimulated the authorities and community to play a more active part in the regulation of domestic morality and in the promotion of upper-class ideals of family and marriage. It is particularly interesting that wives from the middle and popular sectors had greater access to the legal process and used this process as an arena for airing marital discord. This access encouraged greater public sanction of marriage relationships, principally with regard to cases of men's tyrannical abuse of their familial power, and contributed to a heightened appreciation of the benefits of marital companionship.

A. J. Hammerton, writing about Victorian England, argues that "this common thread of disillusion with patriarchal marriage, stemming from men's apparent failure to live up to companionate ideals, marked a fundamental turning point in thinking about conjugal relationships."[10] This change of thinking in marital and gender relations merely civilized the husband's patriarchal power rather than eliminated it, reinforcing a sharper idealization of separate spheres and gender roles.[11] The theoretical and methodological foundations of this chapter are drawn on influential writings by Hammerton and E. P. Thompson.[12] Hammerton proposes that it is useful to look at the role gender played in sharply differentiating the experiences of men and women during the modification of marital ideals. Following his approach, it is necessary to conceptualize two marriage ideals, companionate and patriarchal, as embodying elements of each other, rather than seeing them as stark opposites. Finally, it is crucial to focus on the roles played by the community, family, state, and Catholic Church in controlling and shaping domestic life and conjugal relationships—particularly in a society predominantly corporativist and in which marriage alliances as well as marital relations were submitted to constant public scrutiny. In summary, Hammerton's approach is very useful to understand the complex processes of change and continuity in the ideals and perceptions of marriage and conjugal relations in the Central Valley of Costa Rica.

This chapter examines the conditions that allowed marital dispute suits to become an accessible resource for wives in the first half of the nineteenth century. It investigates to what extent wives and husbands of different social backgrounds embarked on legal action. This issue is explored through analysis of spouses' allegations and emphasizes how the ideals and attitudes about marriage varied according to class and gender. The chapter then turns to examine changes in the character of marital relationships during this period. I assess to what extent such variations in marital relationships were related to the strengthening of the administrative apparatus of church and state. Finally, I evaluate the assimilation of the upper-class ideal of conjugal, harmonious, and affectionate marriage.

Accusations and Procedures

The procedures to set and resolve marital disputes before ecclesiastical and civil courts were simple and brief. However, after 1830 the civil courts became the best option for couples in conflict and for women of the middle sector in particular. This study is based on the analysis of 527 charges argued in 252 marital dispute suits filed by wives and husbands before the ecclesiastical and secular courts of the Central Valley during 1732–1850. Of the 252 cases, 173 (69 percent) correspond to the 1830–50 period, and 79 (31 percent) to the 1732–1829 period.[13]

The couples in conflict were from all social sectors. Using the terminology of the era, I have classified the couples into two groups, *familias principales* (principal families) and *familias del común* (common families). The classification of the first group was based on their own conceptualization and on the identification of brides and grooms by name. Couples from the familias principales were from the emerging urban agricultural and commercial bourgeoisie in San José, Cartago, Heredia, and Alajuela. The second group, the couples from the familias del común, consisted of everyone else, mostly rural families—small and medium rural producers, farmers, prosperous artisans, poor peasants, and day laborers. In this study, the terms *familias principales* and *familias del común* are significant because they reveal how ideological and attitudinal differences in the perception of marriage and marital relations varied according to social origin.[14]

One of the major criticisms of using this type of judicial suit as a source for the study of marital life is the problem that not all unhappy couples filed claims before the authorities. Despite the validity of such criticism, this study is based on the assumption, as Hammerton states it, that "common themes in the hard cases before the courts were echoed in a much wider discourse, crossing ideological boundaries, which focused on marital conflict and sought varying measures of reform and regulation of married life."[15]

I now turn to an analysis of the accusations in marital dispute cases and how such accusations were filed. During the colonial period, this type of claim was filed before the local priest, the only person authorized to deal with it.[16] After 1821, the main change was the gradual loss of exclusive power of the ecclesiastical authorities in the resolution of marriage conflicts, except in cases of divorce. This change was fostered by the centralization of the liberal state, which brought with it the expansion of the judicial apparatus and a greater coverage of the population, especially for the popular sectors in provincial capitals.[17] Moreover, the development of the judicial apparatus was reinforced by state politics, which normalized the gender order through the enactment of the Código General of 1841 and the Reglamento de Policía of 1849; both endorsed the legal prerogative of civil authorities to regulate domestic morality and suggested the type of penalties that should apply.[18] The expansion of the civil judicial apparatus and its power to regulate domestic morality can be seen in the fact that 78 percent of the cases were set before civil tribunals in the 1822–50 period.

After hearing an accusation in the civil courts, the mayor would name two *hombres buenos* (good men or partners) to speak on behalf of the involved parties. Together with the judge or mayor who heard the case, they acted as mediators in the judicial process—attempting to establish the facts, to reconcile the couple, and to propose some sort of settlement. As for the process of reconciliation, the secular response was not very different from the ecclesiastical; both stressed the upper-class ideal of marriage. The hombres buenos, with the judge, tended to insist that the couple restore harmonious relations and attempt to fulfill the Christian upper-class model of marriage.

This upper-class marriage ideal had a differentiated emphasis according to gender. Whereas wives stressed the companionate, affective, and self-sufficient breadwinner ideal partner, husbands stressed the submissive and domestic ideal partner. This differentiated emphasis in the upper-class marriage ideal according to gender was clearly specified in the Código General of 1841, which established that

> spouses mutually owe each other fidelity, aid and assistance. . . . The husband must protect his wife, and she will be obedient to her husband. . . . The wife is obliged to live with her husband, and follow him to wherever he deems convenient to reside. [The] husband is obliged to . . . give her everything necessary to live, according to his abilities and status.[19]

Is it not strange that church and state should be so concerned about harmonious marital relations? Not if we consider that both of these institutions tried to sustain the patriarchal norms of masculine domination, the institution of marriage and the family, and marital harmony and residence (see Varley's chapter in this volume). This attempt can be seen in the following communication sent by the bishop of Nicaragua, José Antonio de la Huerta, to the Costa Rican clergy on 19 August 1797. He declared that

> requiring married couples to live jointly and in conjugal consortium, we have known that there are many of them [married couples] in this bishopric, as well as from other distant provinces, who causing a great hurt to their souls, live separate for long periods, without any legitimate cause which is

approved by sacred canons. To resolve this situation and to fulfill our ministerial duties, I require to all priests to investigate in their parishes, married
couples who live separated and divided and who do not cohabit as husband
and wife, . . . and to persuade and admonish them to jointly live in conjugal consortium; and if you do not succeed by subtle methods, require the
Royal justices of your respective districts to compel them to follow such
requirement[s].[20]

The growing intervention by civil authorities in the first half of the nineteenth century was part of a gradual process of separation of the roles of
the church and the state in the regulation of domestic morality and in the
normalization of the gender order. The church was left to the doctrinal
regulation of marriage and the registration of vital statistics. The liberal
state began to take on a more active role in the regulation and transformation of the domestic life among the popular classes according to the dominant class values.[21] Paradoxically, it seems that when the morality of the
popular sectors was most regulated, they also had greater and more rapid
access to legal resources. Thus, the expansion of the judicial apparatus may
have contributed to a greater "democratization" by extending access to the
law to the popular sectors—especially women, who may have used the
courts to confront, resolve, and regulate their everyday conflicts. Therefore, the courts constituted the key framework within which class conflicts
and domestic, gender, familial, and community conflicts were mediated.[22]
Harmony was a key concept within the liberal doctrine of order, progress,
and civilization. The liberal state promoted patriarchal domination, harmony, and moral discipline of families, spouses, and neighbors, with the
objective of securing the labor discipline and peace necessary to launch the
capitalist development project.[23]

Wives and the Causes of Marital Conflicts

Wives accused their husbands more than husbands accused their wives
before the courts. Of the 252 cases in which the accuser is known, wives
filed 166 suits (66 percent), but husbands presented only 86 cases (34 percent). In other words, marital dispute denouncement was primarily a feminine resource.[24]

There was a sharp contrast between the number of demands filed by couples of the familias principales and those filed by couples of the familias del común. In terms of social strata, in the 252 cases, 208 demands were filed by couples of the familias del común and 44 by couples of the *familias de la élite*. In the cases of the familias del común, 141 wives accused their husbands (68 percent), and 67 husbands accused their wives (32 percent). Of a total of 44 cases of the familias de la élite (principales), 25 wives accused their husbands (57 percent), and 19 husbands accused their wives (43 percent). These numbers indicate that both elite and common wives tended to take the initiative to accuse their husbands. However, among the couples of the familias del común, there was a sharper contrast in the proportion of accusations made by wives and husbands (68 percent of wives, 32 percent of husbands). For their part, elite husbands filed accusations against their wives (43 percent) on more occasions than did their commoner counterparts (32 percent). What factors might help to explain this contrast?

Regarding the right of the wife to resort to the courts, the Código General of 1841, like the colonial legislation, determined that the wife must obtain her husband's permission to testify in a trial or to give away, relinquish, mortgage, or acquire any asset.[25] However, she was granted the right to accuse her husband of abuse.[26] Pertaining to this last point, the law specified that the wife could resort to the tribunals

> when a husband, due to his misconduct or mistreatment of his wife, that not be in deed, may give rise to justified complaints on her part, [in such cases] he will be reprimanded by the judge, and if he resumes his excesses, he will be arrested or put in a correctional house for the time considered adequate, which shall not surpass one year, to which the judge will proceed in light of renewed complaint by the wife, if it turns out to be true.[27]

Based on their right of redress of marital abuse, women formulated complaints against their husbands, demonstrating in the majority of the cases that they had indeed suffered some type of abuse. However, having this right did not allow them license to exaggerate the facts. Charges needed to be corroborated by the judge, who would name two "good men" to interrogate the parties meticulously. In addition, they would call witnesses to promote the couple's reconciliation.

Fourteen main types of charges were filed by wives against their hus-

TABLE I. Wives' Charges against Husbands: Familias Principales and Familias del Común, Central Valley of Costa Rica (1732–1850).

Type of Complaint	Familias Principales		Familias del Común		Total	
	No.	%	No.	%	No.	%
Physical abuse	13	22.8	97	29.2	110	28.3
Verbal and physical abuse	4	7.0	18	5.4	22	5.6
Threats to life	2	3.5	19	5.7	21	5.4
Adultery	11	19.3	48	14.5	59	15.2
"Illicit relationship"	0	0.0	15	4.5	15	3.8
Having a child with another woman	2	3.5	3	0.9	5	1.3
Abandonment	3	5.2	11	3.3	14	3.6
Abandonment / Lack of financial support	8	14.0	46	13.9	54	13.9
Spent their assets	3	5.3	14	4.2	17	4.4
Drunkenness	0	0.0	9	2.7	9	2.3
Vicious and vagrant	0	0.0	10	3.0	10	2.6
Did not allow wife to see relatives	3	5.3	5	1.5	8	2.0
Meddling relatives	3	5.3	25	7.6	28	7.2
Objectionable place of residence	5	8.8	12	3.6	17	4.4
Total of Complaints*	57	100.0	332	100.0	389	100.0
Total of Cases*	25	15.1	141	84.9	166	100.0

Source: Archivo Nacional de Costa Rica and Archivo de la Curia Metropolitana (1732–1850), San José.
*See difference between total of complaints or charges argued by wives and total of cases or suits filed by wives against their husbands.

bands. As we can see in table 1, 166 wives filed suits against their husbands. Of the 166 complaints in which the causes are known, the most frequent on the list is physical abuse. Taken together, physical and verbal abuse account for 34 percent of the charges. Furthermore, wives frequently claimed that they were abandoned and lacked food and necessary clothing, and that their husbands had squandered their assets (22 percent), or that husbands had been unfaithful or were living with other women (20 percent). Other women accused their husbands of constantly threatening to kill them (5 percent) or of being friends of vice and alcohol (5 percent). Finally, women sometimes claimed that their husbands made them live in places they did not like (4 percent) and did not allow them to visit their families (2 percent), or that his relatives interfered in their affairs, thus provoking conflicts (7 percent). (See Ann Varley's chapter.)

In addition, the type of charges varied according to the wives' social origin (see table 1). It is evident that domestic violence was not a practice exclusive of popular sectors. However, common wives tended to place more emphasis on charges associated with physical and verbal abuse and with death threats perpetrated by their husbands (40 percent), as compared to the affluent wives (33 percent).

Among the cruel methods employed by husbands against their wives, the following stand out: yanking or cutting off their braids, tearing their clothes, slapping, lashing with twigs and horsewhips, and threatening their lives with knives, rocks, machetes, and other weapons. According to the Código General of 1841, the penalty for this type of abuse varied according to whether the consequences of violence (wounds, hits, and bad treatment) impeded the victim from working temporarily or permanently,[28] underlining the fact that in a predominantly agrarian society, centered on coffee production and characterized by a shortage of labor, the ability to work was taken seriously.[29]

Abandonment and lack of economic support constituted another of the most important charges filed by wives against their husbands (see table 1). These charges were reported by common wives in 17 percent of the cases and by elite wives in 19 percent. Besides, elite wives did not report accusations of vagrancy or alcoholism. The greater tendency among common wives to file for abandonment and lack of economic support underlines the importance of a husband's economic contribution. It was particularly serious if he did not fulfill the ideal of the self-sufficient breadwinner. In sum, material conditions of the familias del común made it more difficult for husbands to adjust to the upper-class ideal of the self-sufficient breadwinner and of the caring and respectful husband.[30]

The following case illustrates both the difficulty experienced by the popular and middle sectors in adjusting to the upper-class marriage model and the role of drunkenness as a cause of domestic violence and lack of financial support. José Segura, a tailor, was sued by his wife (whose name was not registered) for always being drunk, provoking public scandals, punishing her, and not fulfilling his duties as a provider. In April 1844, the judge sentenced Segura to jail for habitual drunkenness, and because of this vice he scandalizes the neighborhood where he lives. . . . [H]e does not fulfill his marital duties in that he does not provide the necessaries for his wife, and wants to kill her when he is drunk. . . . [He] sets a bad example and abuses Jesus Herrera, an orphan in his care, who being so young does not talk, and is a little deaf and cannot manage alone. . . . Even though said Segura is a tailor, he does not work because of this accustomed vice.[31]

The husband defended himself from these charges by arguing that even though drunkenness often prevented him from working, when he was sober, he was still able to work and provide food for his family. This argument can be appreciated in the following declaration: "[it is] true [that] he is accustomed to drinking liquor and when he drinks, it affects him. . . . As they say he scandalizes the neighborhood, but to say that he abuses and does not provide for his wife is false, because when he is sober he works to support his obligations."[32]

Based on these allegations, the judge ruled that the husband had to fulfill

two months of public service, and once this sentence is completed, he will be turned over to his brother Francisco until he be redeemed. . . . Regarding the orphan, he will be turned over to Mr. José María Aguilar, second-degree relative, and good man trusted by this Court, to administer his goods and with them provide for the mentioned orphan.[33]

It is interesting to analyze the extent to which certain changes in ideals toward couple relationships and gender roles can be detected in the period from 1750 to 1850. There was a marked increase in the number of judicial accusations of marital disputes, particularly in the period 1830–50. Also, there was a general tendency toward change in the order of importance of the types of charges made by wives in the two periods, 1750–1829 and 1830–50, expressed in an increase in charges of physical and verbal abuse (from 24 to 40 percent) and of familial (in-law) interference. The incidence of charges for drunkenness and vagrancy (6 percent) and "life in jeopardy" (5 percent) did not change. However, the following diminished in frequency: charges for adultery (from 29 to 13 percent) and for abandonment and lack of financial support for households (from 20 to 14 percent). Also, the charge "objectionable place of residence" diminished in importance. However, according to the social origin of wives, certain subtle differences can be appreciated.

Whereas elite wives more often charged physical and verbal abuse and threats to their lives, more humble wives tended to charge abandonment, lack of financial support, and drunkenness and vagrancy.

In summary, changes in the emphasis on certain kinds of charges formulated by wives suggest that they increasingly tended to reflect in their discourse some elements of the Christian upper-class marriage ideal. For elite wives, that ideal meant a husband capable of offering his wife companionship, respect, affection. For common wives, it meant a husband fulfilling the role of head of house and self-sufficient breadwinner. One element that promoted the assimilation of the upper-class marital ideal among wives of the popular or middle strata was the expansion of the civil judicial apparatus. This development allowed wives, particularly of the familias del común, the legal means to confront abusive husbands and a method to obtain certain support from the community and family, both of which established, if not a radical improvement in wives' condition, at least some change in the balance of power between wives and husbands.

Husbands and the Causes of Marriage Conflicts

How did husbands' complaints differ from those made by wives? Analysis of claims made by both spouses is essential to understand better the role played by gender and social condition in perceptions of conjugal relationships and the extent to which these perceptions were modified in Central Valley society between 1750 and 1850. Although marital dispute suits were predominantly a feminine resource, husbands' accusations against their wives increased in the 1830–50 period.

Unlike wives, however, husbands of both groups more often tended to charge their spouses with infidelity (38 percent), abandonment (20 percent), disobedience and failure to accomplish duties (23 percent), interference by in-laws in marital affairs (8 percent), verbal abuse (6 percent), and threats to life (2 percent). (See table 2.) Accordingly, the main grounds alluded to by husbands were adultery, abandonment, insubordination, and lack of fulfillment of domestic duties. In other words, husbands emphasized those patriarchal elements that fit the model of the ideal upper-class wife: submissive, obedient, faithful, and completely dedicated to domestic chores.

In spite of husbands' shared perspective regarding the patriarchal marital

TABLE 2. Husbands' Charges against Wives: Familias Principales and Familias del Común, Central Valley of Costa Rica (1732–1850).

Type of Complaint	Familias Principales		Familias del Común		Total	
	No.	%	No.	%	No.	%
Adultery	12	41.4	38	34.9	50	36.2
"Illicit relationship"	0	0.0	3	2.8	3	2.2
Having a child with another man	1	3.5	3	2.8	4	2.9
Abandonment	7	24.1	20	18.3	27	19.6
Does not obey / follow	3	10.3	20	18.3	23	16.7
Does not accomplish domestic duties	1	3.5	7	6.4	8	5.8
Verbal abuse	2	6.9	6	5.5	8	5.8
Meddling relatives	2	6.9	9	8.3	11	7.9
Threats to life	1	3.4	2	1.8	3	2.2
Drunkenness	0	0.0	1	0.9	1	0.7
Total of Complaints*	29	100.0	109	100.0	138	100.0
Total of Cases*	19	100.0	67	100.0	86	100.0

Source: Archivo Nacional de Costa Rica and Archivo de la Curia Metropolitana (1732–1850), San José.
*See difference between total of complaints or charges argued by husbands and total of cases or suits filed by husbands against their wives.

ideal, table 2 suggests certain differences in the emphasis placed on accusations according to social origin, although the differences were less marked among wives. Elite husbands tended to question their wives' faithfulness. Whereas 69 percent of elite husbands accused their wives of adultery or abandonment, common husbands reported this complaint only in 58 percent of the cases. Common husbands tended to focus on disobedience and lack of compliance with the obligation to serve him and the family (25 percent), but upper-class husbands complained of this problem in only 14 percent of the cases.

Certain factors caused these differences in the accusations formulated by husbands and wives. The greater fears of elite husbands about their wives' infidelity may stem, in part, from the weightier influence of social and familial considerations and from the seclusion of elite wives in the domestic sphere. In this context, contact with the opposite sex was taken much more seriously. Moreover, among the dominant class, honor was conceived of in corporativist rather than individual terms and was related to social and familial considerations. Thus, an elite husband was inclined to pressure the authorities to "reestablish" the honor and reputation of his wife and, therefore, of himself and of his family.[34]

The third ground for accusation listed by husbands—that wives did not submit to their authority or fulfill their domestic duties—is an interesting one. Fourteen percent of elite husbands made these charges; 25 percent of commoners made them (see table 2). What tentative explanations can be offered regarding common husbands' greater emphasis on submission? Probably, submission was associated with a husband's limitations in exercising the role of main household authority, given that, first, their spouses made complementary contributions to the maintenance of the home; second, their wives had greater freedom to mobilize and work out of the home, which increased their contact with other people;[35] and third, husbands had their own financial difficulties in providing adequate living space and food and clothing for the family, especially in the first years of marriage.[36]

That husbands (well to do and commoners alike) would resort to the tribunals reveals a certain level of frustration at not being able to resolve the contradiction between ideals and everyday realities. This frustration was particularly associated with the sensation of loss of authority in the home, a sensation that could manifest itself in husbands—particularly common husbands—verbally or physically abusing their wives or squandering the wives' assets or those assets produced jointly. Table 1 substantiates the latter, showing that in wives' accusations against their husbands, 4 percent corresponded to complaints of husbands squandering or taking away their assets. However, this complaint was slightly more common among the elite wives (5 percent).

Masculine impotence before the expected ideal of self-sufficient bread-winner and main authority in the nuclear family is demonstrated in the case of Domingo Arce against his wife, filed before the court of Heredia in March 1843. Arce

accus[ed] his wife, Mersedes Chacón, of having ignored his authority that he rightfully has over her and his house. [Thus], he lives an insufferable life, because he is not the owner of anything of his house, nor does he govern [his house]. [T]herefore, he ask[ed] the Court to establish his right to govern his wife in his house, according to his rights granted him by law, as husband.[37]

Mercedes Chacón granted power of attorney to Mr. Cayetano Morales, who stated on her behalf that

the charges made by her husband seem to be nothing more than whims. . . . [He] himself has confessed that his wife is hard working, as can be seen by the articles in their home which were acquired by her. [S]he [also] plants corn and beans, makes clothes for herself and her children, and even for her husband. [A]nd, although he works, she has no idea what he does with the money because as can be proved, having been absent from the house for one year and eight months, he had not brought any food or clothing for his family. . . . [F]inally, so as not to discredit him, she declines to make other declarations, and . . . asks the Court to sentence him as deemed convenient so that in the future he fulfill his obligations.[38]

After hearing the depositions of the two spouses, the judge explained the sentence by emphasizing feminine subjugation:

considering that a woman is obligated to respect, and be submissive and obedient to her husband, as well as observe the duties imposed upon her by Article 133 of the civil code, which gives the husband the right to govern her and what concerns his home. [A]nd, [considering] a husband's duty is to feed her, keep his job and love her amorously. [T]herefore, based on Articles 132 and 135 of the same code, I find that the accused should observe in the future the obligations placed on her by the cited articles, and the husband should also comply with the parts that correspond to him which I have made known to both parties.[39]

Finally, it is necessary to analyze the extent to which certain changes in ideals toward marriage relationships and gender roles can be detected in the period between 1750 and 1850. In this respect, there was an increase in the number of judicial accusations about marital discord, particularly in the period of 1830–50. Also, like wives, husbands showed a change in the charges they brought against their wives between the two periods, 1750–1829 and 1830–50 — with an increase in the incidence of charges having to do with lack of compliance with domestic duties and abandonment (from 17 to 26 percent), disobedience (from 8 to 30 percent), verbal abuse (from 3 to 11 percent), and rejection of relatives' interference in their conjugal life. However, husbands from one period to the next filed fewer accusations relating to charges of adultery (from 60 to 28 percent) and threats to life.

However, there were no clear differences in the kind of charges husbands, in contrast to wives, made according to their social origin.[40]

In summary, changes in the emphasis on certain kinds of charges formulated by wives and husbands suggest that they tended increasingly to emphasize in their discourse some elements of the Christian upper-class marriage ideal. More precisely, whereas wives stressed the ideal upper-class model of husband as a supportive, respectful, caring, and self-sufficient breadwinner, husbands tended to focus on the patriarchal subjection of their wives, who in turn should fulfill their domestic obligations to him and the family.

Concluding Remarks

This analysis indicates changes as well as continuities in ideals of and attitudes toward marriage and marital relations in Costa Rica in the first half of the nineteenth century, a process that varied according to gender and social origin. As a product of state formation and centralization, the development of the civil judicial apparatus played a key role in those changes. It stimulated the authorities and the community to play a more active role in the regulation of domestic morality and the normatization of a gender order. In addition, the possibility of recourse to the courts promoted an upper-class ideal of harmonious, affectionate marriage and the ideal family form, consisting of a male self-sufficient breadwinner and a dependent homemaking wife subjected to domestic space. Extension of the judicial apparatus made it more likely for wives, particularly from middle and popular sectors, to enjoy greater access to the legal arena for airing marital discord, thus creating greater public sanction of marital relationships.

In the marital disputes aired in tribunals, spouses placed different emphasis on specific aspects of the upper-class marital ideal. Whereas wives alleged that their husbands abused them excessively or did not fulfill the role of primary breadwinner (the companionate ideal), husbands accused wives of not bowing to absolute masculine authority or failing in their domestic chores (the patriarchal ideal). In short, this process of changes as well as continuities in marital ideals resulted in a growing idealization of the separation of spheres and gender roles in which the patriarchal domain was subject to greater regulation at the same time as it was reinforced.

This analysis of charges formulated by couples suggests that in the everyday life of the familias del común, it was difficult to put into practice this upper-class marital ideal. Because wives contributed significantly to the maintenance of the home, common husbands found it difficult to enforce their absolute authority there and to subject their wives to their control. This difficulty may have been accentuated by the fact that common wives had greater freedom than elite wives to mobilize and work out of the home, which gave them increased contact with other people. In addition, this study shows that common couples faced obstacles in achieving the upper-class marital ideal because they lacked the financial resources to provide adequate living space, food, and clothing for the family, especially in the first years of marriage. Finally, the community played a significant role in policing marital affairs. "Privacy and intimacy" in conjugal relations were difficult to attain on an everyday basis.[41]

These findings tend to question the assumptions that, on the one hand, women were mere victims of patriarchal dominance, incapable of resisting and impugning male dominance, and that, on the other hand, women—particularly from popular sectors—ruled in their homes, where there was no room for male dominance.[42] The analysis of marital disputes in Costa Rica in the century from 1750 to 1850 shows that domestic gender relations were dynamic and subject to constant negotiation and that wives from different social sectors tried to subvert or at least to establish a certain balance in patriarchal dominance.

In summary, it should be concluded that a redefinition in the ideals of marriage and gender roles occurred, but in the end the ideological discourse of upper-class companionate and affective marriage both hid and legitimated patriarchal dominance. Nevertheless, the ideal marriage based on companionship and affection constituted more than an attenuated version of the patriarchal ideal. It is in this light, then, that the growing criticisms of masculine and feminine conduct and of the legal reforms, which civilized rather than eliminated the husbands' patriarchal power, should be viewed.[43]

Notes

This research was made possible by a doctoral research fellowship from the Joint Committee on the Latin American and the Caribbean of the Social Science Research Council and the American Council of Learned Societies (1994–95), under the auspices of the Assistant Rectorate of Research and the Center for Historical Research of Central America of the University of Costa Rica (1993–95). I wish to thank Muriel Nazzari, Jeffrey Gould, and Peter Guardino, my dissertation tutors at Indiana University, for their comments. Also, I want to thank Elizabeth Dore, Iván Molina, Steven Palmer, María Tatiana Krot, and Jeanina Umaña for their suggestions. Finally, I thank Paulina Malavassi for her research assistance.

1 Lowell Gudmundson, *Costa Rica Before Coffee: Society and Economy on the Eve of the Export Boom* (Baton Rouge: Louisiana State University Press, 1986), 88; Eugenia Rodríguez, "From Brides to Wives: Changes and Continuities in the Ideals of and Attitudes towards Marriage, Conjugal Relationships, and Gender Roles in the Central Valley of Costa Rica, 1750–1850" (Ph.D. diss., Indiana University, 1995), 140–89; Eugenia Rodríguez, ed., *Violencia doméstica en Costa Rica: Más allá de los mitos*, no. 105, *Cuadernos de Ciencias Sociales* (San José: FLACSO–Costa Rica, 1998).

2 Moritz Wagner and Carl Scherzer, *La República de Costa Rica en la América Central,* 2 vols. (San José: Ministerio de Cultura Juventud y Deportes de Costa Rica, 1974), 1:224–25. Unless otherwise indicated, all translations from the Spanish are mine.

3 Gudmundson, *Costa Rica Before Coffee,* 169–71.

4 Héctor Pérez, "Deux siècles d'illegitimé au Costa Rica 1770–1974," in *Marriage and Remarriage in Populations of the Past,* ed. H. Dupaquier et al. (London: Academic, 1981), 481–93; Rodríguez, "From Brides to Wives," 30–31.

5 Iván Molina, *Costa Rica (1800–1850): El legado colonial y la génesis del capitalismo* (San José: Editorial Universidad de Costa Rica, 1991); Iván Molina and Víctor Hugo Acuña, *Historia económica y social de Costa Rica (1750–1950)* (San José: Editorial Porvenir, 1991); Iván Molina and Steven Palmer, *The History of Costa Rica* (San José: Editorial Universidad de Costa Rica, 1998); Mario Samper, *Generations of Settlers: Rural Households and Markets on the Costa Rican Frontier, 1850–1935* (Boulder, Colo.: Westview, 1990).

6 Molina and Palmer, *History of Costa Rica,* 64.

7 Ciro Cardoso and Héctor Pérez, *Centro América y la economía occidental (1520–1930)* (San José: Editorial Universidad de Costa Rica, 1977), 144–45.

8 Molina and Palmer, *History of Costa Rica,* 65. In addition, there was a redefinition in the ideological models of gender and the family in the period 1880–1930. The liberal reforms and the expansion of press, education, and feminism promoted a broad and systematic diffusion of these models. The modernized discourse on gender and the family stressed, first, the model of a conjugal, monogamic, harmonic, and affective family capable of stimulating economic modernization and preserving the social order; second, the ideal model of marriage by love and companionship; third, a growing idealization of the separation of spheres and

gender roles, consisting of a male self-sufficient breadwinner and head of household, and a dependent homemaking wife subjected to domestic space; fourth, the promotion of modern "scientific" motherhood as a woman's "natural" destiny and urgent social mission to raise healthy, productive, and morally upright children; and fifth, for both males and females, the development of adequate education, work opportunities, family responsibilities, sexual conduct, and public roles (see Eugenia Rodríguez, "Matrimonios felices: Cambios y continuidades en las percepciones y en las actitudes hacia la violencia doméstica en el Valle Central de Costa Rica (1750–1850)," in Rodríguez, ed., *Violencia doméstica en Costa Rica*, 9–30. For the Brazilian case, see Susan K. Besse, *Restructuring Patriarchy: The Modernization of Gender Inequality in Brazil, 1914–1940* (Chapel Hill and London: University of North Carolina Press, 1996), 92.

9 See the first chapter of this book. Dore bases her argument on Philip Corrigan and Derek Sayer, *The Great Arch: English State Formation as Cultural Revolution* (Oxford and New York: Basil Blackwell, 1985).

10 A. James Hammerton, *Cruelty and Companionship: Conflict in Nineteenth-Century Married Life* (London: Routledge, 1992), 7.

11 Hammerton, *Cruelty and Companionship*, 13.

12 A. James Hammerton, "Victorian Marriage and the Law of Matrimonial Cruelty," *Victorian Studies* 33, no. 2 (winter 1990), 269–70; Hammerton, *Cruelty and Companionship*, 1–10, 168–69; E. P. Thompson, "Happy Families," *New Society* (8 September 1977), 499–500. A. J. Hammerton and E. P. Thompson criticize the approaches of E. Shorter and L. Stone. See Edward Shorter, *The Making of the Modern Family* (New York: Basic Books, 1975); Lawrence Stone, *The Family, Sex, and Marriage in England 1500–1800*, ab. ed. (New York: Harper Torchbooks, 1979); Lawrence Stone, *Road to Divorce: England 1530–1987* (Oxford: Oxford University Press, 1990); Lawrence Stone, *Broken Lives: Separation and Divorce in England 1660–1857* (Oxford: Oxford University Press, 1993).

13 The marital dispute suits are located in the Archivo de la Curia Metropolitana and the Archivo Nacional de Costa Rica. Comparing the number of marriages (29,116) to the number of cases of marital disputes (268) in the period between 1750 and 1850, I found that these cases represented a fluctuating proportion of a minimum of 0.4 percent of marriages (between 1801 and 1829) and a maximum of 2.2 percent of marriages (between 1840 and 1850). See Héctor Pérez, "Reconstrucción de las estadísticas parroquiales de Costa Rica, 1750–1900," *Revista de Historia* 17, no. 1 (January–June 1988): 211–77.

14 Rodríguez, "From Brides to Wives," 73–139.

15 Hammerton, *Cruelty and Companionship*, 7.

16 Ricardo Blanco, *Historia eclesiástica de Costa Rica* (San José: Editorial Costa Rica, 1967), 315–16; Claudio Vargas, *El liberalismo, la iglesia, y el estado en Costa Rica* (San José: Ediciones Guayacán, 1991), 65–82. Spanish colonial law about marriage continued in force with few changes in Costa Rica, as well as in other parts

of Latin America, during the nineteenth century. See Costa Rica, *Código General de la República de Costa Rica (1841)* (1841; reprint, New York: Imprenta de Wynkoop, Hallenbeck y Thomas, 1858), Libro I, Arts. 53, 84–160; Marielos Acuña and Doriam Chavarría, "Endogamia y exogamia en la sociedad colonial cartaginesa (1738–1821)," *Revista de Historia* 23, no. 1 (January–June 1991): 107–44; Silvia Arrom, *The Women of Mexico City: 1790–1857* (Stanford: Stanford University Press, 1985), 55; María Gabriela Leret, *La mujer: Una incapaz como el demente y el niño (según las leyes latinoamericanas)* (Mexico City: B. Costa-Amic Editor, 1975), 55, 65; Guillermo F. Margadant, "La familia en el derecho novohispano," in *Familias novohispanas siglos XVI al XIX: Seminario de historia de la familia centro de estudios históricos*, ed. Pilar Gonzalbo (Mexico City: El Colegio de México, 1991), 27–56.

17 Some studies of the first part of the nineteenth century have shown that as a result of the process of state centralization, the military and police corps increased the number of members. See José Luis Vega Carballo, *Orden y progreso: La formación del estado nacional en Costa Rica* (San José: Editorial Porvenir, 1981), 231–80; Mercedes Muñoz, *El estado y la abolición del ejército 1914–1949* (San José: Editorial Porvenir, 1990), 15–33. Unfortunately, no specific studies have been done about the development of the bureaucratic apparatus and its different occupations.

18 Costa Rica, *Código General*, libro I, art. 148, and libro II, arts. 443–544; Costa Rica, *Reglamento de Policía del 20 de Julio de 1849* (1849; reprint, San José: Imprenta Nacional, 1876).

19 Costa Rica, *Código General*, libro I, arts. 130–32. See Ann Varley's chapter in this book, which shows evidence of these tendencies in marriage legislation regarding marital residence in Mexican family law.

20 19 August 1797, Sección Fondos Antiguos, Serie Documentación Encuadernada, caja 31, fol. 51, Archivo de la Curia Metropolitana (hereafter ACM).

21 Rodríguez, "From Brides to Wives," 190–94; Dain Borges, *The Family in Bahia, Brazil, 1870–1945* (Stanford: Stanford University Press, 1993), 112–13, 122–28; Asunción Lavrin, *Women, Feminism, and Social Change in Argentina, Chile, and Uruguay, 1890–1940* (Lincoln and London: University of Nebraska Press, 1995); Besse, *Restructuring Patriarchy*.

22 The strong legalist tendency among the Costa Rican peasantry of the Central Valley during the nineteenth century has been signaled by Iván Molina, *La alborada del capitalismo agrario en Costa Rica* (San José: Editorial Universidad de Costa Rica, 1988), 61–152; Silvia Castro, "Estado, privatización de la tierra y conflictos agrarios," *Revista de Historia*, nos. 21–22 (January–December 1990): 207–30. In addition, the analysis of incest and child molestation cases upholds the hypothesis of prevalent legalist tendencies. See Eugenia Rodríguez, "Tiyita Bea lo que me han echo," in *El paso del cometa: Estado, políticas sociales y culturas populares en Costa Rica, 1800–1950* (San José: Editorial Porvenir, Plumsock Mesoamerican Studies, 1994), 19–45.

23 See note 8. For further discussion of the historical evolution of the role of the Costa Rican liberal state in social policing and in redefining the gender ideological system between 1850 and 1930, see Steven Palmer, "Sociedad anónima, cultura oficial: Inventando la nación en Costa Rica," in *Héroes al gusto y libros de moda: Sociedad y cambio cultural en Costa Rica (1750–1900)*, ed. Iván Molina and Steven Palmer (San José: Editorial Porvenir, Plumsock Mesoamerican Studies, 1992), 169–205; Steven Palmer, "Confinement, Policing, and the Emergence of Social Policy in Costa Rica," in *The Birth of the Penitentiary in Latin America: Essays on Criminology, Prison Reform, and Social Control, 1840–1940*, ed. Carlos Aguirre and Ricardo Salvatore (Austin: University of Texas Press, 1996), 224–53; Eugenia Rodríguez, "La redefinición de los discursos sobre la familia y el género en Costa Rica (1890–1930)," *Populaçao e Família* (Agost 1998): (July–December 1999): 147–82. Rodríguez, "Matrimonios felices," 9–30.

24 These tendencies have been discovered in other case studies in which the grounds for divorce and marital conflict charges are analyzed. For Western Europe and the United States, see Hammerton, *Cruelty and Companionship*, 34–67, 102–33; R. L. Griswold, *Family and Divorce in California, 1850–1890: Victorian Illusions and Everyday Realities* (Albany: State University of New York Press, 1982), 19–20, 69–80, 100–101; Merryl D. Smith, *Breaking the Bonds: Marital Discord in Pennsylvania, 1730–1830* (New York and London: New York University Press, 1991), 103–178; Stone, *Broken Lives*, 3–29; Jöelle Guillais, *Crimes of Passion: Dramas of Private Life in Nineteenth-Century France* (New York: Routledge, 1990), 27; Jeffrey Watts, *The Making of Modern Marriage: Matrimonial Control and the Rise of Sentiment in Neuchâtel, 1550–1800* (Ithaca and London: Cornell University Press, 1992), 224–25. For Latin America, see Arrom, *Women of Mexico City*, 228–49; María Beatrice Nizza da Silva, "Divorce in Colonial Brazil: The Case of São Paulo," in *Sexuality and Marriage in Colonial Latin America*, ed. Asunción Lavrin (Lincoln and London: University of Nebraska Press, 1989), 319–33; Eduardo Cavieres and René Salinas, *Amor, sexo, y matrimonio en Chile tradicional* (Valparaíso: Instituto de Historia, Vicerrectoría Académica, Universidad Católica de Valparaíso, Serie Monografías Históricas, no. 5, 1991), 113–33; Borges, *The Family in Bahia*, 138–43; René Salinas, *El ideario femenino chileno, entre la tradición y la modernidad siglos XVIII al XX* (São Paulo: Estudos Cedhal, no. 8, 1993), 31–49; Eugenia Rodríguez, " 'Ya me es insoportable mi matrimonio': El maltrato de las esposas en el Valle Central de Costa Rica (1750–1850)," *Revista de Ciencias Sociales*, no. 68 (1995): 73–93.

25 See note 16. The Código General of 1841 was preceded by colonial legislation such as the Leyes del Toro (1505), the Concilio de Trento (1563), the Fuero Juzgo, Las Siete Partidas, and the Real Pragmática de Indias (1778). See Acuña and Chavarría, "Endogamia y exogamia," 109–14; Margadant, "La familia," 41–47; Arrom, *Women of Mexico City*, 65–70. A few changes were included in marriage legislation in the Código General of 1841 by comparison to the Real Pragmática.

Among other things, these changes were related to administrative procedures to manage civil matters of ecclesiastical divorce, legal procedures to set marital disputes before civil courts, and the widow's right to assume all the father's authority—or the *patria potestas* (paternal authority)—over their children. See Costa Rica, *Código General,* libro I, arts. 81, 133, 135; libro II, art. 448.

26 Costa Rica, *Código General,* libro I, arts. 133, 135.

27 Costa Rica, *Código General,* libro II, art. 448. Interestingly, if abuse were to produce a lifelong infirmity, or the loss of an organ or limb, and permanent incapacity to work, the sentence would be from three to five years public service or a fine. If the sickness or incapacity lasted between eight and twenty-nine days, the punishment would be six to thirty days in jail or a fine of five to ten pesos. If the incapacity lasted between two and seven days, the penalty would be three to twenty days arrest, but if it lasted less than two days, the sentence would be three to fifteen days arrest. Moreover, the law imposed double sentence in cases of premeditation in insults, assaults, and homicides (Costa Rica, *Código General,* libro III, arts. 521–25).

28 Costa Rica, *Código General,* libro III, arts. 521–25.

29 Molina and Acuña, *Historia Económica y Social,* 69–108; Gudmundson, *Costa Rica before Coffee,* 100–103; Samper, *Generations of Settlers.*

30 Gudmundson, *Costa Rica before Coffee,* 93–103; Virginia Mora, "Los oficios femeninos urbanos en Costa Rica (1864–1927)," *Mesoamérica* 15, no. 27 (June 1994): 127–55; Sidney Chalhoub, *Trabalho, lar, e botequim: O cotidiano dos trabalhadores no Rio de Janeiro da belle époque* (São Paulo: Editora Brasiliense S.A., 1986), 137–44; Hammerton, *Cruelty and Companionship,* 13–67.

31 2 July 1844, Jurídico, exp. 3700, San José, fol. 95–96v, Archivo Nacional de Costa Rica (hereafter, ANCR).

32 Ibid.

33 Ibid.

34 See Rodríguez, "From Brides to Wives," 73–139, for statistical analysis and elaboration of the argument in this section.

35 Gudmundson, *Costa Rica before Coffee,* 100–103.

36 Martine Segalen, *Love and Power in the Peasant Family: Rural France in the Nineteenth Century* (Oxford: Basil Blackwell, 1983), 38–56. Regarding the homes of the average peasant and artisan families in the Central Valley in the early nineteenth century, as compared to the homes of the dominant class, there was no clear distinction between social, work, domestic, and "private" spaces that would have allowed for greater intimacy in couple relationships. See Arnaldo Moya, "Cultura material y vida cotidiana: El entorno doméstico de los vecinos principales de Cartago (1750–1820)," in Molina and Palmer, eds., *Héroes al gusto y libros de moda,* 9–44; Iván Molina, "Viviendas y muebles: El marco material de la vida doméstica en el Valle Central de Costa Rica (1821–1824)," *Revista de Historia de America,* no. 116 (July–December 1993): 59–91.

37 11 March 1843, Jurídico, exp. 3572, Heredia, fol. 61–62, ANCR.

38 Ibid.

39 Ibid. See also Costa Rica, *Código General,* libro I, arts. 131–33, 135.

40 Percentages in this section are drawn from statistical analysis presented in Rodríguez, "From Brides to Wives," 168–70 and 178–80.

41 Rodríguez, "From Brides to Wives," 181–87.

42 Chalhoulb, *Trabalho, lar, et botiquim,* 143–44.

43 Hammerton, *Cruelty and Companionship,* 168–69.

María Eugenia Chaves

Slave Women's Strategies

for Freedom and the Late Spanish

Colonial State

The nature of colonial government in Spanish America has been the subject of much debate.[1] On the whole, the controversy has centered on the degree of efficiency with which the colonial bureaucracy actually carried out the orders and decrees of the Crown of Castile. On the one hand, the colonial government has been seen as efficient—in Weberian terms, as rational bureaucratic—even though the persistence of patrimonial elements or features have been recognized.[2] On the other hand, these very features have been seen as fundamental, and therefore particular powers and interests are considered to have decisively affected and influenced the extent to which the colonial bureaucracy complied with the royal orders and instructions.[3] However, common to both of these lines of interpretation has been the acknowledgment that the Crown's control over its American colonies loosened during the seventeenth and early eighteenth centuries.

In the course of the eighteenth century, the Spanish Crown launched a wide-ranging reform program with the aim of restoring its hegemonic position in the colonies.[4] These reforms, known as the Bourbon Reforms, attempted to reorganize all aspects of colonial society, including the institutions of government, administration, and justice.[5] In this essay, I consider the effects of reformist discourses on subaltern subjects—in particular, on slave women's strategies for freedom.

The hierarchical character of the colonial social structures was informed by racial criteria from the very outset of Spanish rule. Since the late fifteenth century the idea of race, at first associated with lineage, increasingly incorporated into its meaning ideals of purity of blood *(pureza de sangre)*, which in the Americas was further complicated by the presence of African slaves.[6] In mature colonial society, the original emphasis on cultural features such as birthplace or language, present in the early meaning of race, was overtaken by criteria connected with physical appearance, skin color, or *calidad*.[7] The stigmatizing experience of slavery had an impact on this change and also made for a difference in the ways in which Indians and Africans—as well as their descendants—were conceived of within colonial discourse.[8] This modern mutation of the traditional concept of *raza* (also known as calidad) came to be used most frequently in the design of typologies that defined levels of superiority or inferiority among the colonial population.[9]

The system of privileges that governed the colonial order thus depended on strict racial separation between whites, Indians, and blacks. At the same time this order was continually eroded by the persistent practice of interracial mixing *(mestizaje)*, the result of which was an increasing population of mestizos.[10] In order to distinguish between mestizos in terms of relative proximity to "whiteness," people with African ancestry were given the general label *castas*, which was a pejorative term.[11] It embraced the negative medieval meaning associated with a kind of "animal-like" sexual conduct (promiscuous, irregular, etc.) and with the idea that children inherited not only their parents' physical traits but also their vices.[12] Much of the Crown's reformist program was directed at reducing the social mobility of this subaltern population and at clearly defining each subject's status.

Ultimately, the onus of executing the laws and norms of racial designations rested with the functionaries of the church who assigned racial identities on the basis of their perception of physical appearance.[13] In 1768, the Cathedral Chapter (Cabildo Eclesiástico) of Cartagena explained in a correspondence with the Council of the Indies the difficulty of registering the *mestizos de casta* in the ecclesiastical records and proposed that the offspring borne of Spanish men and black women in wedlock should be considered white. The council, however, declined the petition, arguing that "the letter of the law" alone cannot alter the "conjugal consortium," thereby making a black woman white, nor take away from the children of interracial marriages the calidad of mulattos.[14]

However, the criteria of skin color could be replaced when it came to establishing the identity and status of colonial subjects. This change was achieved through various means facilitated by the vagueness of the terms *mestizo* and *casta*. The imprecision was a key factor in the practice of evading the payment of tribute by Indian and casta males who could aspire to mestizo status by fulfilling conditions that sufficiently proved their "whiteness." It was also possible for individuals of average means to purchase legal exemption of the casta status, a *cédula de gracias al sacar,* which made them legally white.[15]

Thus, racial designations were not simply a matter of subjective determination by the authorities, but could also become the object of negotiation between individuals and the colonial government, which has given rise to the question of how central racial criteria really were to eighteenth-century discourses on the stratification of colonial society. Opinions vary as to the weight given to the racial factor versus economic factors. However, the persistence of the racial criteria in the process of social exclusion is acknowledged in one way or another.[16]

This debate could be enriched by an approach that conceives of the process of social differentiation as resulting from the productive capacity of colonial discourse itself.[17] Most of the normative colonial discourses were applied through judicial means, with the aim of creating and imposing a sharply delimited identity on subaltern subjects. At the same time, these discourses also offered subaltern subjects discursive tools that could be made to serve the individual in her or his quest for personal freedom, social ascent, and identity claims. From this perspective, the normative discourses can be seen as an active force in the constitution of legal and social subjects and not simply as a formal recognition of subjects already constituted.[18]

Two of these juridical discourses that enabled the functioning of racial hierarchy were the "Normativa para la declaración de mestizos" issued in Bogotá in 1764 and the Sanción Pragmática, which regulated marriages and was promulgated in New Spain in 1778.[19] They were based on the perceived need to reinforce racial categories, most especially in the case of the casta population, and formed part of the broad spectrum of the Bourbon Reforms. Nevertheless, the criteria of social exclusion that these discourses employed not only served to reinforce social barriers but also provided a basis for social mobility for the subaltern population.

The Sanción Pragmática reinforced the patriarchal power of the father and the state to intervene in order to prevent interracial marriages, especially those that involved persons of African or slave ancestry. Similarly, the Normativa for mestizos was an attempt at defining social categories for taxation purposes.[20] It stipulated that legitimate interracial marriages guaranteed exemption from tribute demands for the offspring only if the father was white or mestizo with no African ancestry. In the case of illegitimate sexual relations by white women, the offspring were always guaranteed exemption from tribute demands, irrespective of the status of the father. A legitimate marriage between a white or mestiza woman and an Indian or casta man entailed a decline in the social rank of her descendants.

Two criteria of social exclusion that interacted in a complex manner could be discerned in both the Sanción Pragmática and in the Normativa. The first criterion, explicit in the discourse, is racial. The second, less evident, is *honor*. These two documents assume that slaves and mestizos de casta are subjects lacking honor and therefore prone to sexual excesses, lust, and vice.[21] Consequently, they were deemed to be incapable of ensuring the legitimacy of their offspring. In colonial discourse, illegitimacy was an a priori feature of slaves' identity, and the same applied to mestizos de casta. This mark of illegitimacy ensued from an interaction between gender discourse and the discourses of race and honor.

The discourse of honor defined gender identities and imposed strict requirements regarding sexual and social conduct. Honor was central to the very idea of whiteness as a relational notion that served to identify white men and women and to differentiate them from the mestizo and casta population. Thus, it was a recurrent theme in colonial discourses that the codes of honor of white women demanded of them chaste sexual behavior, whereas women of "black blood" were free of honor requirements and thus were predisposed to "sexual ardours." This dichotomy allowed the creation of a hierarchy of female roles that, in turn, served to uphold social exclusion along racial lines.[22]

Although the image drawn here is of a racial dichotomy, the reality was much more complex. Illegitimacy and transgressive sexual relations were by no means unusual among women of the social elite, who were expected to uphold the codes of honor.[23] The casta and slave women, on the other hand, in spite of being excluded from the codes of honor, often adhered to those codes to secure social recognition for themselves and their descendants.[24] Such attempts are illustrated in the case of slave women who near the end of colonial rule put forward arguments in defense of their honor when they confronted their owners in the colonial courts.[25]

It is well known that slave women actively participated in efforts to achieve social ascent for themselves and their children, employing two mutually dependent strategies in their attempts to secure their freedom: they sought to take advantage of the relationship with their masters or mistresses by engaging in illegitimate sexual relations and by forming ties of affection and gratitude; or they relied on the masters' willingness to agree to their buying their own freedom or that of a family member.[26] However, a third avenue, their use of the colonial courts has, so far, received less attention.[27]

In the next section, I discuss the case of a slave woman in Guayaquil who went against the dominant discourse that excluded her from the practice of honor, deploying her "stained" honor as the basis for a lawsuit in an effort to gain her freedom from slavery.[28] Taking this case as a point of departure, I explore how the social context and the discursive relations interacted to open up conditions that enabled slave women to change their social status and identity in the colonial order.

The Honor and Freedom of María Chiquinquirá

During the final years of the eighteenth century, the administrative jurisdiction known as the Audiencia of Quito (which after 1830 became the Republic of Ecuador) belonged to the viceroyalty of New Granada. The port city of Guayaquil, where the majority of the slave population of the region resided, was also the viceroyalty's door to the world.[29] In the city, the life and work of many slaves were conditioned by the practice of *jornal*. The *jornalero* slaves enjoyed considerable independence. They had the right to work for themselves, and their duties to the master were confined to the payment of a daily sum called the jornal. In Guayaquil, the labor market for jornalero slaves flourished because manual work, especially in the city's important shipyard, was largely performed by both free and slave casta subjects. Slave women were able to work inside private houses or outdoors.[30]

Slavery in Guayaquil cannot be seen solely as an urban phenomenon; on the contrary, slaves worked temporarily on the agricultural properties in the hinterland of the city or in the mines further north. This spatial and labor diversification was the result both of the diverse economic activities of the slaveholders and of the opportunities slaves had gained when it came to offering their labor to fulfill the payment of the jornal required by their owners.[31] The existence of the jornal had preoccupied the Council of the Indies since early colonial times, the authorities fearing that it could undermine prevailing social relations.[32]

In the colonial port of Guayaquil, as in other colonial ports in the region, master-slave relationships at the end of the eighteenth century were to a great extent conducted on the basis of very flexible yet precarious negotiations.[33] As expected, the slave was always in a weaker position in this relationship. However, as the case I discuss here illustrates, slaves were not entirely defenseless because even when possibilities for negotiation with the master or mistress were exhausted, they were sometimes able to resort to legal action.[34]

In Guayaquil in May 1794, María Chiquinquirá Díaz, identified as a mulatto woman, initiated legal proceedings against her master, the presbyter Alfonso Cepeda y Ariscum, demanding her own and her daughter's freedom.[35] The daughter, María del Carmen Espinoza, was the only child of María Chiquinquirá's marriage to a free tailor. The tailor carried out his work in a shop in the basement of the presbyter's house, where the family lived. At the time of the lawsuit, María Chiquinquirá was a jornalera slave.

In the plea for María Chiquinquirá's freedom, the defense counsel presented two arguments. The first involved her real identity and the story of how her mother had been granted enforced manumission after being abandoned by her master—the father of the presbyter Cepeda. This story implied that she was born to a manumitted mother and consequently had never been a slave. The second argument concerned the ill-treatment María Chiquinquirá and her daughter suffered in the presbyter's house. It was declared that despite being aware of her free status, she had accepted serving the Cepeda family as a slave because she had always been treated with kindness—that is, until the day that her present master, the presbyter, began to ill-treat her and her daughter, which was the reason for her present demand for freedom.

At the outset of the trial, taking into consideration the ill-treatment María Chiquinquirá and her daughter were subjected to by their master, their defense counsel requested that the judge grant the slaves their freedom in order to litigate—in other words, that they be allowed to leave the house of the master for the duration of the trial. The judge ruled in favor of the slaves, permitting them to leave the master's house and authority *(potestad)*. The evidence that proved fundamental to the judge was a statement made by the court clerk, the only witness to the ill-treatment suffered by María Chiquinquirá and her daughter. He testified that he heard the presbyter insult María del Carmen:

> [The presbyter said that she was] a filthy bitch who stank of goats from consorting with the blacks and the zambos of the streets where she spent most of her time. That she had been pawed by those brutes . . . [and I was informed that] that girl was worse than a whore, a prostitute and lascivious. (fol. 34r)

The ill-treatment reported by María Chiquinquirá was not of a physical nature, but rather represented an affront to her honor, an inconceivable claim to the presbyter. He protested angrily against the de facto freedom that the slaves had been granted and did not recognize the insults the court clerk had overheard as valid evidence of excessive cruelty, stating the following:

> What insults could be these that it is insisted here have caused these slave women to be wronged and to suffer infamy and injustice; when slaves in general, because of their wretched state, *do not have a place in the republic nor in the political government, suffering, as it were, a civil death* [muerte civil] *by virtue of their servile condition?* When slaves are not even in control of their natural actions and live wholly subject to the will and disposition of their master, who could think or say that their master can then not discipline and punish them, not only verbally but also physically, with moderation when it is deserved? *How could slaves, who by their nature cannot possess honor and lack all sense of virtue, suffer infamy or defamation because of insulting words uttered by their master? If this were the case, masters could not be the arbiters to discipline slaves errors of word or deed, and slaves could do as they pleased, assured that they could be neither reprimanded nor disciplined.* If this were as I say, slaves would no longer be servile and the institution of slavery would instead be a kind of freedom. . . . I repeat that slaves can never suffer insult or offense from any words of the kind with which their masters might treat them, *for those who*

have neither the capacity nor the aptitude for receiving honor, nor have the least esteem, rank or position in the political state, can also not suffer infamy at the hand of their master. (fol. 168, emphasis added)

This discourse assigned the slave a civil death *(muerte civil)* because she had "no political status in the republic" and was incapable of possessing honor.[36] In this case, the presbyter argued that the status of master implied the right and the duty to punish slaves physically and verbally in order to "contain their sexual desires." Therefore, such punishment could not be considered excessive cruelty:

> Excessive cruelty arises from nothing other than immoderate ill-treatment and excessive punishments. . . . all that occurred was, that from a tender age when she was still single, Doña Estafanía Cepeda, being the owner [of María Chiquinquirá], sister of my client, punished her persistently for acting as a prostitute and being reckless, with no other aim than to subdue her and to contain her desires, resulting from her depraved way of life. (f. 169v)

Due to this differentiation, the master, the subject of honor, could discipline a slave both physically and verbally without committing an offense. It was the duty of the masters to punish and contain the excesses of their slaves.[37] Presbyter Cepeda's discourse echoes a number of assumptions regarding the character of slaves shared by colonial slaveholders and authorities at the end of the eighteenth century.[38] For her part, María Chiquinquirá called into question the honor of her master. Sharing the Cepeda family's everyday life for such a long time put her in possession of a great deal of information about her master's conduct, which she used to discredit him when she accused the presbyter's father of having been sexually promiscuous with his slave women and even of having sired children with them. With this statement, she undermined the differentiation the master had utilized to justify her identity as a slave. Despite all the master's protests, the court did not punish the slave woman for "such slanderous accusations." Rather than being dismissed by the court of the Gobernación, the accusations provided the basis for further investigation into the matter.

After a three-year process, the ruling of the court demanded the return of the two women to the Cepeda family. However, María Chiquinquirá was determined to take full advantage of the law by appealing to a higher court. However, in the meantime, which could well run into years, this "slave" woman could at least live in de facto freedom while the slow wheels of the law ground on.[39]

Honor, Possession, and Power:
Women Slaves and the Colonial Order

The fact that at the end of the eighteenth century a slave woman was able to successfully employ a statement of honor to define herself, thus thwarting the dominant discourse of differentiation, requires a discussion of two issues. The first concerns the nature of the criteria of honor and the internal contradictions in colonial discourses concerning the applicability of the concept to slaves. The second refers to the relation of authority and possession that the master establishes with the slave and to the complex relations the slaves maintained with the rest of colonial society.

In colonial discourses, we find contradictory usages of the criteria of honor. In some of them, such as in the Sanción Pragmática or the Normativa, honor was a factor of social differentiation; therefore, those who were explicitly granted honor acquired social privileges denied to those who were legally excluded from the practices of honor. However, in 1789, the Crown promulgated the "Instrucción para el gobierno de los esclavos," which recognized the right of the slaves to demand redress if they were offended by anyone other than their master or the overseer.[40] The Instrucción contradicted the other discourses of social exclusion and gave rise to a reaction on the part of the cabildos, or governing councils, of several cities, whose members strongly and effectively opposed it. Nevertheless, the Instrucción became sufficiently widespread among the colonial bureaucracy to influence the judges to accept the fact that a slave woman could argue about her honor.[41] The discourse María Chiquinquirá used to define her identity emphasized her free-born condition and her status as a married woman. These characteristics bore with them the possibility of entry into the world of the "honorable," which helped to reinforce the argument of her "stained" honor.[42]

These changing and contradictory uses of the key concept of honor demonstrate that, far from belonging to a stable structure, it was subject to discursive struggles in the context of judicial contestations.[43] Slave women could in certain situations become active agents in the discursive arena and claim legal recognition of their freedom—that is, the status and identity of free women. They could deploy notions such as honor as long as contesting interpretations of those notions resonated with already existing moral and judicial discourses.[44]

Identities were determined by means of legal discourses and sanctioned by them, and therefore could be questioned within their framework. However, relations of power and knowledge upheld the normative discourses and determined whether slaves could accede to legal procedures and the bureaucratic machinery. Two interrelated factors played important roles in slave women's capacity to pursue judicial strategies for freedom. First, slave women commonly developed a network of social relations that was not limited to the master or mistress bondage experience. Second, they acquired and mobilized certain experiences and knowledge to negotiate the colonial world and its discourses.

The exercise of *posesion* was a key factor in defining the master-slave relationship. The changes that it suffered through time are of primary importance in understanding the relations between master and slaves in the late colonial Spanish Empire. Ownership conferred on the owner the power of possession over the slave, as guaranteed by law. A slave was defined as the property of a master; consequently, the owner had the right to make decisions regarding her or his life and labor. Nonetheless, the power of possession was not absolute; it was, rather, relativized both by conflicting principles within the body of legal codes themselves and by the dynamic and complex character of the slave-master relationship.[45] For one, the master's power over the slaves had already been tempered as far back as in the medieval Castilian legal codes, which in turn formed the basis of the Laws of the Indies.[46] By means of these changes in the power of possession, slaves were granted a series of rights, among others the possibility of acquiring and managing their finances or *peculio,* or of claiming their freedom if the master exposed them to prostitution or abandonment.[47]

In Guayaquil, as in other port cities such as Cartagena and Lima, the practice of the jornal was one of many ways in which the master-slave relationship could be resolved. This practice implied a relaxation of the master's power of possession and enabled the slaves to establish varied relations with the rest of the colonial society.[48] In this way, they could strengthen their position by acquiring a support network that sometimes extended beyond the urban limits and was made up of a collection of people—a shapeless, diverse, and anonymous mass, living on the margins of society, into which runaway slaves, former slaves *(libertos),* as well as criminals could easily blend and disappear. As María Chiquinquirá struggled for her freedom, this almost anonymous support network came to life as the lawsuit progressed. She was able to call on dozens of witnesses, from town and countryside alike, who repeatedly recounted the story of her mother and the details of her own life.[49]

The social relationships established by slaves were not limited to the marginal world. Those slaves serving powerful families frequently found themselves involved in their masters and mistresses' social networks and took advantage of their masters' adversaries and allies. The knowledge slaves garnered through their intimate relationships with their masters could easily be translated into legal arguments within a judicial system where the private sphere seeped into the exercise of the law.[50] Such information was fundamental to their courtroom strategies.

María Chiquinquirá exploited such knowledge throughout the trial and instructed her defense counsel on who the presbyter's supporters and opponents were. Thus, through various legal mechanisms, her defense counsel accused individuals within her master's sphere of influence and power, thereby preventing them from affecting decisions in the trial.

Another characteristic of the administration of colonial justice was the decisive role that lower-ranking officials played in the course of legal proceedings. The responsibilities of these officials included dealing with different petitions and appeals, preparing the documentation, informing the parties, and writing and copying the proceedings of the court. Their access to this information enabled them to influence the court proceedings.[51] In the case of María Chiquinquirá, as we have seen, the early testimony of the court clerk was crucial in the court's decision to grant the slaves temporary freedom in order to litigate. Throughout the trial, the presbyter Cepeda complained about the clerk, whom he said was in receipt of presents and money from the slave woman and thereupon took it upon himself to mix up the papers, complicate proceedings, and support the slave in her objectives. Complaints of this nature against court clerks can be found repeatedly in legal documents of the time.[52]

The case analyzed in this essay demonstrates that in the final years of the colonial order, the discourses of the colonial state not only created and imposed social closure, but at the same time informed the contestatory practices developed by subaltern subjects, among them slave women, who attempted to redefine their identity and status. The contestatory discourses appropriated important notions of the official discourses of identification, such as honor. We have also seen that the agency of the slaves in intervening in the judicial process and influencing the arguments in favor of their freedom depended on the degree of knowledge they could acquire and on the extent to which they could mobilize a support network for their cause.[53] The newly acquired confidence of the slaves in their legal pursuit of freedom—their "juridical awakening"—was one among other factors by which the institution of slavery was slowly eroded.[54]

By the end of the eighteenth century, slaves in increasing numbers had secured their freedom and were slowly joining a new social group: the *plebe*. This designation was applied to people of different color and condition belonging to the lower-urban social strata, who through their growing numbers aroused fear among the elite. In spite of this fear, slaves and people of the plebe were mobilized by the rival sides of the colonial elite, the *criollos* and Spaniards, during the struggles for independence.[55]

Slave women, for their part, continued to play the role of protagonists in legal proceedings where their own freedom was at stake.[56] In tune with the times, they began to refer to themselves as "citizens" in spite of their continued status as slaves.[57] The conflictive first decades of the nineteenth century witnessed the emergence of a new discursive regime, but the way in which this new repertoire was mobilized and appropriated by slave women and other subaltern subjects has yet to become the object of major research.[58]

Notes

This article was written as part of the research project "Ethnicity and Power in Urban Contexts: Comparative Studies on Social Closure and Social Control in Tropical Port Cities" supported by the Swedish Agency for Research Cooperation with Developing Countries (SAREC). I appreciate the comments of Professor Emeritus Magnus Mörner and the advice and suggestions of Assistant Professor Lars Trägårdh. Translated by Pam Decho.

1 Magnus Mörner, *Region and State in Latin America's Past* (Baltimore and London: Johns Hopkins University Press, 1993), 3–18, presents an enlightening overview of the debate.

2 Horst Pietschman, *El estado y su evolución al principio de la colonización española* (Mexico City: Fondo de Cultura Económica, 1994), 20–37, 160–63.

3 John L. Phelan, *The Kingdom of Quito in the Seventeenth Century: Bureaucratic Politics in the Spanish Empire* (Madison: University of Wisconsin Press, 1967), 321–37.

4 See the analysis of the "recentralization" process of the Bourbon regime in Claudio Véliz, *The Centralist Tradition of Latin America* (Princeton: Princeton University Press, 1980), 70–89.

5 Cf. Mark Burkholder and D. S. Chandler, *De la impotencia a la autoridad: La Corona española y las Audiencias en América, 1687–1808* (Mexico City: Fondo de Cultura Económica, 1984). The impact of the Bourbon Reforms in the Audiencia of Quito has been studied by Federica Morelli, "Las reformas en Quito: La distribución del poder y la consolidación de la jurisdicción municipal (1765–1809)," *Jahrbuch für Geschichte von Staat, Wirtschaft, und Gesellschaft Lateinamerikas* 34 (December 1997): 183–207.

6 At this time, the word *etnia* was used in two ways: one referred to birthplace or *nación,* and the other to pagan or non-Christian individuals. For a good description of the efforts of the Spanish priests in identifying African slaves in relation to their language and place of birth, see Alonso de Sandoval, *Un tratado sobre la esclavitud africana* (1627; reprint, with an introduction by Enriqueta Vilar Vilar, Madrid: Alianza Editorial, 1987), 136–42.

7 Peter Wade, *Race and Ethnicity in Latin America* (London: Pluto, 1997), 7–9; in "Race / Caste and the Creation and Meaning of Identity in Colonial Spanish America," *Revista de Indias* 55, no. 203 (January–April 1995): 149–53, Robert Jackson points out that the meaning of the word *calidad* could include other physical attributes or signify a general idea of social reputation (152).

8 Wade, *Race and Ethnicity,* 25–30, discusses this difference and its effects in the Latin American republics. In *Marriage, Class, and Colour in Nineteenth-Century Cuba: A Study of Racial Attitudes and Sexual Values in a Slave Society* (Cambridge: Cambridge University Press, 1974), 74–76, Verena Martínez-Alier points out the importance of slavery for the process of social differentiation. See also Roland Anrup and A. Perez, "De la hostia a la horca: El delito de un mulato en Cartagena de Indias del siglo XVIII," *Anales* (Institute for Ibero-American Studies, University of Göteborg) 2d ser., no. 1 (1998): 80–83.

9 See the illustrated list of race typologies in Pedro O'Crouley, *A Description of the Kingdom of New Spain* (1774; reprint translated by Sean Galvin, n.p.: Hohn Howeell, 1972), 19–21. A useful analysis of the influence of the scientific knowledge of the eighteenth century in the construction of racial differences is David Goldberg, *Racist Culture: Philosophy and the Politics of Meaning* (Oxford: Basil Blackwell, 1993), 48–52.

10 For a detailed study of the separatist laws of the Hapsburg era, see Magnus Mörner, *La Corona española y los foráneos en los pueblos de Indios de América* (Stockholm: Institute for Ibero-American Studies, 1970), 94–104. The same author

discusses the term *society of castes* applied to the colonial social structure in *Race Mixture in the History of Latin America* (Boston: Little, Brown, 1967), 53–74. See also Martínez-Alier, *Marriage, Class, and Colour,* 130–41.

11 During early colonial times, the word *mestizo* was applied to the offspring of Indian and Spaniard, but later on it acquired a wider meaning, denoting race mixture generally.

12 Real Academia Española, *Diccionario de autoridades,* 4 vols. (1726; reprint, Madrid: Gredos, 1990), 1:222.

13 Patrik J. Carroll, *Blacks in Colonial Veracruz: Race, Ethnicity, and Regional Development* (Austin: University of Texas Press, 1991), 112–14, rightly points out that the court clerk also played an important role in the racial designations of individuals.

14 Baltasar Gomez al Consejo de Indias, February 1768, Audencia de Santa Fé, legajo 1044, Archivo General de Indias (AGI), Sevilla. Unless otherwise noted, Pam Decho has translated all Spanish-language text used in this essay.

15 María S. Vela, "Mulato 'conocido y reputado por tal,' " *Quitumbe* (Universidad Católica de Quito), no. 9 (June 1995): 77–88, examines the process by which mulattos could legally be declared mestizos in the Real Audiencia de Quito; see also Magnus Mörner, *The Andean Past: Land, Societies, and Conflicts* (New York: Columbia University Press, 1985), 101, and his "Slavery, Race Relations, and Bourbon Reorganization in Eighteenth-Century Spanish America," in *Essays on Eighteenth-Century Race Relations in the Americas,* ed. James Schofield (Philadelphia: Lawrence Henry Gipson Institute, 1987), 8–30. For the case of Indian people, see Karen Powers, *The Indian Migration and Sociopolitical Change in the Audiencia of Quito* (New York: New York University Press, 1990).

16 Mörner maintains that the racial criteria was fundamental in determining colonial social inequality, in spite of the emergent economic classes (*Race Mixture,* 55–73); Julian Pitt-Rivers, "Race in Latin America: The Concept of 'Raza,' " in *Race, Ethnicity, and Social Change: Readings in the Sociology of Race and Ethnic Relations,* ed. John Stone (Belmont, Calif.: Duxbury, 1977), 317–32, conceives *raza* as "relationships of a specific type which exist as a function of a total social structure, but are not reducible to either culture or class structure" (330); Patricia Seed claims that *race* became the major metaphor for social inequality due to the absence in eighteenth-century Spanish colonial language of an alternative word that could signify social difference based on economic and social status (*To Love, Honor, and Obey in Colonial México: Conflicts over Marriage Choice, 1574–1821* [Stanford: Stanford University Press, 1988], 218–25); in *Marriage, Class, and Colour,* Martínez-Alier draws attention to the fact that skin color associated with race "is often used as a symbol for other socially significant cleavages in society" (75–76); Jackson ("Race / Caste") makes clear the inconsistency and subjectivity of race identity and points out that the racial designations cannot define a complex social reality.

17 Cf. Homi Bhabha, "The Other Question: Stereotype, Discrimination, and the Discourse of Colonialism," in *The Location of Culture* (London: Routledge, 1994), 70, 81–83.

18 Cf. Michel Foucault, vol. 1, *The History of Sexuality, An Introduction* (New York: Penguin, 1981), 92–98.

19 Normative para la declaración de mestizos, February 1791, Fondo Mestizos, caja 8, Archivo Nacional de Historia, Quito; the Sanción Pragmática is published in Richard Konetzke, ed., *Colección de documentos para la historia de la formación social de Hispanoamérica 1493–1810*, 3 vols. (Madrid: Consejo Superior de Investigaciones Científicas, 1962), 3:438–42.

20 The definition of social inequality implicit in this normative had the effect of creating the fiction that those of non-African ancestry were equals, a fiction contradictory to the social reality of late-eighteenth-century colonial society. See Seed, *To Love, Honor, and Obey*, 206.

21 Orlando Patterson, *Slavery and Social Death: A Comparative Study* (Cambridge, Mass.: Harvard University Press, 1982), 7–27, 77–97, has argued that the lack of honor that the idiom of power attributed to slaves was a key factor in their social exclusion.

22 Julian Pitt-Rivers, *The Fate of Shechem or the Politics of Sex* (Cambridge: Cambridge University Press, 1977), 1–17, discusses the general structure of the concept of honor.

23 Cf. Ann Twinam, "Honor, Sexuality, and Illegitimacy in Colonial Spanish America," in *Sexuality and Marriage in Colonial Latin America*, ed. Asunción Lavrin (Lincoln and London: University of Nebraska Press, 1989), 118–56.

24 Pablo Rodríguez, *Seducción y amancebamiento en la colonia* (Bogotá: Simón and Lola Guberek Foundation, 1991), 97–124, analyzes how the assumption of the codes of honor influenced matrimonial conflicts among the mulatto and mestizo population in New Granada; in *To Love, Honor, and Obey*, 96–98, Seed studies the change in the perception of concepts such as honor and love in the Mexican case and suggests that the increasing matrimonial practice among the castas and slave women eroded the code of honor of the white women, whose purity and chastity relied on and was legitimized by wedlock.

25 Christine Hünefeldt, *Paying the Price of Freedom: Family and Labor among Lima's Slaves 1800–1854* (Berkeley: University of California Press, 1994), 130–32, 140–42, analyzes several cases in Lima. For New Granada, see Jaime Jaramillo U., *La sociedad neogranadina*, vol. 1, *Ensayos de historia social* (Bogotá: Tercer Mundo, 1989), 50–53.

26 According to Martínez-Alier, slave women and free women of color used concubinage with "white" men as a means of social ascent (*Marriage, Class, and Colour*, 118). María E. Manarelli, *Pecados públicos: La ilegitimidad en Lima, siglo XVIII* (Lima: Flora Tristán, 1993), 101–59, reaches a similar conclusion for the case of Lima.

27 For Guayaquil, the recent article by Camila Townsend pursues this direction: "'Half My Body Free, the Other Half Enslaved': The Politics of the Slaves of Guayaquil at the End of the Colonial Era," *Colonial Latin American Review* 7, no. 1 (June 1998): 105–28.

28 References in the text made to the case henceforth refer to: María Chiquinquirá contra el presbítero Cepeda su amo por su libertad, 1794, Guayaquil, Esclavos, caja 13, exp. 9, Archivo Nacional de Historia, Quito. Parenthetical citations in the text are to the folio numbers.

29 In 1790, the total population of the city was approximately 8,000 inhabitants. Of these, approximately 1,300 were slaves, 4,500 castas and free "blacks," and the rest were supposedly whites. It is estimated that the slave population of the whole Audiencia exceeded 8,000 individuals. Cf. María Luisa Laviana, *Guayaquil en el siglo XVIII: Recursos naturales y desarrollo económico* (Sevilla: Escuela de Estudios Hispano-Americanos, 1987), 126–42; Michael Hamerly, *Historia social y económica de la antigua Provincia de Guayaquil, 1763–1842,* 2d ed. (Guayaquil: Banco Central del Ecuador, 1987), 85–89; and Manuel Lucena, *Sangre sobre piel negra: La esclavitud quiteña en el contexto del reformismo borbónico* (Quito: Abya-Yala, 1994), 57–61.

30 María E. Chaves, *María Chiquinquirá Díaz, una esclava del siglo XVIII: Acerca de las identidades de amo y esclavo en el puerto colonial de Guayaquil* (Guayaquil: Archivo Histórico, Banco Central del Ecuador, 1998), 80–81. The practice of jornal was rare in other regions of the Audiencia of Quito. Cf. Lucena, *Sangre sobre piel negra,* 103–105. See also Franciso Requena, "Descripción histórica y geográfica de la Provincia de Guayaquil," in *Relaciones histórico geográficas de la Audiencia de Quito siglo XVI–XIX,* 2 vols., ed. Pilar Ponce (Quito: Abya-Yala, 1994), 2:502–643. Jornalero slaves were, however, common in other port cities of Spanish America. For Nueva Granada, see vol. 1 of *Relaciones histórico,* Antonio de Ulloa and Jorge Juan, *Viaje a la América Meridional,* ed. Andrés Saumell (Madrid: Graficas Nilo, 1990), 1:76–79.

31 Lucena, *Sangre sobre piel negra,* 96–100, points out that during this period, the majority of slaves of the Audiencia lacked specialization in labor and could be employed in different activities and mobilized throughout the territory.

32 Lucena, *Sangre sobre piel negra,* 188. In the mid–eighteenth century, the council tried, without apparent success, to regulate this practice through norms and sanctions. See the example in "Expediente sobre el maltrato que dan los dueños de esclavos a éstos en Cartagena," 1760, Audiencia de Santa Fé 1023, legajo 3, AGI.

33 For the case of Lima, see Hünefeldt, *Paying the Price,* 167–79.

34 In "'Aquella ignominiosa herida que se hizo a la humanidad': El cuestionamiento de la esclavitud en Quito a finales de la época colonial," *Procesos* 6 (second semester 1994): 23–48, Bernard Lavallé draws attention to the increasing capacity of the slaves of the Audiencia de Quito to utilize the judicial system in order to obtain their freedom.

35 Alfonso Cepeda was the oldest son of one of the most important and powerful families in the Gobernación. Important information about this family can be found in: Testamento de Manuela Ariscum Elizondo, 1759, Protocolos del escribano de Baba, Archivo Histórico del Guayas, Guayaquil.

36 Social death as a characteristic assigned to the slave by the "idiom of power" has been studied in depth by Patterson, *Slavery and Social Death,* 18–28.

37 For a general study of this characteristic in slave societies and its importance in defining the master-slave relationship, see Patterson, *Slavery and Social Death.*

38 There are many examples of this type of discourse from the various regions of the colonial empire: Los dueños de esclavos al cabildo de la ciudad, Expediente sobre educación, trato, y ocupaciones de los esclavos, Popayán 1792, Cedularios, caja 16, fols. 220–22, Archivo Nacional de Historia, Quito. See also Lucena, *Sangre sobre piel negra,* 83–95.

39 Court proceedings were often not completed, or the case dragged on. This particular characteristic regarding the administration of justice under the Spanish colonial state in the Indies is analyzed in Tamar Herzog, *La administración como un fenómeno social: La justicia penal de la ciudad de Quito (1650–1750)* (Madrid: Centro de Estudios Constitucionales, 1995), 116–17.

40 Real Cédula de su Magestad sobre educación, trato, y ocupaciones de los esclavos, 1790–94, Esclavos, caja 16, Archivo Nacional de Historia, Quito; see also a detailed study on the Código Negro of Bourbon reformism in Manuel Lucena, *Los Códigos Negros de la América Española* (Alcalá de Henares: Universidad de Alcalá, 1996).

41 For the analysis of the effects of the Instrucción on the relations between masters, slaves, and colonial authorities in Guayaquil, see my article "La mujer esclava y sus estrategias de libertad en el mundo hispano colonial de fines del siglo XVIII," *Anales* (Institute of Ibero-American Studies, University of Göteborg) 2d ser., no. 1 (1998): 109–14.

42 In 1780 in Guayaquil, more people were single than married. Cf. Hamerly, *Historia social,* 98. The frequency of marriage among the slave population in Guayaquil is unknown. Interestingly, Hünefeldt has pointed out that in Lima the practice of marriage among the slaves during the first decades of the nineteenth century implied a link with the codes of honor dictated by society (*Paying the Price,* 159, 207).

43 Some feminist theorists have underlined the problems with the conceptual structure of honor and how it relates to the social roles of women. See Carol MacCormack and Marilyn Strathern, *Nature, Culture, and Gender* (Cambridge: Cambridge University Press, 1980); Joyce Riegelhaupt, "Saloio Women: An Analysis of Informal and Formal Political and Economic Roles of Portuguese Peasant Women," *Anthropological Quarterly* 40, no. 3 (July 1967): 109–26; and Jane Schneider, "On Vigilance and Virgins: Honor, Shame, and Access to Resources in Mediterranean Societies," *Ethnology* 10, no. 1 (1962): 1–24.

44 I am referring here to Michel Foucault's analysis of power / knowledge relations and of the crucial role subaltern "knowledges" may play in them. See "Two Lectures," in *Power / Knowledge: Selected Interviews and Other Writings, 1972–1977*, ed. Colin Gordon (New York: Pantheon, 1980), 80–83; *Discipline and Punish*, trans. Alan Sheridan (London: Penguin, 1991), 26–30.

45 A criticism of the notions of property and possession has been developed by Roland Anrup, "Disposition over Land and Labor," in *Agrarian Society in History*, ed. Mats Lundahl and Thommy Svensson (New York: Routledge, 1990). See also Roland Anrup, *El taita y el toro: Sobre la configuración del sistema hacendatario cuzqueño* (Stockholm: Nalkas Boken Förlag, 1990), 22–25. Patterson, *Slavery and Social Death*, 20–32, draws attention to the fact that absolute ownership is a legal fiction created by the idiom of power—that of Imperial Rome—to justify the exploitation of slaves, emphasizing its relative and relational character.

46 Slavery was defined as a *contra natura* condition that could be rectified through manumission. Cf. Alfonso el Sabio, *Las siete partidas*, partida cuarta, tit. 21, ley 1 (1555; reprint, Madrid: Boletín Oficial del Estado, 1974), 2:54r. This definition of the medieval code was appropriated by the judicial discourse in support of María Chiquinquirá's freedom.

47 These changes were part of those that affected the exercise of the patria potestad of the father since Roman times. For a discussion of these changes in Spanish colonial society in reference to the family, see Silvia Arrom, *The Women of Mexico City, 1790–1857* (Stanford: Stanford University Press, 1985), 71–80.

48 The ease with which slaves reclaimed their freedom—in other words, took "possession" of themselves—was a constant and growing concern for the authorities during the eighteenth century. Good examples of manifestations of these fears are the claims of the cabildos opposing the Pragmática for the slaves found in the following: Indiferente General 802, Archivo General de Indias, Sevilla; see also Lucena, *Sangre sobre piel negra*, 83–95.

49 This capacity to obtain the cooperation of a large number of people who could testify in their favor can be observed in other cases where slave women of Guayaquil claimed their freedom.

50 Herzog, *La administración*, shows how the networks of power and private interests were intimately related to the administration of justice (131–42 and 230–37).

51 Ibid., 37–38.

52 Cf. Jorge Lujan Muñoz, *Los escribanos en las Indias Occidentales* (Mexico City: Instituto de Estudios y Documentos Históricos, 1982), 122–24.

53 Hünefeldt, *Paying the Price*, has also pointed out the importance of the slaves' support network in their strategies for freedom.

54 Lavallé, has labeled as "juridical awakening" the increasing capacity of the slaves of the Audiencia of Quito to use the colonial courts (" 'Aquella ignominiosa' ").

55 For a general view, see John Lynch, *The Spanish American Revolutions, 1808–1826* (New York: W. W. Norton, 1973), 204–60.

56 "Angela Batallas por su libertad," 1823, Judicios 698, Archivo Histórico del Guayas, Guayaquil, is one of the most interesting cases of this period in Guayaquil. It has been studied by Townsend, " 'Half My Body Free.' "

57 See Camila Townsend, "En busca de la libertad: Los esfuerzos de los esclavos guayaquileños por garantizir su independencia después de la independencia, *Revista Ecuatoriana de Historia,* no. 4 (first semester 1993): 73–85.

58 Townsend's " 'Half My Body' " is an important and pioneering contribution in this field in the case of Guayaquil.

Rebecca Earle

Rape and the Anxious Republic

Revolutionary Colombia, 1810–1830

It is widely accepted that the French and American Revolutions were accompanied (or perhaps preceded) by profound changes in gender relations. Although there is no consensus about the precise nature of these changes, historians such as Joan Landes, Lynn Hunt, and Linda Kerber have elaborated impressive accounts of the revolutionary years that focus specifically on relations between men and women. They and other scholars have examined whether women's rights and duties were redefined by the revolutionary process and how constructs such as masculinity, femininity, or romantic love evolved during the revolutionary period.[1] Historians have only begun to examine such questions in the context of revolutionary Spanish America. There are no sustained studies of the impact of the Spanish-American wars of independence on relations between men and women, or of the meaning of these terms to the revolutionaries. Did the Spanish-American wars of independence invest the image of women with new political meaning? In what ways did the revolutionary process itself redefine views of women's proper role? What position did women occupy within the revolutionary project? Answering such questions will help us understand the relationship between women and the new republican states that formed across Spanish America in the aftermath of independence. It will also shed some light on the nature of the revolutionary processes themselves. This chapter looks specifically at revolutionary Colombia, although it attempts to maintain a broader comparative horizon.

Amazon or Ingenue?

It should be said from the start that this chapter is not a rescue exercise aiming at recovering the forgotten role played by American women in the

Spanish-American independence process. Not only would such a topic be unexciting, it would also be unnecessary. A number of studies have already documented the widespread female involvement in the wars of independence. From such works we can construct an overview of female participation in Colombia's war of independence.[2] Most scholars stress that women from all classes supported the republican movement that opposed Spanish rule. However, this fact by no means indicates that the region's women unanimously supported independence, nor does evidence suggest that republicanism found disproportionate favor among women. The historiographical focus on republican women reflects scholarly bias rather than historical reality. Royalist women have been very little studied; historians have hitherto shown scant interest in feminine support for the Spanish Crown.

The experience of war varied widely. Some regions, such as Panama, saw little active fighting. Women residing in the capital city, Santa Fe de Bogotá, on the other hand, experienced four significant changes of government in the years between 1810 and 1819. Geography was not the only factor leading to difference. Women of different classes responded to the upheavals of war in very different ways. In the absence of regular funding, both royalists and republicans relied on the region's women to provide many of the services needed to maintain an army. If nothing else, officers expected women to sew uniforms, wash clothing, and prepare food. Those who did not volunteer might be obliged to do so by force. As the royalist officer Francisco Warleta remarked sardonically, "the fair sex has never failed to accede to our requests."[3] Conscription and arrest also deprived women of male family members. Elite women, with greater access to the colonial and new republican bureaucracies, vigorously petitioned for the release of captured relatives and rejected demands that they support the military in unwelcome ways. Doña María Manuela de Angulo, a devout royalist, was outraged at being ordered to sew trousers for the Spanish army. She reminded officers of her noble lineage, suggesting they look elsewhere for seamstresses.[4] Plebeian women had less to fall back on when confronted with army demands. Little documentary evidence remains of the responses of the many plebeian women obliged to act as cooks and laundresses. Such women could consider themselves lucky if they were paid half a real for a day's work.

Not all feminine involvement in the war was coercive, and it is on voluntary participation that I would like to focus. Wealthy women provided money and supplies to the insurgent armies. Moreover, the war also led some patrician women to begin performing tasks usually left to the nonelite. Elegant señoras volunteered in hospitals, tending the sick, while other aristocratic women happily mimicked plebeian seamstresses, stitching uniforms for the troops. Doña María Manuela de Angulo's attitude toward sewing was not necessarily typical. Meanwhile, nonelite women played important politico-military roles, much to the distress of some contemporaries. The sight of market women attacking the homes of wealthy royalists was greeted with considerable ambivalence by republican leaders in Santa Fe de Bogotá. Plebeian *mujercillas* (women of low social standing) acted as spies, relaying reports across cities. Such women also accompanied their partners on campaign, despite the regular efforts of officers to proscribe camp followers. On occasion, women even shouldered arms; in a number of well-documented cases, large groups of armed women, inevitably referred to as "amazons," combined to repel an enemy attack on their town. Some women were also drawn into the political debate, the "war of words," that mirrored the military campaign.[5] Doña Concepción Loperena de Fernández de Castro, a signatory of the Province of Valledupar's 1813 declaration of independence, publicly advocated separation from Spain despite being the daughter of wealthy Spaniards. It was a delegation of elite women who convinced Viceroy Antonio Amar y Borbón to abandon the capital in 1810.

Voluntarily or involuntarily, Colombian women equipped both royalists and republicans with clothing and food, nursed ailing soldiers, provided information, articulated opinions, and occasionally participated in armed combat. Many women, in other words, engaged actively with the political and military upheavals of 1810–25. Such activities may seem marginal, and one should certainly not exaggerate their importance in shaping the overall outcome of the war of independence. However, these contributions to the war have a meaning beyond their immediate impact on military events. Their activities subtly repositioned women within the newly emerging republic.[6] Although political action was not new to the viceroyalty's women, as the literature on colonial riot and rebellion amply demonstrates, the war provided women of many different classes with an unusually protracted opportunity to act publicly.[7] "Acting publicly" should be interpreted broadly. Soliciting funds for the troops should certainly be seen as a public, political act. However, even an activity as uncontroversial as volunteering to sew uniforms might bear some small political charge. As Linda Colley remarked of the anti-Napoleonic sewing circles in England, this form of public sewing represented "the thin edge of a far more radical wedge." Speaking of British women, Colley notes, "By extending their solicitude to the nation's armed forces, men who were not in the main related to them by blood or marriage, women demonstrated that their domestic virtues possessed a public as well as a private relevance. Consciously or not, these female patriots were staking out a civic role for themselves"[8] In Colombia, too, the war allowed some women, consciously or unconsciously, to stake out a civic role for themselves. Precisely what this civic role might be was another matter. Colley's remarks should lead us to suspect that this new role would stress the public utility of a gendered domestic order. The behavior of armed amazons might lead one to a quite different conclusion. If nothing else, we should acknowledge that the period of independence saw substantial mobilization of women.

Studies of the participation of women in Colombia's war of independence tend to comment on the ironic fact that women's involvement went virtually unacknowledged. In particular, despite the notable service provided by many sectors of the female population to the republican cause, republican leaders failed to show any real appreciation of their debt to women. On the contrary, figures such as Simón Bolívar stated explicitly that women ought not to involve themselves in political movements. In 1826, for example, Bolívar reminded his sister that "it is very improper for women to concern themselves with political affairs."[9] What is the meaning of this apparent contradiction? It is not simply that Colombia's political leaders did not appreciate their female supporters. Rather, the ways in which the political elite spoke (or didn't speak) about women's wartime activities reveals a deeper anxiety about the significance of the war itself.

Both revolutionaries and royalists understood the war, in part, as a familial drama. The rejection of royal authority was described as a radical break between parent and child. King Ferdinand VII of Spain, drawing on the well-established image of the monarch as the father of his subjects, referred to the American revolutionaries as rebellious sons, wantonly rejecting a father's loving guidance. The republicans described themselves as grown children rejecting their father's unreasonable tyranny. This familial imagery is clearly illustrated in Simón Bolívar's 1815 Jamaica Letter, an eloquent justification for the independence of Spanish America composed while Bolívar was in temporary exile in Jamaica. In this exposition, Bolívar made repeated use of the parent-child metaphor in order to subvert Spain's claims to authority: Spain, unwilling to allow its children to leave the family home, had forced Americans into "a sort of permanent infancy." Indeed, through its actions, Spain had forfeited all claim to paternal authority. In Bolívar's text, Spain is feminized as an "unnatural stepmother":

> We are threatened with the fear of death, dishonour, and every harm; there is nothing we have not suffered at the hands of that unnatural stepmother— Spain. . . . We have been harassed by a conduct which has not only deprived us of our rights but has kept us in a sort of permanent infancy with regard to public affairs. . . . When the French invasion . . . routed the fragile government of the Peninsula, we were left orphans.[10]

The Spanish monarch, far from being a loving father, had become a hateful stepmother. Antonio Nariño, leader of the revolutionary state of Cundinamarca during the first years of the war, manipulated this metaphor with consummate skill in his newspaper *La Bagatela*. Here he dissects the term *Madre Patria*, which, he complains, is "so often used in our newspapers":

> This patriotic maternity, or maternal paternity, has left me utterly bewildered, unable to understand the tangled strands of our political genealogy. . . . I've enquired repeatedly about the Grandmother Patria *[Abuela Patria]*, the Sister Patria *[Hermana Patria]*, the Cousin Patria *[Prima Patria]*, the Aunt Patria *[Tia Patria]*, but the only one that I've actually met is the Stepmother Patria *[Madrastra Patria]*, who treats her descendants like strangers, and her children like slaves.[11]

Such familial imagery was not unique to revolutionary Colombia. Mary Lowenthal Felstiner has documented the use of very similar language during Chile's revolutionary period.[12] She attributes this language to specific features of Chilean independence: Chile's revolutionaries were generally creoles, sons of Spanish fathers and creole women. The colonial struggle, she suggests, was inevitably understood as a familial drama dividing fathers from sons. Yet this interpretation overlooks the frequency with which this metaphor was employed elsewhere during the so-called Age of Revolution.

Jay Fliegelman has convincingly demonstrated that some forty years earlier both Tories and revolutionaries depicted the American Revolution in similar terms. There, too, the colonial war was cast in part as family drama.

Fliegelman charts the changes in child-rearing practices in the eighteenth century and notes the decline in parental control over their children's marriages.[13] The eighteenth-century family, he argues, was in itself a site of considerable intergenerational strife. Familial conflict was thus the natural metaphor through which to understand political unrest. The use of familial imagery to depict revolution has been particularly well-documented for the French Revolution. Lynn Hunt, among others, has traced the ways in which the revolution was represented as a struggle between father and sons.[14] Colombian revolutionaries were thus drawing on established metaphors when they cast Ferdinand VII as a neglectful father or spiteful stepmother.

However, by interpreting the revolution in this way, the revolutionaries inevitably raised worrying questions. What would become of the family itself while the sons fought the father? This question must be read on two levels. The nascent family of American states was certainly imperiled by the conflict with Spain. In the Jamaica Letter, Bolívar predicted that, after independence, the "orphaned" American states would seek a new, loving father; he considered Mexico a suitable parental figure.[15] Yet the metaphysical family of American states was not the only family placed at risk by the war. After the overthrow of the paternal figure of the king, what would become of the patriarchal social order? Republican leaders certainly did not want to dismantle the basic social structures that had ordered colonial society. Despite the revolutionaries' frequent depiction of Americans as oppressed slaves, few advocated the outright abolition of slavery. On the contrary, individuals such as Bolívar expressed fears that the new republic might degenerate into a pardocracy, a government run by the people of color. Denunciations of the metaphorical slavery to which creoles had been reduced were not intended as comments on the institution of slavery. Rather, they served as a powerful invocation of weakness and dependence.[16] Similarly, calls to overthrow Spain's paternal authority were not intended to alter relations within real families. It was one thing for men to overthrow paternal authority, but quite another for women to do so. Female mobilization during the war thus posed troubling questions about women's nature and about their proper place in the new republican society.

Historians of the French and American Revolutions have argued that female mobilization was very disquieting for male revolutionaries. Moreover, in France and North America, female participation in the revolutionary process prompted very explicit attempts to exclude women from the world of politics. French republican leaders felt "great uneasiness" about women acting in public ways. Consequently, particularly after 1793, male republican leaders condemned women's political clubs, rallies by women, and public political appearances by women.[17] In the case of the American Revolution, Sylvia Frey has argued that male revolutionaries were "profoundly ambivalent" about women's participation in trade boycotts and other political activities. There, too, male revolutionaries moved to exclude women from public space and to depict women as vulnerable and dependent.[18] To what extent did similar processes occur in Spanish America? Were male revolutionary leaders in Colombia "profoundly ambivalent" about female participation in the war? Did women's varied political activities result in their later exclusion from public political space? Did Gran Colombia's republican leaders strive to depict all women as passive and dependent?

I want to start my analysis with a specific text—a proclamation by Simón Bolívar from 1813, during the so-called Campaña Admirable. In the text, Bolívar praises the valor of women from the Province of Trujillo in Venezuela when they had fought alongside republican men in a recent military encounter. This is what Bolívar says:

> even the fair sex, the delight of humankind, our amazons have fought against the tyrants of San Carlos [that is, the royalists] with a divine valor, although without success. The monsters and tigers of Spain have shown the full extent of the cowardice of their nation. They have used their infamous arms against the innocent feminine breasts of our beauties; they have shed their blood. They have killed many of them and have loaded them with chains, because they conceived the sublime plan of liberating their beloved country. . . . Soldiers: even the women of this country fight against the oppressors and compete with us for the glory of defeating them.[19]

What is Bolívar saying in this passage? He is very ambiguous about the role played by the women of Trujillo. On the one hand, he explicitly praises them for taking up arms. They are amazons, who fight with divine valor. That is to say, they were active combatants. On the other hand, Bolívar castigates the royalists ("the monsters and tigers of Spain") for their cowardly attack on innocent republican women: "They have used their infamous arms against the innocent feminine breasts of our beauties; they have shed their blood." The same women whose active fighting Bolívar has just praised suddenly become naive feminine victims of royalist brutality. Are they amazons or innocents?

This short passage is emblematic of the ambivalent way republican leaders understood female participation in the war. Political leaders might laud women for supporting them, but their praise was qualified by the insistence that women were innocent victims of the war. Moreover, comments like Bolívar's that praise women's martial valor are relatively uncommon. The occasional amazon flits across the rhetorical stage, but women are much more likely to appear in political discourse in a rather different role: that of pure victim. When women are invoked, it is in ways that emphasize both their passive suffering and the enemy's bestiality. According to republican leaders, royalists publicly flogged respectable matrons, accused innocent men of insurgency in order to gain sexual access to their wives and daughters, and cruelly imprisoned the blameless wives of republican leaders.[20] Women's bodies, especially elite women's bodies, were a matrix of republican suffering. As occurred in revolutionary North America, the suffering woman in Colombia became the "distinctive feminine image of revolutionary virtue."[21]

We can see this image most clearly in one particularly striking accusation. Over and over again republican leaders accused the royalists of raping innocent widows and virgins, raping innocent widows and virgins in churches, threatening to rape nuns in churches. It is to this accusation that we now turn.

When I first began working on this topic, I was struck by the number of republican texts that deplored the impious rape of women within church confines. In 1814, for example, the insurgent city council of Cali issued a condemnation of the behavior of royalist troops in their city. "Everyone knows," they asserted, "that the Lord's temple has been profaned and the honor of widows and the virgins has been injured." José Manuel Restrepo, republican politician and author of a monumental history of the revolution, denounced the libidinous acts committed by royalist soldiers in the churches of Quilichao, Paniquitá, and El Tambo. Insurgents in Socorro deplored the behavior of royalist troops who came "profaning temples, dishonouring virgins and mutilating patriots." Indeed, it wasn't only the royalists who were accused of rape and sacrilege. During the early years of the war, contending groups of insurgents accused each other of "killing priests, raping women, profaning temples."[22]

Several observations may be made about this imagery. First of all, we should note that it is, primarily, imagery—which may seem obvious; wartime propaganda has often revolved around the victimized body of a woman. It is well known that British propaganda during the First World War made effective use of rape-based atrocity stories in order to rally opposition to Germany, for example.[23] Indeed, Jean Bethke Elshtain has argued that the image of woman as quintessential victim of war is virtually universal.[24] I would like, nonetheless, to insist that these Colombian denunciations of rape serve specific, rather than universal, symbolic purposes. First, however, it is useful to consider the particular context in which the denunciations were made.

In revolutionary Colombia, the new official concern about rape as a violent crime against innocent women contrasts strikingly with the general lack of interest in the prosecution of rape prior to the outbreak of hostilities. During the colonial period, what we would call rape was generally lumped together with breach of promise ("seduction") as a crime of relatively minor importance. The usual punishment for convicted rapists (or seducers) was a fine paid to the victim. Because of the perceived overlap between seduction and rape, the victim herself might also be disciplined. A women who claimed to have been seduced might be confined to a convent for a time.[25] Thus, during the colonial period, rape was not generally seen as a violent act committed against innocent women. Rather, rape (or seduction) revealed some level of moral failing on the part of both participants, each of whom might shoulder a share of the blame. The heightened political concern about rape during the war of independence and the interpretation of rape as a violent assault on entirely blameless women thus reflect a new understanding of the offense. How do we account for this change?

One might argue that the change simply reflects the increased incidence of rape during the war.[26] Perhaps the denunciations of rape were not mere propaganda. It is probable that the frequency of rape increased during the revolutionary period, but this does not in itself explain the new language. During the colonial period, not all "rapes" fitted very comfortably into the category of "seduction," yet that is how they were understood legally. Similarly, during the wars of independence, the propagandistic denunciations of enemy atrocity bear only partial relation to women's lived experience. To begin with, these denunciations of rape suggest that the victims were only certain groups of particularly vulnerable women: virgins, nuns, widows. In reality, wartime rape did not affect only respectable virgins. The (admittedly scanty) military records of actual trials for rape certainly do not bear out the charge that sexual assault fell disproportionately on these groups. Moreover, when republican troops were themselves accused of raping women, their officers responded with a shrug of the shoulders. Such things, the officers explained, were a natural occurrence in times of war.[27] Outage over the violation of innocent maidens operated on a different plane from the wartime reality of rape. The new concern was not a simple reflection of the changes in the frequency and nature of actual cases of rape or of the universal imagery of female victimization. It was, I would suggest, an anxious response to increased female mobilization.[28] The repeated insistence on the victimization and rape of women expresses anxiety about a very different reality. Far from being uniquely passive victims, many women were actively participating in the process of independence, some in ways that directly challenged existing class and sexual hierarchies, as we have seen. This uncomfortable reality was neutered by the monotonous insistence that women, particularly respectable women, were the principal, exemplary victims of war. That is why Bolívar's amazons slipped uncontrollably into innocent feminine beauties. The virgin raped inside a church epitomized the image of women as passive victims, countering the reality of them as active participants in wartime activities.

Revolutionary anxiety about women's mobilization does not manifest itself uniquely in denunciations of rape. Other victimization legends also thrived. Like the mythologized accounts of rape, these stories stressed that the war violated the lives of respectable women, forcing them to behave in ways contrary to their feminine natures. Most importantly, women were represented as vulnerable and defenseless. For example, after the royalist reconquest of 1815–16, stories circulated that the triumphant royalists were obliging respectable republican women to attend dissolute parties at the very moment that their husbands, fathers, and sons were being executed. Beautiful and unprotected republican women were forced to cavort with licentious royalist officers, exposing themselves and their grief to disrespect and humiliation.[29] Elite women, such stories stressed, were particularly persecuted during the war. In contrast, nonelite women, with little honor to lose, became the focus of republican opprobrium. Prostitutes, the classic example of women in the public view, particularly alarmed republican leaders. Republican officers worried that royalist women, acting as common prostitutes, might undermine the integrity of their army through an assault on the very bodies of their soldiers: women's public sexuality might weaken the body politic. In one deeply alarming incident, "royalist" prostitutes allegedly incapacitated republican soldiers by serving them *aguardiente* laced with hallucinogens.[30] Consorting with "enemy prostitutes" was thus strictly forbidden.

Concerns about women's relations, sexual or otherwise, with the new republican state were not confined to independence-era Colombia. I have already noted similar concerns in revolutionary France and America. Nor was Colombia the only Spanish-American state where republican leaders expressed ambivalence about female mobilization. Rather, comparable anxieties also appeared in the other Spanish-American republics established after the outbreak of war in 1810. In early republican Buenos Aires, women's increased participation in the independence movement coincided with an outpouring of anxious rhetoric about prostitutes. Abandoned jails were reopened with the express purpose of housing prostitutes, whose unchecked behavior was blamed for the city's ills. Meanwhile, all women were banned from political events. Women with political ambitions were publicly lampooned. In Río de la Plata, too, the incorporation of women into the new republican state proved problematic.[31] These tensions were perhaps inherent in the republican project of the long eighteenth century, from the War of the Spanish Succession to the end of Spanish colonial rule about 1825. Recent work on both France and North America has emphasized the degree to which the republican ideals of freedom and liberty were constructed around the explicit exclusion of certain groups of dependent beings— particularly women and, in the case of North America, slaves. As Joan Landes argues, "the [French] Republic was constructed against women, not just without them."[32] We are not yet in a position to show whether this was true for Spanish America. However, it is clear that in Spanish America, too, women occupied a contested seat at the revolutionary banquet. Lynn Hunt, in her analysis of revolutionary France *(The Family Romance of the French Revolution),* has asserted that such tensions were due to deep-seated male anxieties about paternal control. She notes that revolutionary republicans were rarely certain what to do with women after the overthrow of the patriarchal king. One need not ascribe to Hunt's neo-Freudianism to accept the truth of this observation for revolutionary Colombia.

Symbols and Supporters

I have been arguing that the alarming reality of female participation in the war was met by a steady rhetorical insistence on women's role as victim. Does this then mean that political leaders were completely uninterested in gaining the support of the female population? On the contrary, political leaders were generally delighted when women expressed enthusiasm for their side. Revolutionaries were very proud of any support offered to them by groups of women because female support was considered an indication of the naturalness of their philosophy: even untutored women could see its truth. But their responses further demonstrate that the period of the war saw a sustained effort to confine women to a nonparticipatory political sphere. As in revolutionary France and North America, political leaders appreciated feminine support as long as it remained passive and purely symbolic.[33] We should consider an illustrative example. In 1811, a group of women from the Venezuelan province of Barinas wrote to the governor, offering to enlist in the republican army: "we are not unaware that you, attending to the weakness of our sex, perhaps have tried to excuse us from military hardships; but you know very well that love of country animates crueler beings than us and there are no obstacles so insurmountable that it cannot conquer them."[34] This offer was naturally rejected. More significantly, however, it was also printed in the *Gaceta de Caracas* in order to publicize the women's signal patriotism. What was, at least on the surface, an offer of active support was thus converted into a gesture of symbolic support. Women's support was celebrated as long as it remained on this level. Once decoupled from active involvement, female patriotism functioned as a powerful symbol throughout the war. Women symbolized liberty in triumphal pageants; women planted liberty trees; images of women, especially of Indian women, symbolized the new independent nation.[35] The degree to which this imagery diverged from issues of real political power is clear. Indian women, who exercised no accepted authority whatsoever, might represent the republic. Young women still subject to their father's authority might impersonate liberty. Appropriate female patriotism was thus depicted as passive and symbolic. Again we may usefully compare Colombia with independence-era Río de la Plata. Francine Masiello has argued that in Buenos Aires the independence period "produced a series of mythologies about women devoted unconditionally to the nation."[36] As in Colombia, these mythologies revolved entirely around symbolic displays of support for the new republic. One celebrated group of patriotic women provided their husbands with rifles engraved with their own names. The women were thus symbolically present in battle without actually taking part in any fighting. This sort of patriotism is quite removed from that of the armed amazon who participates in actual battle. In both Argentina and Colombia, symbolic displays of patriotism were rewarded as long as they remained purely symbolic. If necessary, active displays of patriotism could be reglossed as symbolic, as occurred with the offer made by the women from Barinas Province.

In Colombia, a particularly interesting example of the conversion of an active participant into a passive symbol is provided by the career of republican heroine Policarpa Salavarrieta, a young woman from a poor family living in the capital, Santa Fe de Bogotá.[37] Salavarrieta, or La Pola as she is fondly known in the historical literature, worked as a seamstress, with a sideline in illegal aguardiente distillation. in 1817, she conceived a bold plan to subvert royalist troops in the Santa Fe garrison. Using a network of contacts, she hoped to induce royalist soldiers to defect to the republicans. Her plan, although ambitious, was ultimately unsuccessful, and she was captured and executed by the royalists in November 1817.

With her death, Salavarrieta was rapidly elevated to a special, indeed unique, place in the pantheon of republican heroes. She was virtually the only woman to be executed in the capital, and her death inspired a substantial hagiographic literature, which is not surprising, for Salavarrieta was in many ways a perfect feminine hero. She displayed unmistakable patriotism, but any discomfort about her too active leadership of the plot to subvert the troops was quickly neutralized by the martyr's death she suffered at the age of twenty. Contemporary commentaries stressed not her valiant attempt to undermine the royalist garrison, but rather her beauty, her virtuous female character, and her unswerving determination to die for the fatherland. Her name was immediately made into the anagram "yace para salvar la patria"

("She lay down her life to save the fatherland"), and various atrocious verses were composed honoring her willingness to pour out her blood for the fatherland.[38] It is worth noting that eyewitness accounts of Salavarrieta's actual execution lend no support to the claim that she wished to die for the patria. Such accounts instead describe her as railing against her executioners until the last minute.[39] Nonetheless, hagiographic accounts soon converted her into a symbol of willing sacrifice for the republic. Policarpa Salavarrieta, the female martyr, remains to this day the supreme emblem of female participation in Colombia's war of independence.[40]

"The Anxieties Attendant upon a Revolutionary Project"

What then were the appropriate places for Colombian women in the process of political transformation?[41] On the one hand, women's engagement with the military and political revolution has been documented. Although substantially more work remains to be done, it is clear that many different classes and groups of women were mobilized by the war. Women's involvement in the war ranged from the unwilling preparation of food to armed combat. On the other hand, this varied female involvement in the war prompted republican leaders to represent all female participation as passive suffering. What conclusions can we draw about the role of gender in the construction of the republic?

Historians of the nineteenth century in Latin America have stressed that the family was intended as the fundamental unit of the new republican nation. The beatification of the family began early in the lives of these republics. Republican leaders wished to overthrow Ferdinand VII of Spain, symbolic father of the Spanish Empire, but they certainly did not want to destroy male authority within the family itself. On the contrary, the male was confirmed as the official head of both the new nation and the individual household. As Colombia's revolutionary constitutions proclaimed (echoing the French Constitution of 1795), "no one can be a good citizen who is not a good father, good son, good brother, good friend, and good husband."[42] The patriarchal family, in other words, lay at the center of the new republic, and a man's public role was modeled on his role within the family.

Women's relation to the state was also mediated through this metaphor.

A woman's role in the new republic was to mirror her role within the family. That familial role was to consist primarily of uncomplaining sacrifice for the greater good. Policarpa Salavarrieta's symbolic (as opposed to actual) death thus displayed impeccable republican virtues: she willingly gave up her life for the sake of the new republican family.

Women did not need to sacrifice *themselves* to be good patriots. Innumerable women remain immortalized in Colombian historical hagiography for having offered up their sons to the new republic; Doña Dolores de Picón, the wife of a republican leader, sighed in 1814: "I give thanks to God, because my sons have poured out their blood for the fatherland."[43] What Linda Kerber has called "Republican Motherhood"—the rearing (and sacrifice) of patriotic sons—thus offered an additional role to women, still without suggesting that they should be active outside the home.[44] Republican mothers contributed to the republic by educating their sons to be good citizens. Bolívar described the central role assigned to women in his "virtuous republic" in his famous appendix to the 1819 Venezuelan Constitution. This "virtuous republic" established a separate "Poder Moral" or Moral Power intended to oversee the morality and education of Colombian citizens.[45] A special Cámara de Educación, organized by the Poder Moral, was to supervise education throughout the republic. The Cámara explicitly acknowledged the importance of women in the education of republican citizens. Affirming that "the cooperation of women is absolutely indispensable for the education of children in their earliest years," the appendix ordered that all women in the republic be provided with "concise and simple" information on this civic responsibility.[46] From the earliest days of the republic, they were to exercise their influence from within the home, not from without. Beyond education, motherhood itself offered a further model for feminine patriotism. In revolutionary France, a woman who nursed an orphaned child was accorded the title of "precious citizen," although without acquiring thereby any political rights. Her citizenship was purely symbolic.[47] In Spanish America, as in revolutionary France and North America, republican motherhood was celebrated, although such motherhood in itself never accorded women further political rights. Moreover, the image of the republican mother was itself intended essentially for the middle classes, on whom all civic life was modeled. As Sarah Chambers has found in her study of revolutionary Arequipa, poor women had difficulty living up to the image and therefore in claiming the status that republican motherhood was intended to afford them.[48] Moreover, how this model was received by Colombian women, not all of whom were in a position to adopt its benevolent domesticity, remains a topic for further research. The official position was clear: women were to relate to the republic via their subordinate position within the family.

The family and women's place within it were thus central concerns of the republican elite from the republic's inception. Subsequent chapters in this volume illustrate the continued vitality of these concerns. Elizabeth Dore, for example, documents the efforts by local elites to police and regulate both family life and gender roles in post-independence Central America. Yet, in Colombia, attempts to construct a republic on a model of male activity and female passivity were confronted with the uncomfortable reality of women's actual wartime activities, which were a source of anxiety and tension for the political elite, who both welcomed and feared female participation in the war. The war thus heightened anxieties about the proper role of women without in any way resolving them. Gender relations in the nineteenth-century republics were thus conceived, at least in part, in the revolutionary process itself.

Notes

1 See, for example, Linda Kerber, *Women of the Republic: Intellect and Ideology in Revolutionary America* (Chapel Hill: University of North Carolina Press, 1980); Jay Fliegelman, *Prodigals and Pilgrims: The American Revolution against Patriarchal Authority, 1750–1800* (Cambridge: Cambridge University Press, 1982); Ruth Bloch, "The Gendered Meaning of Virtue in Revolutionary America," *Signs* 13 (1987): 37–58; Joan Landes, *Women and the Public Sphere in the Age of the French Revolution* (Ithaca, N.Y.: Cornell University Press, 1988); Olwen Hufton, *Women and the Limits of Citizenship in the French Revolution* (Toronto: University of Toronto Press, 1992); Madelyn Gutwirth, *The Twilight of the Goddesses: Women and Representation in the French Revolutionary Era* (New Brunswick, N.J.: Rutgers University Press, 1992); and Lynn Hunt, *The Family Romance of the French Revolution* (Berkeley: University of California Press, 1993).

2 For Colombia, see José Dolores Monsalve, *Mujeres de la independencia* (Bogotá: Academia Colombiana de Historia, 1926); Oswaldo Díaz Díaz, *La reconquista española,* 2 vols. (Bogotá: Ediciones Lerner, 1967); Evelyn Cherpak, "The Participation of Women in the Independence Movement in Gran Colombia, 1780–1830," in *Latin American Women: Historical Perspectives,* ed. Asunción Lavrin

(Westport, Conn.: Greenwood, 1978), 219–34; and Aida Martínez Carreño, "Revolución, independencia, y sumisión de la mujer colombiana en el siglo XIX," *Boletín de Historia de Antigüedades,* vol. 79 (1989): 000–000.

3 Colonel Francisco Warleta is quoted in José María Restrepo Saenz, *Gobernadores de Antioquia, 1517–1819,* 2 vols. (Bogotá: Imprenta Nacional, 1932), 1:291–92.

4 See Testimony of Doña María Manuela de Angulo to Sala Capitular de Popayán, Popayán, 19 June 1817, Audiencia de Santa Fé, legajo 631, Archivo General de Indias (henceforth AGI), Sevilla.

5 The phrase is François-Xavier Guerra's. See François-Xavier Guerra, *Modernidad e independencias: Ensayos sobre las revoluciones hispánicas* (Madrid: MAPFRE, 1992), 275–318.

6 By "republic," Colombia's revolutionary leaders generally meant a constitutional, representative democracy. The precise mechanisms ensuring representation and the degree of centralization were the subjects of a fierce debate. For a discussion of these issues, see the useful prologue by Carlos Restrepo Piedrahita in *Actas del Congreso de Cúcuta, 1821,* vol. 1 (Bogotá: Biblioteca de la Presidencia de la República, 1989).

7 Women were active participants in many colonial riots. For an overview, see Anthony McFarlane, "Civil Disorders and Popular Protests in Late Colonial New Granada," *Hispanic American Historical Review* 30 (1984): 17–54.

8 Linda Colley, *Britons: Forging the Nation, 1707–1837* (London: Vintage, 1996), 275.

9 Simón Bolívar to María Antonia Bolívar, 10 July 1826, Magdalena, in Simón Bolívar, *Escritos del libertador,* 25 vols. (Caracas: Sociedad Bolivariana de Venezuela, 1977), 3:89–90.

10 Simón Bolívar to Henry Cullen, 6 September 1815, Kingston, in Vicente Lecuna, ed., *Selected Writings of Bolívar,* 2 vols. (New York: Colonial, 1951), 1:103–22.

11 Antonio Nariño, *La Bagatela,* no. 8, 1 September 1811; Or consider *La Bagatela,* issue 8, no. 1, 15 September 1811.

12 Mary Lowenthal Felstiner, "Family Metaphors: The Language of an Independence Revolution," *Comparative Studies in Society and History* 25 (1983): 154–80.

13 Fliegelman, *Prodigals and Pilgrims.* Comparable processes occurred in eighteenth-century Spanish America. See, for example, Robert McCaa, "Gustos de los padres: Inclinaciones de los novios y reglas de una feria nupcial colonial, Parral, 1770–1810," *Historia Mexicana* 40, no. 4 (1991): 579–614, for a brief discussion of parental control over their children's choice of a partner.

14 Hunt, *Family Romance.*

15 Bolívar's explicit call for a replacement father figure may be compared to the elevation of George Washington to the status of "founding father" in the years following the American Revolution. See Fliegelman, *Prodigals and Pilgrims,* 199. Hunt argues that the absence of "founding fathers" of the French Revolution illustrates the degree to which the very idea of fatherhood became problematic for the leaders of the French Republic. See *Family Romance,* 71–80.

16 The Jamaica Letter again provides clear examples of the Americans-as-slaves

metaphor. Identical metaphors are documented for revolutionary Chile in Fel-stiner, "Family Metaphors." For an incisive discussion of the use of slavery metaphors in the British colonies, see Kathleen M. Brown, *Good Wives, Nasty Wenches, and Anxious Patriarchs: Gender, Race, and Power in Colonial Virginia* (Chapel Hill: University of North Carolina Press, 1996), especially pp. 370–73.

17 Landes, *Women and the Public Sphere;* Hufton, *Women and the Limits of Citizen-ship;* and Hunt, *Family Romance,* p. 81, for "great uneasiness."

18 Sylvia Frey, "Gendering the Republic," unpublished seminar paper, Depart-ment of History research seminar, University of Warwick, 30 October 1997.

19 Proclamation of Simón Bolívar, 22 June 1813, Trujillo, in Bolívar, *Escritos,* 4:325–26. Cf. Cherpak, "Participation of Women."

20 See, for example, José Manuel Restrepo, *Historia de la revolución de Colombia,* 6 vols. (Medellín: Editorial Bedout, 1969), 2:148–50.

21 Bloch, "Gendered Meaning," 45.

22 Sala Constitucional de Cali to Congress, 30 January 1814, Cali, Papeles de Cuba, legajo 897, AGI; Díaz, *La reconquista,* 2:163; Restrepo, *Historia de la revolución,* 2:148; and Pedro María Ibáñez, *Crónicas de Bogotá* (Bogotá, Colombia: Tercer Mundo, 1989), 3:114–16. Or see various examples in Hermes Tovar, "Guerras de opinión y represión en Colombia durante la independencia (1810–1820)," *Anuario Colombiano de Historia Social y de la Cultura,* no. 11 (1983): 187–233.

23 Nicoletta F. Gullace, "Sexual Violence and Family Honor: British Propaganda and International Law during the First World War," *American Historical Review* 102, no. 3 (1997): 714–45.

24 Jean Bethke Elshtain, "Reflections on War and Political Discourse: Realism, Just War, and Feminism in a Nuclear Age," in *Just War Theory,* ed. Jean Bethke Elshtain (New York: New York University Press, 1992), 260–79.

25 For examples from colonial Mexico, see Asunción Lavrin, "Sexuality in Colonial Mexico: A Church Dilemma," in *Sexuality and Marriage in Colonial Latin Amer-ica,* ed. Asunción Lavrin (Lincoln: University of Nebraska Press, 1989), 47–95, McCaa, "Gustos de los padres"; Ramón Gutiérrez, *When Jesus Came, the Corn Mothers Went Away: Marriage, Sexuality, and Power in New Mexico, 1500–1846* (Stanford: Stanford University Press, 1991); and Richard Boyer, *The Lives of the Bigamists: Marriage, Family, and Community in Colonial Mexico* (Austin: Univer-sity of Texas Press, 1995). For colonial New Granada and Venezuela, see Kathy Waldron, "The Sinners and the Bishop in Colonial Venezuela: The Visita of Bishop Mariano Martí, 1771–1784," in Lavrin, ed., *Sexuality and Marriage;* and Pablo Rodríguez, *Seducción, amancebamiento, y abandono en la colonia* (Santa Fe de Bogotá: Editorial Ealon, 1991), in particular 29–72.

26 A seminal, although problematic, text on rape during wartime is Susan Brown-miller, *Against Our Will: Men, Women, and Rape* (New York: Bantam, 1975).

27 For a particularly clear example, see Luis Francisco de Rieux to Gabriel de Torres, 27 August 1821, Turbaco, Papeles de Cuba, legajo 717, AGI.

28 In this regard, the work of Anna Clark on the meaning of rape in eighteenth-

century England is particularly suggestive. Clark notes an interesting discrepancy between the perceptions and the reality of rape during this period. Although criminal records suggest that working-class women were most likely to be assaulted by members of their own class, this is not reflected in English popular discourse on rape. On the contrary, there is a rich popular literature about the rape of working-class women by licentious aristocrats, despite the fact that such assaults were apparently relatively uncommon. The myth of aristocratic assault on defenseless working-class girls, Clark argues, displays concerns about the impact of the economic transformation under way in England: "the image of the poor maiden victimised by the aristocratic libertine provided a very specific symbol of class exploitation." Thus, Clark asserts, the popular language used to discuss rape in eighteenth-century England did not correlate directly to its actual incidence, but referred to other concerns of the English working class. Clark labels this popular imagery of rape a myth—as story that symbolically expresses anxieties bought about by social crisis. I would argue that a comparable mythologizing force was at work in revolutionary Colombia. See Anna Clark, "The Politics of Seduction in English Popular Culture, 1748–1848," in *The Progress of Romance: The Politics of Popular Fiction*, ed. Jean Radford (New York: Routledge and Kegan Paul, 1986), 47. This thesis is elaborated further in Anna Clark, *Women's Silence, Men's Violence: Sexual Assault in England, 1770–1845* (London: Pandora, 1987).

29 For repeated examples, see Monsalve, *Mujeres de la independencia*.

30 Report by Sala de Gobierno de Popayán, 6 June 1822, Independencia MI-3j, sig. 6874, Archivo Central del Cauca, Popayán. Official reports identify prostitutes as either royalist or insurgent. See, for example, Sala Capitular to Francisco de Montalvo, Popayán, 5 July 1817, Audiencia de Santa Fe, legajo 631, AGI; and Report on a republican prostitute, Archivo Anexo, Guerra y Marina, tomo 152, f. 240, Archivo Histórico Nacional de Colombia, Bogotá.

31 Mark Szuchman, *Order, Family, and Community in Buenos Aires, 1810–1860* (Stanford: Stanford University Press, 1988), 118–19.

32 Landes, *Women and the Public Sphere*, 12. Much of the recent work on the role of race in the Enlightenment and in the American Revolution builds on ground first ploughed by Edmund Morgan. See Edmund Morgan, *American Slavery, American Freedom: The Ordeal of Colonial Virginia* (New York: W. W. Norton, 1975).

33 See Kerber, *Women of the Republic*, 105–10, for a lucid discussion of this phenomenon in North America.

34 Cherpak, "Participation of Women," 223.

35 For a liberty tree, see José María Caballero, *Diario* (Bogotá: Editorial Villegas, 1990), 201. For patriotic Indians, see the portrait of Simón Bolívar in David Bushnell, *The Making of Modern Colombia: A Nation in Spite of Itself* (Berkeley: University of California Press, 1993); and Hans-Joachim König, "Símbolos nacionales y retórica política en la independencia: El caso de la Nueva Granada,"

in *Problemas de la formación del estado y de la nación en Hispanoamérica,* ed. Inge Buisson, Günter Kahle, Hans-Joachim König, and Horst Pietschmann (Cologne: Bohlau, 1984), 395. For a woman representing Liberty, see Ibáñez, *Crónicas,* 4:150. E. McClung Fleming, "The American Image as Indian Princess, 1765–1783," *Winterthur Portfolio* 2 (1965): 65–81, and E. McClung Fleming, "From Indian Princess to Greek Goddess: The American Image, 1785–1815," *Winterthur Portfolio* 3 (1966): 000–000, discuss the comparable iconography of the American Revolution.

36 Francine Masiello, *Between Civilisation and Barbarism: Women, Nation, and Literary Culture in Modern Argentina* (Lincoln: University of Nebraska Press, 1992), 19.

37 For information about Policarpa Salavarrieta, see Díaz, *La reconquista,* vols. 1 and 2.

38 Díaz, *La reconquista,* 1:384–85.

39 Caballero, *Diario,* 238.

40 See Rafael Gómez Hoyos, *La independencia de Colombia* (Madrid: MAPFRE, 1992), 198.

41 The phrase in the subhead is from Hunt, *Family Romance,* 194.

42 This phrase is repeated in virtually all of Colombia's revolutionary constitutions in the years between 1811 and 1819. See the Constitución de la República de Tunja, 1811, capítulo II; Constitución del Estado de Antioquia, 1812, sec. 3, art. 4; Constitución de la República de Cundinamarca, 1812, art. 28; Constitución del Estado de Mariquita, 1815, título II, art. 6, Constitución de la Provincia de Antioquia, 1815, Deberes del Cuidadano, art. 4; all in Manuel Antonio Pombo and José Joaquín Guerra, eds., *Constituciones de Colombia,* 2 vols. (Bogotá: Biblioteca Popular de Cultura Colombiana, 1951); Constitución de Neiva, 1815, in Gómez Hoyos, *La independencia de Colombia,* 201; and Constitución de Angostura, 1819, sec. 2, art. 5, in *Actas del Congreso de Angostura, 1819–1820* (Bogotá: Biblioteca de la Presidencia de la República, 1988), p. 148.

43 Monsalve, *Mujeres de la independencia,* 72.

44 The concept of Republican Motherhood is elaborated in Kerber, *Women of the Republic,* chap. 9. Jan Lewis discusses the related figure of the Republican Wife in Jan Lewis, "The Republican Wife: Virtue and Seduction in the Early Republic," *William and Mary Quarterly* 44, third series (1987): 565–85. See also Sarah Chambers, "Gendered Meanings of Virtue and Citizenship in Early Republican Spanish America," unpublished conference paper delivered at the American Historical Association, Atlanta, 7 January 1996.

45 "Apéndice a la Constitución relativo al Poder Moral," in Pedro Grases and Tomás A. Polanco, *El libertador y la Constitución de Angostura de 1819* (Caracas: Banco Hipotecario de Crédito Urbano, 1970). The phrase "virtuous republic" is from sec. 2, art. 5 of the Poder Moral.

46 Poder Moral, sec. 3, art. 2.

47 Hufton, *Women and the Limits of Citizenship,* 64.

48 Chambers, "Gendered Meanings."

Elizabeth Dore

Property, Households, and

Public Regulation of Domestic Life

Diriomo, Nicaragua, 1840–1900

Between independence and the coffee revolution, when nation-states were weak throughout Central America, municipal governments exercised considerable power. Central to their rule was the public regulation of domestic life. This chapter examines changes in the gender order in an Indian pueblo in Nicaragua in that interregnum. It·analyzes landed property, household headship, and public control over so-called private morality, and considers how these elements were influenced by the coffee economy. I argue, first, that the rise of private property significantly altered gendered arrangements in the Indian pueblos of southwestern Nicaragua, and second, that public regulation of domestic morality was pivotal in constructing state power at the local level.

Scholars of Central America agree that the rise of coffee was a historical turning point, particularly in the development of land and labor systems and in the process of state formation—although, for the most part, they have agreed to disagree about how to interpret those changes. Virtually absent from the debates has been the question of how the coffee revolution affected prevailing gender regimes and whether the transformation of gender was of any great importance.[1] This chapter addresses these neglected issues and concludes that a gendered analysis significantly broadens our understanding of how the coffee revolution altered land tenure, household composition, and everyday state formation in rural Nicaragua. The question of labor I treat elsewhere.[2]

First, some definitions. The analytical distinction between *household* and *family* is clear: the former refers to residence, the latter to kinship. This is a study of the household, the social unit in evidence in census materials. A caveat, however, must be attached to the meaning of *headship*. The category *female household headship* has been popularized by social policy debates, but all too frequently there is ambiguity about what headship means.[3] In this study, imprecision regarding headship derives from the historical sources; nineteenth-century Nicaraguan censuses indicate the sex of household heads but fail to explain how headship was defined. I am confident, therefore, in quantifying female and male heads of household, but cautious in giving meanings to those categories.

Courting the risks involved in defining something as complex and protean as the state, I mean by it the array of political institutions that foster and endeavor to reproduce the rule of the dominant classes. Although states present themselves as governing in the general interest, this self-definition rarely reflects their inner nature. First, societies have no "general interest" that overrides all class, gender, and racial divisions. Second, such an interpretation ignores the major power inherent in the operation of the state, power that derives from the expropriating classes. It is more useful then to think of the state as ruling in the general interest of an ensemble of dominant classes—for instance of capitalists, landlords, merchants, bankers, and so on. In this perspective, within the state there occurs negotiation of rule, but in their vast majority the protagonists in this contest share the worldview of the propertied classes. They attempt in this process to make the world conform to their view of what constitutes legitimate or natural class, gender, ethnic, and race relations.

As in much of the rest of Latin America in the nineteenth century, Nicaragua had neither a capitalist economy nor a capitalist state. However, even more than in other countries, the Nicaraguan state in the latter part of the century was still in embryonic form. The subject of this essay is the gendered process of state formation or the state politics of gender. For this inquiry, the approach pioneered by Philip Corrigan and Derek Sayer is useful.[4] To uncover the hidden histories of state formation, they examine long-term processes that contribute to the construction of new social relations and that destroy old ways of life. They demonstrate how, largely through regulation of the mundane activities of life, the state—the organized power of the ruling classes—naturalizes a specific form of class, gender, and racial domination. In most countries, this naturalization has been accomplished insidiously. Gradually one historically unique form of rule comes to be thought of as normal, as the only way society could be organized. Alternative social relations and identities are rendered abnormal, made to seem subversive, and suppressed.

In Central America, with the absence of viable nation-states between independence and the nineteenth-century coffee boom, municipal governments took the lead in regulating the social order. In doing so, they became central to the consolidation of secular authority in the public sphere; they were the vanguard of the emergent liberal state. There are vast theoretical and historical differences between consolidation of the English bourgeois state that Corrigan and Sayer describe and the patronage state in nineteenth-century Nicaragua. Nevertheless, "state formation as cultural revolution" allows us to understand how, following the collapse of the Spanish colonial state in Central America, a ladino, male peasant elite consolidated its class, gender, and ethnic domination in towns throughout the countryside. This chapter examines how one sector of society remade its "world"—an Indian town in Nicaragua—in its own image. The study of the regulation of gender within rural society forms part of the hidden history of state formation in Latin America.

This essay is a case study of Diriomo, an Indian community radically transformed by the coffee boom of the late nineteenth century. The town of Diriomo and its rural *caseríos* (hamlets) are located on a *meseta* formed by the Managua-Granada-Jinotepe triangle in southwestern Nicaragua. It is in the cluster of villages and towns known today as "Los Pueblos." The history of Diriomo is, with certain variations, the story of the Meseta de los Pueblos.

My argument is developed in four parts. The first part describes the gendered nature of common property regimes and the regulation of domestic morality before the rise of coffee. The second treats transformations in land tenure, and demonstrates that land privatization had a different meaning for the women of the Comunidad Indígena (Indian Community) than for its men. The revolution in landed property expropriated some Indian men, albeit a minority, but it expanded female land rights and facilitated women's acquisition of land. The third part examines the relationship between changes in the social organization of land and household headship. It finds that land privatization may have accentuated a preexisting tendency toward nonmarrying behavior in the pueblo. The fourth part analyzes public regulation of domestic life and how this fortified the local elite and their instrument of rule, Diriomo's municipal government. Finally, the conclusion argues that public regulation of gender was an important aspect of state formation in Nicaragua.

Patriarchy and Common Property

In Diriomo, the coffee revolution altered the nature of property, local power, and the gender order more, perhaps, than anything else since the cataclysm of conquest. In the colonial period, the Crown granted Diriomo, a rural community on the outskirts of the city of Granada, the status of Comunidad Indígena, and with this about one square league of common land (4,350 acres). Until the mid–nineteenth century, that land—*el común*, which included fields, pastures, forests, rivers, and lakes—was held in the name of the community and administered by its leaders. Although land was not privately owned, by the nineteenth century Indian society was stratified by differential wealth in the form of *mejoras*, or improvements to the land, such as hedgerows, fruit trees, crops, and cattle.

Stratification by wealth was modest and sometimes difficult to discern; in contrast, property differentiation by gender was stark and transparent. Common property rights were male rights, membership in the Comunidad Indígena was restricted to adult males and mejoras were owned by men. Evidence of this restriction comes from three sources. In the first, a land claim from the 1860s, the claimant described the old system of rights to el común.[5] In the second, the mayor of the municipality itemized property in mejoras owned by individuals within the Indian Community in the 1840s. No women were on that list.[6] In the third, petitions for private land filed in the throes of the coffee revolution, Indian women invoked fathers' traditional usufruct rights to the commons, but no mention was made of mothers' land rights.[7]

It seems then, that Indias' formal access to the commons derived from male kin. This contrasts with men's membership in the Comunidad Indígena, which inherited through matrilineal descent. In this particular community and probably other Comunidades Indígenas in nineteenth-century Mesoamerica, rights to common resources passed through women, yet passed them by.[8] *Cofradías*, which owned and administered an important part of the collective wealth of the community—in particular, herds and pastures—also concentrated power in domains from which women were excluded. In summary, women's formal access to the material resources of the community was mediated through kinship relations with men.

Political power within the comunidad was another masculine domain. As community members, only adult males had voice and vote in communal deliberations.[9] Governance of the community was entrusted to a male civil-religious hierarchy led by the *alcalde indígena,* which allocated usufruct rights, adjudicated disputes, administered the treasury *(caja de comunidad),* and organized religious fiestas.

The relationship between these male-dominated economic-political institutions and conjugal-residence patterns in Diriomo's Indian population prior to the coffee boom remain something of an enigma. Information on family forms in Nicaragua's Indian townships between the late eighteenth and late nineteenth centuries is scarce. Some evidence about marriage behavior prior to independence is found in the Bula de la Santa Cruzada of 1776, a census administered for religious purposes throughout Central America. According to the Bula, approximately 30 percent of Indian men and women in Diriomo were unmarried,[10] a number consistent with the pattern of nonmarrying behavior found throughout Latin America at that time, especially among the popular classes.[11]

In the late colonial period, ladinos—people of mixed Spanish, Indian, and African heritage—settled in the pueblos of southwestern Nicaragua, renting land from the Indian communities.[12] In 1776, 7 percent of the population of Diriomo was described as ladino.[13] Subsequently, Indian and ladino identities gradually blurred, contributing to a process of ladinoization in the region. Yet by the 1850s, this process was not far advanced in Los Pueblos. In Diriomo, the major signifier of Indianness remained men's usufruct rights to the commons. As long as the Comunidad Indígena controlled access to land, Indian identity survived.[14]

After Central American independence, ethnic categories were abolished in law, but in practice they did not disappear. In Nicaragua, with a vacuum of power at the level of nation-state, political authority devolved to the regions and locales. Municipalities with their governing body, the Junta Municipal, were superimposed on Comunidades Indígenas, a prior ethno-political jurisdiction. Tensions inherent in the coexistence of the Indian and municipal jurisdictions intensified in Diriomo when it became apparent that municipal politics was de facto a ladino sphere. Nicaragua's first constitutions conferred citizenship and the vote exclusively on men of property.[15] Although those charters did not explicitly exclude Indians from citizenship, as they did women, no man of the *casta indígena* participated in Diriomo's Junta Municipal. Indian and ladino political spheres were separate and increasingly unequal, the former subordinated to the latter.

Diriomo's ladino citizens, fifty or so men of the rich peasantry, elected the Junta Municipal. At its head sat the *alcalde municipal,* the main political force in Diriomo. He was simultaneously the town's mayor, civil and criminal judge, bailiff, notary, and sometimes scribe. No man on the Junta Municipal claimed private ownership of land, yet all fulfilled the property requirement for citizenship. Like the Indian leaders, they owned mejoras, or the products of labor; unlike Indians, their property included more substantial items such as mills and carts.[16] Property in the products of labor, modest as it was, formed the economic basis of class stratification within the pueblo. Most men, whether Indian or ladino, had little property besides their clothes, rustic houses, small domestic animals, and machetes.

By the mid–nineteenth century, ethnic differentiation in this region of Nicaragua was only remotely related to "racial" origin. Whether families were Indian or ladino increasingly depended on a mix of wealth, culture, and politics. The first provided the possibility of social mobility that could effect ethnic transubstantiation. The second, a question of self-identification and labeling by others, was manifested concretely in land rights. The third, municipal power, was at the heart of increasing ethnic, class, and gender disparities in the pueblo. The Junta Municipal became the motor of peasant differentiation, although in the mid–nineteenth century this process was still at an early stage.

Gender relations, both within and between the Indian and ladino communities, rested on a mixture of material, ideological, and biological elements. In the first two—the material and ideological—control over property was central to gender differentiation, although it was ruled by different customs and laws in the two ethnic communities. In the case of Indias, exclusion from direct access to property was customary and pertained to all females of the comunidad, regardless of marital status. In the case of ladinas, exclusion from property reflected Hispanic law, which differentiated women by marital status. According to Nicaragua's civil code, single women and widows could control property, if they were fortunate enough to have any, but married women could not.[17] In conclusion, social relations of patriarchy, understood as senior male authority over everyone in the household, were substantively different in the two ethnic communities in Diriomo.

As the Junta Municipal consolidated its power in the pueblo, it eroded preexisting ethnic differences in gender regimes—a process that might be called the ladinoization of gender. Like the process of ladinoization itself, this process was still in an incipient stage in the middle nineteenth century. Tribunals, comprised of the alcalde and two *hombres buenos* (good men) adjudicated disputes involving honor, domestic violence, and rape. Before the rise of coffee cultivation, thus before conflicts over land and labor engrossed the attention of the Junta Municipal, a small group of rich ladino peasants increasingly imposed their moral ethos on the community at large. This fraternity normalized two separate codes of conduct for women of the pueblo: one for elite ladinas, another for poor women, mostly Indias. For the former, the junta enforced an honor code, which included sexual purity before marriage and monogamy afterward; for the latter, Diriomo's elite ladinos encouraged a different model of sexuality, one in which neither marriage nor female purity was considered the norm.

Both gender regimes precipitated an assortment of struggles within the juridical sphere. In one case, a ladina matron spent months and a small fortune to defend her honor. In a trial that polarized the elite of the pueblo, Juana Carballo accused Olaya Vásquez of "bringing about the loss of my publically recognized honor as a good wife and mother."[18] The heart of the dispute was whether Vásquez initiated the rumor that Carballo had had sexual relations with Vásquez's husband ten years earlier. At the trial, Carballo declared, through the intermediation of her husband, that "as the public judges people's honor, I cannot allow the evil that directly spoiled my person and reputation to pass in silence." Seventeen male witnesses provided testimony about the character and conduct of Carballo and Vásquez, as well as about their husbands and families. In the end, the *juzgado* (tribunal) ruled that Vásquez defamed Carballo and sentenced her to prison.

The case is interesting for a number of reasons. It demonstrates the power of the pueblo's male elite to regulate gender norms, an authority that the Junta Municipal gradually appropriated from the Catholic Church. Furthermore, it underlines the public nature of a woman's honor and its importance to the extended family. The litigants, witnesses, and judges all repeatedly described honor as a public virtue, which stood in stark contrast to the fact that a married woman had virtually no public legal persona. In the eyes of the law, she was for most purposes her husband's chattel. Finally, married women's invisibility was evident in the courthouse drama. Both women stood silently; their spouses spoke for them. The courtroom was a Kafkaesque theater where married women had no voice, where their existence was acknowledged only through the words of their husbands, and where the town's patriarchs sat in judgment on domestic morality.

In a different vein, the alcalde and his appointees regulated the sexuality of poor women. Not infrequently, humble women accused wealthy ladinos of sexual assault. Although the majority of those charges were dismissed by the tribunal for insufficient evidence, the accusations alone stand as evidence that some women of the popular sectors did not accept the elite's bifurcated morality.[19] Few plaintiffs were as successful as Gertrudis Banegas, who accused a member of the Junta Municipal of raping and kidnapping her daughter. In line with local custom, Banegas's denunciation was dismissed by Diriomo's tribunal. However, the case was transferred to Granada, possibly because Banegas had access to cash or to a political patron.[20]

In the period the Junta Municipal was consolidating its power in the community, numerous accusations were made that elite ladinos had sexually abused poor Indias—which raises the question whether the patriarchs' routine, possibly systematic violation of poor women, mostly poor Indias, was one means of fortifying ladino authority in the pueblo. There are at least two possible explanations for the increased visibility of what today we call sexual abuse. First, such practices had been endemic to the exercise of class and ethnic domination in Latin America since the Conquest.[21] Nevertheless, in the pueblos of Nicaragua, they may have assumed a more public dimension with the social transformations that accompanied the coffee revolution. Alternatively, the post-independence establishment of municipal tribunals in the Indian pueblos might have precipitated public denunciations of elite male behavior, behavior that in the past attracted little official attention.[22]

Another case sheds light on the ways in which class and gender hierarchies were sustained in rural Nicaragua. In 1869, Marcelino Cano accused Diriomo's parish priest of illegally detaining his wife.[23] On two occasions, when Cano tried to remove his wife from the priest's house, the curate struck him. At first, Cano took no action against the clergyman because, in his words, "the priest is a person of dignity." However, he complained to the bishop of Granada a second time, after he lost the use of his left eye and could not work. Angered by the bishop's lack of response and the priest's ongoing mistreatment of townspeople, Cano denounced the priest to the town's civil tribunal. The juzgado refused to adjudicate the case—not, however, because it fell within an ecclesiastical jurisdiction. Permitting the case to proceed, said the alcalde, "would encourage men of Cano's social standing to show disrespect for people in authority."[24] In this matter of local state making, by extending his authority to regulate morality, the alcalde municipal reproduced the class-gender domination of the township's elite.

Between independence and the coffee revolutions, power was exercised mostly at the local level in Central America. It was an era of municipal government formation and the consolidation of regional ruling elites. Central to these processes was the public regulation of sexuality by municipal authorities. With the emergence of the liberal state, weak though it was in Nicaragua, the mid–nineteenth century saw early moves toward the secularization of society. Where before the church monopolized the regulation of marital relations and sexual behavior, incipient municipal governments took on this role as their own. Insofar as this legitimated municipal political authority in an area so central, yet traditionally sacred, as control over the body and the sacrament of marriage, this was a bold move. In Diriomo, the Junta Municipal united the customary powers of the church and the family patriarch.

We know little in the case of the ladino minority, less in the case of the Indian majority, about gender relations within the household. I am not suggesting, therefore, that social control over women or the regulation of gender norms—and the two are not the same thing—occurred mostly within the public sphere. My argument is that the patriarchal household was not the only, probably not even the primary, site of regulation and contestation of gender relations. The construction of gender is a social rather than an individual process. In rural Nicaragua, that process was an important part of the everyday formation of municipal government in the nineteenth century. Municipal juntas regulated gender norms and sexuality, and in exercising that authority fortified their political power. This was an important part of the process of state formation in Nicaragua.

The premise that state formation is intimately tied up with the regulation of gender is one of the major leitmotifs of this volume. In different historical-temporal contexts, Rodríguez, Earle, Guy, Vaughan, Rosemblatt, Gotkowitz, Fisher, and Molyneux all describe how the consolidation of state power is a gendered process. Each of these case studies examines the ways that specific states sought legitimacy in and through the normalization of a particular gender regime.

From Common to Private Property

The privatization of coffee lands in Diriomo began in the 1860s, ended sometime around 1930, and can be roughly divided into three periods.[25] In the first, almost before anyone in Diriomo understood the meaning of private property in land, oligarchs from Granada appropriated some of the best coffee lands in the pueblo. Next, Diriomo's rich peasants—its ladino elite—became aware that the tide was turning toward private property in land and claimed what they could of the Indian commons and the municipality's *ejidos* (common property of the Corporación Municipal). Finally, realizing that a revolution in landed property had changed the nature of their world, poor Diriomeños, Indian and ladino, struggled to acquire title to the plots they and their ancestors had cultivated.

This political upheaval fortified the authority of Diriomo's Junta Municipal. The process involved little buying and selling of land. Wealth and power lubricated what was on one level a legal procedure, but more profoundly was a political system built around patronage and clientelism. By 1930, taken as a whole, land privatization created a socially differentiated peasantry in Diriomo, as it did in the other regions of western Nicaragua. A central element of that upheaval was a transformation in gendered property relations. Within the Indian Community, it broke the male monopoly on land rights and ushered in female landholding. In the township at large, it was associated with women's expanded participation in the cash economy and a rising proportion of female household heads.

Nineteenth-century liberalism in Nicaragua was not the political expression of a bourgeois revolution.[26] It was associated, nonetheless, with consolidation of the nation-state, land privatization, and codification of individual rights—all differentiated by gender. Civil codes enacted as part of a liberal agenda throughout Latin America confirmed the Hispanic legal tradition of bilateral or partible inheritance. Latin American women in the middle nineteenth century could own, inherit, and bequeath property. For married women, however, this right was heavily encumbered, more so even than in the colonial period. With the rise of private land, marriage took on particular importance as a property relation, and the codification of private property in land in the late nineteenth century went hand in hand with a redefinition of marriage. Paternity and maternity, to an extent fluid categories in colonial law, were defined more explicitly and restrictively in Latin America's new civil codes.[27]

Nicaragua's Civil Code of 1867 spelled out the terms whereby a husband controlled his wife's property and sexuality. A woman retained property she owned before marriage; however, its control passed to her spouse. Wealth acquired during marriage *(gananciales)* was jointly owned, administered by the husband, and divided equally upon the death of either partner. In several ways, death emancipated married women. Widows and deceased wives acquired "male" rights to property: the former to control it, the latter to bequeath it.

Largely for reasons of private property, Nicaragua's Civil Code of 1867 and then of 1871 regulated sexuality. To facilitate inheritance, the law sought to simplify identification of biological parents. To that end, it granted a husband legal control over his wife's womb and thus by extension over her sexual practices.[28] A wife's legal rights, such as they were, pertained only if she was "decent," defined as monogamous and obedient to her husband. In cases of marital separation, a husband could confine his wife "con una familia honrada" for ten months. Although the code does not elaborate on this point, it seems the objective was to ensure that if she gave birth, the child would be the husband's offspring.

In addition to provisions protecting rights of the father, the code virtually legalized uxoricide or wife killing. If a husband could prove his wife's adultery, he enjoyed legal impunity if he killed her. However, if he was the adulterer, so long as his infidelities were not flagrant, his wife had no legal recourse to redress the situation. In other words, whereas a wife's infidelities were grounds for murder, a husband's did not even justify separation. Impunity for husbands who murdered their wives was struck from Nicaragua's Civil Code in 1904; however, male adultery was legally sanctioned for fifty years more, which may explain, in part, why extralegal polygamy remained widely tolerated in Nicaragua even at the end of the twentieth century.[29]

Nicaragua's Civil Code of 1867, particularly its property provisions, had unintended consequences for the gendered order in rural society. Around 1880, when middle and poor peasants in Diriomo came to realize they could not reverse the property revolution, they sought to join it. Men and women of the rural poor embarked upon the lengthy and bewildering legal process of titling land, which began with a claim of prior possession. For men of Diriomo's Indian Community, this claim was relatively straight-forward because it rested on their usufruct rights to the commons. For women of the community, it was more ambiguous. Because they did not have parallel land rights, their petitions regularly invoked the rights of their fathers.[30]

Following an assortment of affidavits, testimonies, surveys, and fees—all facilitated by a *patrón*—the Junta Municipal awarded fortunate claimants *derecho de posesión* (right of possession). Many people who petitioned for land rights, especially poor Indians and ladinos, were unsuccessful. Some were unable to muster the support of a patrón, others sold their claims, and many others never had that opportunity. Someone with more power or a more powerful patrón simply appropriated their land. What is unexpected, however—especially given the emphasis in Nicaraguan historiography on peasants' wholesale loss of land in the coffee revolution—is *not* that many small peasants never acquired land, but that so many did.[31] Even more surprising is the number of women who succeeded in their claims.

In the early stages of land privatization in Diriomo, dominated by the formation of larger holdings, women who acquired land were elite ladinas. Poor women became active participants in the property revolution at a later stage, one marked by the creation of a landed peasantry with small *parcelas* (plots). Land records indicate that by 1920 about 15 percent of small holdings in Diriomo were owned by women. Given Indias' former exclusion from land rights and women's absence from the formal political sphere, the number of female landowners was relatively high. The question, and one not easily answered, is what enabled poor peasant women to engage in the process of land privatization in Los Pueblos? I suggest that the answer lies in a combination of factors: the decline of the Indian Community, the ethnic blindness of property law, and a rise in female-headed peasant households.

It is evident from the historical record that the whole idea of private property in land, especially of land rights for females, was new in Diriomo and not readily understood. Repeatedly, alcaldes spelled out why and how a woman could own and bequeath land. On one of many such occasions, the alcalde municipal invited the public to the *chagüite* (farm) of a deceased ladina. There he explained in detail how the law regarding private property worked:

> the deceased Antonina contracted matrimony with Juan Evangelista, neither one brought any property to the marriage, but they acquired, during their union, the goods listed above. . . . These should be divided equally, as they are the product of the marital union, and one half will be given to the surviving spouse and the other half divided between the two children.[32]

The property revolution in Nicaragua altered the gendered system of landholding among the rural majority. With the rise of private property, the regime of male common property rights gave way to a peasant society in which men and women owned plots of land. This change in the gender order was not a consequence of the revolution in landed property; it was central to that revolution.

Coffee production for export contributed to the commercialization of the local economy, a process the Junta Municipal struggled to manage. It required merchants and artisans to buy commercial licenses and pay taxes to the junta.[33] An 1883 census of Diriomo indicates that women played an active role in the emerging cash economy, with an equal number of women and men listed as artisans and merchants.[34] About 65 percent of female artisans and merchants in the township were unmarried, either single or widowed. Two factors might explain the preponderance of unmarried women among economically active females. The first is the feminization of poverty: women in households without an adult male had to earn cash to supplement the household economy. But this same data can be read differently; because females could earn cash, they could head households. They had less need to be economically dependent on a man. In addition, the legal requirement that a married woman have her husband's explicit consent to enter into contracts might have had a dampening effect on married women's activities in the cash economy.

Artisanal work was gendered along lines we have come to expect: cooking, sewing, baking, and washing clothes were "female" occupations; carpentry, woodworking, quarrying, and smithing were "male" ones. In commerce, however, the gendering of work was less in evidence. Of the town's twenty-five licensed merchants, ten were women. As many authors have pointed out, commerce on a grand scale in Latin America was the province of men, but petty trade the domain of women. This pattern was reproduced in Diriomo. Men were wholesale and long-distance merchants; women were shopkeepers and local market traders.[35]

Land privatization gradually ate away at the Indian Communities on the Meseta de los Pueblos. There was a decline in Diriomo's Indian population in a period of little more than one hundred years. In 1776, 92 percent of the population of Diriomo was listed as Indian; by 1883, that figure had been reduced to 74 percent.[36] Notwithstanding this decline, the important point here is how Indian the pueblo remained in 1883, even after the onslaughts of the coffee revolution, not how ladino it had become. The preponderance of Indians is striking, particularly in light of the tendency in nineteenth-century Central American censuses to underreport the Indian population.[37]

In conclusion, the coffee revolution was associated with a significant transformation in gendered property relations in Diriomo. The male monopoly on land that characterized the common property regime gave way to an agrarian system in which women as well as men were peasant proprietors. In addition, the expansion of the cash economy was associated with an increase in women's participation in commerce and artisanal work.

Private Property and Household Headship

The social upheavals that accompanied the coffee revolution left their mark on household headship in Diriomo. In 1882, 40 percent of households in the pueblo were headed by women, and it appears that marriage was less widespread than it had been a century earlier.[38] Whereas 31 percent of the adult population was single in 1776, 51 percent was single in 1883.[39] Although we do not know whether for census purposes "married" meant in a conjugal union, legal or otherwise, the comparative data suggest a rise in nonmarrying behavior. Combined with the high incidence of female-headed households in 1883, we have a very different picture of peasant society in rural Latin America than the one we have been routinely offered. The traditional view of the peasant household as extended and male headed, with at least two working adults, is not applicable to Diriomo or, as I have argued elsewhere, to most of rural Latin America in the nineteenth century.[40]

This evidence suggests a link between the coffee revolution and disintegration of the traditional patriarchal household. That strong conclusion merits careful scrutiny, however. Such a premise rests on the notion that the patriarchal household was pervasive in the preceding historical period. Although that might have been the case, as indicated by a higher incidence of marriage in 1776, I believe the evidence here remains inconclusive for a number of reasons, not least that the 1776 census was administered by the church, the institution charged with ensuring that the population married. Instead, I offer a weaker hypothesis. Women's landownership and participation in the expanding commercial economy provided certain material possibilities for female household headship that did not exist previously. It is also possible that an inclination toward nonmarrying behavior on the part of women of the upper and middle stratas was enhanced by patriarchal law. A single woman retained control over whatever resources she might possess—if married, she forfeited control. Yet for most women such advantages of nonmarital independence may well have been offset by disadvantages, both economic and social, associated with remaining unwed.

Although the image of the female household head may bring to mind unwed mothers, the stereotype of contemporary policy debates, widows headed about 35 percent of female-headed households in nineteenth-century Diriomo. This means, of course, that 65 percent of those households were headed by single women, mostly mothers. In another epoch, both widows and single mothers might have been subsumed into a male-headed household. It is possible, however, that expanding opportunities for female landholding and participation in the cash economy gave those women the wherewithal to maintain a separate residence.

The evidence of female household headship combined with a tendency toward nonmarrying behavior underlines connections between women's economic dependence and male control over female property, labor, and sexuality. When women enjoyed some degree of economic independence, modest though it might have been among the peasants of Diriomo, we find a society in which marriage was not a universal norm, nor male household headship all-pervasive.

The fact that almost 40 percent of households in Diriomo were female headed in the late nineteenth century is of major significance for understanding the unfolding process of peasant differentiation. It may partly explain the relatively high percentage of peasant land titles held by women and women's active participation in the cash economy. Although more re-search is needed to understand the ways in which gender affected social dif-ferentiation and vice versa, the story so far suggests a strong link between male monopoly over productive resources and the male-headed household. When women became small peasant landholders and participated in the cash economy, there was a very high incidence of female-headed house-holds in the pueblo. This history sustains the idea that property relations are sexual relations in another form. Friedrich Engels pointed out this connec-tion, but his formulation was flawed by romanticism about gender equality in "primitive" societies and by ahistoricism about capitalist development.[41]

Family Patterns and Local State Making

Faced with a large and seemingly growing number of single mothers in the pueblo, the governance of gender norms took on a different character. Before the rise of coffee, municipal tribunals expended their efforts in polic-ing sexual behavior. With the changing property regime, local government became more involved in the regulation of paternity and maternity. Ad-judicating cases of child support and inheritance reinforced the authority of the elite in the conflictive processes of elaborating family values and sexual identities. The tribunals' role was particularly conspicuous in many cases involving single women who claimed child support from wealthy ladinos of the pueblo, cases that reveal the mechanisms of public regulation of so-called private life.

At least 128 child support claims were logged in Diriomo's civil tribunal between 1850 and 1875. In one case, Señora Josefana Bermúdez asked the alcalde to compel Señor Eufreciano Alfaro to support his infant son, the offspring of their illicit union. The Código Civil required fathers to support their children after the age of three, the customary age of weaning.[42] Señora Bermúdez asked the judge to waive the law on account of her poverty and requested the father assume this obligation immediately.[43] The señora recounted how, as a single mother, she struggled to sustain her four children in conditions of extreme poverty. Although she testified that she had never been married, the scribe titled her "señora" in the court record. He did the same for all mothers, regardless of marital status. Whether this practice was common in rural Nicaragua or his own idiosyncrasy remains a mystery. However, it served to reinforce the elite's moral code of universal marriage.

In the course of the trial, the defendent, Señor Alfaro, struck a bargain with the alcalde. He offered child support in return for custody. Such bargains were commonplace; elite men of the pueblo regularly bartered recognition of paternity for custody, especially of sons. For some men, willingness to assume responsibility for out-of-wedlock children might have stemmed more from material than sentimental attachments. The aspiring entrepreneurs of Diriomo frequently complained to the Junta Municipal about the labor shortage. They found extrafamilial labor hard to come by because most of the population worked within a household economy. In this milieu, where children were productive assets and paternity gave men control over the labor of their progeny, it is possible that elite ladinos regarded paternity, at least in part, as a social relationship of production.

In the Alfaro-Bermúdez dispute, the town patriarchs presented the señora with an offer she could hardly refuse. Either she could keep her son and let him go hungry, or she could collect child support and surrender him to his father on his tenth birthday, the customary age at which a child could work for wages. Bermúdez's dilemma was shared by many of the rural poor. Parents frequently gave away or sold the most valuable asset they had, their children. In another case, Santiago López, representing himself and his wife, asked the alcalde to order the return of their two sons. In López's words, "a year before they had given away [*regalado*] the children, but the two young boys were continually working, from morning to night, in tasks too heavy for their ages."[44]

State regulation of parental obligations was not always pro-patriarchal. Luiza Vallecío, a ladina artisan and single mother, demanded that Andrés Marcía, Diriomo's former mayor, recognize paternity of his two *hijos naturales* and "pasarle alimentos" (provide them with food).[45] Marcía agreed, with the usual patriarchal bargain: food now for custody later. Throughout the trial, however, Vallecío flaunted the gendered arrangements normalized by the town fathers. First, she refused to accept the patriarchal bargain. Second, she dispensed with the charade of presenting her behavior in terms of the feminine ideal of purity and honor. After two years of litigation, the tribunal ordered Marcía to pay child support and awarded Vallecío permanent custody of the children. Yet justice remained beyond her reach because Marcía ignored the ruling. Beyond issuing several writs demanding he comply with the sentence, the tribunal did nothing, maybe because Marcía was part of the ladino fraternity that governed Diriomo. Marcía's sexual exploits apparently inflicted no long-term damage to his political career. Several years later he was reelected mayor for a second term.[46]

Local government in Diriomo was actively engaged in constructing families and domestic values. Interpretation and implementation of the Civil Code, with all of its intricacies, gave the junta wide berth to legitimate particular class, gender, and ethnic concepts of family, motherhood, and fatherhood. Family law was explicitly differentiated by gender; in practice, it was differentiated by class and ethnicity as well. As a result, the tribunal's regulation of paternity and maternity consolidated the patriarchal households of the rich ladino peasantry. The patriarchal ideal was a privileged household, an institution to which the less privileged may have aspired, but rarely achieved.

The municipal government's regulation of motherhood was contradictory. Their decisions fortified an ideal of the patriarchal family, a model that did not fit the life experiences of the numerous single mothers of the pueblo.[47] Despite the tribunals' bias in favor of this model, single women— and not exclusively those of the middle and upper strata—continued to turn to the legal system to resolve conflicts in their domestic arrangements. Women who appealed to the Junta Municipal hoped the patriarchs would redress situations the plaintiffs considered unjust. Their expectations were partly grounded in the tensions within family law—in particular, between provisions that fortified patriarchal authority and those designed to protect women and children from arbitrary rule. Also, in a milieu in which peasants habitually turned to their patrón for support in time of need, women appealed to the benevolence of the town fathers. These tensions—both legal and social—made the tribunal an arena of struggle over the ideology and everyday practices of family life. In Diriomo, municipal intervention did not always have negative consequences for the individual women embroiled in the judiciary. Yet class, race, and gender biases so infused the interpretation of the law and of the entire social order, for that matter, that the overall effect of municipal regulation was to fortify the ladino elite's gender, class, and ethnic domination.

Other chapters in this volume arrive at similar conclusions regarding the role of the judiciary in the normalization of what might be considered elite gender regimes. Rodríguez, Chaves, Guy, and Varley all show how the courts provided opportunities for contestation regarding legitimate marital and sexual behavior. Throughout Latin America, in different times and places, women and men readily turned to the courts in their quest for what they considered to be conjugal justice. These studies conclude that although the courts facilitated litigation over gender norms, they tended to fortify social relations that reflected the class, gender, and ethnic worldviews of the elite.

Conclusions: Gender, Class, and State

Politics in the rural pueblos of Nicaragua was not high in the sense that it was some rarefied sphere that touched only the lives of the elite. Municipal politics dominated by rich ladino peasants regulated people's everyday practices of birth, child raising, work, marriage, sex, and death. This practice gave the local elite wide-ranging powers to regulate family values, which in turn fortified their expanding political power. Like the case of republican Colombia, as described by Rebecca Earle, the governance of gendered norms was an important aspect of everyday state formation in Nicaragua in this era.[48]

The emerging local state, with its ample powers of regulation and surveillance, reshaped the mundane activities of people's lives. The authority of the juzgado to call in endless witnesses to testify about the sexual behavior and family mores of their neighbors was a daily reminder of the sway of local politicians. People knew that the powers of the alcalde, the Junta Municipal, the hombres buenos, and the tribunals were not limited to regulating land and labor, as extensive as it was. They also had the capacity to intervene in the routines of domestic life. Some behaviors and customs they encouraged, others they tolerated, and quite a number they branded as deviant.

The coffee revolution was a period of great social upheaval. The fabric of community, family, and household within the Indian pueblos of rural Nicaragua became unraveled; it was rewoven under the direction of the municipal government. The process of negotiation and consolidation of power at the local level was as much about reconfiguring the gender order as it was about reconstructing class and ethnic relations. The society that emerged in Nicaragua in the early twentieth century was seigneurial, sustained by patron-client relations far more than by commodity relations.[49] In a social order where patronage provided the major link between society and the state, municipal institutions became central actors. They expanded the political powers of the pueblo's patriarchs. As part of the process of peasant differentiation, the upper strata of the ladino peasantry fortified the Junta Municipal and made it into an instrument of class, ethnic, and gender rule. Within the municipality, tribunals became a major focus of gender politics. Public contestation over gender norms took place predominately within the judicial sphere, which enhanced and legitimated the powers of the local state apparatus. Possibly of greatest significance, the tribunals fortified— ideologically and materially—the patriarchal family at a moment when 40 percent of households in Diriomo were female headed.

This history of gender offers a new way of thinking about the coffee revolution and state formation in Latin America. Gradually, in what once were Indian pueblos, a ladino peasant elite established its authority in Nicaragua. With a hold on municipal government, they reshaped social relations and regulated people's everyday lives. Through the array of regulatory agencies at their disposal—juzgados, land registers, state labor drafts—the municipal elite suppressed communal relations and consolidated relations of subordination to the emerging patrons of Nicaragua. Petty caudillos in the countryside forged bonds with politicians in regional and national government.[50] This bonding was part of the everyday formation of Nicaragua's patronage state, which was swept away by the Sandinista Revolution in 1979.

Notes

I thank Maxine Molyneux, Lowell Gudmundson, Muriel Nazzari, Steven Topik, Jeffrey Gould, Donna Guy, Silvia Arrom, Florencia Mallon, and John Weeks for comments on earlier drafts of this essay. Research for this study was supported by grants from the Fulbright Commission, the American Philosophical Society, the American Academy of Learned Societies, the National Endowment of the Humanities, the British Academy, and the University of Portsmouth. An earlier version of this chapter was published in the *Journal of Latin American Studies* 29, no. 2 (October 1997): 591–611.

1 Lowell W. Gudmundson is among the few historians of Central America who has analyzed this issue; see *Costa Rica Before Coffee: Society and Economy on the Eve*

of the Coffee Boom (Baton Rouge: Louisiana State University Press, 1986). Verena Stolcke calls attention to this lacuna in "The Labors of Coffee in Latin America: The Hidden Charm of Family Labor and Self-Provisioning," in *Coffee, Society, and Power in Latin America,* ed. William Roseberry, Lowell Gudmundson, and Mario Samper Kutschbach (Baltimore and London: Johns Hopkins University Press, 1995), 65–93. For gendered analyses of other Latin American coffee economies, see Verena Stolcke, *Coffee Planters, Workers, and Wives: Class Conflict and Gender Relations on São Paulo Plantations, 1850–1980* (Basingstoke: Macmillan 1988); and Heather Fowler-Salamini, "Gender, Work, and Coffee in Córdoba, Veracruz, 1850–1910," in *Creating Spaces, Shaping Transitions: Women of the Mexican Countryside, 1850–1999,* ed. Heather Fowler-Salamini and Mary Kay Vaughan (Tucson: University of Arizona Press, 1994), 51–73. For analyses of gender and state formation in Latin America, see Steve J. Stern, *The Secret History of Gender: Women, Men, and Power in Late Colonial Mexico* (Chapel Hill and London: University of North Carolina Press, 1995); Donna Guy, *Sex and Danger in Buenos Aires: Prostitution, Family, and Nation in Argentina* (Lincoln: University of Nebraska Press, 1990); E. Bradford Burns, *Patriarch and Folk: The Emergence of Nicaragua, 1789–1858* (Cambridge, Mass.: Harvard University Press, 1991); Mark Szuchman, *Order, Family, and Community in Buenos Aires, 1810–1860* (Stanford: Stanford University Press, 1988); and Marjorie Becker, "Torching La Purísima, Dancing at the Altar: The Construction of Revolutionary Hegemony in Michoacán, 1934–1940," in *Everyday Forms of State Formation: Revolution and the Negotiation of Rule in Modern Mexico,* ed. Gilbert M. Joseph and Daniel Nugent (Durham, N.C.: Duke University Press, 1994), 247–64.

2 Elizabeth Dore, *The Myth of Modernity: Nicaragua, 1840–1979,* work in progress.

3 For a critique of the category *female household headship,* see Ann Varley, "Women Heading Households: Some More Equal than Others?" *World Development* 24, no. 3 (1996): 505–20.

4 Philip Corrigan and Derek Sayer, *The Great Arch: English State Formation as Cultural Revolution* (Oxford and New York: Basil Blackwell, 1985).

5 Diego Cano pide al Alcalde Municipal, 18 May 1868, rama Corporación Municipal, Sec. Alcaldía Municipal, asunto Tierras Ejidales, Archivo Municipal de Diriomo (hereafter, AMD). Similar male property systems have been found in Indian peasant communities in Chihuahua, Mexico, and the Central Highlands of Peru. For Mexico, see Daniel Nugent and Ana Maria Alonso, "Multiple Selective Traditions in Agrarian Reform and Agrarian Struggle: Popular Culture and State Formation in the Ejido of Namiquipa, Chihuahua," in Joseph and Nugent, eds. *Everyday Forms of State Formation,* 209–46. For Peru, see Florencia E. Mallon, "Patriarchy in the Transition to Capitalism: Central Peru, 1830–1950," *Feminist Studies* 13, no. 2 (summer 1987): 379–407.

6 Prefectura Departamental al Alcalde Constitucional de Diriomo, 3 March, 6 May, 11 June, 26 July 1849, Correspondencia, AMD. In response to requests from the Prefectura Departamental in Granada for information about individ-

ual wealth for the purposes of levying a war tax, the alcalde of Diriomo sent lists of owners of property and mejoras, which included members of the Indian Community.

7 "Entre Josefa Ramírez y Víctor Ayala por la compra de una huerta," 19 July 1867, 19 October 1864, 8 December 1865, 9 March 1865, rama Corporación Municipal, sec. Alcaldía Municipal, asunto Tierras, Libro de Demandas Verbales, AMD.

8 It would be foolhardy to generalize about indigenous gender relations in indigenous communities in Latin America from one or two cases. Nevertheless, there may be a certain romanticism in the theories of so-called pre-Western or pre-capitalist gender equality. For the first, see Mona Etienne and Eleanor Leacock, eds., *Women and Colonization: Anthropological Perspectives* (New York: Praeger 1980), v–vi; for the second, Friedrich Engels, *The Origin of the Family, Private Property, and the State* (Hammondsworth: Penguin, 1986).

9 Documents from a nearby Indian Community, Nindiri, indicate a practice of collective male decision making. Participation by men only is documented by an incomplete record of deliberations about whether the community should sell its lands. Deliberaciones: Comunidad Indígena de Nindirí, 18 February 1878, rama Agricultura, AMD.

10 Bula de la Santa Cruzada, 3 July 1776, A.39 (5), exp. 28130, leg. 1749, Archivo General de Centro América (hereafter cited as AGCA), Guatemala City. This population count was administered by ecclesiastical authorities for the purpose of selling indulgences. According to the bula, 64 percent of the adult Indian population in Diriomo was married, 31 percent was single, and 4 percent widowed. It is not apparent what the categories *married* and *single* meant—for instance, whether people in consensual unions were considered married or single. Also, it is unclear whether the data refer only to the town center or also to rural hamlets.

11 For a critical analysis of the Latin American historical literature on female household heads in the eighteenth and nineteenth centuries, see Elizabeth Dore, "The Holy Family: Imagined Households in Latin American History," in *Gender Politics in Latin America: Debates in Theory and Practice,* ed. Elizabeth Dore (New York: Monthly Review, 1997), 101–17. Also Silvia Marina Arrom, *The Women of Mexico City, 1790–1857* (Stanford: Stanford University Press, 1985).

12 Following Spanish convention, *ladino* and *Indio* refer to men, *ladina* and *India* to women. I use the masculine form *(ladino / Indio)* to refer to collectivities of men and women.

13 Bula de la Santa Cruzada, 3 July 1776, leg. 1749, AGCA. A total of 1,116 adults lived in the township in 1776. 1,027 (92 percent) were Indian, 73 (7 percent) were ladino (mestizo and mulatto), 1 percent were Spanish.

14 On ladinoization, see Jeffrey L. Gould, " '¡Vana Ilusión!' The Highlands Indians and the Myth of Nicaragua Mestiza, 1880–1925," *Hispanic American Historical Review* 73, no. 3 (August 1993): 393–429.

15 On the constitutions of 1826 and 1838, see Burns, *Patriarch and Folk,* 133.

16 Until the 1860s, property transactions in Diriomo involved the buying and selling of mejoras—improvements to the land—not land itself. This system of ownership is apparent in bills of sale, wills, and disputes over property, which recorded frequent transactions involving animals and crops, none involving land. See, for example, El Sr. Tiffer intentando la prohibatoria a Don Vicente Espinosa sobre una huerta . . . , 23 January 1864, Juzgado Unico Constitucional de Diriomo, AMD.

17 For details on gender differentiation in Nicaraguan property law, see Luis Zuñiga Osorio, 'Patria Potestad', tesis para el doctor en derecho (Managua, 1935), 32–38.

18 Demanda verbal motivada por Juana Carballo y Olaya Vásquez por difamación de delito, 14 November 1865, Juzgado Municipal de Diriomo (hereafter cited as JMD), AMD. For a similar case, see Demanda motivada por La Sra Juana Isabel López, 14 March 1843, JMD, Libro de Conciliaciones, AMD. Unless otherwise noted, all translations from the Spanish are mine.

19 In twenty-three years, 102 accusations of rape, sexual assault, and battery were lodged by women. 83 of those charges were dismissed by the alcalde for insufficient evidence. Libros de Terminaciones Verbales, 1851–1873, AMD.

20 Gertrudis Banegas expona que el Sr. Tomás Vasconcelos ha perpetrado los delitos de rapto y estrupo en mi hija . . . , 11 June 1869, Libro de Terminaciones Verbales, AMD.

21 Cecilia Salinas, *Virtud sumisa, amor rebelde* (Santiago: Centro de Estudios de la Mujer, 1994); Sonia Montesinos, *Madres y huachos* (Santiago: Centro de Estudios de la Mujer, 1991).

22 Eugenia Rodríguez suggests, for the case of Costa Rica, that the creation of municipal tribunals might have effected a certain democratization of power, especially in the regulation of gender relations. See her chapter in this volume.

23 Sr. Marcelino Cano contra el cura de almas de este pueblo Parroco Don Aureliano Gutierres, 18 February 1869, Libro de Terminaciones Verbales, AMD.

24 Ibid.

25 Elizabeth Dore, "Land Privatization and the Differentiation of the Peasantry: Nicaragua's Coffee Revolution, 1850–1920," *Journal of Historical Sociology* 8, no. 3 (September 1995): 303–26.

26 David McCreery calls this aborted liberalism. *Rural Guatemala, 1760–1940* (Stanford: Stanford University Press, 1994).

27 Silvia Arrom, "Changes in Mexican Family Law in the Nineteenth Century: The Civil Codes of 1870 and 1884," *Journal of Family History* 10, no. 3 (fall 1985): 376–91.

28 Although the Nicaraguan Civil Code does not explicitly refer to "the womb" as such, it was not uncommon to do so at this time in Latin America. The Rio Branco Law of 1871 in Brazil was called the "Law of the Free Womb." It decreed that children born of slave mothers would be free upon reaching the age of majority.

29 The 1904 amendment to the Civil Code of 1867 stated that a wife could be granted a divorce on grounds of "el concubinato del marido, siempre que tenga a la mujer en su propia casa, o notoriamente en otro sitio, o cuando en el hecho concurren tales circunstancias que constituyan una injuria grave para la esposa y finalmente el abandono manifesto." Zuñiga Osorio, "Patria Potestad," 40.

30 Entre Josefa Ramírez y Víctor Ayala por la compra de una huerta, 19 July 1867, rama Corporación Municipal, sec. Alcaldía Municipal, asunto Tierras; 19 October 1864, 8 December 1865, 9 March 1865, Libro de Demandas Verbales, AMD.

31 Influential historians of Nicaragua argue that the coffee revolution created a rural proletariat. See Jaime Wheelock Román, *Imperialismo y dictadura: Crisis de una formación social* (Mexico City: Editorial Siglo XXI 1979), and Oscar René Vargas, *La revolución que inició el progreso, Nicaragua, 1893–1909* (Managua; ECO-TEXTURA, 1990). For a counter interpretation, see Dore, "Land Privatization."

32 Inventario y tasación de los bienes . . . de Antonina Jiménez, 6 April 1861, AMD.

33 Actas de la Junta Municipal, 16 January and 18 February 1873, AMD.

34 Censo de la Población: Diriomo, Año 1883, caja 191, leg. X7, fol. 152, Archivo Municipal de la Prefectura de Granada (hereafter cited as AMPG), Granada, Nicaragua. Approximately 7 percent of adult women and the same percentage of adult men participated in the cash economy: for women, 48 out of a total of 716; for adult men, 51 out of a total of 676.

35 For details on women's participation in the cash economy, see Elizabeth Dore, "Patriarchy and Private Property in Nicaragua," in *Patriarchy and Economic Development,* ed. Valentine M. Moghadam (Oxford: Clarendon, 1996), 56–79.

36 Bula de la Santa Cruzada, 3 July 1776, A.39 (5), exp. 28130, leg. 1749, AGCA, and Censo de la Población: Diriomo, Año 1883, caja 191, leg. X7, fol. 152, AMPG. Although ethnic labels in censuses are notoriously unreliable, I consider census data before the twentieth century useful as a gross indicator of ethnic identity in Diriomo.

37 Gould, " '¡Vana Illusión!' "; Justin Wolfe, "Becoming Mestizo: Ethnicity, Culture, and Nation in Nicaragua, 1850–1900," paper presented at the Tercero Congreso Centroamericano de Historia, San José, Costa Rica, 15–18 July 1996.

38 Censo del Departamento de Granada, Año 1882, caja 175, leg. 486, fol. 121, AMPG.

39 Censo de la Población: Año 1883, AMPG. Of all adults, 40 percent were married, 51 percent were single, 9 percent were widowed.

40 Dore, "The Holy Family," 101–17.

41 Engels, *Origin of the Family.*

42 The Spanish legal language for child support was "pasar alimentos."

43 La Sra. Bermúdez contra el Sr. Eufreciano Alfaro, 30 April 1866, Juzgado Municipal de Diriomo, AMD.

44 Reclamo de Santiago López, 18 June 1860, Libro de Conciliaciones, AMD.

45 Luiza Vallecío contra Andrés Marcía por alimentos, 21 March 1874, Libro de Terminaciones Verbales, AMD. Child support cases in the previous decade

spelled out that "pasar alimentos" meant providing food and firewood. Although the language of this case referred to "pasar alimentos," the judge said that support in this instance should take the form of money payments. This decision may have reflected a certain monetization of the economy associated with the coffee revolution or the fact that Marcía was one of the richest men in the pueblo, one of the first to participate in the regional cash economy.

46 Ibid.

47 Legally, neither single mothers nor widows exercised patria potestad (paternal authority over children). They had legal responsibility to support their offspring, but not the authority that, for fathers, accompanied it.

48 For analysis of state control over gender and sexual practices, see R. W. Connell, "The State, Gender, and Sexual Politics: Theory and Appraisal," in *Power / Gender: Social Relations in Theory and Practice,* ed. H. Lorraine Radtke and Henderikus J. Stam (London and Thousand Oaks, Calif.: Sage, 1994), 136–73.

49 On the seigneurial nature of rural society in Nicaragua, see Dore, "Land Privatization." For the case of Brazil, see Richard Graham, *Patronage and Politics in Nineteenth Century Brazil* (Stanford: Stanford University Press, 1990).

50 This interpretation of the Somoza dynasty is developed in Dore, *Myth of Modernity.*

Donna J. Guy

Parents Before the Tribunals

The Legal Construction of Patriarchy in Argentina

Father, protect your son; Children, honor your father.
—Juan Carlos Rébora, *La familia*

Shortly before midnight on 10 November 1903, the family problems of Spanish immigrants became a matter for the Argentine state to adjudicate. Señora Carmen R. de Fernández went to a Buenos Aires police station to denounce her husband Eugenio. In a fit of pique over a poorly cooked meal, a drunken Eugenio had beaten his wife and seven-year-old son. Carmen, visibly bruised, turned to the state for protection. She had to report the fight because her son, a minor, could not do so. When her husband was taken to trial in June of the following year, his attorney claimed that it was a *riña de familia,* a family fight that did not merit punishment. In contrast, the prosecuting attorney rejoined: "a father can moderately punish his children, but to beat them up with his fists does not fit this description." The judge evidently agreed, and Eugenio's rights to control his wife and children were removed by a sentence of two years' imprisonment, a decision upheld by an appeals court.[1]

Buenos Aires at that time was filled with European immigrants, many of whom had their own ideas of how families should be governed. Although male patriarchs were usually allowed to exercise unfettered control over their families, the police had to respond if adult family members complained. Furthermore, the behavior of poor men, both immigrant and native born, came under great scrutiny by state officials, and, unlike in Costa Rica, only judges dealt with family issues.[2] The combination of a highly diverse population and a well-developed judicial system enabled many women and children to lodge complaints of unjust behavior by male relatives.

Although Buenos Aires had one of the highest rates of foreign-born populations in Latin America in the early twentieth century, it was not alone in its goal to prosecute errant fathers and mothers. All throughout post-independence Latin America, civil and penal codes contained provisions to restrict, punish, or remove patriarchal authority from fathers and mothers who failed to provide food, clothing, and education for their children, or who abandoned and abused their children. Some states added other justifications. Bolivia, for example, included incest as grounds for rescinding patriarchal authority, and Mexico and Ecuador were among the first to give women equal governance rights over their children.[3] The existence of laws in Latin America delineating the rights of male heads of family to govern their families enabled these issues to come to court.

What is the definition of a patriarch, and how has it changed over time? Are fathers only providers, or are they expected to show care and feelings for their children? Do they expect complete control over their family, and how do they react to the intrusion of governmental authorities? Are there cultural differences that permeate the concept of fathering, differences that can be traced historically?

Some scholars ignore fathering, this very important aspect of masculinity, or assume it to have immutable traits linked to biological patriarchal rights. Others argue that modern patriarchy is linked solely to the male's economic support of the family. The definition of patriarchy I utilize in this essay is the male ability to govern a family through a combination of power, economic responsibility, and emotional relationship.[4]

In nineteenth and early twentieth century Argentina, some fathers believed that patriarchy gave them complete control over minors in the family, whereas others contended that their patriarchal responsibilities, including their financial obligations to the family, were contingent on their own desires. Fathering to some meant unfettered sexual access to their children, and to others it meant serving as pimps. There were good fathers, and ones universally condemned. Nevertheless, there was a broad range of opinion about the attributes ascribed to fathering. Furthermore, these opinions derived from a perception of changing masculine rights within the family. Rooted in belief in male governance over children, they merit a historical analysis.

In Argentina, the concept of fathering is, on the surface, easy to study because the civil and penal codes in statute law clearly delineated the normative practices for fathers and mothers for the entire nation. This delineation did not mean that everyone agreed with these laws, but they emphasized an extensive body of beliefs and practices associated with this important aspect of masculinity.

How and when the modern Argentine state contested patriarchal rights and gender relations is the subject of this essay. I cover the period that begins with independence—focusing principally on cases and laws that followed the enactment of the Argentine Civil Code in 1871—and ends in 1985, when women were granted joint legal custody over their children. Other critical moments in Argentine law include the passage of the Ley Agote in 1919 that enabled the state to rescind patriarchal rights over delinquent children and a series of laws in the late 1940s that eliminated a range of patriarchal restrictions associated with illegitimate children, permitted complete adoption for the first time, and punished errant parents who did not support their children.

From the colonial period onward, the Latin American colonial and postcolonial state envisioned the family as the basic unit of society. Imperial civil legislation informed Spanish and Portuguese subjects about the rights and privileges of family heads. These behavioral norms carved out extensive gendered spheres of influence for male patriarchs, as well as more restricted spaces for married women and for unmarried or minor children, both male and female. Nevertheless, just as the state protected patriarchy by granting rights and privileges, it could also restrict or deny such powers if the men went to jail or if children served monarchy or religion by joining the army or a religious order.

The wars of independence in Latin America from 1810 to 1820 marked the beginning of a long, slow process of state formation, part of which included the passage of civil codes in the second half of the nineteenth century to replace imperial legislation. The history of the modern nation-state in Latin America is thus directly linked to the evolution of parenting, childhood, and gender relations. Within the family, social relations between and among fathers, mothers, and children shaped both the social order and the construction of the political and economic world. Latin American patriarchy, often thought to be unfettered by state control until recent times, was always a potential site of tension, contention, and conflict between family members and the state. Fathers often thought their rights over their

wives and children were absolute, yet children resisted overbearing parental authority by private as well as public acts. Wives, even without complete
divorce, often sued their spouses for legal separation and used accusations
of patriarchal violence toward themselves or their children as grounds for
separation. The state also had vested interests in preventing what it deemed
to be inappropriate marriages as well as abuse by parents. These tensions
had been Latin American realities since the colonial era, and their persistence thereafter demonstrates the contested nature of patriarchy.[5]

In 1974, Nadia Haggag Youssef raised a series of questions regarding the
origins of a Latin American patriarchal system less rigorous than that of
Middle Eastern countries. She suggested that such a system might have
been created by "historical or social conditions peculiar to Latin America"
and that these conditions might have led to situations that prevented "the
institutionalization of ideal family norms."[6] Youssef then examined the
impact of conquest practices that led to concubinage and miscegenation,
and the inability of the church to promote legal, stable marital relationships
among the poor. These conditions—added to the reality that poor women
needed to leave home to work, often as domestic servants for more powerful families—all served to weaken patriarchy.

In addition to these factors, I would argue that the state (the complex set
of ideologies, laws, and normative practices that exist independent of individual rulers), even during the colonial period, chose to weaken the absolute authority of the patriarch so that it could intervene in family and
gender relations. The state saw patriarchal rights as contingent upon the
age of the child and the willingness of the father to obey public laws. Failure
to fulfill patriarchal responsibilities threatened, but did not guarantee, the
restriction or removal of patriarchal privilege.

The vigor with which independent Latin American nation-states pursued errant fathers and mothers depended upon a combination of legal
statutes and the willingness of officials to intervene. Because the Argentine
state brought many patriarchs to the courts, these cases provide an intimate view of state-family interactions. These interactions were tempered
by other factors as well, however. The first Argentine Civil Code was written in the 1860s and became law after 1871. Subsequently, massive waves of
European immigrants flooded the country from 1880 to 1914, bringing their
own concepts of patriarchy as an absolute right. The simultaneous rise of

industrial capitalism and a chronic labor shortage in different regions of Argentina led to ad hoc state efforts to appropriate family labor without patriarchal consent before and after 1880.[7]

High rates of infant abandonment by single mothers further confused the situation of the patriarchal family—a problem not addressed by national legislation until the first overhaul of the Argentine Civil Code in 1926, when the state reaffirmed that single mothers exercised patriarchal authority *(patria potestad)* over their children and that mothers and daughters could choose their own professions and keep their wages. Over the years, additional reforms of the civil codes—particularly those enacted after the return to civilian government in 1983 after years of military rule—finally gave mothers and fathers shared patriarchal rights and privileges over their children. Nevertheless, for almost one hundred years, gender relations within the family were contested and resolved by Argentine judges.

The basic structure of both patriarchy and fatherhood in Argentina is rooted in the legal term *patria potestas*—or, as it is known in Spanish, *patria potestad*. According to the Roman tradition, a father's control over his child was absolute and perpetual. Fathers not only had the right to choose their child's profession, but could also sell them into slavery or even kill them under certain circumstances. This right continued for as long as the father lived. In contrast, Germanic laws defined the right as contingent and limited only to those children who had not reached the age of majority. Although Gothic legal traditions permitted mothers to exercise such rights, most other legal traditions excluded them. Spanish colonial law allowed fathers strong prerogatives and released children from parental authority only when they reached the age of majority.[8] Like other Latin American nations, Argentina did not grant patria potestad to married mothers until the twentieth century—specifically, not until 1985.

By the time the first Argentine Civil Code was put into effect in 1871, Germanic, canon, and Roman legal traditions had been drawn upon to define the legal family for purposes of inheritance and the maintenance of social order. The ideal Argentine family was based upon a religious marriage, the offspring of which had the right to inherit from both parents. In return, children had the obligation to obey their parents and perform chores without wages. Parents were expected to provide food and clothing, educate their children, and govern them until they married or reached the age of majority. The head of the family was presumed to be the father, and only he or a single mother could be taken to court for failing to provide food and clothing.[9]

Families formed without the benefit of legal marriage were more complicated. Children of sacrilegious or adulterous relationships never had the privilege of their father's authority until Peronist legal reforms in 1948. Under this system, their fathers could neither govern them nor leave them an inheritance even if they wanted to. Children of consensual relationships between unmarried individuals were at the mercy of their parents. They could be recognized or denied by either parent. Single mothers had additional impediments because they could never take men to court on paternity charges. In these cases, fathers were fathers only if they chose to be recognized as such. Once they acknowledged paternity, however, they were expected to provide for their *hijos naturales,* or natural children.[10]

These laws, if enforced, raised a basic question about male privileges. Could men truly govern their biological children? Was this a "natural" right or one that was contingent upon legal statute? Could they ignore these rights if they wanted to? In other words, how absolute was the concept of patriarchy? To the dismay of jurists and fathers, Argentine law was never completely clear about the extent of men's authority over their family. Unlike Brazilian laws, which granted men extreme power over their family, the Argentine codes tempered male prerogatives. They could not kill their unfaithful wives, and they could be taken to court if a father were considered unfit.[11] These rights were delineated in a general way, but by the end of the nineteenth century, legislators began their quest to expand state jurisdiction over the family.

The impetus for civil code reforms of patriarchy stemmed from the political consequences of European immigration. Familiar with European anarchist, syndicalist, and socialist philosophies, many urban immigrant workers joined with Argentines in espousing the restriction of patriarchal privilege. Labor unions began to promote strikes to improve working conditions, and by the 1890s the Argentine Socialist Party became active.[12] It, too, was concerned about the ability of fathers and husbands to keep female workers from striking.

The economic crash of 1890 and the subsequent lean years had a clear impact on the family. More and more children were abandoned in state-supported orphanages, and older children were set out to work to help the family survive. Many native-born Argentines saw child labor as a form of "moral abandonment," however, and sought legislation to enable government officials to deal with these problems. The main obstacle was the patriarchal rights of fathers. To incarcerate a child in a reformatory necessitated parental willingness to suspend their patria potestad, for the period of incarceration.

As early as 1894, advocates of child rights targeted patria potestad as an outmoded principle. Concerned that the state should protect children from bad parents, a noted public health physician and reformer, Benjamín Dupont argued that patria potestad "was a feudal right." Fathers should enjoy these powers so long as they were good, and unfit parents should hand over their parental rights. Within the unfit category, he identified two groups: "the indifferent and the criminal."[13]

In order to eliminate this legal problem, to deal with juvenile delinquency, and to send a clear message to parents that they risked losing their children to the state, more precise state parameters were defined in the Ley Agote of 1919. This law provided the first major revisions of the Argentine Civil Code. It was specifically designed to enable the state to remove patria potestad from parents whose minor children had been arrested for criminal behavior. The children (boys) were then sent to a reform school until the state determined that they were rehabilitated. A new institution, the Patronato Nacional de Menores, was also established. Comprised of judges, or *defensores de menores* (defenders of minors), the patronato would oversee the operations of the reform schools. At the time the law was debated, Carlos Melo, a member of the new middle-class Radical Party, argued that there were twelve thousand abandoned children in Buenos Aires. For this reason, he wanted "the *patronato* of the Argentine state, from this day forward, to aid minors who are abandoned or delinquent, and give them the protection, the direction, and the support they have lacked. In this way they will be able to learn how to work and form their sense of morality." In other words, he wanted the state to replace their errant fathers.[14]

In 1926, Argentine legislators enacted the second major revision of the Civil Code. Following the lead of previous socialist efforts to improve the conditions of married and working women, the code enabled married women to select their own occupations and to keep their salaries. It also confirmed that single mothers had patria potestad over their children, but it retained the exercise of patria potestad with regard to fathers of legitimate children, stipulating that it was still subject to vigilance of the state.[15]

Reforms enacted between 1890 and 1926 indicate that the strong language of the Civil Code empowering and insisting that men govern their family was put into doubt by the ability and occasional willingness of the state to intervene in family matters. The results of this tension enable us to retrieve the thoughts and beliefs of fathers in Argentina, and show that legal practices tended to favor fathers, even after national laws began to equalize governance rights between fathers and mothers. Men were usually deprived of their parental rights because of child abandonment or child abuse, but the courts exercised this right with great reluctance. In contrast, single mothers were more frequently challenged by the law for their lack of moral correctness and more easily lost custody of their children. These conclusions are based upon an examination of patria potestad cases encountered in the Archivo General de la Nación (Argentina) and in several provincial archives between 1880 and 1930. The cases offer us an opportunity to see how men were criticized as fathers and how they responded to the charges. Most of these fathers were poor, often illiterate. Many were immigrants from other countries. What they shared in common was their willingness to present their views of fathering and how they as men responded to the challenges of the courts.

Several governmental entities existed to deal with children whose parents couldn't or wouldn't take care of them. In 1823, the government of Buenos Aires created an elite women's society, the Sociedad de Beneficencia, and among its responsibilities was the admission of infants into its orphanages. This responsibility became more important as the city expanded. The year the society was founded, only 143 children entered its orphanage. The annual number continued to be less than 200 until the 1860s, but in 1878 it increased to 417. Ten years later, more than 700 children were abandoned or ophaned annually.[16] Between 1870 and 1895, when there were 186,320 and 663,854 inhabitants in Buenos Aires, respectively, the number of infants deposited annually at the Sociedad increased from 644 to 1,817.[17] The Defensoría de Menores, the department that defended minors and the poor, existed after 1829 to protect older abandoned and wayward children. Even children living with their biological parents came under the scrutiny of provincial and national governments if they were poor and did not work.[18] The defenders confronted increased numbers of vagrant, discarded, and abused children. In 1885, the two city defenders received 809 children, and within three years this number had jumped to 1,307. 1,878 children entered the care of three defenders by 1898; thereafter the numbers began to taper off. The plight of these youngsters, the majority of whom were not infants, was even graver than that of those who entered the Sociedad de Beneficencia's portals because the Defensoría de Menores did not operate orphanages. It either had to find a place for them within the Sociedad's institutions, send them to local jails, or place them in some kind of foster care. Defensores had great difficulty finding foster parents for older boys, and many of the girls sent to private homes ran away because they were exploited as domestic servants. Many boys and girls ended up on the streets or in jail for the crime of being homeless and abandoned.[19] Similar charitable organizations and defensores operated in the provinces. Thus, there was a long history of tension between the state and the desire of men, particularly lower-class men, to govern their families without interference.

Some children came under the scrutiny of state officials even if their fathers wanted to be the ideal parent. Because parenting was part of a legal structure designed to ensure inheritance rights, certain children were destined to be fatherless according to the law. This legal reality became bitterly clear to Juan Martín Pelliza when, in 1885, he asked his lawyer to petition the Sociedad de Beneficencia for patria potestad over his daughter, Elena Enríquez. Everyone, including Pelliza's attorney, recognized Pelliza's claims as invalid because Elena's mother had been married to someone else at the time of the child's conception. Consequently, Lucio Vicente López, Pelliza's attorney, suggested that, at best, Pelliza be allowed to visit the child every two weeks under the watchful eye of household employees. "As a pretext for such visits Sr. Pelliza should be construed only as the child's protector, because there exists only a justifiable sense of caring since this is a man who may be a father, but lacks all rights as such." In this case, everyone but Pelliza agreed that a man had to be legally eligible as well as biologically responsible in order to "father."[20]

Blanca Gontrán and her lover Miguel Lani discovered this unpleasant truth in 1897 when Blanca went to court to get custody of their daughter, Julia Artemisa. Blanca claimed she never knew that Miguel was married, and not only had he tricked her, but he had taken Julia Artemisa when she was less than five years old, a time when mothers almost always had custody. Miguel saw the situation very differently. He insisted that he had been open about his marriage, and that Blanca had abandoned both of them. Miguel defended himself by claiming that

A caring and affectionate father [*un padre cariñoso y afectuoso*] can not snatch a child to hand it over to a mother who never showed any affection and, on the contrary, mistreated the child from the first day. . . . A father with an unblemished reputation and who possesses the necessary means to take care of his daughter—to whom he has given his name and for whom he works to give her an easy life, will never hand his daughter over.[21]

In this plaintive statement, Miguel placed as much emphasis on his emotional attachment to his daughter and his standing in the community as on his ability to provide for her. Unfortunately for the child, the courts frowned on the adulterous relationship. The attorney for the Defensoría de Menores argued that neither parent had the rights of patria potestad over this unfortunate child, and thus on 12 August 1899, the judge awarded custody of Julia Artemisa to a nonrelative.[22] In this way for almost fifty years, entire groups of men were denied their legal right to be fathers, and this reality provided the underpinning for Peronist demands that fathers could adopt their out-of-wedlock children.

Although mothers were supposed to care for babies, particularly those who had not been weaned, some fathers insisted upon taking the child away from an unfit mother. Fathers then had to obtain the services of a wet nurse. In 1925, Casilda Freire de Basilia, an eighteen-year-old woman, went to court in Santa Rosa, La Pampa, to insist that her husband return her unweaned one-and-a-half-year-old infant daughter, Nafla. Salvador, a twenty-five-year-old "Arab," a merchant with fourteen years residence in Argentina, complained that Casilda had abandoned their home and that he intended to maintain custody of the child unless he were forced to give her up. Unlike the defensores de menores in Buenos Aires, who usually sided with the mother if the child was not weaned, the appointed official in La Pampa declared that only the husband had patria potestad. Furthermore, husbands also had the right to administer possessions, so Salvador was under no obligation to hand over any of Casilda's clothing.[23]

Not all men were so intent on taking care of their children, and they believed that this, too, was within their masculine rights. Some men simply refused to "father" their children. In 1880, Servilana Alegre took her presumed father, Pedro Alegre, to court—arguing that he was obligated to provide her with food and clothing. Although Pedro recognized that he had one daughter with Servilana's mother, he claimed to have no more relations with the woman after that child died. When the judge first decided on the case in 1882, he argued, "Paternity is an aspect of nature that is a mystery," and sided with Pedro. To him, a central aspect of masculinity was the willingness to recognize a natural child. If a man refused, no one could make him accept his fatherly duties.[24] Once again, it was not until the 1940s that legal reforms ensured children that even if their fathers did not want to "father" them, they could at least be freed of the social stigma of having the term illegitimate placed on their civil documents.

Children took their parents to court, but they rarely won unless the parents admitted they had been wrong. Occasionally men agreed to divest themselves of their fatherly responsibilities. In one case, the father felt it was better to relinquish his rights to cover up his marital scandals. In 1893, Alberto Vidal went to court to request that his father Jacques be denied patria potestad over Alberto's sister Blanca. Alberto claimed his father was living a scandalous life with his mistress María, his mother's former servant. During the course of their affair, Jacques and María had a child. Alberto's mother, Catalina Etchegaray, then demanded a legal separation and declared that her husband was no longer considered worthy of exercising patria potestad over his legal children. Jacques was accused of trying to cover up his relationship with María by forcing her to marry José Correro, who conveniently disappeared. María continued to live with Jacques, ostensibly as his maid, and had another child with him.[25]

Blanca's family was much better off than many of those who went to court to fight patria potestad cases; her older brothers sent her to Europe, and her uncle paid for her expenses. Her father paid no attention to her, but after her mother died, he was accused by his legal family of misappropriating Blanca's inheritance from her mother. When confronted by these statements, Jacques's lawyer claimed that Jacques refused to respond, and only to avoid additional scandal would he be willing to give up his patria potestad over Blanca. He then requested that Blanca pay the court costs.[26]

Although Jacques was willing to dispense with his fatherly privileges, the courts were not. The judge in the case claimed that individuals could give up only rights that pertained to themselves. In this case, the rights pertained to family governance issues, so the judge could not accept the offer.[27] The judge's decision provoked an extensive debate regarding the difference between the rights and privileges of a father. Jacques Vidal's attorney, Juan

Traut, argued that the Civil Code was flawed because it did not distinguish between rights and privileges. All fathers had a duty to feed and educate his children. These were *irrenunciables*. At the same time, no one could force someone to be a father if he did not want to be, even if it was his duty. Finally, the judge agreed with Juan Traut that he could not force Jacques to be a good father, and after considering the scandals underlying the case, he removed Jacques's patria potestad.[28]

Judges sometime dealt with patria potestad issues by refusing to give opinions. Alejandro Albarrasin tried for years to get the courts to remove his father's patria potestad over him, but to no avail. In Buenos Aires, Alejandro found himself with no money to pay for his education or, even more importantly, for the medicines for his heart condition. His father had spent years in Europe and left him beholden to his brothers to pay his expenses. After four years, Alejandro went to court in April 1880, but it was not until 24 November 1880 that the courts finally agreed to allow Alejandro's bank to release the funds. In the meantime, Alejandro's father was asked to appear in court. When he failed to do so, the court continued to make no decision on the case until Alejandro announced in September 1881 that he was celebrating his twenty-second birthday and was therefore an adult.[29]

If children had difficulty forcing the courts to liberate them from the control of their fathers, the courts were almost always more willing to take the word of a presumed father over that of a mother in a family dispute. In 1891, José Andreu claimed that his wife had hidden her pregnancy from him because it was not his child. He believed that the child had been given the first name of the presumed father. The attorney for the Defensoría de Menores accepted José's claim that the child was not his and insisted that a guardian be named for the child rather than leave him under the control of his mother.[30]

Mothers rarely won custody battles against their husbands. In 1886, five years after she was granted an ecclesiastical divorce, Margarita Suffern de Smith asked for patria potestad over her son. From the time of her separation, her husband Carlos had never shown interest in or provided for his son. Margarita offered a letter from James P. Kavanaugh of the Holy Cross School testifying that she was the sole support of her child. Carlos never responded to these charges. Despite all evidence pointing to Margarita's dedication to her child, the court determined that Carlos's failure to respond to the court's inquiry was insufficient proof that he had no interest in his son. All that Margarita could obtain from the courts was the right to keep the child in her custody.[31]

Estela Spraggon D'Amico fared equally badly. In 1899, she went to court to ask that her husband Santiago be denied patria potestad over their children. Since 1891 her husband had disappeared from five to six months at a time, and when he returned, he was often drunk. He threatened to kill her as he said goodbye. She also claimed that he had never concerned himself with educating his children. Santiago retaliated by getting a judge to insist that Estela turn the children over to him, the person with the legal right to govern them. Yet according to Estela's attorney, Santiago had promised to leave her and the children alone if she paid him four thousand pesos.[32]

Like many other cases, the matter dragged on until 1903 when the judge finally released his opinion. Although he found the father's attempt to sell his children disgusting, he believed that neither patria potestad nor marriage was negotiable. Therefore, he refused Estela's request. When she appealed the decision, he refused to change his mind. In fact, even though he admitted that the legal separation between the D'Amicos was not Estela's fault, he thought it was inappropriate that a wife should go to court to accuse her husband. "And if she isn't a good wife, how could she be a good mother?" questioned the judge. For all those reasons, he insisted that Santiago retain his fatherly rights.[33]

Juana María Ghezzi de Mateo initially thought she could have her husband's patria potestad taken away. In 1922, she asked the court to remove her husband's patria potestad over their four-year-old son Angel Dionisio and give it to her. She claimed that just one year after their marriage he began behaving badly and beating her. He then abandoned the household and their son. When they received a legal separation, he had promised to pay her for child support, but had never done so. Nevertheless, he continued to visit his child, which Juana María considered an intrusion on her work schedule as a seamstress.[34]

In his own defense, Dionisio Mateo claimed that Juana María and her parents did everything to make it difficult for him to keep in contact with his son. He accused them of "inculcating in my son sentiments of hatred and disdain for me, giving him the most perverse instructions regarding his conduct during my periodic visits." During one interview in a judge's office, his son was so aggressive with him that a nonfamily member had to restrain the child. When Dionisio began to comfort his now calmed child, he claimed that the child told him "that I was bad with you because otherwise my mother would have punched me."[35] He also claimed his son received no dinner that evening.

Dionisio Mateo openly admitted that he had not paid any child support and had abandoned his home, but he insisted that he had abandoned neither his son nor his rights over the child. As far as he was concerned, the court had no right to take away his fatherly rights. He proclaimed: "neither the current Civil Code nor any other law in the world, could impose the removal of patria potestad."[36]

Some fathers thought their control over their children was absolute, a belief that sometimes led to cases of extreme and brutal treatment of children. The courts in Buenos Aires were still inconsistent about the way they decided these cases, however. Juan Botto was arrested for acting as a pimp for his daughter, Abrina Santos Botto, in 1881. The thirteen-year-old girl, already employed as a baby-sitter, was supposedly sent to live with a family in Rosario, whose patriarch met her father in a bar. When it later became clear that Abrina was not working as a baby-sitter in Rosario, her mother confronted Juan and found out that he had sold their daughter for 1,800 pesos to a bordello madame. When the case went to court, the government attorney argued that what Juan had done was not statutory rape (since he had no relations with his daughter), and he therefore had been charged under the wrong statute. Eventually Juan was freed, although the man from Rosario was convicted.[37] Because the father was acquitted, his patria potestad remained intact.

Pedro Berruti, a fifty-year-old Italian immigrant, was not so lucky. In 1907, he openly admitted having forced sexual relations with one of his daughters, María, because "his fellow countrymen [from Italy] believed that it was commonplace to have relations with their daughter in order to avoid getting venereal diseases from prostitutes." As for his other daughter, Enriqueta, he argued that she had submitted without threats of violence and with her own consent.[38] María offered a poignant description of her father's actions, and Enriqueta contradicted her father's version by claiming that her father threatened her with a pistol as he raped her.[39] Because there were no laws against incest and his two daughters were under fourteen, he was accused of statutory rape. María was rewarded for her testimony by being incarcerated in the women's jail. Enriqueta and her brother

Santiago were sent off to the Sociedad de Beneficencia. Their father was convicted of rape and deprived of all rights to govern his daughters.[40]

In other cases of cruelty, children were temporarily separated from their fathers, but patria potestad was not taken away. Miguel José García accused his father in 1909 of treating him abominably ever since his mother had died ten years earlier and his father had remarried. He begged the courts to release him from his father's control, but they would agree to do so only for a short period of time. Perhaps Miguel José had less luck because, unlike Pedro Berruti's daughters, he had never had the police come to the house. Furthermore, his case was different because it did not deal with sexual abuse, so it was difficult to corroborate his story.[41]

Once again, such confident legal pronouncements obscured more complicated situations. Sometimes both fathers and mothers were at a loss about how to raise their difficult children. If these children were arrested, government authorities became extremely interested in rehabilitating them. However, those authorities needed parental permission, or they insisted that parents temporarily relinquish their patria potestad so that the state could place such children in reform institutions. The archives of the Ministry of the Interior are replete with pleas from parents asking the government to assume temporary custody over an errant child.

Before the Boys' Reform School (Asilo de Reforma de Menores Varones) opened up, there were few places to send errant boys. For that reason, the mother superior in charge of the women's jail wrote to President José F. Uriburu in May 1895, requesting permission to set up a wing to house poor adolescents so that they could be educated and supervised until they turned twenty-two. In response, the defensores de menores strongly opposed the idea because the Civil Code empowered "parents to moderately correct their children, and when given permission by the Judge, to detain them in an establishment for one month. If the children were sent to jail, parents would be deprived of their responsibilities."[42]

In 1898, the first Boys' Reform School was opened. From the outset there were far more requests for admission than places for boys. Both mothers and fathers, desperate to keep their boys out of trouble, voluntarily offered their patria potestad over their sons for a month in return for state care of their children. In 1904, for example, Roberto Gagnebien went to court to seek help after his son had run away several times and had often been arrested. Because he could no longer prevent his child from getting into mischief, he wanted the judge to place him in an institution. David Gagnebien was sent to the Boys' Reform School. By relinquishing his rights over David, Roberto had acknowledged his limitations as a father.

Felipe di Camillo had less luck. Burdened by poverty as a common laborer and the father of many children, he was dismayed by the conduct of his fifteen-year-old son, Alfredo, who had developed *hábitos de holgazón* (idle habits). Felipe was fearful that Alfredo would not become *un ciudadano útil* (a good citizen). Thus, Felipe wanted his son sent to the Marcos Paz Reform School. Felipe proved that he was Alfredo's natural father, but the request was denied because there was no room in the reformatory.[43]

Some boys were sent away without their parents' permission. In response to complaints about gangs of street urchins, the Buenos Aires defensor de menores, who covered the lower-class southern side of Buenos Aires, announced in 1907 that during the past year he had petitioned courts to remove the patria potestad of boys whose parents were "unable, inappropriate, or who had abandoned" their sons. During the next few years, there was an intensive campaign to rid the city of these boys by sending them, under court order, to work on ranches or "industries" in the national territories. Most of them ran away from their caretakers, who used them as cheap labor.[44]

Decreased immigration to Argentina after 1914 did not diminish the state's desire to reform families and deprive unsatisfactory fathers of their parental privileges. Equally important, fathers continued to resist the intrusion of the state into their families, just as Argentine judges were still reluctant to remove patria potestad permanently. Although some fathers wanted to be relieved of unruly sons and daughters, others relished the task of shaping their children's personalities, character, and sense of morality.

Governments and political parties of all different types pondered the role of the state in family governance. Additional socialist-inspired reforms of the Civil Code in 1926 gave women significantly more power within the family. During the era of political fraud from 1930 to 1943, the alliance of conservatives, with sectors of the socialist and radical parties, both permitted and encouraged a wide range of family reform bills to be presented in Congress. In 1932, they proposed the formation of a children's bureau, similar to the U.S. Children's Bureau, to help mothers and children. The deputies who introduced the bill talked about the rights of children and mothers to receive state aid, but not about fathers.[45] Although deputies from several parties tried to get the proposal a fair hearing, the plan languished in committee. In 1936, a new proposal emerged to create a mothers' and children's bureau, an idea that eventually led to the formation of a maternity fund for working mothers and of other laws to protect women and children.[46]

By the time the Perón administration began to examine how patriarchal powers had affected Argentina and what the state might do to deal with these issues, several generations of Argentine men had gone before the tribunals to express their contempt for state interference in the family. They almost all argued that they had biological rights of governance, which they were as free to acknowledge as to ignore. In challenging his wife's custody rights over their children, Isaac de Tezanos, for example, argued that as a father he "satisfied an intimate caring for his children that no one could dare to doubt, and all my activities are adjusted to the various responsibilities associated with a father's patria potestad." For that reason, no court could deny him his children.[47] Yet jurists contradicted these innate rights. Dr. Jorge E. Coll, a prominent children's rights specialist, argued in 1931 that times had changed and so too had concepts of family. According to him, "When a man cannot fulfill his [social] duties, society must intervene, remove this right [patria potestad] and take control of the children to educate them according to the needs of the larger society."[48] Single mothers also protested. The attorney for Rosa Garnica, an unmarried woman who unsuccessfully sought to have her son returned to her by her former lover, argued that "a deceived woman, a good mother subject to ridicule is an inferior person before the Courts [la Justicia], and even more importantly, her prestige as a mother can be questioned by any unsubstantiated accusation. . . . as if it were normal that most mothers are bad and deserve to have their sacred rights taken away."[49] Until these tensions were resolved or subdued, men would continue to challenge legal interference into family matters.

Over the years, politicians, legal specialists, and feminists made a conscious effort to redistribute governance rights within the family. It seemed as though women had won by the 1950s. In 1952, an officially sponsored elementary school textbook put out by the government of Juan Perón (1946–55) defined the new father and his relationship to his child. In contrast to the earlier vision, this one acknowledged the father's importance, but dismissed his role in governance issues compared to the mother's:

"Papa is strong. He works all day, and when he comes home, he chats with Mom or plays with us. At times he helps us with our homework or explains a lesson to us." In contrast, mothers were described as the *almas tutelares de la casa* (the spiritual guardians of the house). The term *tutelar* also implied that married women had custody over a minor, thereby replacing an absent or nonfunctioning father. In a similar way, the wife of the president, Eva Perón, was proclaimed the alma tutelar of all children, and President Perón was the national embodiment of the father.[50]

It is perhaps no coincidence that during the first Peronist administration, there were strong debates in the Argentine Congress over the modern Argentine family. New laws were passed that gave inheritance rights to all children, allowed divorce, and permitted complete legal adoption. During the course of these reforms, a number of bitter debates were waged in which some legislators protested the perceived weakening of the patriarchal rights of fathers. Members of Perón's own political party argued that it was a man's right to have a child to pass on his name, wealth, and status. According to these legislators, children—particularly male children—were the property of the men in the family, not of the women. Men had important roles in the family that could be carried out only with the presence of children.[51] Peronist ideology attempted to place women in positions of authority in the family, but many men disagreed.

The battle over patria potestad did not end with Peronism. In 1993, Julio López del Carril, a distinguished conservative Argentine law professor, emphatically stated that patria potestad was a natural, not a legislated, right: "Patria potestad, whatever might be its origins and concepts, precedes the existence of the law. Thus even when men had not elaborated the law, it was understood that they could and should govern and direct the lives of their children until they became men and women."[52] The issue is not so easily resolved, however. In stating that fathers and single mothers (and by 1985 all mothers) had the right to make key decisions for their children, López del Carril was ignoring the issue of how adoptive parents obtained rights to parent their children, and how the Argentine state consistently contested the parental rights of men whom the courts considered inappropriate fathers.

López del Carril was aware of alternative opinions. He admitted that one of Argentina's neighbors, Uruguay, had a Civil Code that *conceded* to parents' rights over their children. He knew that some parents could be abusive, but he disdained those who argued that children had inherent rights, "as if their parents were their enemies." He did accede, however, that the state had the right to intervene, but only in extreme cases if fathers could not govern wisely.[53]

Challenges to the masculine right of patria potestad have continued to the present day, and despite changing legislation, judicial approaches remain similar. Although the Argentine Congress tried to reform power relations within the family, the courts were very reluctant to take governance privileges away from men and to deprive mothers of child custody. Thus, we can make some observations regarding the ways that men in Argentina have defined their masculinity in terms of fathering. Even though Argentine laws perceived fathering to be linked directly to inheritance, men in Argentina did not always agree. They tended to perceive fathering more in terms of governance than inheritance. Some insisted on being fathers even if their children were precluded by law from receiving their parents' property. Others believed that they had the right to determine not only whether they considered themselves fathers, but also under what conditions they would agree to honor the economic and governance rights linked to such recognition. Peronist men, on the other hand, wanted to extend their rights over children to include their illegitimate or adoptive children.

Many fathers talked about their emotional links to children, yet some believed that these emotions could have sexual as well as social content. Their masculinity could be expressed sexually with their children, and they believed they were above the law. Their beliefs were reaffirmed by the lack of laws criminalizing incest. Finally, fathers believed—a view often supported in the courts—that their rights to govern the family transcended the rights of their wives to do so. For good or for bad, they were the fathers, and besides their economic responsibilities, they had clear governance rights. Both wives and children had to offer exceptional proof of abuse to break patriarchal rights.

Notes

I would like to thank Gary Hearn, Ursula Lamb, Osvaldo Barreneche, and Eva Johnson for their comments on earlier drafts. This research was sponsored by various grants from the Social and Behavioral Research Institute, College of Social and Behavioral Sciences, University of Arizona, a University of Arizona Sabbatical Fellowship, and a National Endowment for the Humanities Fellowship, and a University of Arizona Vice President for Research Summer Research Grant.

1 Eugenio Fernández, acusado de lesiones corporales a su esposa Carmen R. de Fernández e hijo Eugenio, 10 November 1903 to 5 September 1904, Tribunales Criminales, letra F., 1903, legajo 83, Archivo General de la Nación (hereafter AGN), Buenos Aires. The quotes were on fol. 38. Unless otherwise noted, all translations from the Spanish are mine.

2 Eugenia Rodríguez S., "Civilizing Domestic Life in the Central Valley of Costa Rica, 1750–1850," in this volume.

3 Bolivia, *Código Civil boliviano con secciones de legislación, doctrina y jurisprudencia,* comp. Hugo Sandoval Saavedra (La Paz: Fundación Universitaria "Simón I. Patiño," 1955), título 9, art. 194, 153.

4 Robert Griswold, for example, defends the U.S. definition of fathering that is completely economic. Robert L. Griswold, *Fatherhood in America, a History* (New York: Basic Books, 1993).

5 Basic works on colonial patriarchy include Patricia Seed, *To Love, Honor, and Obey in Colonial Mexico: Conflicts over Marriage Choice, 1754–1821* (Stanford: Stanford University Press, 1988; Asunción Lavrin, *Sexuality and Marriage in Colonial Latin America* (Lincoln: University of Nebraska Press, 1989); and Silvia Arrom, *La mujer mexicana ante el divorcio eclesiástico, 1800–1857* (Mexico City: Sepsetentas, 1972).

6 Nadia Haggag Youssef, *Women and Work in Developing Societies* (Westport, Conn.: Greenwood, 1976), 86.

7 Donna J. Guy, "Lower-Class Families, Women, and the Law in Nineteenth-Century Argentina," *Journal of Family History* 10, no. 3 (fall 1985): 318–31.

8 José Arias, *Derecho de familia,* 2d ed. (Buenos Aires: Editorial Kraft, 1952), 360.

9 Donna J. Guy, "Niños abandonados en Buenos Aires (1880–1914) y el desarrollo del concepto de la madre," in *Mujeres y cultura en la Argentina del siglo xix,* comp. Lea Fletcher (Buenos Aires: Feminaria Editoria, 1994), 219.

10 Linda Lewin, "Natural and Spurious Children in Brazil Inheritance Law from Colony to Empire: A Methodological Essay," *The Americas* 48, no. 3 (1992): 351–96.

11 Susan K. Besse, "Crimes of Passion: The Campaign against Wife Killing in Brazil, 1910–1940," *Journal of Social History* 22, no. 4 (1989): 653–66; Asunción Lavrin, *Women, Feminism, and Social Change in Argentina, Chile, and Uruguay, 1890–1940* (Lincoln: University of Nebraska Press, 1995).

12 Iaacov Oved, *El anarquismo y el movimiento obrero en Argentina* (Mexico City: Siglo XXI, 1978); Richard Walter, *The Socialist Party of Argentina* (Austin: University of Texas Press, 1977).

13 Benjamín Dupont, *Patronato y asistencia de la infancia; Consideraciones sobre la*

necesidad inprescindible de una ley de protección á la primera infancia y estudio socio-lógico sobre la necesidad de reformatorios para los ninos moral y materialmente aban-donados (Buenos Aires: Tipo-Lito del Sport, de E. Sarniguet y Cía., 1894), 10.

14 Argentine Republic, Congreso Nacional, Cámara de Diputados, *Diario de sesiones* (1919), 2:708–9.

15 Lavrin, *Women, Feminism, and Social Change*, 208–211.

16 Buenos Aires City, Intendencia Municipal, *Patronato y asistencia de la infancia de la capital de la república* (Buenos Aires: El Censor, 1892), 10–11.

17 Alberto B. Martínez, *Censo general de la población, edificación, comercio e industrias de la ciudad de Buenos Aires,* 3 vols. (Buenos Aires: Cía Sudamericana de Billetes de Banco, 1910), 2:64.

18 Guy, "Lower-Class Families."

19 Argentine Republic, Ministerio de Justicia e Instrucción Pública, *Memorias* (1886), 1:69, 72; (1889), 1:131, 136; (1899) 120, 141.

20 Letter from Lucio Vicente López to the Sociedad de Beneficencia, 14 August 1885, Sociedad de Beneficencia, Asuntos Legales, leg. 57, fol. 34, AGN.

21 Gontrán, Doña Blanca, solicitando la entrega de su hija Julia Artemisa, Tribunales Civiles, letra G, 1897, leg. 31, fols. 12–13, AGN. The quote is on fol. 13.

22 Ibid., fol. 34. In the original document, "Ministerio" was used for "Defensoría." Since the Defensoría did not have ministerial status, it is assumed that the word was used to refer to its general ministering to minors.

23 Freire Casilda de Basilio, reclama ropas y una hijita de 1½ años, Fondo Justicia, Juzgado Letrado Jaramillo, leg. 243, Archivo Histórico de La Pampa, Santa Rosa, La Pampa.

24 Servilana Alegre contra Pedro J. Alegre, sobre paternidad, Tribunales Civiles, 1880–85, letra A, leg. 221, AGN. fol. 377. Servilana appealed the case, but finally gave up in 1885.

25 Don Alberto Vidal contra Don Jacques Vidal sobre pérdida de la patria potestad de la hija menor del este Doña Blanca Vidal, Tribunales Civiles, 1893–94, letras V–W, leg. 17.585, fol. 4, AGN. Alberto had been named legal guardian of his sister in order to initiate the lawsuit.

26 Ibid., fols. 4–12.

27 Ibid., opinion of 30 November 1893, fol. 26.

28 Ibid., fol. 112, final judgment of 14 December 1894, fol. 123.

29 Alejandro Albarrasin solicitando cése Francisco Albarrasin ejerciendo la patria potestad, Tribunales Civiles, 1880, letra A, leg. 222, fols. 1–35, AGN.

30 Don José Andreu negando la paternidad a Don Manuel Andreu, Tribunales Civiles, 15 November 1891, letra A, leg. 320, fol. 9, AGN.

31 With the exception of 1954 (the last year of the Peronist government), until the 1980s, there was no complete divorce in Argentina. Instead, two forms of legal separation were available: religious and secular. Usually the grounds for a woman winning a separation was abuse to herself or her children, or her husband's impotence. Suffern de Smith, D. Margarita, solicitando patria potestad,

División Poder Judicial, Fondo Tribunales Civiles, August 1886–27 March 1888, letra S, leg. 16.33, AGN.

32 Spraggon D'Amico, D. Estela, contra D'Amico, Don Santiago, por pérdida de la patria potestad, Fondo Tribunales Civiles, 20 October and 15 November 1899, letra S, leg. 16.256, fol. 1 and fol. 7, AGN.

33 Ibid., 3 February 1903, fol. 331; court of appeals, July 1903, fol. 378.

34 Da. Juana María Ghezzi de Mateo contra Dionisio Mateo, División Poder Judicial, Fondo Tribunales Civiles, 1922 letra G, leg. 198, fol. 4, AGN.

35 Ibid., fol. 8.

36 Ibid., fol. 10.

37 Botto, Juan, por corrupción de su hija María, División Poder Judicial, Fondo Tribunales Criminales, 1881 letra B, leg. 16, fols. 4 and 11, AGN.

38 Pedro Berruti, por violación de sus hijas, 17 July 1909, Tribunales Criminales, 1907–8, letra B., leg. 112, fol. 5, AGN.

39 Ibid., 18 July 1909, fols. 7–8.

40 Ibid., Letter from Alvina Praet de Sala, Sociedad de Beneficencia, to Juez de Instrucción de la Capital, Dr. Jaime Llavallol, 9 August 1909.

41 García, Miguel José, sobre privación de patria potestad a Valentín García, undated, División Poder Judicial, Fondo Tribunales Civiles, 1904, letra G, leg. 61, expediente 57, fol. 1, AGN.

42 Ministerio de Justicia e Instrucción Pública, 21 May 1895, letra C, expediente generales, leg. 38, exp. 308, fols. 1–2, AGN.

43 Ministerio de Justicia e Instrucción Pública, 6 December 1911, letra D, Dirección de Justicia, leg. 112, expediente 127, AGN.

44 Ministerio de Justicia e Instrucción Pública, *Memoria* (1906), 110; (1910), 115–16.

45 Ibid., (1932), 2:120–21.

46 For a compilation of socialist Alfredo Palacios's efforts to enact family legislation, see Alfredo Palacios, *La defensa del valor humano: Legislación social argentina* (Buenos Aires: Editorial Claridad, n.d.).

47 Isaac de Tezanos sobre patria potestad de sus hijas, 24 March 1879, Tribunales Civiles, 1886, letra T, leg. 16.923, fol. 1, AGN.

48 Dr. Jorge E. Coll, "Legislación y tribunales para menores," *Boletín del Museo Social Argentino* 19, nos. 112–14 (October–December 1931): 387–97.

49 Rosa Garnica contra Don Manuel Alvarez Pereyra sobre entrega de un hijo, División Poder Judicial, Fondo Tribunales Civiles, 1922, letra G, leg. 195, fols. 24–25, AGN.

50 *El alma tutelar: Libro de lectura para 1er Grado Superior,* 4th ed. (Buenos Aires: Editorial Luis Lasserre, 1952). The quote is on p. 10, the definitions on pp. 7–11.

51 Donna J. Guy, "From Property Rights to Children's Rights: Adoption in Argentina, 1870–1948," unpublished paper.

52 Julio López del Carril, *Patria potestad, tutela, y curatela* (Buenos Aires: Ediciones Depalma, 1993), 8–9.

53 Ibid., 13–14, 139–40.

Mary Kay Vaughan

Modernizing Patriarchy

State Policies, Rural Households, and

Women in Mexico, 1930–1940

Most feminist scholars concur that patriarchy was retained, perhaps even strengthened, by the Mexican Revolution of 1910.[1] However, by the 1930s, the postrevolutionary state's policies envisioned a modernization of patriarchy in peasant households. The intent was not to emancipate women and children but to subordinate the household to the interests of national development. Nonetheless, policies suggested empowering women and children in new ways. Government reformers drew from social ideas articulated in a transnational professional milieu and adapted them to suit their definition of national needs, but policy implementation varied greatly across the heterogeneous terrain of rural Mexico. The purpose of this essay is to engender Mexican rural development policy and implementation in the 1930s and to pose research questions for studying the interaction among state policies, peasant households, and women between 1940 and 1960.[2]

Defining the State

Max Weber defined the state as a compulsory association claiming control over territories of people. States are administrative, legal, extractive, and coercive organizations that attempt to structure relations within civil society and between civil society and public authority. Theda Skocpol has drawn from Weber and Otto Hintze to argue that states have their own interests independent of the societies they govern. They function in a transnational milieu ever cognizant of the need to secure their interests in a global arena of competition and domination and of shifting patterns of trade, investment, and development.[3]

But as essays in this collection show, states are not closed entities developing disciplinary projects in isolation from society or carrying out behavioral revolutions from above. State and society are mutually constituted through complex historical interaction. Neither is monolithic; both are highly variegated. Agencies of the state are among many disciplining and socializing bodies that interact in intricate, often contradictory ways within a particular society.[4] States also function as arenas of struggle among different social groups with distinct policy agendas and varying degrees of power to promote and sustain them.

In this essay, I want to stress how states are limited in their implementation of policy by factors of capacity and will: by economic resources, the number and quality of technically competent personnel, as well as competition and conflict between and among state agencies and other governmental institutions.[5] Effective implementation of policy also depends on how policy converges with social values and needs, interests, and capacities. The state's lack of capacity and will and a weak or absent social convergence empower subjects to contest the disciplinary intent of policies, although not always in emancipatory ways.

Finally, the relation between the modern Latin American state and the capitalist class, domestic and foreign, continues to be a thorny and unresolved debate now weakened by Marxist theory's fall from fashion. The debate is pertinent to this examination of Mexican rural development policy in the 1930s. Although state actors in the 1930s envisioned property redistribution and forms of cooperative and state enterprise as correctives to free-market capitalism, they did not envision an immediate socialist revolution. For their part, national and foreign capitalist circles effectively maneuvered against such a possibility from inside and outside their respective states.[6]

Contextualizing the Modernization of Patriarchy: The Transnational Milieu (1920–40)

The social policy of the postrevolutionary Mexican state drew from a transnational discourse engaging European, U.S., and Latin American professionals and reformers. To engender that policy, I borrow from Victoria de Grazia's analysis of what others have called developmentalism.[7] She argues that at the turn of the twentieth century, Western states faced a "demographic crisis" of population management. The crisis lay at the intersection between an emerging mass society brimming with political demands and social ills and the state's need to control and mobilize society for purposes of national survival and development in an increasingly competitive global order. World War I accentuated the crisis by rallying mass societies around militarized nationalism. In its aftermath, it unleashed an unprecedented cacophony of political movements, dislocations, social demands, and experiments, which resonated in a context of mounting international conflict and competition. Each state devised social policies to nationalize citizens in the interests of order, development, and military defense.

In particular, the new social policies involved the rationalization of domesticity. De Grazia sees this as the major shift in gendered politics between the nineteenth and early twentieth centuries. The nineteenth-century state was built upon male citizenship with women relegated to the private, domestic sphere—characterized as an irrational space of sentiment, feeling, and emotional primitivism. Twentieth-century states sought to rationalize this sphere. Mothers had to be educated for scientific, hygienic household management and child raising in order to produce healthy, efficient, patriotic citizen-workers. Public appropriation of reproductive activities such as education, hygiene, and health care demanded new interactions between households and the public sphere: the appointed household actor was the woman, the mother. The rationalization of domesticity did not involve the immediate granting of full citizenship rights to women, however. In most instances, the interests of women were subordinated to those of the patriarchal family and national development.

The articulation and implementation of social policy involved the emergence of a transnational professional class. Along with other Latin Americans, Mexicans shared assumptions and ideas drawn from a milieu created through publications, international conferences, professional organizations, and training centers. Exchange between U.S. and Latin American professionals intensified through Pan American organizations after 1880, and Latin American communication with Europeans expanded through the League of Nations.[8]

Although transnationally nurtured, social policy varied from country to country. Within countries, it changed with shifting political coalitions, mobilizations, and geopolitical configurations. Mexico's demographic crisis was the revolution itself: masses of people, urban and rural, in armed rebellion, social movement, and dislocation, marked by hunger, violence, and rapid mobility. From the perspective of the embryonic state arising from this upheaval, the population had to be brought to order in a progressive manner. The "race," understood in transnational professional jargon to be degenerate and diseased, had to be revitalized and its energies harnessed for development and participation in a modern, competitive global order. Like their counterparts in the United States and in other Latin American countries, Mexican policymakers were preoccupied with the urban poor and working classes. Unlike their Latin American counterparts, however, they were also preoccupied with rural development, for they aimed to domesticate a rebellious peasantry.

The revolutionary conflagration made Mexican development policies progressive compared with those of other countries. In the eugenics debate over nature versus nurture, Mexican policymakers and professionals unquestionably chose environmental over biological determinism. Artists and educators orchestrated the browning and mestizoization of Mexican national culture in defiance of prerevolutionary social Darwinism, and endowed this coloring with legitimacy and integrity at a time when racialist discourse dominated intellectual and professional circles in much of Europe and the United States. Further, although accepting the biologized notion of a diseased social body, Mexican policymakers linked degeneration to structural, class issues: peasants were sick and lethargic because of rapacious landlords, priests, and an unjust distribution of property and wealth. Redistributive rural policy promoted land reform. Persistent sociopolitical agitation, the massification of politics, and the need for the state or party to establish effective control over a far-flung and highly mobilized society led to a radicalization of policy, which reached its peak during the presidency of Lázaro Cárdenas from 1934 to 1940.[9] Thus, in keeping with the distinction made in this volume between liberal and populist states in Latin America, the progressive aspects of Mexican social policy, although suggested in the 1920s, became dominant in the populist 1930s.

On the other hand, policy formulation occurred within a transnational context with a new imperialist configuration. As European interest in Mexico receded after World War I, Mexico was left face to face with the aggressive Colossus of the North. Still, a revolution and nationalistic postrevolutionary governments on its huge southern border challenged the U.S. government, which had to balance relations with Latin America, Europe, and Japan in the unstable period between two world wars. U.S.-Mexican relations were too contentious, complex, and tentative to speak of a simple imposition of U.S. interests or ideologies on Mexican social policy. Between 1920 and 1938, when Cárdenas's nationalization of oil brought strong pressure from U.S. (and domestic) capitalist circles, the new configuration may have constrained and shaped the progressive and innovative aspects of Mexican social policy, but it did not cripple them. In the field of education, Mexicans appropriated U.S. notions of progressive pedagogy and implemented them in what was one of the most creative and unique rural education programs in the world.[10] By contrast, in health policy, the Rockefeller Foundation practically created the Mexican Departamento de Salubridad, bankrolled it, shaped its priorities, programs, and methodologies, and trained its staff.[11] However, in the 1930s, Rockefeller-trained Mexican officials countered the foundation's disease-specific medical interventionist approach with more comprehensive policies that emphasized prevention through the elimination of poverty and provision of public sanitation.[12]

If in comparative perspective Mexican social policy appeared progressive, in certain ways it was not. First, unlike the United States, Mexico did not generate a strong middle-class women's movement to articulate and implement a maternalist approach to social policy.[13] Whereas religiosity had been a factor in building the U.S. women's movement, the intense antireligiosity of Mexican male revolutionaries bifurcated any potential middle-class women's reform initiative in Mexico. Those women who entered state bureaucracies (in small numbers as policymakers and administrators in education, family welfare, and juvenile justice; in large numbers as teachers; and in initially small but growing numbers as nurses and social workers) did so to carry out social policies of governments increasingly vocal in their antireligiosity. Middle- and upper-class Catholic women, whose notions of domestic reform had much in common with those of the state, rallied against the government in defense of religion, as did legions of nonelite women.[14] Second, the progressive, cross-class, community-based women's movement pressuring the government for women-centered measures was weaker in Mexico than in countries such as Chile.[15] Most progressive women were linked to state and official organizations overwhelmingly dominated by men. Third, in contrast to policies in the Russian and Chinese Revolutions, Mexican social policy ignored the core of rural women's oppression by only indirectly challenging the patrivirilocal extended family that predominated among the peasantry.[16] Finally, in the 1930s, the rationalization of domesticity was the most derivative component of Mexican rural development policy and, as such, was remarkably unadapted to conditions prevailing in most of the countryside and insensitive to women's local knowledge and practice.

Modernizing Rural Patriarchy: The Articulation of Federal Policy, 1930–40

Rural development policy in Mexico in the 1930s can be viewed as a family-oriented policy envisioning a modernization of patriarchy. Articulated in agrarian, educational, and health programs, it aimed at destroying regional, often precapitalist, patriarchal networks of power and at provisioning in favor of national, horizontal, market-linked networks. It sought to remake the family—men, women, and children—in the interests of nation building and development. It rested upon a restructuring of male productive practices and sociability, a mobilization of children for patriotic development, and the rationalization of domesticity.[17]

The male campesino's production would be commercialized and nationalized. New, horizontal, state-linked *ejidos* (land reform units), cooperatives, and marketing networks would replace his old reliance on vertical, local networks for resource allocation, provisioning, and trade. His social behavior was to be sanitized—his drinking, gambling, praying, womanizing, and violence curtailed. No longer would a swig of *aguardiente* seal a high-interest loan from the landlord. This act would be replaced by handshaking and document signing at sober ceremonies between *ejidatarios*, their elected officers, and the ejidal bank.

The male campesino was to be encouraged to read agrarian law and technical manuals and to listen to the radio and its government broadcasts rather than to priests. Forsaking blood sports—cockfighting and bullfighting and boxing—he was to play basketball and baseball. Modern team sports would encourage his health and sobriety, and develop in him the proper mix of competitiveness and cooperation appropriate to autonomous, self-disciplined performance in the anonymous modern world.

The school would mobilize his children for national development. Independent of parents and the church, this space fell under the state's discursive and normative dominion. It would be coeducational. Boys and girls would learn together a similar curriculum promoting patriotism and modernity. Girls were as important as boys to the development effort because they could become reproductive workers, consumers, and marginal income earners. Together they would engage in patriotic learning through cooperative gardening and marketing, the formation of 4-H clubs, competitions in rural crafts and agriculture, and the organization of sports teams as well as folkloric dance and singing ensembles for patriotic civic festivals.

Rationalization of the domestic sphere focused on mothers in households. Policymakers urged teachers to promote the civil registration of conjugal unions, births, and deaths—a secularizing process of state regulation begun in the previous century. They also propagated new "scientific" discourses on human development, nutrition, hygiene, and disease. Campesino homes were to be redesigned for health, comfort, and sexual propriety. Windows were to be installed for light and air; animals were to be ejected from the living quarters, and rooms partitioned to prevent "promiscuity." The hearth was to be raised from floor to waist level and a chimney installed to preserve women's backs, eliminate smoke from the house, and reduce accidents. The corn-grinding mill *(molino de nixtamal)* and sewing machines were to be introduced.

Campesina mothers were to learn more nutritional ways of feeding their families. Teachers and health workers would fight *curanderas* (healers), witchcraft, and homespun midwives. They would peddle modern medicines and inoculate against small pox and other contagious diseases. Sanitation was an urgent matter. Soap should be made and used, latrines built, garbage burned, flies swatted, and water boiled. Integral community development envisaged a new feminine sociability disassociated from the church and linked to civic, secular action. This sociability was an extension of domesticity. Women would gather not to dress the Virgin for festival, but to crusade for the moral and physical health of the community. They were to organize antialcohol leagues and to serve on the school's parent council. They would combat dirt and disease, get rid of standing pools of water, push for the installation of potable water, and set up first aid teams.

Based upon urban, imported models, the prescriptions for rationalizing domesticity suggested the use of rural women as conduits for the realization of state interests, rather than the elaboration of a woman-centered project. The effort showed ignorance and contempt for rural women's knowledge, skills, beliefs, and social organization within the separate female sphere arranged around reproductive functions. Its attack on religiosity did much to alienate campesinas from the more progressive, emancipating aspects of policy. The state's interest in domestic violence was not a concern for wife abuse per se but for the pernicious effects of alcohol on production and family welfare. Designed to promote population growth, policy never articulated women's right to control their bodies and their sexuality. It denied or denigrated their knowledge and practices related to the human body. Women were to make a pact with new medical professionals and cede control of their bodies and those of their children to them. As Anne Emanuelle Birn shows, Rockefeller public health teams working for the federal and state governments in Morelos aimed at breaking into and breaking up spheres of female expertise and sociability built around childbirth and the pre- and postnatal care of women and babies.[18]

Although the project to rationalize domesticity threatened to violate and disorganize existing female spheres of sociability, power, and knowledge, it was not part of a larger policy that attacked rural women's oppression at the core. Such a policy would have challenged peasant inheritance patterns, which were customarily between fathers and sons. As Ann Varley explains in her essay in this volume, the patrivirilocal extended family obliged young women to leave their families to enter their spouses' households, where they occupied near servant status under the dominion of mothers-in-law and husbands. Because they married out, girls could also be discriminated against in family investments in education and welfare. With its emphasis on ejidal plots for male heads of household, agrarian policy aimed theoretically at destroying this extended family and replacing it with the nuclear farming family. However, we have yet to study how the two interfaced in practice, and we know that the patrivirilocal extended family persisted in much of rural central Mexico that experienced land reform.[19] Marginal women's groups defended women who tried to acquire ejidal plots, but masculine patterns of possession and inheritance persisted. With regard to the latter, rural policy failed to address the vulnerable position of female heads of household, whose numbers had probably increased through the violence, mobilizations, and dislocations of revolution.

Nonetheless, the projected rationalization of domesticity challenged rural patriarchy in ways that potentially opened new spaces and behaviors for women. First, new technologies such as the molino de nixtamal freed women from hours of labor regarded by husbands as protected, regulated time in physically enclosed space.[20] Women might invest their new-found time in the public sphere—mobilizing for community improvements, serving on the parents' school council, marketing their crafts and garden produce. Second, the rationalization of domesticity implicitly undercut dominion of male heads of household by creating a relationship between wives and female teachers or nurses, messengers of potentially subversive information about women's rights and options. Such relationships, however, might also undermine female networks of reproductive knowledge, skill, and power based upon the accumulated prestige of the oldest women, who in turn upheld the patriarchal order. Policy suggested weakening the power of the elders in favor of youth, the conjugal couple, the nuclear family, and, ironically, the female head of household, and promoting the direct interaction of these entities with the educative state and marketplace.

In other ways as well, policy suggested a possible restructuring of socialization practices at the expense of abusive male authority. The promotion of schooling for girls and coeducation was to correct what was perceived to be male disparagement and mistreatment of women. The policy's condemnation of male drinking often pilloried in theater and rhetoric the drunken husband who abused his wife and children. Its effort to substitute patriotic sports events for male-exclusive blood sports and their alcoholized bonding might improve the quality of life for women and children.

Implementing Federal Policy: 1930–40

There was, however, a big gap between policy formulation and implementation. As previously noted, policy implementation must consider issues of state capacity: available resources, the quality and competence of personnel, and the degree of horizontal (federal-level agencies of education, agrarian reform and health) and vertical (federal, state, and local officials) inter-governmental collaboration. Although Mexican federal bureaucracies had expanded and matured since the 1920s, they were still incipient, under-staffed, underfunded, and competitive with regional and local authorities and with each other. At the level of communities, policy implementation ultimately depended on active support within the community as well as on the community's willingness and capacity to release resources necessary for policy implementation—all of which were problematic given the cultural distance between the state's vision and the feistiness and poverty of most rural societies.

In my book, *Cultural Politics in Revolution,* I examine the implementation of educational policy in four peasant societies in northern and central Mexico in the 1930s. A brief recap here of the findings related to the rationalization of domesticity from two case studies of communities undergoing agrarian, educational, and health reform demonstrates a range of implementation experiences. These communities are located on the left bank of the Yaqui River in the northern state of Sonora and in Tecamachalco, a former hacienda region of Puebla on the central Mexican highland plateau.

Between the Cárdenas government and the immigrant mestizo agricultural workers and *colonos* (settler farmers) on the left bank of the Yaqui River in Sonora, there was an unusual convergence of state capacity and community support.[21] Here, in 1937, at Cárdenas's initiative, government agencies developed a coordinated, relatively well-financed program of community development inclusive of land reform, irrigation, cooperative production and marketing, state credit and technical assistance, education, health, and sanitation. The state had the advantage of operating in a rich agricultural region among an enthusiastic population. Migration from other parts of Mexico, the nature of work in the valley, and the frontier character of the newly settled region eroded aspects of peasant culture.[22] Communities were incipient, and organized religion weak. Male heads of household had lost control over production and worked for wages as did other family members—male and female—in diverse jobs in agricultural camps, food processing, transportation, and services. The situation created new spaces for women and youth. Migration, the nuclearization of families, and dependence on the market had broken down intergenerational female hierarchies built around reproductive practices. Male team sports— notably baseball—had already taken hold, privileging male youth and nurturing in them new forms of solidarity at workplaces, in unions, and in campesino organizations.

Fantasies of modernity captured people's imaginations. They had come to escape the hardships of rural life and now saw "the promised land." Before agrarian reform, they embraced modernist hopes generated by Hollywood movies and the technological revolution exploding around them. Motorbikes, cars, agricultural machinery, corn-grinding mills, store-bought pain relievers, sewing machines, and Sears catalogs made their dazzling appearances and demonstrated their utility. Political and social mobilization for land reform, schools, community, and household improvements occurred in tandem with state encouragement and cooperation, but without violence. The mobilization incorporated women in household reforms, education, and community development, while excluding them from the politics of land reform, agrarian association, and public office.

The convergence of interests, values, and resources between the Mexican state and the Yaqui Valley ejidatarios was rare in rural Mexico, however. More typical was the encounter between state agents and peasants in Tecamachalco, an impoverished, arid region of ejidatarios who had violently struggled to retrieve village lands from surrounding haciendas.[23] They had succeeded in doing so despite, not because of, the state. In place of a coordinated development program in the 1930s, agrarian reform authorities and representatives of the ejidal bank sparred with education and health personnel as each strained to carry out their agency-specific mandates and to obtain local support. All federal agents were poorly financed, minimally trained, and inclined by circumstances to improvisation. For example, to patch over the collapse of prerevolutionary networks of production, provisioning, and marketing, agricultural agents encouraged campesinos to cultivate maguey. This dryland plant produced the alcoholic beverage pulque, for which there was strong local demand. From the perspective of educators and health workers, pulque was sheer poison for the already diseased bodies of the campesinos. It was the source of the degeneration they sought to reverse: alcoholism, lethargy, illness, violence, and the squandering of time and money. Although the revolution had broken down vertical patriarchal relations between villagers and haciendas in Tecamachalco, it had reinforced patriarchal relations in peasant households as they returned to subsistence farming and reduced exchange with the outside world. Persistent violence stemming from intercampesino and peasant-landlord strife kept women isolated and secluded in their homes. Kidnapping, assault, robbery, and rape were commonplace. Tecamachalco women could have used state assistance when drought in the early 1930s aggravated already precarious conditions of reproduction. Borne by dusty winds, viruses swept regularly through towns, sickening and killing the young and old. Male migration for work left many women in charge of *milpa* (peasant plot), animals, and children. But, instead of building a cooperative relationship, teachers and health agents were widely separated from most Tecamachalco women.

The instructions teachers received from the Secretaría de Educación Pública (SEP), school inspectors, and health officials in training seminars were at odds with local cultural practices, resources, and the organization of power. Women teachers were told to visit campesino homes to instruct mothers in proper household management, puericulture, and hygiene only to find their entry blocked by women and men who valued the privacy of the hearth. Official prescriptions encouraged teachers to see local reproductive practices as irrational, ineffective, and ensconced in primitive superstition. However, the teachers had few resources to demonstrate the effectiveness of their "science." Their recommendations for improving nutrition and sanitizing households and communities ran up against the scarcity of water. Homogenizing peasant women as ignorant, education and health officials did not seek out local female specialists whose proven skills and prestige could have brokered in exotic innovations. Instead, campaigns to inoculate against contagious diseases were often tactlessly carried out. Teachers and Departamento de Salubridad brigades would descend on towns on market days to vaccinate en masse—sometimes accompanied by police and soldiers.

Critically, most Tecamachalco women associated state agents with antireligiosity in an area where deep local religious sentiment meshed with an exogenous Catholic political movement. Even after popular opposition forced the government to call off its antireligious campaign in 1936, most Tecamachalco women showed mistrust and timidity. In large part, although not exclusively, the tainting of state reform efforts with godlessness inhibited women's engaging in new forms of sociability and association that might have empowered them in new ways. Antialcohol and community improvement campaigns that engaged women were rare or weak, and men maintained control over community affairs and the parents' school councils. In contrast to women, campesino men developed new forms of solidarity in their ejidos, cooperatives, political organizations, and basketball teams. Sports competitions between teams of different communities in civic celebrations and campesino associations' weekend encounters offset the debilitating inter- and intracommunity divisions that had plagued campesino mobilization in the region. While they helped to fortify a peasant organization linked to the state, they also probably contributed to a sense of class solidarity and political empowerment for campesino men.

In the 1940s, conditions became more favorable for the modernization of patriarchy envisioned by social policy. This observation goes against the grain of prevailing scholarship, which sees 1938 as the year property redistribution and social spending were curtailed, and 1940 as the date ushering in decades of conservative political control by the Partido Revolucionario Institucional (PRI). However, it can be argued that economic growth associated with relative political stability from 1940 to 1960 enhanced state capacity in certain aspects of social policy while creating conditions for greater convergence between policy and local society in regions such as Tecamachalco. In the 1940s and 1950s, the state provided Tecamachalco campesinos with tractors, ploughs, seeds, credit, and marketing assistance. The federal government financed irrigation works and the digging of deep-water wells to alleviate the age-old problem of water. Completion of the highway between Puebla and Tehuacán opened possibilities for crop diversification, marketing, migration, and alternative sources of employment.

Local support for household reform expanded. Women and children began to experience the twin effects of state policies and market growth: introduction of the molino de nixtamal, the waist-level hearth, water sources closer to home, paved highways, and state-subsidized fleets of buses—all of which freed women's labor and facilitated mobility precisely at a moment when meeting family subsistence needs required their greater participation in markets and nonlocal work sites.[24] Mothers saw that children survived epidemics when vaccinated and so asked for shots. Child mortality fell with the introduction of antibiotics. Child nutrition improved with the availability of canned foods, especially sardines. Beer and soft drinks replaced pulque as drinks of choice, and basketball continued its ascendance over blood sports. Girls' literacy rose in tandem with boys'.[25]

It was not simply material conditions or the time factor required to break in new practices that accounted for the rising demand for schools and modern health measures in Tecamachaclo. Through practice, state agents honed their skills as negotiators between distinct cultures, instead of acting like singular imposers of a correct modern project. Government health programs became more successful once they identified female community leaders and practitioners as partners in the dissemination of modern medicine and health practices. Women teachers came to understand the logic of campesino ways. They had learned, for instance, that it was rational for mothers to give children small amounts of pulque as a nutritional liquid in an arid region without safe drinking water. Teachers themselves used herbal medicines as well as modern drugs and cures. For women teachers to become brokers between cultures was not that difficult. Although their social mobility and professional identity were strongly bound up with the revolutionary, state mystique of modernity, they themselves were usually from a rural social milieu just a notch above that of the campesinas. If state prescriptions pushed their understanding of local culture to the backs of their minds, carrying out their revolutionary mandate to improve campesino well-being required that they recall and use that understanding. Begun in the 1930s, this communication between female agents of the state and local women was facilitated in the 1940s by the relaxation of religious tensions and the achievement of relative sociopolitical peace.[26]

Ironically, female heads of household—the group the state entirely overlooked in the countryside—may have benefited more from education and health policies than married women. Oral histories from Tecamachalco and the Yaqui Valley and Judith Friedlander's study of Hueyapan, Morelos, uncover the experience of single mothers who took advantage of the opportunity schooling offered them to create a nonlanded "patrimony" or inheritance they could leave their children: new skills that would enhance their income-earning opportunities as adults. We find single mothers associating with female teachers not only as enablers for their children but as role models. Similarly, they were often the first to join state health practitioners, sharing with them their local knowledge of curing and caring, learning how to give shots, and peddling modern medicines.[27] They perhaps had greater freedom to associate and experiment than did married women, and they may also have had greater need. The subject would benefit from further quantitative and qualitative research.

Toward a Gendered Analysis of State Policy, Rural Households, and Women (1940–60)

Feminist social scientists have made critical contributions to studies of rural Mexico in their gendered analyses of development policies and processes, their challenge to the construction of the peasant as male, and their alternative focus on the peasant household as a gendered site of power constantly engaged in devising and implementing strategies for survival. Primarily concerned with contemporary dilemmas confronting Mexican campesinas, they have made certain assumptions about the Mexican Revolution and the trajectory of the peasantry after 1940. For some, the 1940s was a utopic period of a subsistence peasant economy created by Cardenista land reform—nourished by economic growth only to be sabotaged by it. Sometime in the 1950s, capitalist growth combined with population growth and urban-, male-, and agribusiness-biased government policies undercut and undid the peasant economy—disorganizing communities, deepening poverty, diversifying income-producing activities, and sending migrants to cities in search of survival.[28] Another approach, premised on a pessimistic view of the revolution's agrarian reform, argues that because the latter failed to provide peasants with sufficient, cultivable land, its negative consequences for the peasantry were immediately visible in increased impoverishment and out-migration after 1940.[29]

A gendered analysis of development policy in the 1930s and case studies such as those of Tecamachalco and the left bank of the Yaqui River call for a historicization of the post-1940 period, beginning with the decades between 1940 and 1960. Gendered in conceptualization, as well as microhistorical and comparative in approach, such historicization should yield more specific understandings of the intersection among state policy, rural households, and campesina women.

In historicizing this period, we must recognize gendered legacies of the revolution. In many regions, important foci of traditional patriarchal power such as the patrivirilocal, extended family and many recreational customs survived the revolution. At the same time, new centers of male power emerged in political organizations and state bureaucracies. Although the revolutionary process opened political and bureaucratic channels for redressing grievances and making claims, these channels were male-dominated and not easy for women to navigate. However, women gained some space in the state around reproductive issues and politics. This space expanded in the 1940–60 period as government programs grew and as women health and educational workers adopted more positive ways of interacting with community women. By contrast, rural economic policy paid no direct attention to women and offered them little direct state support.

Historicizing the post-1940 period also requires a gendered understanding of development processes and policies that considers technologies of reproduction as seriously as it measures those of production. The impact of factors affecting reproduction—antibiotics, vaccination, the molino de nixtamal, buses, clinics, canned and powdered foods, bottled soft drinks, wells, and schools—must be more carefully assessed. To what extent did these factors improve the quality of life and expand the labor force participation of women and their children? Analysis of such factors will help us to understand family gender dynamics, women's economic participation, generational change, and campesino / a negotiations with the state.

In historicizing and engendering rural experience, we should focus on the campesino household as principal actor. We have to ask to what degree, under what circumstances, and in what form do women participate in the making of family strategies? How does such participation differ according to their position as wives, daughters, mothers-in-law, daughters-in-law, widows, and single women? What new spaces, activities, and powers do women in these positions create for themselves, and through what kind of interaction with familial and extrafamilial actors, spaces, and processes? What forms of female knowledge, skill, and power are lost or marginalized—for instance, through formal education and interaction with state health agencies—and with what consequences for women? What new forms of female knowledge, skill, and power are created?

How do campesina women maneuver in what appears to be a triple vise of "traditional" familial patriarchy, an overwhelmingly masculine state politics, and a conservative trend in national cultural politics? In relation to the latter, we have to assess the impact of Cold War ideology, a continuing and renovated Catholic social mobilization, and the new mass media of comic books, cinema, and radio on rural women and family life.

Among the compelling reasons for historicizing this period is the need to examine the "population explosion." This international, professional elite construct harbors in its imaginary a vision of the culprits: ignorant, uneducated, manipulated peasant women. Feminist sociologists have a different opinion: in a period of relative rural prosperity and opportunity, large families had, for a time, a comparative advantage.[30] Thus, improved welfare, rising incomes, and female educational levels did not immediately result in declining fertility. Microhistorical, comparative analysis should help us to understand rural women's margins of maneuver, strategies, and decision-making roles in Mexican population politics between 1940 and 1960.

Notes

1 The bibliography is long. For a relatively recent, theoretical, and comparative analysis, see Sandra McGee Deutsch, "Gender and Socio-Political Change in Twentieth-Century Latin America," *Hispanic American Historical Review* 71, no. 2 (1991): 260–76.

2 The following analysis is taken from Mary Kay Vaughan, *Cultural Politics in Revolution: Teachers, Peasants, and Schools in Mexico (1930–1940)* (Tucson: University of Arizona Press, 1997), a study primarily of the implementation of educational policy and secondarily of agrarian and health policies in four rural societies in the 1930s. My analysis is also informed by essays in Heather Fowler-Salamini and Mary Kay Vaughan, eds., *Creating Spaces, Shaping Transitions: Women of the Mexican Countryside (1850–1990)* (Tucson: University of Arizona Press, 1994). Heather Fowler-Salamini and I articulated the main lines of argument in this essay in "What Difference Does Gender Make to the Agrarian Politics of the Mexican Revolution?" a paper presented at the Conference on Latin American History, Chicago, Ill., January 1995.

3 See Theda Skocpol, "Bringing the State Back In: Current Research," in *Bringing the State Back In,* ed. Peter B. Evans, Dietrich Rueschemeyer, and Theda Skocpol (Cambridge: Cambridge University Press, 1985), 5–8; Alfred Stepan, *The State and Society: Peru in Comparative Perspective* (Princeton, N.J.: Princeton University Press, 1978), chaps. 3 and 4.

4 Current debate is situated between two extremes: a Foucauldian approach that emphasizes dispersed, multiple sites of discipline and power, and an approach that stresses state agency in shaping and regulating social behavior. The latter is well exemplified by Philip Corrigan and Derek Sayer, *The Great Arch: English State Formation as Cultural Revolution* (Oxford: Basil Blackwell, 1985). For Foucault's position, see Michel Foucault, *Discipline and Punish: The Birth of the Prison* (Harmondsworth, Eng.: Penguin, 1979); "Governmentality," in *The Foucault Effect: Studies in Governmentality,* ed. Graham Burchell, Colin Gordon, and Peter Miller (Chicago: University of Chicago Press, 1991), 7–105; "Two Lectures," in *Culture / Power / History: A Reader in Contemporary Social Theory,* ed. Nicholas B.

Dirks, Geoff Eley, and Sherry Ortner (Princeton, N.J.: Princeton University Press, 1994), 200–221, especially Lecture Two, 210–21.

5 On state capacity, see Skocpol, "Bringing the State Back In," 2, 17–18; Theda Skocpol and Kenneth Finegold, "State Capacity and Economic Intervention in the Early New Deal," *Political Science Quarterly* 97 (1982): 268–78.

6 To date, no study has surpassed Nora Hamilton's *The Limits of State Autonomy: Post Revolutionary Mexico* (Princeton, N.J.: Princeton University Press, 1982), a Marxist analysis of the relationship between the state and foreign and domestic capitalist circles. New research has revealed pressures placed on the Cárdenas government by regional power formations and conservative social movements, which corroborate rather than contradict her argument.

7 Victoria de Grazia, *How Fascism Ruled Women in Italy, 1922–1945* (Berkeley: University of California Press, 1993), 1–76.

8 Francesca Miller, *Latin American Women and the Search for Social Justice* (Hanover, N.H.: University Press of New England, 1991), 82–102; Donna Guy, "The Pan American Children's Congresses, 1916–1942: Pan Americanism, Child Reform, and the Welfare State in Latin America," *Journal of Family History* 23, no. 3 (1998): 272–91.

9 See Vaughan, *Cultural Politics,* chap. 2.

10 The bibliography on education in the Mexican Revolution is mammoth. On rural education, see, among others, Ramon Eduardo Ruiz, *Mexico: The Challenge of Poverty and Illiteracy* (San Merino, Calif.: Huntington Library, 1963); Josefina Vazquez, *Nacionalismo y educación* (Mexico City: El Colegio de México, 1970); David Raby, *Educación y revolución social* (Mexico City: Sepsetentas, 1976); Isidro Castillo, *México y su revolución educativa* (Mexico City: Editorial Pax Mexicana, Librería Carlos Cesarman, S.A., 1965); Mary Kay Vaughan, *The State, Education, and Social Class in Mexico: 1880–1928* (Dekalb: Northern Illinois University Press, 1982); and Vaughan, *Cultural Politics.*

11 See studies by James McLeod, "Public Health, Social Assistance, and the Consolidation of the Mexican State, 1888–1940" (Ph.D. diss., Tulane University, 1990); Armando Solorzano, "The Rockefeller Foundation in Revolutionary Mexico: Yellow Fever in Yucatán and Veracruz," in *Missionaries of Science: The Rockefeller Foundation and Latin America,* ed. Marcos Cueto (Bloomington: Indiana University Press, 1993), 52–72; Anne Emanuelle Birn, "Local Health and Foreign Wealth: The Rockefeller Foundation's Public Health Program in Mexico, 1924–51" (Ph.D. diss., Johns Hopkins University, 1993).

12 Birn, "Local Health and Foreign Wealth," 259–325; Ana Maria Kapelusz-Poppi, "Dr. Enrique Arregun Velez: Leftist Public Health Programs in Twentieth-Century Mexico," paper presented at the XXI International Congress of the Latin American Studies Association, Chicago, Ill., 23–25 September 1998.

13 See Theda Skocpol, *Protecting Soldiers and Mothers: The Political Origins of Social Policy in the United States* (Cambridge, Mass.: Harvard University Press, 1995), 311–524.

14 See Randall Hanson, "Mujeres Militantes: Las Damas Católicas and the Mobilization of Women in Revolutionary Mexico, 1912–1929," paper presented at the Conference on Latin American History, New York, January 1997; Barbara Miller, "The Role of Women in the Mexican Cristero Rebellion: Las Señoras and las Religiosas," *The Americas* 40, no. 1 (1984): 303–32; and Marjorie Becker, "Torching La Purísima, Dancing at the Altar: The Construction of Revolutionary Hegemony in Michoacán, 1934–1940," in *Everyday Forms of State Formation: Revolution and Negotiation of Rule in Modern Mexico,* ed. Gilbert M. Joseph and Daniel Nugent (Durham, N.C.: Duke University Press, 1994), 247–64.

15 See Karin A. Rosemblatt, "Gendered Compromises: Political Cultures, Socialist Politics, and the State in Chile, 1920–1950" (Ph.D. diss., University of Wisconsin–Madison, 1996), and Corinne Pernet, "Mobilizing Women in the Popular Front Era: Feminism, Class, and Politics in the Movimiento Pro-Emancipación de la Mujer Chilena (MEMCH), 1935–1940" (Ph.D. diss., University of California–Irvine, 1996).

16 On the Chinese and Russian Revolutions, see Maxine Molyneux, "Family Reform in Socialist States: The Hidden Agenda," *Feminist Review,* no. 21 (winter 1985): 47–64.

17 The information on these pages, except where noted, is taken from Vaughan, *Cultural Politics,* chap. 2, 25–46. It is based on Secretaría de Educación Pública, *Memorias,* 1932–38; *Plan de Acción de la Escuela Primaria Socialista,* 1935, and the training publication for teachers, *El Maestro Rural,* 1932–34; federal school inspectors' reports contained in the Archivo Histórico de la Secretaría de Educación Pública; and the following school textbooks: Gabriel Lucio, *Simiente: Libro tercero para escuelas rurales* (Mexico City: Secretaría de Educación Pública, 1935); *Serie SEP, primer año, lectural oral* (Mexico City: Secretaría de Educación Pública, 1938); Manuel Velazquez Andrade, *Fermin* (Puebla: Premia, 1986; orig. pub. 1929). My presumption to read from educational documents a shared intent and conceptualization for overall rural policy (inclusive of agrarian and health policies) stems from my analysis of the implementation of such policies in the states of Sonora and Puebla in the 1930s. This analysis (Vaughan, *Cultural Politics,* 47–76) draws from materials in the Archivo General de la Reforma Agraria, Mexico City; the Archivo de la Reforma Agraria, Puebla; the Archivo Administrativo General del Estado de Sonora, Hermosillo; and the Acervos Presidentes (Ortiz Rubio, Abelardo L. Rodríguez, and Lázaro Cárdenas del Rio) in the Archivo General de la Nación, Mexico City, in addition to material from the Archivo Histórico de la Secretaría de Educación Pública, Mexico City.

18 Birn, "Local Health and Foreign Wealth," 190–98.

19 See, for example, among others, essays in Fowler-Salamini and Vaughan, *Women of the Mexican Countryside:* Gail Mummert, "From *Metate* to *Despate:* Rural Mexican Women's Salaried Labor and the Redefinition of Gendered Spaces and Roles," in particular 194–195; Soledad Gonzalez Montes, "Inter-

generational and Gender Relations in the Transition from a Peasant Economy to a Diversified Economy," in particular 181–82; Maria da Gloria Marroni de Velazquez, "Changes in Rural Society and Domestic Labor in Atlixco, Puebla, 1940–1990," in particular 215.

20 Oscar Lewis, *Life in a Mexican Village: Tepoztlán Revisited,* 5th ed. (Urbana: University of Illinois Press, 1963), 99, 107–8, 323.

21 My analysis of this region, drawn from Vaughan, *Cultural Politics,* 163–88, relies on correspondence in the Acervos Presidentes (Pascual Ortiz Rubio, Abelardo L. Rodriguez, Lázaro Cárdenas del Rio, Manuel Avila Camacho); Archivo General de la Nación, Mexico City; Archivo General de la Reforma Agraria, Mexico City; Archivo Administrativo del Estado de Sonora, Hermosillo; U.S. State Department Records relating to the Internal Affairs of Mexico, 1930–1940, Washington, D.C.; federal school inspectors' bimonthly reports, those of the SEP director in Sonora, and other data in the Archivo Histórico de la SEP, Mexico City; interviews with men and women who had experienced schooling and land reform of the 1930s; a particularly wonderful collection of oral histories engagingly compiled and edited by Mayo Murrieta and Eugenia Graf, *Por el milagro de aferrarse: Tierra y vecindad en el Valle del Yaqui* (Hermosillo, Son.: Colegio de Sonora, Instituto Tecnologico de Sonora, Instituto Sonorense de Cultura, 1992); and the autobiographical novel, Gerardo Cornejo, *La sierra y el viento* (Hermosillo, Son.: Arte y Libros, 1977).

22 The Yaqui Indians had inhabited this rich valley, but the majority of them had been forced out of the valley by Mexican armies by the first decade of the twentieth century. In the 1930s, many had returned to the valley but were cordoned off in a camp on the right bank of the Yaqui River, policed by the Mexican army.

23 For more complete analysis, see Vaughan, *Cultural Politics,* 77–106; *Women of Mexican Countryside,* 106–24; "Economic Growth and Literacy in Nineteenth-Century Mexico: The Case of Puebla," in *Education and Economic Development Since the Industrial Revolution,* ed. Gabriel Tortella (Valencia: Generalitat, 1990), 155–62. Sources used include Acervos Presidentes, Archivo General de la Nación, noted above; Archivo Municipal de Tecamachalco; Archivo de la Reforma Agraria, Puebla; and Archivo General de la Reforma Agraria, Mexico City; bimonthly inspector reports and the archives of individual federal schools found in the Archivo Histórico de la Secretaría de Educación Pública, Mexico City; oral interviews with teachers and students from the period; and census data, 1895–1960.

24 On the importance of cheap bus transportation for rural women, see especially Judith Friedlander, *Being Indian in Hueyapan: A Study of Forced Identity in Contemporary Mexico* (New York: St. Martin's, 1975), 1–24, 62–64; on the introduction of household technology in rural central Puebla, see Marroni de Velázquez, "Changes in Rural Society," 210–24; on household technology, roads, schooling,

and women in Tepoztlán, Morelos, see Wendy Waters, "Revolutionizing Child-hood: Schools, Roads, and the Revolutionary Generation Gap in Tepoztlán, Mexico, 1928–44," *Journal of Family History* 23, no. 3 (1998): 292–311.

25 For an optimistic assessment of the impact of these factors on the lives of women and children, see Waters, "Revolutionizing Childhood," 292–311.

26 Mary Kay Vaughan, "Rural Women's Literacy and Education during the Mexican Revolution: Subverting a Patriarchal Event?" in Fowler-Salamini and Vaughan, eds., *Women of the Mexican Countryside,* 117–21; "Women School Teachers in the Mexican Revolution: The Story of Reyna's Braids," *Journal of Women's History* 2, no. 1 (1990): 154–62.

27 See Vaughan, *Cultural Politics,* 163, 169, 188; and "Rural Women's Literacy," 116, 119. Interviews with Victor Alva, Puebla, 2 July 1991, 22 July 1989; Agustina Barrojas de Caro, Puebla, 6 July 1991; Reyna Manzano, Puebla, 12–15 July 1989; Marcelina Saldivar de Murrieta, Hermosillo, 7 April 1989. See also Murrieta and Graf, *Por el milagro,* 84–94; Judith Friedlander, "Doña Zeferina Barreto," in Fowler-Salamini and Vaughan, eds., *Women of the Mexican Countryside,* 125–39. For more on the survival strategies of Doña Zeferina, see Friedlander, *Being Indian in Hueyapan.*

28 Lourdes Arizpe and Carlota Botey, "Mexican Agricultural Development and Impact on Rural Women," in *Rural Women and State Policy: Feminist Perspectives on Latin American Agricultural Development,* ed. Carmen Diana Deere and Magdalena Leon (Boulder, Colo.: Westview, 1987), 73–80.

29 Patricia Arias, "Three Microhistories of Women's Work in Rural Mexico," in Fowler-Salamini and Vaughan, eds., *Creating Spaces,* 165.

30 Arizpe and Botey, "Mexican Agricultural Development," 77.

Laura Gotkowitz

Commemorating the Heroínas

Gender and Civic Ritual in Early-Twentieth-Century Bolivia

In Bolivia's most acclaimed and extensively circulated nineteenth-century novel, *Juan de la Rosa* (1885), by Nataniel Aguirre, the narrator discovers and describes what would hitherto be Bolivia's perhaps most memorable battle of the wars for independence. This now mythical moment, learned each year by millions of Bolivian schoolchildren, is the one protagonized by Cochabamba's valiant mestiza-chola market women,[1] the Heroínas, who fought and died on 27 May 1812, when royalist forces returned to Cochabamba to extinguish the last flames of resistance in this rebellious region. Faced by a shortage of soldiers and the cowardly example of the few men who remained in the town, a blind grandmother led the women of Cochabamba to the city's highest hill, the Coronilla, where they perished in a noble battle to the cry "there are no men."[2]

With the principal exception of Aguirre, Bolivia's nineteenth-century writer-politicians virtually ignored the mestizas' 1812 battle. In the first decades of the twentieth century, however, this unusual confrontation became the object of extensive commentary and attention: Commencing with a grandiose celebration on the 1912 centennial, Cochabamba elites organized an annual procession to honor the Heroínas. In 1926, following years of planning and a highly publicized debate, a monument dedicated exclusively to the mestiza heroines was inaugurated on the historic Coronilla. During the 1940s, a populist military regime in turn transformed the local celebration for the Heroínas into a national holiday: Mother's Day.

This essay traces the transformation of the regional celebration for the Heroínas of Cochabamba into a national holiday for Bolivian mothers. Of numerous regional celebrations in Bolivia, to my knowledge the celebration for the Heroínas is the only such festival ever converted into a national holiday. In Bolivia, Mother's Day is not exclusively focused on the mother, but directly linked and conflated with a civic ritual that serves to teach the nation's history and to inculcate patriotic sentiments. Further, the historical narratives associated with this national holiday privilege the experience of one particular region, making the mestizas of Cochabamba the source of a national character. Essentially overlooked in the nineteenth century, the heroic mestizas were transformed into a formative figure of Bolivia's modern political culture in the early twentieth century, at the height of contentious struggles over public space, public culture, citizenship, and nationhood. Mestizas were situated at the very heart of these conflicts—not just as symbols, but as agents of competing policies and projects.

If Cochabamba's mestiza heroines emerged as a key political symbol with the rise of the liberal-oligarchic state, the class and cultural identity of personages associated with the patriots nevertheless shifted at two key turning points: the 1920s decade of heightened intra-elite conflict, urban popular mobilization, and feminist organization; and the 1940s era of populist pacts when the military officer Gualberto Villarroel ruled in loose alliance with the Nationalist Revolutionary Movement (MNR), which would subsequently lead Bolivia's 1952 revolution. In Aguirre's 1885 novel, the heroines had been identified with the blind grandmother and the mestiza market women she mobilized. In the 1920s, however, the oligarchy instead portrayed the patriots as writers, agents of an illustrious culture without connections to lower classes. During the 1940s, mestiza market women took the place of lettered women. I argue that this latter shift was the result of a complex interaction between a precarious populist state seeking to incorporate urban labor and the local agendas of new middle sectors: mestiza merchants.

The changing representations of the Heroínas in the 1920s and 1940s highlight key aspects of the relationship between state making, civic ritual, and gender in twentieth-century Bolivia. In Bolivia, as elsewhere in Latin America, the process of nation-state making was marked by the promotion of civic rituals and holidays, in the course of which particular manifestations of popular culture were transformed, suppressed, eliminated, or replaced with "invented traditions."[3] Voicing explicit moral and social agendas, civic ceremonies intersected with efforts to regulate and reorder public space and custom; they enacted official historical narratives to foster identification with common symbols and new collectivities.[4] Like other forms of official history such as national novels, these civic rituals were in turn structured by specific logics of gender.[5] For Bolivia's oligarchic liberals, women's 1812 defense of the city against invading Spanish forces was a sign of the nation's level of civilization or "title of nationality."[6] Populists also exalted women's role in the wars for independence as a sign of devotion and national virtue, but diverged from oligarchic narratives in making the mestiza icon of such allegiance to the nation. Moreover, populists went further than liberals in actually mobilizing women politically and endorsing gender-specific social provisions.[7] Populist civic ritual thus simultaneously adjusted racialized and gendered boundaries of the nation, vindicating mestizas and *mestizaje* (the mixture of races)—but ambivalently. More than a sign of their own heroic deeds or even of the region, the Heroínas emblem became a terrain of struggle over citizenship and the "memory of the nation"[8]—its founding traditions, racial origins, and identity. Who would belong to the nation? Who embodied its cultural and historical essence?

Bolivia's populist state commodified the image of Cochabamba's rebel patriots, making the mestiza market women an idealized sign of cultural and political integration, and condensing the multiple meanings of their complex history into a figure of national unity.[9] But the populist performance also built upon multilayered traditions shaped by diverse local actors, centrally the market women who asserted their own honor and status through participation in the parade. Though it served to legitimize a precarious, modernizing regime, Mother's Day as Heroínas Day was not simply imposed by the state, but the product of ongoing struggles and alliances between women's movements, organized labor, municipal government, and the populist state.

The Oligarchy's Heroines

Modeled on the protagonists of Aguirre's 1885 novel, carved in Italy, and slated for Bolivia's 1925 centennial celebrations, the bronze monument for the Heroínas sparked a heated controversy about the space this statue of women should occupy and about the very meaning of the independence war history, the traditions, and the identity of the region. At stake were the social and cultural origins of the women, the Heroínas, who had participated in one of Cochabamba's foundational battles, and whether they had been protagonists or elements of a larger crowd. Should Cochabamba's patriotic traditions be symbolized by anonymous plebeian women, Indias, and cholas? Or by both common and acclaimed individuals, both men and women?

The gradual, contested effort to create this monument embodies an increasingly divisive and violent urban political culture. Following Bolivia's 1899 civil war, a centralized, La Paz–dominated state was consolidated under the auspices of the triumphant Liberal Party. With the revival of political rivalries around 1914, divided elites appealed to and mobilized urban mestizo sectors in electoral conflicts loosely drawn along regional lines. Regrouped in the Liberal, Republican, and Genuine Republican Parties in the 1920s, oligarchic groups forged clientelistic alliances with urban popular sectors that they mobilized for votes, moral instruction, and electoral violence. Elites, however, were also pressured by increasingly independent labor movements—which in urban areas included a strong core of domestic servants and market women.

At the level of urban space, this era of liberal state making was also characterized by ongoing struggle over public and popular space, culture, and economy. In Cochabamba, the most critical battle was waged around *chicherías,* which were gradually excluded from the center of the city—a symbol of power.[10] More generally, elites sought to transform and suppress popular festivals, simultaneously promoting civic ones designed to "solemnize" such celebrations and awaken the "spirit of the people, accustoming them to more dignified spectacles."[11]

Civilizing and "dignifying" the plebe was clearly common motivation for various organizations to be involved in the Heroínas celebration and monument. From its inception in 1912, the elite-led Heroínas festival was a "ritual of rule,"[12] a means both to cultivate common symbols and sentiments and to dignify the urban popular sectors zealously summoned to participate. But the extended conflict over the monument also reveals points of tension. Certainly the monument became a kind of political weapon as elite divisions deepened in the early twentieth century. The icon also attests to regionalist strife: the Heroínas celebration could be read as the protest of a marginalized region against a centralizing state; the festival lavishly exhibited regional history and culture, calling attention to Cochabamba's central role in the formation of the Bolivian nation-state. Further, the project was marked by disputes over women's role in the national past (and present)—especially when oligarchic women began to press for a more gendered celebration in the 1920s. The story of the monument and its long-delayed inauguration thus points to the complex ways disputes over gender, race, and class together shaped the cultural dynamics of liberal state making.

Existing data indicates that a project to honor the Heroínas was first conceived in 1912, the centennial of the 1812 battle. The work was initiated by the Comité Ejecutivo de las Fiestas del Centenario de 1912, which grouped together "with preference the descendants of Esteban Arze and other independence leaders"[13] and was presided by Sara Salamanca, wife of the prominent Cochabamba landlord and future president, Daniel Salamanca. Among the many elements of the celebration this committee planned, one key moment was the official inauguration of a monument already established in 1910, on the highest, most meaningful point of Cochabamba's historic Colina de San Sebastián, the Coronilla. This first monument, the *obelisco escolar,* had been modeled on an obelisk recommended by Nataniel Aguirre in his 1885 novel, *Juan de la Rosa.* In recommending its creation, an 1893 pamphlet detailed the Heroínas battle in the context of a discussion of the four "bloodiest battles of the war for independence."[14] The 1910–12 monument was designed to commemorate Cochabamba's independence war heroes in general; it did not single out the Heroínas but claimed them as part of a regional tradition, one sign of Cochabamba's peculiarly patriotic past. In contrast, the 1926 statue was made specifically by and about women. The 1912 centennial was characterized in press reports as a dazzling display of social and regional unity, but the 1926 Heroínas monument sparked controversy.[15]

In Aguirre's *Juan de la Rosa,* the narrator suggests a simple monument to reflect the heroic spirit of the Heroínas: a canon, an harquebus, and a stone column. But the 1926 monument does much more than what is explicitly advocated in the novel: it takes the story literally and reproduces the battle fought by women and led by a blind grandmother brandishing her cane. This design, moreover, was selected from two possible proposals. The other alternative would have represented "the defense of the heroines; and in the middle the symbolic figure of Faith, supporting a mortally-injured woman and whose left hand is pointing out to her the statue of the Sacred Heart."[16] It is not entirely clear if the representation of the "defense of the heroines" would have differed in the two models, nor are the details of the decision-making process available. But it is obvious that the alternative design differed significantly from the one chosen because it includes the symbols of sacrifice and Faith. The image selected emphasizes the battle itself, and although it includes signs of renunciation, it accentuates more aggressive, fighting poses. It privileges the figures of the grandmother and her granddaughter, Clara, clamoring for protection at her knees. Attached to the base of the monument, three bronze scenes from Aguirre's novel further illustrate the valor of the grandmother and the market women. High above them hovers a prominent statue of Christ.

In contrast to the 1910 monument, the 1926 statue was a strictly private initiative that had to struggle for municipal support and approval. With backing at key junctures from the national government and private sponsors, the fund-raising for the project, although difficult, seems to have proceeded apace. Just when the monument was finally to be completed, however, in January 1925—in time for Bolivia's centennial that August—the organizing committee faced perhaps its most serious obstacle: the municipality declined its wish to situate the statue on the Colina de San Sebastián. The organizers wanted to place the monument at the very top of the Colina, the Coronilla, where it would necessarily replace the 1910 obelisco escolar, which honored both male and female, elite and subaltern independence fighters of Cochabamba. In 1924, the women of the committee began to make appeals to the municipal council to "see whether they could obtain the transfer of the obelisk to another space since they believed that the Coronilla was the most adequate for the Monument to the Heroínas."[17] In January 1925, however, Sara Salamanca received a letter informing her that the council had decided the monument should occupy not the Coronilla but what had previously been the Plaza de Toros,[18] on the lower side of the historic site, where bullfights were (infrequently) held.[19] The Plaza de Toros was also much closer to the disorderly maze of markets, chicherías, mestizo-cholo residences and workshops that encompassed the hill.[20]

As the Heroínas monument neared completion, an intense debate arose over the women's proposal to move the 1910 obelisk from the Coronilla so the Heroínas monument could occupy the highest, most meaningful point. The Cochabamba newspaper El Heraldo published texts objecting that the monument privileged the Heroínas, "as if the virile people in mass" would not have made the same sacrifice,[21] or that it depicted all of the women who perished on the colina as "indias and cholas."[22] One article criticized the exclusive reference to the 1812 battle; the first monument (the 1910 obelisk) was considered more representative because it commemorated "bellicose *actions* and multiple traditions of Cochabamba's glory," including the interventions by both anonymous and well-known heroines.[23] There were even accusations that the women had tried to destroy the obelisk.[24] Finally, some objected that the icon had a more "religious than patriotic character."[25] Despite strong opposition to the Heroínas monument, no one fully dismissed the project, yet critics continued to object to the transfer of the obelisk. In the end, the question was which of the two commemorative works embodied the regional and national spirit, and thus belonged at the very top of the historic hill.

If the opposition was straightforward in delineating its position, Salamanca's motivations in struggling to create the 1926 monument are more ambiguous. In her correspondence, she principally linked the project with patriotism, religion, and a kind of grandness; she said, for example, that the monument would be "without dispute the best in the city" and perhaps in the entire republic. She also stressed women's role in the commemorative project and claimed that the 1812 battle had been the "most heroic and abnegated of independence war actions."[26] Although she privileged the Heroínas, Salamanca nevertheless rarely and only subtly referred to their class and cultural identity. Still, while local elites rejected both gender and ethnic referents of the monument, she did seem to believe that the *hijas del pueblo* (the cholas) had played the principal role in the 1812 battle, particularly the association of *chifleras*,[27] and thus that the monument should represent the mestiza market women.

If race and class were main lines of contention, the controversial aura of the Heroínas monument was also heightened by the burgeoning activism of Bolivia's first elite feminist associations, created in the twenties. There is no evidence that Salamanca was connected with Bolivia's most prominent women's organization of the time, the Ateneo Femenino, but as cofounder of a "society to protect the poor," La Olla del Pobre, she was certainly immersed in the charitable work that typified feminist activity of the era and may have viewed the Heroínas project in line with such protectionist endeavors. In a general sense, the kinds of social intervention characteristic of early twentieth-century feminism both valorized the civilizing role of motherhood and demanded respect and protection for mothers and families. In turn, this work could provide a bridge to the public for elite women.[28]

Although the controversy over the Heroínas monument seemed to be based on and to generate competing historical narratives, the missives exchanged between the municipality and the organizing committee regarding the *space* the monument should occupy also reveal a kind of affinity regarding the civic objective of the new icon. The Plaza de Toros, the site recommended by the municipality, could be easily identified as a popular or marginal space. The Coronilla, which the women preferred, could be attributed, on the other hand, with great historic significance as the site of battles that had contributed to and culminated in the formation of the Bolivian nation-state—from the 1730s tax revolt led by the mestizo Alejo Calatayud to the women's 1812 battle. In one plea, it was suggested that in situating the monument near the "ruinosa plaza taurina," which was referred to as a reminder of the "barbarie civilizada," a magnificent plaza could be created on this northern plane.[29] If it was thus reasoned that the symbol would transform the space, the women instead seemed to fear the space would make the meaning: perhaps the Plaza de Toros would suggest a link between the monument and the "barbaric" customs of the mestizo plebe, diverting attention from the civic intentions invested in the monument. Naturally, the more straightforward question of visibility also mattered: the desire to capture and control the most central and legitimate historical message.[30]

The monument for the Heroínas approached completion at a particularly significant if potentially volatile moment: the centennial of the Bolivian nation, which coincided with the 1925 presidential elections and the convocation of Bolivia's Second Workers' Congress at Oruro, a sign of the growing strength of organized labor.[31] The advent of the centennial itself intensified struggles over city space as elites sought to create an idealized and "civilized" image for the international gaze.[32] In La Paz, where the culminating aspects of the festivities were slated to take place, all streets were to be repaved and houses painted the color of cement or pearl-gray.[33] But undoubtedly the most forceful measure enacted was a centennial-year decree prohibiting Indians from entering La Paz's main plaza and seat of government. Although it is not known what import this particular ordinance had in Cochabamba, Indians were periodically denied entrance to the city's central plaza even in this culturally fluid, mestizo region—probably precisely on such occasions as the centennial.[34]

At this volatile political moment, oligarchic elites—who competed to control and contain the voice and votes of the plebe—could conflate the interventions, demands, and pressures of emerging women's and labor movements. One news article, for example, associated Sara Salamanca with the risks of women's political incursions, asserting a link between "the distinguished matron" and the political violence of the cholo plebe, especially the *matarifes* (butchers).[35] Not coincidentally, the article was published just when Sara Salamanca was struggling to bring the monument to completion against the objections of local critics; in January 1925, she had in fact written to a señora who had contributed to the 1912 centennial celebrations, requesting her assistance with fund-raising for the monument by initiating a collection among the so-called hijas del pueblo or cholas.[36] The negative press, moreover, coincided with Daniel Salamanca's campaign for the presidency; Sara Salamanca, standing for her husband—then presidential candidate for the Genuine Republicans (1925) and future president of the republic (1931–34)—became a target of attacks against him.[37] In sum, 1925 was a portentous year of heightened political and social tensions, both cause and consequence of maneuvers to reorder the city and its symbols, which quite literally forced certain people from the center.

Notwithstanding local criticisms of the monument and an inauspicious political climate, the Comité Ejecutivo led by Sara Salamanca in the end reached an agreement with the municipal council to move the 1910 obelisk so that the Heroínas monument could be placed on the highest point of the hill, as the committee had hoped to do from the beginning.[38] Despite this favorable conclusion, the delays and negotiations experienced by the committee reveal the complex web of interests that emerged and operated around the meaning and allocation of this contested urban space. The conflicts that arose suggest an underlying debate about history and identity, about which historical events and personages both the site and the monument should represent, and about who should ultimately decide.

Indeed, the extended conflict over the women's statue was perhaps only truly resolved when the monument was finally inaugurated in May 1926, at which point the newly elected Bolivian president Hernando Siles entered the picture, situating the icon squarely within the conflictive elite political arena.[39] Sara Salamanca, who had died six months previously, was honored on this highly publicized occasion. But the male dignitary in a sense replaced her as author, mapping his own meaning onto the icon. As in 1912, the press lauded the May 1926 celebration on the Coronilla, claiming more than twenty thousand people in attendance. Words were heard from Modesta Arauco, representative of the "First Section of the Market," and delegates of women's groups from Oruro and La Paz also spoke.[40] The president himself, arriving at the foot of the monument, received a "clamorous ovation" from the crowd and participated in customary kinds of activities after the ceremony, meeting with workers and local dignitaries.[41]

But the 1926 festivities for the Heroínas also included an unusual twist: the inauguration of the monument was linked with the coronation of Bolivia's premier poetess, Adela Zamudio. On the evening of May 27, the Social Club held a soiree in its salons to honor the president, his wife, and the poet Zamudio; on May 28, the poet was crowned in the Teatro Achá, located in the center of Cochabamba just off the main plaza.[42] Though Zamudio was Bolivia's pioneering and perhaps most radical feminist, the coronation—attended by some of the nation's most renowned intellectuals—above all called attention to her cultural accomplishments and sheer brilliance. As one well-known writer later observed, Cochabamba's major newspapers paid more attention to the coronation than to any other aspect of the presidential visit.[43] Indeed, the inauguration ceremony and the coronation were so closely linked that Zamudio could easily have been perceived as the central figure—heroine—of the three-day festivities. As the coronation thus diverted attention from the mestiza market women represented high on the city's historic hill, the monument could be read as an image of Cochabamba's distinguished women—as opponents had wished.

Cochabamba elites opposed the representation of their independence war heroes as Heroínas only; the region's heroic past could not be portrayed as the action or glory of women alone. But their deepest objection was that Indias and cholas personify the regional (national) traditions. The conflict over Cochabamba's statue of women wasn't exclusively about gender; it was about the kind of nation women in this context could represent: an unruly mestizo plebe or a poetic, intellectual, civilized, and cultured elite.

Although the Heroínas monument was finally accepted and inaugurated with great fanfare, the orchestration of the events attached to the unveiling diverted attention away from the bronze mestiza market women who had managed to occupy the very top of Cochabamba's most historic hill. In addition to the coronation of Adela Zamudio, the inauguration coincided with the installation of Cochabamba's Veinte-cinco de Mayo market,[44] the city's finest, most modern commercial space reputedly styled by French designers and complete with decorative iron work and marble tables for meat sales.[45] A kind of compromise had been struck. The prominent image of market women—meticulously modeled on the ragged, Quechua-speaking vendors of Nataniel Aguirre's *Juan de la Rosa*—was recontextualized and balanced with references to a cultured class, signs of progress and modernity. The oligarchy would not draw inspiration from anonymous campesinas and urban mestizas alone; instead, their muse was an acclaimed, lettered woman, a poet.

Mestiza Protagonists in Villarroel's Mother's Day

A deep, fundamental connection between Cochabamba's mestiza market women, Mother's Day, and the Bolivian nation was forged only in the 1940s under the auspices of the populist-military president, Gualberto Villarroel. In turn-of-century commemorations for heroes and heroines of Cochabamba's most celebrated independence war battles, subtle references only occasionally linked the May 27 heroines of San Sebastián with the Mother, and an explicit commemoration of Mother's Day was decreed in 1927 by the Bolivian government for May 27, to be celebrated in all schools. But in 1944 Villarroel's populist regime (1943–46) declared this "homage" to the Mother a national holiday.[46] During the 1940s, moreover, Aguirre's *Juan de la Rosa* began to be incorporated into Bolivia's secondary-school curriculum.[47] In the new era of populist pacts, the mestiza market women of the novel became national protagonists.

At a moment of precarious consolidation, Villarroel's well-publicized support for the Heroínas and Mother's Day marked a politically strategic move by his government toward particular corporate entities, especially urban labor. But his support for the Heroínas parade also had deeper ideological significance. The populist performance, like the president's public discourse, linked social rights with motherhood, patriotism, honor, and the nation. Oligarchic regimes of the twenties had at times invoked the family and private life, but after Bolivia's devastating loss to Paraguay and the profound social upheavals of the Chaco War era (1932–35), military-socialist and populist governments put the family and morality at the very center of political discourse. In the late 1930s, military socialists passed laws to protect working mothers and families that organized labor had been demanding since the 1920s; stipulated an interventionist state responsible for providing work or unemployment compensation to all citizens; and began to address the long-standing political demands of bourgeois women. These governments passed laws expanding women's civil rights, initially proposed in 1925, and approved a highly controversial measure declaring the legal equality of "natural" and legitimate children.[48]

The Villarroel regime took further steps to liberalize family law and expand women's political rights. Its 1945 Constitution essentially replicated the military socialists' 1938 charter, but also granted literate women the vote in municipal elections, bringing some mestizas into the electorate—among them necessarily small-scale merchants. The Villarroel Constitution, furthermore, gave concubinage the status of marriage. This controversial measure brought working-class families more fully within the regulatory reach of the state—just as it granted honor and potentially greater economic security to poor women.[49] Finally, the Villarroel regime made the mestizas emblems of the nation, thus redeeming them.

Under Villarroel, Heroínas-Mother's Day staged a nationalist myth of cultural and political integration rooted in Nataniel Aguirre's 1885 story of Cochabamba, mestiza heroism, and the nation's historical origins. The Heroínas and Mother's Day parade, diffused by various media throughout the nation, would inspire sentimental and moral investment in the patria. Still, this script wasn't Villarroel's alone. The mestiza market women became national symbols as a result of the interaction between the local aims of small-scale merchants and the national agenda of a populist military facing political challenges from left and right.

As in the 1920s, the key reference for the new Mother's Day celebration was the sacrificial battle led by the blind grandmother in Aguirre's *Juan de la Rosa,* but the organization of the holiday changed hands. In the 1940s, the Heroínas parade was no longer convened by elite patriotic associations. Instead, the Hijas del Pueblo, a mutual aid society of market vendors, emerged as the principal spokesperson for the event. One highlight of the 1944 celebration was the coronation of the queen of the Hijas del Pueblo at a *verbena popular* (popular soirée) in the working-class neighborhood Cara-Cota.[50] In 1926, a poet had been crowned at the Heroínas celebration; in the 1940s, the queen was instead a market vendor.

The Hijas del Pueblo was originally established in 1923 by vendors in Cochabamba's Veinte-cinco de Mayo market, and grouped together *arroceras* (rice sellers), chifleras, and *mañazas* (meat sellers) all cholas or hijas del pueblo. Its primary objective was to provide mutual assistance to its members and charitable service; the organization claimed a civic, apolitical status. Especially in the 1940s, the group participated actively in civic processions, wearing a special uniform—blue *polleras* (skirts)—it had adopted for all such public appearances. But it was also established to organize against "abuses of authority." Like associations of market women in La Paz, the formation of the group was motivated by the expulsion of sellers from their *puestos de venta* (vendors' stands) and by increases in the price of renting a stand. The original spark for the Cochabamba organization was a proposed 1923 municipal ordinance to raise the price of stalls in the Mercado Central or to evict sellers altogether. The initial organizing effort produced a great uproar in the market, which led to the intervention of the police and the detention of several vendors.[51]

Little is known about the internal structure of the Hijas del Pueblo, and it is unclear if the original 1923 group had outside support from women's groups or the church, as it did in the 1940s. During the Chaco War, the organization dispersed and was essentially disbanded. In the late 1930s, it was reestablished, bringing together the principal vendors of the Veinte-siete de Mayo and Veinte-cinco de Mayo markets, which were located in the center of Cochabamba and which likely catered to an elite clientele.[52] The principal institutional affiliations of the association in this period were the church and the military;[53] it had no formal connections with organized labor. The Hijas clearly had widespread support, boasting six hundred members of the "popular classes" in 1944.[54]

Villarroel's extensive backing of the Hijas' Heroínas Day parade was surely linked with the regime's efforts to cultivate support among urban mestizo cholos who comprised the labor movement—the regime's weakest link. Isolated from international supporters and besieged by internal opposition from mineowners and the right, Villarroel sought to develop new sources of popular support in the months after his December 1943 coup.[55] Principally, the regime promoted the increasingly powerful mine workers, granting recognition to their national federation—the Federación Sindical de Trabajadores Mineros Bolivianos (FSTMB) in June 1944. But it also courted urban labor, with much less success. The principal party associated with labor organizations during the 1940s was not the Nationalist Revolutionary Movement (MNR), Villarroel's chief ally, but the Party of the Revolutionary Left (PIR), which enjoyed great support among Cochabamba's urban workers.[56] It is plausible to think that the Villarroel regime courted the Hijas, which was not affiliated with the PIR-associated labor federation, as part of its strategy to create an alternative labor movement independent of the PIR-led Federación Obrera Sindical (FOS). With the Heroínas celebration, the regime identified the market women as potential mediators between it and urban labor, in turn exhibiting its affinity with workers and the poor.[57]

But the regime's support for the Heroínas celebration also points to the special role gender played in populist state making: market women—one of the most autonomous sectors of the labor movement and critical providers of urban sustenance—were simultaneously well poised to pressure the regime and to be incorporated by it. In the post–Chaco War juncture, demands for social and political reforms from both bourgeois and working women intensified—partly because the war had greatly enhanced women's economic participation and importance, partly because of the renewed force of labor movements in general. Further, not all women's unions were incorporated by the PIR-led labor movement, which opposed the Villarroel regime and swept up male unions in the postwar context.[58] Within urban labor, market women were thus the regime's most viable political target. The marketplace, moreover, was itself ripe symbolic terrain, signifying all that the populist state sought to offer: abundance, welfare, integration. This message had utmost importance as waves of rural strikes threatened to interrupt harvests, prevent transport of agricultural goods to urban markets, and destabilize prices—problems that were often blamed on mestiza merchants and that could potentially topple the precarious regime.[59]

The principal moments of the 1944 Heroínas celebration indeed focused attention on the market women grouped in the Hijas del Pueblo. The centerpiece of the 1944 Heroínas celebration was the *romería* (pilgrimage) to the Coronilla led by the Hijas del Pueblo on the morning of May 27. Sandwiched between a "Jura de la Bandera de los Premilitares en el Monumento a Bolívar" and a lunch for the "Guarnición en la Escuela de Armas," the romería filled a two-and-a-half-hour slot that culminated in a ten o'clock mass for the Virgen de las Mercedes.[60] The Hijas del Pueblo carried the image of the Virgin from the cathedral to the Coronilla, which was bedecked by Villarroel and his wife, several top-ranking government officials including the minister of defense and the minister of education, and two local authorities, the prefect and mayor.[61] By order of the mayor's office, all public markets in the city were closed.[62]

The founding president of the Hijas del Pueblo, Teodosia Sanzetenea de Terrazas, gave one of three principal speeches delivered on the Coronilla that May 27. Directing herself to the "Excelentísimo señor Presidente de la República," she claimed that the light of the Virgin Mercedes had guided Cochabamba's humble women in love and defense of the patria:

> One day like today, May 27, 1812, the humble Women of the Market desperately searched for men to defend Cochabamba from the claws of the tyrant Goyeneche. Together all anxious to defend the city, the women prayed that the Virgen of the Mercedes would illuminate their sentiments and give them courage for the defense; the Sacred Image of War opened in the hearts of the humble market women—Rice sellers, chifleras, butchers, grocers, and women of other trades—ardent love for the Fatherland and its liberty.[63]

Sanzetenea's words were not just stock, patriotic refrains but point to the market women's deep investment in this historic moment. In their 1941 founding statement, the Hijas vowed to "solemnize every year the heroic deed of May 27, 1812, as they [were] direct heirs."[64] Additionally, for Cochabamba's September 14 celebration, the association organized a float that authenticated the 1812 Heroínas battle.[65] In taking up the historical narrative publicized by the oligarchy, the Hijas thus substituted protagonists: they claimed themselves, market women, to be true descendants of the Heroínas, in turn asserting Cochabamba's mestizo-cholo origins.

In news articles of the forties, other interpretations of the 1812 battle continued to circulate alongside the Hijas' parade. Cochabamba's leading newspapers at times associated the hitherto anonymous Heroínas with the names of particular, illustrious women or with a more abstract mother figure. Nevertheless, the Hijas' version, which gave the name Heroínas to "the humble women of the market," succeeded in being that most broadly publicized by the regime. During the Villarroel presidency, the Cochabamba celebration was broadcast by radio so that it would reach homes throughout the republic.[66] The parade might be read, moreover, as an official reading of Aguirre's novel because its promulgation coincided with the incorporation of *Juan de la Rosa* into the secondary-school curriculum.

What was the Hijas' stake in this apparent alliance with Villarroel and municipal authorities? Rather than achieving full-scale incorporation, their organization gained a certain political clout and even autonomy.[67] Just after Villarroel's overthrow in 1946, a conflict regarding appointment of the *jefe de mercados* (director of markets) perhaps best illustrates the Hijas' gains and motivations.[68] Petitions, rallies, a butchers' strike, even street fights marked an intense struggle over this regulatory post—evidence of "profound popular anger."[69] One jefe, Augusto Tardio, had been charged with allowing a free reign for speculators and vending from the ground, corrupt deals between agents and vendors, and general disorganization of markets. The Hijas backed the reinstatement of another jefe, Guillermo Aldunate, acclaimed for order, price controls, hygiene, honesty, and concern for the public interest.[70] An anonymous letter added "insolence and vulgarity of the vendors" to the grievances,[71] and a note from "mothers and heads of households" decried abuses committed by providers of primary goods.[72] The Hijas themselves demanded a "resolution that satisfie[d] not only the aspirations of the Sociedad Hijas del Pueblo but the whole population"[73] and that resulted in fair prices for an "undernourished people."[74] For the ultimately triumphant supporters of Aldunate, the main problems were the price hikes and feigned shortages by meat sellers, tolerated by Tardio. According to Tardio, however, the issue was the end of patronage for other vendors; he claimed a group of arroceras had used the Hijas to denounce his own efforts to control prices—to suppress "personal favors to families that had previously been treated preferentially."[75] For spokespersons on both sides, the question was which vendors a particular jefe favored.

The populist regime took the Hijas' rendition of the 1812 battle for its own legitimizing myth, evidence of its alliance with the people. In the process the Hijas perhaps became an arm of the municipality, helping to ensure order, hygiene, and stable prices in the marketplace. Yet the arrangement was reciprocal. Price controls might be acceptable, but also a market the Hijas themselves valued—one that had order, hygiene, and protection for vendors with established stalls. A primary objective for the Hijas del Pueblo, moreover, was the ritual itself. One aspect not mentioned in news reports is the extent to which local authorities and Aldunate himself backed the Hijas in their celebration of the Heroínas, requiring all vendors to attend the romería and offering support for a great fiesta in the market.[76] The market women's procession to the Coronilla predated the populist celebra-

230   *Laura Gotkowitz*

tion, but involvement by Villarroel, the military, and the jefe de mercados made it a much grander commemoration. The populist state swallowed up popular culture, but the state-directed holiday was also a chance to reconstitute local traditions and the networks of power on which they were based.[77]

Conclusion

Rather than a straightforward manifestation of "official" or "popular" culture, public rituals like the Heroínas march are uneven processes, halting and fissured sites and rites of subjection and contestation simultaneously.[78] The 1940s Heroínas festival enacted an alliance between populists and mestiza cholas. The mestizas were situated as Villarroel's urban allies, mediators, and potential integrators; incorporated into the national pantheon as a new political and symbolic force, they claimed their own honor and civic rights.[79] In Cochabamba's complexly stratified commercial terrain, the Hijas del Pueblo also must have affirmed their social standing at such public ceremonies. But the Mother's Day parade they led was also Villarroel's story. The mestiza market women no longer stood for the acclaimed women the oligarchy declared to be Cochabamba's heroines, yet the heroines were no longer rebels. Instead, the populist parade represented Cochabamba mestizas as patriotic mothers and loyal clients of the populist state.

In the populist context of multiclass coalitions, reformist leaders publicized the mestiza merchants' revisionist history, which valorized Cochabamba's mestizo-cholo origins. The mestizos/as had been at best the object of an ambivalent gaze in the oligarchy's nation. In the formative decade of the forties, which witnessed the rise of mestizo middle sectors and the incorporation of previously excluded political actors, the martyred mestizas of Aguirre's novel became protagonists of Bolivia's national history, its founding mothers. Yet the narrative the mestizas then protagonized had been and in many respects still was an oligarchic story based on ambivalent identification, ambiguous union, limited citizenship. The populist state commodified and domesticated the mestiza heroines, turning them into symbolic mothers and patriotic images of valor and abnegation to be distributed in all the nation's schools. On the other hand, the mestizas were clearly more than "living symbols," decorative signs of national unity.[80]

They performed the story, taking Cochabamba's central arteries and its most historic, foundational space.

Notes

I thank Rossana Barragán, Katherine Bliss, Elizabeth Dore, Brooke Larson, Laurie Milner, Janet Morford, Michela Pentimalli, Seemin Qayum, and Gustavo Rodríguez for their insightful comments and suggestions on earlier drafts. Research was supported by the Social Science Research Council and the American Council of Learned Societies, with funds provided by the Mellon and Ford foundations, and the Swarthmore College Research Fund. My thanks also go to Anna Chirinos for assistance with research. An earlier version was published in *El siglo XIX: Bolivia y América Latina,* ed. Rossana Barragán, Dora Cajías, and Seemin Qayum (La Paz: IFEA and Historias, 1997), 701–16.

1   Most literally, *mestiza(o)* and *chola(o)* refer to individuals of mixed race, but *cholo* in general connotes greater proximity to Indianness. In early-twentieth-century Bolivia, they were derogatory terms associated with a "dangerous" urban plebe and "predatory" rural elites. See Brooke Larson, "Andean Communities, Political Cultures, and Markets: The Changing Contours of a Field," in *Ethnicity, Markets, and Migration in the Andes: At the Crossroads of History and Anthropology,* ed. Brooke Larson and Olivia Harris, with Enrique Tandeter (Durham, N.C.: Duke University Press, 1995), 5–53, particularly 35–38; and Rossana Barragán, "Identidades indias y mestizas: Una intervención al debate," *Autodeterminación* 10 (1992): 17–44.

2   Nataniel Aguirre, *Juan de la Rosa* (1885, Cochabamba: Los Tiempos / Los Amigos del Libro, 1987), 241–56. All translations are mine.

3   Eric Hobsbawm and Terence Ranger, eds., *The Invention of Tradition* (Cambridge: Cambridge University Press, 1983). On Latin America and Bolivia, see William H. Beezley, Cheryl English Martin, and William French, eds., *Rituals of Rule, Rituals of Resistance: Public Celebrations and Popular Culture in Mexico* (Wilmington, Del.: Scholarly Resources, 1994); and Gustavo Rodríguez, "Fiestas, poder, y espacio urbano en Cochabamba (1880–1923)," *Siglo XIX, Revista de Historia* 13 (1993): 95–118.

4   See Eric Van Young, "Conclusion: The State as Vampire — Hegemonic Projects, Public Ritual, and Popular Culture in Mexico, 1600–1990," in Beezley, Martin, and French, eds., *Rituals of Rule,* 343–74. On monuments as official history, see Barbara A. Tenenbaum, "Streetwise History: The Paseo de la Reforma and the Porfirian State, 1876–1910," in ibid., 127–50; and Mauricio Tenorio Trillo, "1910 Mexico City: Space and Nation in the City of the *Centenario,*" *Journal of Latin American Studies* 28 (1996): 75–104.

5 On the gendered logics of Latin America's national novels, see Doris Sommer, "Irresistible Romance: The Foundational Fictions of Latin America," in *Nation and Narration,* ed. Homi K. Bhabha (London: Routledge, 1990), 71–98; Francine Masiello, *Between Civilization and Barbarism: Women, Nation, and Literary Culture in Modern Argentina* (Lincoln: University of Nebraska Press, 1992); and Julie Skurski, "The Ambiguities of Authenticity in Latin America: *Doña Bárbara* and the Construction of National Identity," *Poetics Today* 15, no. 4 (1994): 59–81.

6 Aguirre, *Juan de la Rosa,* 186–87.

7 Gender reforms under liberal and populist regimes were nevertheless rooted in rather similar logics. See Maxine Molyneux's chapter in part 1 of this volume.

8 Tenorio Trillo, "1910 Mexico City," 89.

9 See Van Young, "The State as Vampire," 367–68; Tristan Platt, "Simón Bolívar, the Sun of Justice and the Amerindian Virgin: Andean Conceptions of the *Patria* in Nineteenth-Century Potosí," *Journal of Latin American Studies* 25, part 1 (1993), 159–85, in particular 166; Ana María Alonso, "The Effects of Truth: Re-Presentations of the Past and the Imagining of Community," *Journal of Historical Sociology* 1, no. 1 (1988): 33–57, 44–45 cited; and Angel Rama, *La Ciudad Letrada* (Hanover: Ediciones del Norte, 1984), 90–92.

10 *Chicherías* are places where maize beer is sold and consumed. Gustavo Rodríguez and Humberto Solares, *Sociedad oligárquica: Chicha y cultura popular* (Cochabamba: Editorial Serrano, 1990).

11 *Fiesta patriótica dedicada a los héroes de Cochabamba* (Cochabamba: Imprenta del Siglo, 1876), 1. See also Rodríguez, "Fiestas, poder, y espacio urbano."

12 Beezley, Martin, and French, eds., *Rituals of Rule.*

13 David Alvéstegui, *Salamanca: Su gravitación sobre el destino de Bolivia,* 3 vols. (La Paz: Talleres Gráficos Bolivianos, 1958), 2:432.

14 *Discurso pronunciado por el presidente del H. Concejo Municipal, D. Luís Frías, al colocar la primera piedra del monumento del 14 de Septiembre de 1810* (Cochabamba: Imprenta El Heraldo, 1893).

15 On the 1912 centennial celebrations, see "Resumen de las fiestas," *El Heraldo,* 29 May 1912, 3; and "La gran romería," *El Ferrocarril,* 29 May 1912, 2.

16 Raquel Salamanca U. de Gumucio, ed., *Sara Ugarte de Salamanca y el monumento a las Heroínas de la Coronilla* (Cochabamba: Ed. Canelas, 1975), 39.

17 Ibid., 25.

18 Ibid.

19 Marie Robinson Wright, *Bolivia: The Central Highway of South America, A Land of Rich Resources and Varied Interest* (Philadelphia: George Barrie and Sons, 1907), 284.

20 See Humberto Solares, *Historia, espacio, y sociedad, Cochabamba 1550–1950: Formación, crisis, y desarrollo de su proceso urbano,* 2 vols. (Cochabamba: Editorial Serrano, 1990), 1:79–80.

21 "El monumento del cerro de San Sebastián debe ser conservado a todo trance, Es conmemorativo de las glorias de Cochabamba," *El Heraldo,* 27 December 1924, 2.

22 "Más sobre el monumento del cerro de San Sebastián," part 2, *El Heraldo,* 10 January 1925, 2.

23 Ibid., my emphasis. See also "Sobre el monumento de la Colina histórica," *El Republicano,* 9 July 1925, 1; and "Sobre el monumento de la Colina histórica," part 2, *El Republicano,* 10 July 1925.

24 Ibid., 25–26.

25 "El monumento a las Heroínas no debió ser religioso," *El Heraldo,* 29 January 1925, 2.

26 Salamanca, *Sara Ugarte,* 24.

27 See the letter to a potential contributor reproduced in Salamanca, *Sara Ugarte,* 34. Chifleras sold fabric, lace, buttons, and other materials used to make clothing.

28 See Asunción Lavrin, *Women, Feminism, and Social Change in Argentina, Chile, and Uruguay, 1890–1940* (Lincoln: University of Nebraska Press, 1995).

29 "El monumento del cerro de San Sebastián debe ser conservado a todo trance," *El Heraldo,* 27 December 1924, 2.

30 See Alonso, "The Effects of Truth."

31 James Dunkerley, *Orígenes del poder militar en Bolivia: Historia del ejército, 1879–1935* (La Paz: Quipus, 1987), 109–37; Herbert Klein, *Parties and Political Change in Bolivia, 1880–1952* (Cambridge: Cambridge University Press, 1969).

32 On the Mexican centennial as the creation of an ideal city, see Tenorio Trillo, "1910 Mexico City."

33 Report on "Celebration of Centennial of Bolivian Independence," 18 March 1925, 2, RG 59, 824.415 / 15 and 824.415 / 6–29, U.S. National Archives, Washington, D.C.

34 Ricardo Azogue O., Gustavo Rodríguez O., and Humberto Solares S., "Proceso histórico de la constitución de Cochabamba," part 1, *Opinion / IESE, Economía y Sociedad,* 3 January 1988, 6.

35 Cited in "Las infames calumnias de la prensa oficial: Justificación necesaria," *El Republicano,* 26 May 1925, 3.

36 Salamanca, *Sara Ugarte,* 34.

37 See Alvéstegui, *Salamanca,* 423–38.

38 Salamanca, *Sara Ugarte,* 37.

39 The first section of the monument was delivered on 7 August 1925. "Programa de las fiestas patrias," *El Republicano,* 1 August 1925, 3.

40 *El Heraldo,* 1 June 1926, 2.

41 "Las fiestas del 27 y 28 de Mayo, grandes manifestaciones a S.E.," *El Heraldo,* 31 May 1926, 2.

42 "Sarao," *El Republicano,* 26 May 1926, 4. See also Augusto Guzmán, *Adela Zamudio: Biografía de una mujer ilustre* (1955; reprint, La Paz: Juventud, 1988), 151–56.

43 Guzmán, *Adela Zamudio,* 152.

44 See "Programa general de festejos con motivo del CXIV aniversario," *El Co-*

mercio, 19 May 1926, 3. On the history of this market and its contemporary social dynamics, see Ruth Marina Mendoza H., "El Mercado 25 de Mayo como espacio comunicacional" (Licenciatura thesis, Universidad Privada del Valle, Facultad de Ciencias Sociales y Administrativas, 1994).

45 Mendoza H., "El Mercado 25 de Mayo," 28–29.

46 See *Anuario Administrativo de 1944* (La Paz: Edición Oficial), 302–3; and *Anuario Administrativo de 1927* (La Paz: Litografías e Imprentas Unidas).

47 Alba María Paz Soldán, "Narradores y nación en la novela *Juan de la Rosa,* de Nataniel Aguirre," *Revista Iberoamericana* 52, no. 134 (1986), 29–52, in particular 29–30.

48 See Klein, *Parties and Political Change,* 235–287; and Gloria Ardaya, *Política sin rostro: Mujeres en Bolivia* (Caracas: Editorial Nueva Sociedad, 1989), 26–28.

49 On support for the measure among La Paz market women, see Ineke Dibbits et al., *Polleras libertarias: Federación Obrera Femenina, 1927–1965* (La Paz: Tahipamu / Hisbol, 1986), 55.

50 "Actos que se desarrollarán durante la visita del presidente provisorio," *El País,* 26 May 1944.

51 Jael Bueno, "La sociedad 'Hijas del Pueblo,' orígenes y desarrollo," *Nosotras / Opinión,* 4–5, and "La mujer cochabambina, En las primeras décadas del Siglo XX," *Nosotras / Opinión.* On market women in La Paz, see Dibbits et al., *Polleras libertarias;* Zulema Lehm A. and Silvia Rivera C., *Los artesanos libertarios y la ética del trabajo* (La Paz: THOA, 1988); and Ximena Medinaceli, *Alternando la rutina: Mujeres en las ciudades de Bolivia, 1920–1930* (La Paz: CIDEM, 1989.)

52 In 1936, Cochabamba's market vendors formed the Sindicato de Comerciantes Minoristas under the military socialist's obligatory sindicalization decree, but the Hijas del Pueblo did not join. Bueno, "Sociedad 'Hijas,' " 4–5.

53 On the connection between the Hijas and Catholic Action, see Raimundo Grigoriu Sánchez de Lozada, "Bolivia," in *El catolicismo contemporaneo en Hispanoamérica,* ed. Richard Pattee (Buenos Aires: Editorial Fides, 1951), 93.

54 "No hubo ayer misa de Campaña debiendo efectuarse recién mañana," *El Imparcial,* 26 May 1944, 4.

55 Lawrence Whitehead, "Bolivia Since 1930," in *Cambridge History of Latin America,* ed. Leslie Bethell (Cambridge: Cambridge University Press, 1991), 8:530.

56 See Jael Bueno, Jesús Mendoza, and Gustavo Rodríguez, "Los trabajadores cochabambinos," *Opinión / IESE, Estudios Sociales,* 17 January 1989.

57 In general, Cochabamba's sindicalist movement remained closely tied to the PIR, which was a key player in the movement that overthrew Villarroel in July 1946. Bueno, Mendoza, and Rodríguez, "Los trabajadores cochabambinos," 6. On the overthrow of Villarroel, see Klein, *Parties and Political Change,* 381–82; and Lawrence Whitehead, "Bolivia," in *Latin America Between the Second World War and the Cold War, 1944–1948,* ed. Leslie Bethell and Ian Roxborough (Cambridge: Cambridge University Press, 1992), 120–46.

58 Lehm and Rivera, *Los artesanos libertarios*, 61–80; Ardaya, *Política sin rostro*.

59 On urban discontent, see Klein, *Parties and Political Change;* and Lehm and Rivera, *Los artesanos libertarios*, 75–80.

60 "Hoy habrá misa de Campaña," *El Imparcial*, 25 May 1944, 8; "No hubo ayer misa de Campaña debiendo efectuarse recién mañana," *El Imparcial*, 26 May 1944, 4.

61 "Notas de sociedad," *El País*, 28 May 1944, 8.

62 "Mañana permanecerán cerrados los mercados," *El Imparcial*, 26 May 1944, 1.

63 "Con celo patriótico actuaron ayer las socias de 'Las Hijas del Pueblo,'" *El País*, 28 May 1944, 8. For a biography of Sanzetenea, see "El día de la madre," *El Imparcial*, 27 May 1947, 4.

64 *Actas de la Sociedad "Hijas del Pueblo 27 de Mayo,"* Primer Tomo, "Acta de Fundación," 25 May 1941. I am grateful to Alcira Patiño, honorary president of the Hijas del Pueblo, for sharing the *Actas* with me.

65 Ibid., "Asamblea general del 25 de Mayo de 1943."

66 "Hoy llegará procedente de Sucre, el Presidente Tcnl. Gualberto Villarroel con su Comitiva," *El País*, 26 May 1945, 4.

67 This parallels the Chilean case as analyzed by Karin Rosemblatt in this volume.

68 On the conflict, see "Muchas razones le asisten al alcalde municipal para destituir al actual jefe de mercados Augusto Tardio," *El Imparcial*, 19 January 1947, 4; "Será destituido el actual jefe de mercados," *Los Tiempos*, 19 January 1947, 1; and "Carta del jefe de mercados, levantando cargos infundados," *Los Tiempos*, 18 September 1946, 5.

69 "El pueblo se impuso ayer en el asunto de la jefatura de mercados," *El Imparcial*, 7 February 1947, 1; "Fue conjurada la carestia de carne," *El Imparcial*, 11 February 1947, 1; and "El pueblo pide la exoneración del actual jefe de mercados Augusto Tardio," *Los Tiempos*, 16 January 1947, 4. The strike was called by the FOS.

70 "El pueblo se impuso ayer en el asunto de la jefatura de mercados," *El Imparcial*, 7 February 1947, 1; and "Fue conjurada la carestia de carne," *El Imparcial*, 11 February 1947, 1.

71 "La administración de los mercados," *Los Tiempos*, 24 January 1947, 3.

72 "Una carta con motivo del nombramiento de jefe de mercados," *Los Tiempos*, 13 February 1947, 2.

73 "El pueblo pide la exoneración del actual jefe de mercados Augusto Tardio," *Los Tiempos*, 16 January 1947, 4.

74 "Las Hijas del Pueblo, realizaron una gran manifestación," *El Imparcial*, 12 February 1947, 1.

75 "El jefe de mercados ante una campaña interesada de prensa," *El País*, 17 January 1947, 5.

76 Interview, Alcira Patiño, Cochabamba, August 1998. Patiño's remarks refer to the 1960s and 1970s, when Aldunate required all vendors to attend the romería and helped support a great fiesta in the market. In all likelihood, Aldunate took similar measures during the Villarroel era.

77 See Gilbert Joseph and Daniel Nugent, "Popular Culture and State Formation in Revolutionary Mexico," in *Everyday Forms of State Formation: Revolution and the Negotiation of Rule in Modern Mexico,* ed. Gilbert Joseph and Daniel Nugent (Durham, N.C.: Duke University Press, 1994), 3–23, especially 17.

78 Philip Corrigan and Derek Sayer, *The Great Arch: English State Formation as Cultural Revolution* (New York: Blackwell, 1985); and Van Young, "The State as Vampire."

79 On parades as an assertion of civic rights, see Mary Ryan, "The American Parade: Representations of the Nineteenth-Century Social Order," in *The New Cultural History,* ed. Lynn Hunt (Berkeley: University of California Press, 1989), 131–53, in particular 137.

80 Ibid., 148–51.

Ann Varley

Women and the Home in

Mexican Family Law

The home is a space that both symbolizes and shapes gender relations. In this chapter, I analyze judicial definitions of "the marital home" in Mexican Supreme Court rulings on divorce cases brought on the grounds of abandonment of the marital home. I apply Ana María Alonso's arguments about the rationalization of patriarchy in nineteenth-century legal reforms to a change that took place in the 1950s in Supreme Court rulings on what constitutes the marital home.[1] This change rejected the practice of couples sharing accommodation and upheld the nuclear family as the ideal household form. I regard the ruling as evidence of state support for the modernization of patriarchy as described by Jean Franco and Steve Stern.[2] The judges' concern to free young wives from the authority of the older generation—and particularly of older women—may be construed as state support for the emergence of a supposedly benevolent, "paternalistic," and "rational" form of patriarchy.

The State, the Family, and Gender Relations in Mexico

In contrast to earlier interpretations that described the state as essentially good or bad for women, more recent approaches regard it "not [as] a unitary structure but [as] a differentiated set of institutions, agencies and discourses, and the product of a particular historical and political conjuncture."[3]

The state is a site of struggle where interests are actively constructed rather than fixed in advance.[4] Consequently, theorists now emphasize "practice and discourse" rather than institutions when discussing the state.[5] Women or other disadvantaged groups can sometimes benefit from state practice, but because states operate *within* society, they are permeated by gender inequalities: "they both influence gender relations and are influenced by them."[6]

State-gender relations need to be understood in the context of broader political imperatives. In Latin America, feminist scholars have argued, "heterosexual love and patriarchy in the domestic sphere" underpinned the consolidation of the nation-state.[7] In the "long, slow process" of nineteenth-century state formation, "the family was equated with the public good."[8] Because the family supposedly transcended ethnic, class, and regional differences, it offered an alternative, nonviolent basis for the emergence of a coherent national identity, creating "family order out of institutional chaos."[9]

Jean Franco argues that when the liberal intelligentsia concerned with nation building in Mexico reluctantly recognized their inability to establish an ethnically homogeneous nation, they opted instead for a "homogeneously modern nation."[10] Women were to receive a limited education to prepare them for their central role in modernizing family life and constructing the nation-state by teaching children patriotism and the work ethic. This role was not to undermine male authority because the husband was "the State's representative in the family, governing his wife and children."[11] Nor was education to undermine female commitment to the domestic sphere.[12] Women who went out to work were portrayed as "mannish or hairy-chested" in Porfirian Mexico.[13]

Liberal recipes for the modernization of the family are echoed by the postrevolutionary state's efforts to "remake the family . . . in the interests of nation building and development," as described by Mary Kay Vaughan.[14] After the revolution, the campaign to "create a new national soul" sought "to penetrate the home and the hearts and minds of men, women, and children" because " '[a]t the root of every social transformation has been and always will be the transformation of the home and the family.' "[15] The task was particularly difficult in the campesino household—regarded, in Alan Knight's words, as a "tenebrous den of vice and ignorance" by education officials in the frontline of the struggle for the allegiance of its members.[16]

Women had played an active role in the revolution of 1910–17, and a feminist movement had started to emerge in these years.[17] At the same time, however, as Ilene O'Malley has pointed out, machismo had been reinforced by the revolutionary obsession with virility. The upheaval had given lower-class men the chance to recover a manhood they had been denied by the *porfiriato,* but frustration with government failure to deliver the promised rewards of revolution led to an embittered form of machismo "manifested as alienation from politics and rejection of the father-figure model of the revolutionary hero."[18]

In the decades after the revolution, the government adopted policies that ran counter to "the traditional gender order," but these policies "subordinated women to the state's construction of a modern family."[19] Commitment to progressive measures was also contingent on political priorities. In the late 1930s, when the Frente Único pro Derechos de la Mujer gathered fifty thousand members to campaign for female suffrage, the government of Lázaro Cárdenas supported the necessary constitutional amendment until it realized that reform might damage the electoral fortunes of his chosen successor.[20] The postrevolutionary state's commitment to feminism was "distinctly ambivalent."[21]

It took until 1953 for Mexican women to gain the vote. By then, however, the state's promotion of economic development had contributed to social changes accompanying industrialization and urbanization that outstripped the effects of its cultural project.[22] As Steve Stern argues, one consequence of Mexico's transformation from a rural to an urban society was a rejection of forms of patriarchal power associated with the old order: "as hegemonic cultural discourse seized upon subaltern machismo as the symbol of a Mexican pathological inheritance, a form of masculinity to be transcended, new spaces and possibilities opened up for women."[23]

In popular cultural forms such as *libros semanales,* women were encouraged to seek different models of family relationships and a role in the paid labor force. These weekly publications invited women to see themselves as being harmed, as Jean Franco puts it, by "the plot of the old Mexico"—traditional machismo.[24] It was specifically the older generation of men whose influence women were to reject, as "the patriarchal biological father" was replaced by "the paternalistic father of the modernization discourse."[25]

Franco's arguments mostly address the way in which older men were portrayed: "In the modernization tale, it is the ingrained habits of the 'typical' Mexican—violence, machismo, and drunkenness—that have to be repudiated, and since men of the older generation do not seem likely to reform themselves, women must simply break away from the traditional family and embrace the work ethic."[26] She touches only in passing on women of the older generation, yet older women's role in the extended family has been described as reinforcing patriarchy.[27] The Supreme Court rulings discussed in this chapter would oppose this role, challenging the domination of young wives by their in-laws.

"Reinscribing" Patriarchy in Mexican Law

Studies of the gender implications of law in Latin America have concentrated on the legislation itself rather than on its judicial application.[28] In Mexico, a rich vein of research has explored court records from the colonial period onward, yet it has mostly focused on the stories behind the cases rather than judicial ideologies, which are equally important.[29] Rulings by the Supreme Court are not restricted to interpreting the law as it applies in specific cases: they can also define its meaning for wider purposes. Once five consecutive rulings to the same effect have been passed in judicial review cases, their interpretation of the legal point at issue becomes binding on all lower courts.[30]

Ana María Alonso has argued that one element of the modernization of patriarchy in Mexico was its "reinscription" in the law. The evidence for her argument comes from the criminalization of domestic violence in the 1871 Criminal Code (Código Penal). A husband's use of a certain degree of violence had previously been accepted by both church and state, and he had the right to kill his wife if he caught her committing adultery. Under the new Criminal Code, domestic violence was to be "penalized regardless of its severity" and penalties imposed for the murder of an adulterous wife.[31]

Alonso describes these changes as part of the liberals' efforts to substitute rational, democratic forms of legitimation for violence: "The redefinition of legitimate authority in the public sphere entailed a reciprocal transformation of authority in the domestic sphere. . . . Though liberals did not question a husband's right to govern his wife, they did redefine the basis of his authority: the subjection of women to man in marriage was to [be] predicated on the legal contract, the epitome of free will, reason and modernity, at odds with physical violence, a signifier of barbarism." Thus, "Purged of the chaos of violence, domestic patriarchy was reinscribed in law, the embodiment of universal reason and progress."[32] Domestic violence was reconstrued as the practice of *deviant* men.

Alonso also examines how the legislation was applied in Namiquipa, Chihuahua. The women who were most successful in gaining conviction of violent husbands were those who "abided by the norms and values of honorable femininity."[33] Thus, changes favoring (some) women can be construed as a "reinscription" of patriarchy in the law.

The terms of that inscription were the subject of further modernization, in family as well as in labor and criminal law.[34] In colonial family law, the subordination of women had been above all a subordination of married women, with widows and single women enjoying more rights than wives.[35] Reforms introduced in the Civil Code of 1870 and then of 1884 did not remove this disparity. Although widowed, separated, and single mothers were granted *patria potestad* (parental authority), the liberals' concern to increase individual freedom did not extend to married women.[36] They feared that giving husbands and wives equal authority would risk the "continual mutiny of the subjects against the established authority."[37] Their concern was primarily for *male* freedom, so inequality between husbands and wives even increased. Whereas infidelity by either spouse had previously been grounds for separation, men's adultery was now condoned except in certain (limited) circumstances. Insofar as the reforms reduced patriarchal control, then, they did so with regard to parental authority. Single adults—who, unless "emancipated," had previously been subject to their father's control until his death—were freed from the patria potestad at the age of twenty-one.[38]

Postrevolution legal reforms were described as a response to "the feminist movement" and the fact that "woman has ceased to be relegated exclusively to the home."[39] Absolute divorce was introduced by Venustiano Carranza in 1914. The 1917 Law of Family Relations, subsequently incorporated into the 1928 Civil Code, granted married women patria potestad and removed the requirement for wives to obey their husbands: "husband and wife shall enjoy equal authority and consideration within the home and shall therefore decide by mutual agreement on everything to do with the running of the home."[40]

Reforms were, nevertheless, limited. Husbands were still obliged to support their wives, and wives to live where their husband decided.[41] In addition, "the management of and responsibility for household work [*los trabajos propios del hogar*] shall be the concern of the wife."[42]

By the 1970s, the legal allocation of responsibility for housework to wives was regarded as so obvious an injustice that this article was one of several repealed in 1974 in anticipation of International Women's Year and the first United Nations' Conference on Women, held in Mexico City in 1975. (Because not all Mexican states adopted these reforms, however, the wife is still responsible for housework in one-quarter of them.)[43]

Twenty years before these reforms, the allocation of responsibility for household work to the wife had underpinned an important change in judicial understanding of the marital home. This change coincided with other legal actions to improve the status of women in Mexico—most obviously, the extension of suffrage in 1953, but also the repeal at the end of that year of the requirement that wives should live where their husbands decided. Spouses were now simply required to "live together in the marital home."[44] This reference was one of several in the Civil Code to *el domicilio* or *la casa conjugal* that were not accompanied by any definition of the concept. It was this absence of definition that was addressed by Supreme Court rulings.

The (Un)acceptability of Shared Housing

Judicial attitudes about the existence of a domicilio conjugal when accommodation was shared with relatives underwent a sea change in the 1950s.[45] Previously, the marital home was deemed to "exist not only when the house is dedicated exclusively to use by a single married couple, but also when the spouses live with other people."[46] Starting in 1954, however, a series of Supreme Court rulings denied the existence of a marital home when couples depended on others for their accommodation. For example, a man from Chiapas sought to divorce his teenage wife for abandoning his parents' home in Tuxtla Gutiérrez. The Court ruled that "It is not possible to give the name of 'marital home' to the house of the mother-in-law, or of third parties in general, where some husbands are accustomed to taking their wives to live as *arrimadas*."[47]

Arrimados are people living with someone else, particularly young couples living with the man's or woman's parents. It was this common practice that the Court began to find unacceptable in the 1950s. By 1961, the "thesis" making this interpretation of the law obligatory had been issued and remains in force today.[48] It has generally favored women protecting wives who leave their in-laws' home because of abuse by their husband or his relatives from being judged "guilty" of abandoning the marital home.

Women and the Home in Mexican Law   243

What was the meaning of this change in judicial interpretation? Why should Supreme Court judges (*ministros*) cease to recognize the sharing of parental accommodation as an acceptable arrangement for the marital home? They were not especially concerned about housing conditions or overcrowding. Indeed, a 1954 ruling explicitly acknowledged that residential options varied with social class. It was not the mere fact of couples sharing accommodation with parents that troubled the judges, but the social relations involved: "The existence of the marital home is not incompatible with living with relatives of the wife or the husband, as is a frequent occurrence amongst certain social classes in our country, *providing that the wife can exercise the rights granted to her by law,* such that in the house or in the rooms to which the couple are restricted she should be the only one to give orders or take decisions about the work to be carried out within the home." What was at issue was the wife's ability to exercise the authority to run the home. The danger to be avoided was that "[the wife who was] living with other people, even relatives, should be subject to their direction."[49]

In these statements, the judges had a specific relative in mind: the woman's mother-in-law. In ruling after ruling, accommodation was described as "the home of the [wife's] mother-in-law" *(suegra)* or "the home of the husband's mother."[50] Hence, "it is not possible to give the name of 'marital home' to the mother-in-law's home."[51] This wording reflects the circumstances in which the cases were brought: in only one was the existence of a marital home denied because the couple were living with the *woman's* mother.[52] It was not, however, because the man's mother was separated or widowed that the home was described as hers; the description was used even in cases where his father was also living there.

The rulings reveal that the home was treated as a feminine space. The judges' decisions on the marital home expressed a desire to assign that space to one, and only one, woman.

Wives' Opposition to Living with Their In-Laws

Court rulings reflected the concerns of the women who brought or contested these cases. The litigants' objectives in fighting the case mostly seem to be fairly clear because the woman or man judged "guilty" of an action that made continuance of the marriage undesirable would forfeit her or his claim to economic support and could lose custody of any children.[53] What is of interest here is that the records also stand testimony to the changing nature of marriage. Although women's accounts of why their marriages failed undoubtedly reflected both their strategic aims and the advice and language of their lawyers, they also yield many insights into the women's expectations of marriage.

In the cases studied, wives often reserved their most bitter complaints for their mothers-in-law. Some claimed they would still be willing to live with their husband if they had a home of their own. One woman had refused to move to her in-laws' home in Coatzacoalcos because, if her estranged husband wanted her to join him there, "it was only with the intention of making trouble [vejacciones] for her as she would be living under the influence of his relatives and it would be impossible for her to live in harmony and tranquillity with them." She was, she said, willing to go back to her husband, but only if he found them a home that was "completely independent."[54] A woman who believed in witchcraft wrote to a *quiromántico* asking for help in getting her husband to take her away from his parents' home in Veracruz City.[55] Another young wife from Tuxtla Gutiérrez left her in-laws' house within four months of her wedding. Her husband, she said, had failed to keep his promise to provide somewhere for them to live "other than his parents' home," although she had "never on any occasion accepted" that they should live there.[56]

Unwillingness to live with one's in-laws clearly predates the change in Supreme Court rulings on the subject. In 1939, for example, a lawyer from Mexico City demanded that his wife come back to him in his parents' home, but she refused to join him until he could guarantee her *"una posición desahogada"*—a "clear" or "comfortable" situation in a home of their own.[57] A woman from the state capital of San Luís Potosí described the time she spent with her in-laws from 1942 to 1944 as a *vida de calvario* (a life full of calvary).[58]

Women also claimed to have been ill-treated and thrown out of the house by their in-laws. In the north of San Luís Potosí, a couple from the small town of Matehuala had gone to live with the man's parents, but "[the wife's] mother-in-law and [her husband] started to give her a hard time [darle mala vida] and . . . threw her out."[59] A woman from Ciudad Madero, Tamaulipas, reported that her mother-in-law had thrown her out several times during the ten years they had shared a home. Her mother-in-law "was always ill-disposed toward [her] and treated her very badly," and witnesses reported hearing the older woman call her "dirty, slovenly . . . a lazy, idle, good-for-nothing slut." On several occasions, they found her "crying in the street" after she had been thrown out.[60] Another woman, who had left her mother-in-law's house in Mexico City only eight months after getting married, said she had been "insulted in a serious and grossly offensive fashion by the mother of the plaintiff, who, without any consideration [for her welfare], threw her and their recently born child out into the street with only the clothes she was wearing."[61] A woman accused of abandoning the marital home in a tiny rural community in the municipality of Palenque, Chiapas, maintained that what had really happened was that "even though she was pregnant . . . her mother-in-law and sister-in-law . . . beat her up and threw her out."[62]

Such complaints must be understood in the light of each woman's strategic aims because being obliged to leave provides legal justification for abandoning the home.[63] In the first of the Chiapas cases cited above, the teenage wife was left with her in-laws in Tuxtla Gutiérrez when her husband, a pilot, went to work hundreds of kilometers away in Yajalón. She claimed that "one night when her mother-in-law was drunk, at about eleven o'clock, she [the mother-in-law] threw her out of the house." Her witnesses would describe how "they found her [the wife] crying at the doors of her in-laws' house, with her little daughter in her arms, when her mother-in-law, *alcoholizada,* threw her out."[64] The Court accepted that she had been forced to leave, although, on cross-questioning, the witnesses also reported and the wife acknowledged that she had gone to the house with her mother and a man in a car to collect her belongings earlier that same evening.

Women, in short, employed a range of strategies in their efforts to avoid having to live with their in-laws and subsequently to gain the support of the courts. Their arguments must be understood in that light. Their stories, however, consistently depict a poor quality of relationship between wives and their mothers-in-law.

Women Reinforcing and Resisting Patriarchy

It might be objected that these cases are deviant ones with no wider relevance. The literature shows, however, that this is not so. It records a long history of difficulties associated with patrilocal residence patterns. Ironically, it is women who, as mothers-in-law, have taken on themselves the task of maintaining control over their sons' wives and, in doing so, of reinforcing patriarchy.

In rural Mexico, young couples have traditionally spent several years living with the man's parents before forming a separate household.[65] In urban areas, the tendency is now weaker but still significant.[66] Financial difficulties preventing establishment of separate households or male labor migration often mean that wives remain under their in-laws' supervision.[67] The consequences of such an arrangement are perhaps most vividly recorded in Hugo Nutini's study of family relations in San Bernardino Contla, where relations between mothers- and daughters-in-law were "always tense." They were, indeed, "[t]he most antagonistic relations in Contla society. . . . The antagonism and tension are so extreme that they leave a lasting impression on both mother-in-law and daughters-in-law."[68]

Many marriages are reported to have failed because of "meddlesome mothers-in-law."[69] Mothers-in-law can even become the "accomplices" of male violence because of their belief that young wives " 'need to learn their place' in their new households."[70]

Valentina Napolitano interprets tensions between low-income mothers- and daughters-in-law in Guadalajara as younger women challenging the equation of motherhood with self-denial *(abnegación)*.[71] They are also challenging what Ruth Behar describes as older women's "reinforcement of the idea that women should be subordinate to their husbands." The extent of that reinforcement is movingly illustrated by the account given by Esperanza, the woman whose life history Behar recorded, of how her mother-in-law reacted to her going to the door of their home to look out:

> Suddenly she grabs me by the hair, by the braids, and pushes me inside. We had been married eight days. "Why did you go out? What are you looking for?" It was the first scolding I got from her. After that I was really sorry I had gotten married. But what could I do? So, she finished pushing, shoving, and hitting me. "So that you'll know that from now on things are not the same as when you were single." . . . "Here you are done with mother. Here you are done with friends. . . . Here, you came to know your obligation towards your husband, nothing else."[72]

Challenging the Authority of the Older Generation

The power yielded over young wives by family elders was challenged by the change in judicial attitudes toward shared accommodation. The change may be regarded as furthering a reduction in the authority of the older generation started in nineteenth-century family law reforms.

In the 1930s, the judges were already displaying an apparent preference for independent accommodation for young couples. A 1938 ruling on a case from Monterrey stated that "If the husband . . . lives with his parents . . . it would be too much to demand that [his wife] be obliged to follow him there in order to avoid rendering herself liable to accusations of abandoning the marital home. . . . [T]he wife is not obliged to live with her husband in the house of a stranger [*en casa de un extraño*], even a relative." Up to this point, the ruling appears sympathetic to the wife's feelings, but it continues with a brief qualification that radically changes the overall meaning: "if she has not been invited to do so by her husband, with the authorization of the head of the house."[73]

The Court thus made the approval of the man's parents the key issue. Interestingly, in this ruling, as in some others, a man living with his parents is described as doing so "with the status of *hijo de familia*." Now used pejoratively to refer to someone considered immature, this phrase was the legal term for adults remaining subject to their father's authority before the liberal reforms emancipated those over the age of twenty-one.

The foregrounding of parental authority was evident in cases from the 1930s and 1940s. In the Mexico City case in which the wife refused to move in with her husband's parents, the couple had originally spent some time with them on getting married. The husband argued that because this arrangement had been acceptable to his parents in the past, it was clearly still acceptable. The judges rejected his "implicit approval" argument.[74] Their reasoning about what constituted approval may seem rather nice, but it shows that the older generation's position was regarded as the crucial issue. This point is confirmed by a 1947 case from the town of Aguascalientes in which a woman quoted the 1938 ruling to support her argument that the house the couple shared with her mother- and sister-in-law could not be regarded as the marital home. The Court, however, emphasized the second part of the ruling. Given that the couple clearly had the permission of the man's mother to live in her home, the wife's displeasure *(disgusto)* was deemed irrelevant, and she lost her case.[75]

Until the 1950s, then, the Supreme Court rulings focused almost exclusively on the authority of the older generation. The change that took place in that decade shifted the focus to the problems facing young wives living with their in-laws.

Domestic Wrongs and Marital Rights

The key concern in Supreme Court rulings about shared accommodation was now that the wife should be able to "exercise the rights granted to her by law" by being the only one to supervise the running of the home.[76] The judges evidently regarded this as a privilege granted to a woman by virtue of her married state. Their arguments echoed the concerns expressed by the women fighting these cases.

Why should having the responsibility for running the home be the subject of such contention? Supervising servants is clearly a different matter from doing the housework oneself, but the people bringing these cases were by no means all able to afford servants.[77] Why should having exclusive responsibility for housework be such a privilege? To argue that women disputed the only source of power available to them—power within the domestic sphere—would *at best* be to argue "by default." What were their *specific* complaints, the specific "rights" for which they fought?

Managing the Household Budget

Women disputed the right to manage the household budget. The woman from Ciudad Madero mentioned above complained "that the person who receives and distributes the money in her home is [her husband's] mother." The Court deemed this situation "a serious affront to the dignity of the wife" in that the husband let "his mother take on the right to dispose and govern *[las facultades de disposición y gobierno]* within the household, relegating the wife . . . to second place."[78] In 1976, the wife of an employee in a rural credit agency in Juchitan, Oaxaca, complained about living with her in-laws because "I do not have the running of the house, as a wife, because in reality I do not know how much my husband earns because I do not receive his salary. . . . My husband does not show any consideration for me as his wife. . . . My mother-in-law . . . controls everything, including my husband's salary."[79]

Who controls the household budget clearly affects how and on whom money is spent. There are practical reasons, then, for women to contest financial arrangements, and yet it is difficult to see these reasons as being of the same order as the desperation that drove poor women in the late colonial period to challenge their husbands' affairs "to reclaim for their households [the] resources and attentiveness channeled to *amasias* [mistresses]."[80] Immediate concerns about material survival seem unlikely to explain fully a wife's anger about her mother-in-law receiving her husband's pay. Wives disputed the implications of such financial arrangements: not having control over the household budget was an affront to their dignity. It was the symbolic as much as the material importance of the handover that offended them.

The Servant Role

Wives' most common grievance was that they were being treated like servants. The woman from Juchitán quoted above linked her husband's failure to give her his pay and her unenviable situation: "I do not receive his salary and have lived only as a servant and an arrimada in the house of his parents."[81]

Wives did not complain about having to do domestic labor for their husband or children; they objected to having to work for their husband's parents. The woman from Tuxtla Gutiérrez who accused her mother-in-law of throwing her out protested, for example, that "she was treated like a servant for her mother-in-law."[82] The other teenage wife from Tuxtla left her in-laws' home because "her husband's parents, in their relations with her, behaved like her bosses [*patrones*] and treated her like a servant. . . . as [they] had her there as a servant and treated her very badly, she told her husband that the situation was intolerable to her."[83] She was not the only one to complain of ill-treatment: a woman living in Toluca, whose husband was unemployed and unable to support them, was "effectively a servant in the house of her in-laws, and had to put up with scoldings and blows from her father-in-law."[84]

It is not surprising that young wives living with their husbands' families should be treated as servants because that is what they have effectively always been.[85] In rural areas, however, the need for assistance with domestic tasks has declined dramatically as a result of technological change. Stern connects the change from hand- to mill-grinding of maize, for example, with a decline in the demand for young wives to function as servants for their mothers-in-law. A telling quote from Oscar Lewis's study of the Martínez family illustrates his argument: "Had it not been for the mill . . . Esperanza would have long before insisted that Felipe, the eldest son, marry and bring home a daughter-in-law."[86]

In these mostly urban mid-twentieth-century cases, however, the young wives' protests were seemingly based on the premise that their role as servants to their in-laws was an extraordinary matter, not something that they might reasonably have anticipated—which says a lot about women's changing expectations of marriage. It is interesting, however, that wives and judges alike depicted the "servant" role not as an anachronistic one but as one that undermined women's marital rights. Furthermore, wives' protests cannot satisfactorily be explained solely in terms of the labor involved because their express wish to have the running of an independent home indicates that much the same work performed in different circumstances would be acceptable to them. Without the authority to run the home, women felt threatened in their identity as wives. A woman apparently gained her wifely identity through the *exclusivity* of her responsibility for domestic labor and authority over the space of the home.

Denial of an Adult Identity

In 1958, a man from an old pueblo on the edge of the city of Puebla sought to divorce the woman to whom he had been married for five years. His wife complained bitterly that "during the day he took me TO WORK AND BE INSULTED in his mother's home. BUT WHEN NIGHT CAME, DAY AFTER DAY HE TOOK ME BACK TO MY MOTHER'S HOME. . . . in reality, I DIDN'T EVEN LIVE WITH HIM BECAUSE EVERY NIGHT HE TOOK ME BACK TO MY MOTHER'S HOUSE TO SLEEP."[87] Working for another woman was especially humiliating when accompanied by the public denial of her relationship with her husband. The wife's outrage at this mockery of a marriage, graphically expressed in the capitalization of her statement, reflects the extreme threat it posed to the integrity of her identity as an adult—a woman old enough to be married and possess her own home space.

A woman's identity as wife apparently depended on her relationship with her husband and on having exclusive responsibility for running the home. Resistance to living with one's in-laws expressed fear of being denied the acquisition of an adult identity.[88] In accusations that their husbands were immature or unmanly, women projected onto them their fears and anger about this denial of their adulthood. The woman living in Toluca said her husband had suggested she return to her parents' home in Mexico City until he was able "to throw off the parental yoke . . . [and] begg[ed] her to forgive his lack of character."[89] The woman from Veracruz who believed in witchcraft called her husband "unmanly [poco hombre], useless, accursed, not worthy of a woman's love."[90]

In their in-laws' homes, then, women remained quasi-daughters, but because they were not in truth daughters of the house, they were in danger of being left with the identity of a servant. The domestic work they performed was therefore resented because it symbolized their lack of a proper wifely identity and adulthood: the denial of their marital rights.

Modernizing Patriarchy, Marriage, and the Family

In her study of changing gender relations in Michoacán, Fiona Wilson observes that "women have come together to fight a practice [living with one's in-laws] they consider wrong and unjust when transposed from an agrarian to an urban setting. Of all the changes taking place in the last twenty-five years, this may be judged as being of the most far-reaching importance for the conditions of women's lives."[91]

The fact that the cases examined here come from (mostly) urban areas as far apart as Veracruz, Monterrey, Tuxtla Gutiérrez, and Ciudad Madero suggests that this description of women's resistance to a practice prevailing in rural areas has far wider relevance. As Stern describes it, "A young wife faced an imposing intergenerational triad of authority: the ruling family patriarch (her father-in-law), her immediate supervisor in labor and physical movements (her mother-in-law), and a patriarch in the making (her husband)."[92] The women fighting these divorce cases, like those described by Wilson, opposed this triad. The change in Supreme Court rulings on the marital home in the 1950s shows judges siding with the wives in this respect. Why should they have done so?

In answering this question, we must first point to other midcentury legal reforms—such as the removal of the husband's prerogative to decide where a couple should live—that improved women's status but can also be read as measures strengthening the institution of marriage. Reforms reducing the ability of the husband and his relatives to impose their will on his wife made it more likely that young couples would stay together and thus supported marriage as an institution. One-third of divorce cases in the early 1950s were brought for abandonment of the marital home, so judges were likely to be aware of the threat to marriage posed by wives' unhappiness about living with their in-laws.[93] Support for marriage may also be seen in the way the 1947 Population Law canceled economic benefits for women living in consensual union that had been instituted by its 1936 predecessor.[94] These benefits had run counter to a general trend of supporting civil marriage started by the liberals and continued by postrevolutionary governments in their efforts to secularize the social order and foster civic virtue.[95]

When the Supreme Court turned against shared accommodation, it also turned away from the older generation. That the state should tolerate or even encourage the erosion of the authority of family elders reflects the postrevolutionary belief that the search for a new Mexican citizen must focus on the younger generation.[96] Older women in particular were mistrusted because they were seen as the enemies of anticlericalism. Their religiosity was linked to their need to control family members—for example, by the denial of communication to the parents of people living together or failing to marry in church. Although anticlericalism had waned by midcentury, a habitual mistrust of the older woman may conceivably have informed the Supreme Court's repudiation of her authority within the household.

Other factors likely to have informed the judicial preference for nuclearization included urbanization and imported cultural discourses. In the 1940s and 1950s, government agencies "built roads and distributed radios . . . [b]ut the roads and the radio brought a different culture: Americanized, consumerist."[97] They did so during a period often depicted as the "golden age" of the nuclear family in the United States. Jean Franco argues that mass culture, including television (introduced in 1950), provided alternative sources of meaning in an urbanizing nation. It devalued loyalty to one's birthplace, the extended family, and the belief that marriage offered "the inevitable source of satisfaction for women." Libros semanales, for example, encouraged women to identify themselves as workers, portraying marriage as a "working partnership" rather than romance, with employment "disguise[d] . . . as emancipation from the violence and oppression of working-class men."[98]

Urbanization and education provided "pathways of escape from a traditional destiny" for women: more opportunities for income generation and increased physical mobility taking them out of the reach of family elders.[99] The 1940s saw a dramatic expansion in the rate of urbanization and a diversification of housing possibilities as *colonias proletarias* began to appear on the urban periphery. Cities offered couples the prospect of access to housing that did not depend on parental resources, while employment for women provided additional income with which to defray the costs of independent accommodation.[100] Urbanization and economic growth thus provided material conditions that made it easier for people to live in nuclear households, and an emerging urban culture—particularly in Mexico City, where the Supreme Court occupies a building just off the *zócalo* (central square), the symbolic heart of the nation—fostered the belief that Mexico had outgrown its rural past. Judicial rulings on the marital home may thus be understood as part of the state's drive for modernity, distancing itself from traditional rural culture.

In conclusion, part of what Steve Stern describes as the repudiation of "pathological" machismo was a rejection of the authority of the elders and state endorsement of a "paternalistic" form of patriarchy. Furthermore, the wives fighting divorce cases owed their formal liberation from the power of their in-laws to a "benevolent" state adjudicating between the competing claims of its citizens. In spite of the nominal equality of wives and husbands, then, the parallels between state authority and male authority within the family reemerged, albeit in paternalistic guise.

As with mass literature, what is absent from the judges' vision of family life in the cases examined is "any form of female solidarity." Just as the libros semanales "reinforce[d] the serialization of women," judicial opposition to extended households reinforced the serialization of the family.[101] The chances of conflict between women living together may have declined, but so too did opportunities for cooperation and solidarity, leaving wives' well-being rather more dependent on their husbands' fitting the paternalistic ideal of the modernization discourse. New spaces may have opened for women, but others were perhaps more firmly closed than before.

Notes

This chapter is based on research carried out in 1996–97 to provide contextual material for the (UK) Economic and Social Research Council–funded project "Gendered Housing: Identity and Independence in Urban Mexico" (1997–2000) on which I am currently engaged. The assistance of Consuelo Méndez (Instituto de Investigaciones Jurídicas, Universidad Nacional Autónoma de México) and the staff of the Supreme Court archive was invaluable. I would particularly like to thank Alicia Pérez Duarte, Juan González Alcántara, Alicia Martínez, and Manuel González Oropeza for helping me to understand more about Mexican family law, and Steve Stern, Nikki Craske, the editors of this volume, and two anonymous readers for their helpful comments.

1   Ana María Alonso, "Rationalizing Patriarchy: Gender, Domestic Violence, and Law in Mexico," *Identities* 2, nos. 1–2 (1995): 29–47.
2   Jean Franco, *Plotting Women: Gender and Representation in Mexico* (London: Verso, 1989); Steve J. Stern, *The Secret History of Gender: Women, Men, and Power in Late Colonial Mexico* (Chapel Hill: University of North Carolina Press, 1995).
3   Georgina Waylen, "Gender, Feminism, and the State: An Overview," in *Gender, Politics, and the State,* ed. Vicky Randall and Georgina Waylen (London: Routledge, 1998), 1–17, 7 cited.
4   Rosemary Pringle and Sophie Watson, " 'Women's Interests' and the Post-Structuralist State," in *Destabilizing Theory: Contemporary Feminist Debates,* ed. Michèle Barrett and Anne Phillips (Cambridge: Polity, 1992), 53–73.
5   Waylen, "Gender, Feminism, and the State," 6.
6   Maxine Molyneux, "Twentieth-Century State Formations in Latin America," in this volume.
7   Alonso, "Rationalizing Patriarchy," 43; Elizabeth Dore, "The Holy Family: Imagined Households in Latin American History," in *Gender Politics in Latin America: Debates in Theory and Practice,* ed. Elizabeth Dore (New York: Monthly Review, 1997), 101–17.
8   Donna Guy, "Parents Before the Tribunals," in this volume; Francine Masiello, "Women, State, and Family in Latin American Literature of the 1920s," in *Women, Culture, and Politics in Latin America,* ed. Seminar on Feminism and Culture in Latin America (Berkeley: University of California Press, 1990), 29; Elizabeth Dore, "One Step Forward, Two Steps Back: Gender and the State in Latin America's Long Nineteenth Century," in this volume.
9   Elizabeth A. Kuznesof and Robert Oppenheimer, "The Family and Society in

Nineteenth-Century Latin America: An Historiographical Introduction," *Journal of Family History* 10, no. 3 (1985): 215–34, 228 cited; Doris Sommer, "Irresistible Romance: The Foundational Fictions of Latin America," in *Nation and Narration*, ed. Homi Bhabha (London: Routledge, 1990), 71–98.

10 Franco, *Plotting Women*, xviii.

11 Silvia M. Arrom, *The Women of Mexico City, 1790–1857* (Stanford: Stanford University Press, 1985), 77.

12 Mary Kay Vaughan, *The State, Education, and Social Class in Mexico, 1880–1928* (DeKalb: Northern Illinois University Press, 1982).

13 William E. French, "Prostitutes and Guardian Angels: Women, Work, and the Family in Porfirian Mexico," *Hispanic American Historical Review* 72, no. 4 (1992): 529–53, 542 cited.

14 Mary Kay Vaughan, *Cultural Politics in Revolution: Teachers, Peasants, and Schools in Mexico, 1930–1940* (Tucson: University of Arizona Press, 1997); quote from "Modernizing Patriarchy: State Policies and Rural Households in Mexico, 1930–1940," in this volume. This similarity was not the only one in the cultural projects of pre- and postrevolutionary regimes: Alan Knight, "Popular Culture and the Revolutionary State in Mexico, 1910–1940," *Hispanic American Historical Review*, 74, no. 3 (1994): 393–444. Both sought, for example, to reform working-class masculinity. For a Chilean parallel, see Karin Alejandra Rosemblatt, "Domesticating Men: State Building and Class Compromise in Popular-Front Chile," in this volume.

15 Knight, "Popular Culture," 402, quoting Calles's Grito de Guadalajara, and 412, quoting Emiliano Pérez Rosa et al., "Proyecto de organización de las brigadas de acción socialista dependientes del sindicato 'Trabajadores de le Enseñanza,'" Morelia, Michoacán, 16 July 1935.

16 Ibid., 405, 424–45. See also Molyneux, "Twentieth-Century State Formations."

17 Shirlene A. Soto, *Emergence of the Modern Mexican Woman: Her Participation in Revolution and Struggle for Equality, 1910–1940* (Denver: Arden, 1990); Anna Macías, *Against All Odds: The Feminist Movement in Mexico to 1940* (Westport, Conn.: Greenwood, 1982).

18 Ilene V. O'Malley, *The Myth of the Revolution: Hero Cults and the Institutionalization of the Mexican State, 1920–1940* (Westport, Conn.: Greenwood, 1986), 142.

19 Molyneux, "Twentieth-Century State Formations"; Vaughan, "Modernizing Patriarchy."

20 Enriqueta Tuñón, *Mujeres que se organizan: El Frente Único pro Derechos de la Mujer 1935–1938* (Mexico City: Universidad Nacional Autónoma de México/Porrúa, 1992); Macías, *Against All Odds*.

21 Knight, "Popular Culture," 424.

22 Ibid., 399, 442.

23 Stern, *Secret History*, 331.

24 Jean Franco, "Plotting Women: Popular Narratives for Women in the United

States and in Latin America," in *Reinventing the Americas: Comparative Studies of Literature of the United States and Spanish America,* ed. Bell Gale Chevigny and Gari Laguardia (Cambridge: Cambridge University Press, 1986), 249–68, 263 cited.

25 Franco, *Plotting Women,* 182.

26 Franco, "Plotting Women: Popular Narratives," 262.

27 Ruth Behar, "Rage and Redemption: Reading the Life Story of a Mexican Marketing Woman," *Feminist Studies* 16, no. 2 (1990): 223–58; Vaughan, "Modernizing Patriarchy."

28 See, for example, María Gabriela Leret de Matheus, *La mujer, una incapaz como el demente y el niño (según las leyes latinoamericanas)* (Mexico City: Costa-Amic, 1975); Universidad Nacional Autónoma de México, *Condición jurídica de la mujer en México* (Mexico City: UNAM, 1975). Notable exceptions include María A. Banchs, "El proceso de administración de justicia en el delito de violación," in *Mujer y sociedad en América Latina,* ed. María del Carmen Feijoó (Buenos Aires: Consejo Latinoamericano de Ciencias Sociales, 1991), 15–61; Nelly González Tapia, "Violencia doméstica al amparo del derecho: La agresión a la mujer por el cónyuge o conviviente," in Feijoó, ed., *Mujer y sociedad,* 109–61; Elizabeth Dore, "Property, Households and Public Regulation of Domestic Life: Diriomo, Nicaragua, 1840–1900," in this volume; Guy, "Parents Before the Tribunals."

29 Arrom, *Women of Mexico City;* Soledad González and Pilar Iracheta, "La violencia en la vida de las mujeres campesinas: El distrito de Tenango, 1880–1910," in *Presencia y transparencia: La mujer en la historia de México,* ed. Carmen Ramos Escandón (Mexico City: Colegio de México, 1989), 111–41; Stern, *Secret History;* Alonso, "Rationalizing Patriarchy."

30 Divorce cases are heard at the district level, appeals at the state level. Either party may then bring an *amparo* appeal for judicial review to the Supreme Court of Justice.

31 Alonso, "Rationalizing Patriarchy," 32.

32 Ibid., 31.

33 Ibid., 41.

34 Alicia I. Martínez, "Mujeres latinoamericanas en cifras: Los derechos de la mujer en México" (Facultad Latinoamericana de Ciencias Sociales, Mexico City, 1991, mimeo).

35 Arrom, *Women of Mexico City,* 77.

36 Silvia M. Arrom, "Changes in Mexican Family Law in the Nineteenth Century: The Civil Codes of 1870 and 1884," *Journal of Family History* 10, no. 3 (1985): 305–17. Colonial law had reserved patria potestad exclusively for fathers.

37 *Nuevo febrero mexicano: Obra completa de jurisprudencia teórico-práctica* (Mexico City, 1850), I, 64–66, quoted in Arrom, "Changes in Mexican Family Law," 310. The phrase provides a striking illustration of Carole Pateman's argument that

the liberal social contract was a fraternal one based on fear of the "disorder of women." See Carole Pateman, *The Sexual Contract* (Cambridge: Polity, 1988), and *The Disorder of Women* (Cambridge: Polity, 1989).

38 Arrom, "Changes in Mexican Family Law." Single women could not leave their parents' home, however, without parental consent until they reached the age of thirty.

39 *Código Civil para el distrito y territorios federales* (1928), "Motivos." Translations from legislation and amparo cases are mine.

40 *Código Civil* (1928), art. 167.

41 Ibid., arts. 164 and 163, respectively.

42 Ibid., art. 168.

43 Alicia E. Pérez Duarte, *Derecho de familia* (Mexico City: Fondo de Cultura Económica, 1994).

44 *Código Civil*, art. 163, reform of 31 December 1953 (*Diario Oficial*, 9 January 1954). A woman had been permitted to refuse to live with her husband only if he chose to live somewhere *"insalubre o indecoroso"* or out of the country (except on government service): *Código Civil* (1928), art. 163.

45 The final rulings in amparo cases considered of wider interest are summarized in the *Semanario Judicial de la Federación* (hereafter *SJF*). Wherever possible I have also consulted the case file in the Supreme Court archive. The seventy-three cases reviewed date from 1928 to 1984. All but twelve originated as divorce cases; the remainder originated either as petitions for economic support from absent husbands or demands that women who had left the home should return to their husbands. These cases are included because they shed light on judicial understanding of what "abandonment" and "the marital home" meant, but some also provoked divorce petitions in response. Three-quarters of the original divorce petitions came from the husband, and only one-quarter from the wife; this proportion remains fairly constant over the decades, although the total number of cases increases.

46 *Amparo directo* (hereafter, AD) 2307 / 45 (9 July 1945), Archive of the Supreme Court of Justice, Mexico City. I follow the usual style of reference to amparo cases except insofar as I omit the appellant's name.

47 AD 5236 / 54 (13 October 1955).

48 The five rulings cited date from 1958 to 1961: *SJF Apéndice 1917–85*, IX: 318, Tesis de jurisprudencia 205. By 1961, however, the Court had already issued at least sixteen rulings to the same effect. Rulings still reject sharing: see, for example, *SJF* 8a Epoca, XIII: 316, Tribunales Colegiados de Circuito (1994).

49 AD 3306 / 53 (4 March 1954), emphasis added.

50 *SJF* 5a Epoca, 131:649 (1956); *SJF* 5a Epoca, CXXXI: 322 (1957); *SJF* 6a Epoca, V: 69 (1957); *SJF* 6a Epoca, LXI: 147 (1962).

51 *SJF* 5a Epoca, CXXVI: 97 (1954); *SJF* 5a Epoca, CXXIX: 49 (1956); *SJF* 5a Epoca, CXXXI: 505 (1957); *SJF* 6a Epoca, XXVII: 82 (1959).

52 *SJF* 5a Epoca, CXXVI: 519 (1955).

53 Pérez Duarte, *Derecho de familia.*

54 AD 5825 / 55 (5 July 1956).

55 AD 7426 / 56 (22 November 1957).

56 AD 3478 / 58 (27 February 1959).

57 AD 5324 / 42 (3 December 1949).

58 AD 49 / 5352 (25 June 1952).

59 AD 782 / 54 (23 September 1954).

60 The insults do not translate easily: "cochina, mugrosa . . . floja, huevona, in-epta." AD 2202 / 56 (9 October 1961).

61 AD 5390 / 72 (7 January 1974).

62 AD 7171 / 67 (20 June 1968).

63 *SJF Apéndice 1917–1985,* IX: 317, Tesis de jurisprudencia 203.

64 AD 5236 / 54 (13 October 1955).

65 Hugo G. Nutini, Pedro Carrasco, and James M. Taggart, eds., *Essays on Mexican Kinship* (Pittsburgh: University of Pittsburgh Press, 1976); Heather Fowler-Salamini and Mary Kay Vaughan, eds., *Creating Spaces, Shaping Transitions: Women of the Mexican Countryside, 1850–1990* (Tucson: University of Arizona Press, 1994).

66 For a review of the literature on this issue, see my "Gender and Housing: The Provision of Accommodation for Young Adults in Three Mexican Cities," *Habitat International* 17, no. 4 (1993): 13–30.

67 Fiona Wilson, *Sweaters: Gender, Class, and Workshop-Based Industry in Mexico* (Basingstoke: Macmillan, 1991); Fiona Wilson, "Workshops as Domestic Domains: Reflections on Small-Scale Industry in Mexico," *World Development* 21, no. 1 (1993): 67–80.

68 Hugo G. Nutini, *San Bernardino Contla: Marriage and Family Structure in a Tlaxcalan Municipio* (Pittsburgh: University of Pittsburgh Press, 1968), 218–19.

69 John M. Ingham, *Mary, Michael, and Lucifer: Folk Catholicism in Central Mexico* (Austin: University of Texas Press, 1986), 64; Oscar Lewis, *Life in a Mexican Village: Tepoztlán Restudied* (Urbana: University of Illinois Press, 1951).

70 Mercedes González de la Rocha, *The Resources of Poverty: Women and Survival in a Mexican City* (Oxford: Blackwell, 1994), 144.

71 Valentina Napolitano, "Self and Identity in a 'Colonia Popular' of Guadalajara, Mexico" (Ph.D. thesis, University of London, 1995).

72 Behar, "Rage and Redemption," 240. It should be noted that mother- / daughter-in-law relations in Mexico are not always depicted in such a poor light. June Nash found more harmonious relations between in-laws in a Chiapas village where couples were equally likely to live with either set of parents: *Social Relations in Amatenango del Valle, Chiapas: An Activity Analysis* (Cuernavaca: Centro Intercultural de Documentación, 1969). Beverly Chiñas reports that "very strong bonds of affection" can form between Zapotec mothers- and daughters-in-law: *The Isthmus Zapotecs: Women's Roles in Cultural Context* (New York: Holt, Rinehart and Winston, 1973), 59. Such benevolence is not found in cases from the

South of Mexico that I have examined, although there are suggestions of a greater willingness on the part of even teenage wives to resist oppressive in-laws. This resistance may reflect a certain softening of patriarchy commonly reported for the indigenous South, where young wives have historically "held comparatively greater rights of physical separation" from their husbands (Stern, *Secret History*, 239). The South is overrepresented in the cases studied, with 33 percent of the total (the North, with 19 percent, is underrepresented; the Center has 48 percent, similar to its population share). Veracruz, with eleven cases, has more than any other state, although the Federal District of Mexico City has the largest number of cases overall (eighteen). In part, this statistic reflects a surprising number of cases (seven) involving men working for PEMEX, the state oil company, although even more involved men working for the national railways (nine). The privileges enjoyed by the workers of these companies and their families as a result of their political significance may have some role to play in explaining this number, possibly raising the stakes in marital disputes or reducing legal costs in some way (I am grateful to Juan González Alcántara for this suggestion).

73 AD 2436 / 37 (21 January 1938).

74 AD 5324 / 42 (3 December 1949).

75 AD 5861 / 47 (16 February 1951).

76 AD 3306 / 53 (4 March 1954).

77 The cases examined include, on the one hand, the divorce of author Antonieta Rivas Mercado, daughter of a wealthy architect and lover of José Vasconcelos: AD 3697 / 28 (24 April 1930). At the other social extreme, some husbands argued that they could not afford independent accommodation: AD 1043 / 77 (13 March 1978); AD 4141 / 58 (4 June 1959). In one Mexico City case, the wife shared a room with her sisters-in-law, while her husband shared with his brothers; he was unemployed and could not afford even to buy their food: AD 3686 / 73 (15 January 1975). A man from Veracruz argued that "it is normal for persons of his social class to live . . . in a single room": AD 4423 / 70 (11 March 1971). A couple from Oaxaca were also living in one room, furnished only with "a bed, two chairs and a table": AD 4512 / 76 (29 April 1977).

78 AD 2202 / 56 (9 October 1961).

79 AD 4512 / 76 (29 April 1977).

80 Stern, *Secret History*, 82; González and Iracheta, "Violencia en la vida."

81 AD 4512 / 76 (29 April 1977).

82 AD 5236 / 54 (13 October 1955).

83 AD 3478 / 58 (27 February 1959).

84 AD 3711 / 72 (30 August 1973).

85 Stern, *Secret History;* Wilson, "Workshops as Domestic Domains"; González and Iracheta, "Violencia en la vida."

86 Oscar Lewis, *Pedro Martínez: A Mexican Peasant and His Family* (New York: Random House, 1964), 469, quoted in Stern, *Secret History*, 335.

87   AD 545 / 61 (30 July 1962). Capitals in original.
88   Stern, *Secret History,* also links the "laboring daughter-servant" role with the denial of women's "acquisition of an adult marital and sexual identity" (93).
89   AD 3711 / 72 (30 August 1973).
90   AD 7426 / 56 (22 November 1957).
91   Wilson, *Sweaters,* 88.
92   Stern, *Secret History,* 336.
93   Interpreting divorce statistics is tricky, particularly for the period before 1971 (when the practice of foreign residents divorcing in Mexico was discontinued). The figure cited excludes a category ("incompatibility") that did not exist in the Civil Code and was apparently used mostly for divorces of foreign residents. Excluding, additionally, mutually agreed divorces, abandonment accounted for three-quarters of 1950 divorces. The divorce *rate* for abandonment has generally fallen since 1950—unlike the rate for mutually agreed divorce, which accelerated dramatically in the 1970s. Data from Instituto Nacional de Estadística, Geografía e Informática, *Estadísticas de matrimonios y divorcios 1950–1992* (Aguascalientes: INEGI, 1994).
94   Martínez, "Mujeres latinoamericanas."
95   Knight, "Popular Culture"; Vaughan, "Modernizing Patriarchy."
96   Vaughan, *Cultural Politics;* Knight, "Popular Culture."
97   Knight, "Popular Culture," 443.
98   Franco, "Plotting Women: Popular Narratives," 258–66, 258 and 266 cited. Mexico ratified the International Labor Organization's declaration on equal wages for women and men in 1955, and 1962 labor legislation reforms instituted equal rights and obligations for men and women; Martínez, "Mujeres latinoamericanas."
99   Stern, *Secret History,* 331–37. Less than one-fifth of the cases studied here came from rural areas, one-third from small towns and one-half from larger cities.
100 See also Steve J. Stern, "What Comes after Patriarchy? Reflections from Mexico," *Radical History Review* 71 (1998): 54–62. Stern's use of the term "rent-free" housing is, however, somewhat misleading: "shantytown" housing is rarely free. See my "Neither Victims nor Heroines: Women, Land, and Housing in Mexican Cities," *Third World Planning Review* 17, no. 2 (1995): 169–82. The significance for the "breakdown of the patriarchy" of material changes that made it possible for young families to survive economically on their own is emphasized by Guillermo de la Peña in his "Ideology and Practice in Southern Jalisco: Peasants, Rancheros, and Urban Entrepreneurs," in *Kinship Ideology and Practice in Latin America,* ed. Raymond T. Smith (Chapel Hill: University of North Carolina Press, 1984), 204–34.
101 Franco, "Plotting Women: Popular Narratives," 266.

Karin Alejandra Rosemblatt

Domesticating Men

State Building and Class Compromise in Popular-Front Chile

Norms of masculine deportment were central to the novel forms of class compromise and state building that took shape in Chile in the 1930s and 1940s. During those years, a series of reformist popular-front coalitions became the determinant force in Chilean national politics.[1] Constituted by the Radical, Socialist, and Communist Parties, the coalitions triumphed in the 1938, 1942, and 1946 presidential elections and won control of the executive branch of the state. More importantly, the popular-front coalitions mobilized popular sectors and promised political democratization while simultaneously implementing a program of capitalist economic modernization attractive to the dominant classes. As part of their efforts to modernize and democratize the Chilean nation-state, the popular fronts sought to reform gender relations.

Like other Latin American states, the Chilean state expanded rapidly in the late 1930s and 1940s: it directed and financed new industrial development projects; set up arbitration and conciliation boards to mediate labor disputes; expanded public education; developed new social assistance programs for children and the indigent; and consolidated an extensive system of health care, social security, and disability benefits for white- and blue-collar workers. Like the populist governments examined by Mary Kay Vaughan and Laura Gotkowitz in this volume and by other authors elsewhere, the popular fronts both mobilized and made concessions to sectors of the popular classes. What set the popular fronts apart, however, was their inability to consistently neutralize or supplant existing popular organizations. More than other Latin American populist leaders, popular-front state officials instigated and validated increased political participation for working-class Chileans and implemented reforms by availing themselves of the cultural resources of established popular organizations. Although state practices altered the nature of popular organizing, popular groups not only retained a degree of autonomy but also gained political influence.[2]

Gender influenced the novel forms of class conflict and alliance that emerged in popular-front Chile and hence the process of state formation. Processes of political convergence and divergence—reflected by and amplified within the state—in turn molded gender. As political leaders validated and promoted a masculine identity that defined men as workers and family heads, they justified increased material benefits and political enfranchisement for men by insisting that men's productive labor and their contributions to their families fortified the nation. Working-class men consequently achieved the status of privileged citizens. Women, too, profited from state reforms as they mobilized to press their gender-based demands, but as nonworkers and dependent family members they were clearly considered secondary citizens. The widespread recognition of their mothering notwithstanding, women were denied tutelage of their children and, until 1949, the right to vote in national elections. Although members of the women's movement, like labor leaders, influenced popular-front policymaking, they were nevertheless subordinate members of the ruling alliance.[3]

This essay focuses on the sometimes contrasting, sometimes convergent politics of policymakers, on the one hand, and organized male workers linked to the Socialist and Communist Parties, on the other. How, it asks, did gendered forms of cultural sharing and conflict determine the concrete nature of each group's participation in reform efforts? The essay begins with a general characterization of the popular fronts and their supporters, noting how each group framed class compromise within discourses of national identity and progress. The next section shows how those notions of nationality and progress were gendered. The essay then discusses multifaceted efforts to define and regulate working-class masculinity, noting how these efforts played into the political negotiations of the popular-front period. Specifically, it looks at the participation of popular-front state officials and working-class activists in antialcoholism crusades and in efforts to stimulate "healthy" recreational pursuits among men. An integral part both of state efforts to define appropriate forms of masculine citizen participation and of working-class efforts to fortify socialist organizations, these crusades became vehicles for turning men into hardworking laborers and reliable breadwinners for their families.

Theoretically, this essay advances a view of state formation as a gendered historical process that traverses civil society and is patterned by popular sectors as well as by political and economic elites. By looking closely at evolving norms of popular masculinity, the essay reveals the complex connections between state policy, on the one hand, and conflict and agreement within civil society, on the other. It also shows how cultural sharing and conflict, which took place within as well as outside the state, varied according to specific historical circumstance.[4]

Progress, Nationality, and Class Collaboration

At the center of the popular-front project was the promise to democratize Chile politically and to modernize it economically. Yet because the popular-front coalitions could not always reconcile capitalist development with efforts to increase the political rights and material well-being of subalterns, they often found it difficult to achieve both goals at once. Although the containment and control of popular protest, which was a by-product of the popular-front strategy, benefited the propertied classes, the expansion of workers' or consumers' rights restricted the rights of employers and proprietors, undermining the capitalist nature of the popular fronts' development project.

As part of the popular fronts' attempts to bridge the contradictions within their program and to generate the political stability that would allow them to govern, the coalitions promoted national identity among popular classes and elites, and represented their project as a national project. In fact, president Pedro Aguirre Cerda and his followers resuscitated the concept of *chilenización* (Chileanization) to describe the process of national identification and consolidation they encouraged. By rousing feelings of *chilenidad* (Chileanness), popular-front leaders encouraged citizens of all social classes and political orientations to view and express their own particular demands in terms of national prerogatives. The forging of a national consciousness aimed to encourage order by harmonizing the perceived interests of rich and poor.[5]

The promotion of economic modernization and industrialization would allow the Chilean nation to progress and overcome its stature as a subordinate nation, and was central to popular-front attempts to encourage national cohesion. Popular-front politicians presented social reform as a national imperative that flowed from required economic changes, claiming that to stimulate modernization and economic independence it was necessary to improve the living conditions of the popular classes. In 1939, Socialist Party member Salvador Allende, who was at the time minister of health, clearly articulated this discursive strategy in a book he penned to present a medico-social reform platform. In that book, Allende warned that without concurrent economic and social reforms, Chile would remain a second-class nation. Linking popular well-being to capitalist development and work, he characterized the working class as the nation's "human capital." If Chile's human capital was healthy and robust, he said, industrialization would proceed apace, and Chile's stature within the community of nations would be secured. But if Chileans remained ill fed, ill housed, and ill paid, Chile would not have the healthy and dense population it needed to assure its national security.[6] Popular-front leaders thus told economic elites that reforms that benefited the nation's "human capital" were good for the dominant classes because they were good for the economy and good for the nation, and they told workers that popular classes would benefit from economic changes—thus, in the process, stimulating cooperation between workers and capitalists.

Although the political parties of the left opposed the dominant classes more frontally than the Radical Party they too contributed to the modernization of capitalist development. Abandoning the calls for immediate revolution that had prevailed prior to the formation of the first popular-front coalition, leftist organizations joined alliances that sought evolutionary change. Insofar as leftists believed that a stage of economic and political progress (democratization and industrialization) was a necessary step in the transition to socialism, they were willing to quell popular resistance for the sake of progress.[7] In return for their contribution to national prosperity, communists, socialists, and labor activists sought and gained influence within the state. Socialists and to a lesser extent communists occupied major and minor positions in state agencies: they served as ministers, governors and intendants, heads of government services, labor and sanitary inspectors, and even rather menial secretaries and administrators. The Confederación de Trabajadores de Chile (CTCh, Confederation of Chilean Workers), a labor confederation that grouped together the majority of the country's labor unions, won representation on government decision-making bodies.[8]

Along with leftists, working-class activists generally supported popular-front bids for national progress. As popular-front leaders affirmed that, in contrast to past leaders, they understood popular well-being as part of the health of the nation, the laboring classes responded with patriotic rapture: "What is useless to the country is useless to socialism," a Socialist Party publication from Arauco asserted in 1941. "That is to say, always the nation above all other considerations, no matter what they may be." Like these Socialist Party members, members of the Communist Party made patriotic proclamations devoid of any explicit class content. In 1946, they described themselves as following in the "honorable tradition" of their "glorious ancestors who lifted the banner of national independence."[9]

However, not all labor and leftist activists were as conciliatory. At times, popular faith in progress and subaltern patriotism took on a more restrained and class-conscious tone. The task of popular-front supporters, communists asserted elsewhere, was not simply to follow in the trajectory of the "glorious ancestors" who had fought in Chile's independence wars, for the independence battles of Chacabuco and Maipú had not liberated all Chileans—most of whom continued to be servile, ill housed, ill clothed, hungry, and exploited. Instead of continuing on that path, what most Chileans needed was a more substantive "second independence" that would give them greater material comforts. Likewise, according to workers at the El Teniente copper mine, "effective patriotism" meant "a better distribution of the benefits of [our] riches." Socialists agreed. They ostensibly wanted changes that transcended the banners of left and right and served the entire nation. But then they made clear the type of reform they had in mind: "The liberation of a social class that has been ferociously exploited by another which made itself powerful at the expense of the secular fatigue of el pueblo."[10]

Still other sectors of the left rejected even more forcefully the twin notions of progress and national fellowship. In an allegorical tale titled "Resignation" and published in the Socialist Party magazine Rumbo, a hungry and tethered young calf asks her mother why she is not allowed to drink the mother's milk. The mother explains that in the days of "barbarie" cows ran free and fed their milk to their children. "But now," the mother continues, "we have progress, civilization, culture." The calf replies with tender innocence: "Of all that progress you just listed I do not enjoy any of it, I'm always cold and hungry." The mother concedes that the cows she knows do not benefit from progress. "[B]ut," she continues, "they say [it benefits] the collectivity." With less embellishment, another Socialist Party publication (which represented a Socialist Party faction that opposed participation in President Pedro Aguirre Cerda's cabinet) stated: "[The] presumed social solidarity that exists in relation to the nation does not exist. And that is why, for us, there is no other solidarity than that of our class, that of the workers. . . . [M]ost of the benefits of civilization do not reach us."[11]

Despite the persistence of such oppositional sentiment, the twin discourses of modernization and national aggrandizement seemed attractive to most members of labor and leftist organizations. Although some leftists put forth a version of nationalism rooted in a more oppositional class identity by insisting that they—and not the oligarchy—would ensure the well-being of the nation, like their more conciliatory comrades they nevertheless tempered their class-based demands. To better understand why this less conflictual formulation won out over others, it is useful to look at how gender played into the discourses of nationalism and progress. As I argue in the next section, the form of class compromise that emerged in Chile—and the limits of that compromise—came about largely because national and grassroots leaders linked national advancement to gendered arrangements that, although they restricted individual male autonomy, buttressed working-class solidarity and granted political, economic, and familial privileges to men as family heads. At the same time, because those gendered arrangements were widely accepted by elites as well as the poor, they served to forge agreements between classes.

Gender and Class Compromise

In both their more elite and their more popular varieties, popular-front discourses on class collaboration, modernization, and national fellowship were fundamentally gendered. Like the national leaders described by Eugenia Rodríguez, Donna Guy, Mary Kay Vaughan, and Ann Varley in this volume, popular-front leaders tried to "modernize" gender relations by consolidating nuclear male-headed families and redefining men's privileges and responsibilities to both their nation and their families. Popular-front leaders used gender and family as powerful yet contested and contradictory symbols of their project—emblems both of their pro-popular sensibilities and of the moral and political sensibilities they shared with the right. In the 1938 presidential campaign, for instance, Aguirre Cerda's competitor claimed that the election of the popular-front candidate would undermine mutual respect among family members and fellow citizens. Although refuting his opponent, Aguirre Cerda did not question the validity of his competitor's ideal: he countered by saying that his government would carry out an economic modernization that would provide youths with jobs and thereby allow young people to make homes for themselves. In fact, most popular-front leaders suggested that the unfavorable economic conditions generated by past governments, and not the popular-front project, undermined family life. Thus, Aguirre Cerda and his supporters linked the reshaping of the economy and the consolidation of a new ruling coalition to the reconstitution of gender relations.[12] Once in office, popular-front leaders would implement a vast array of reforms aimed specifically at constituting and fortifying male-headed nuclear families in which husbands acted as stable breadwinners. To strengthen and stabilize nuclear families, they sought to assure men jobs that would allow them to support women and children.[13] And to stimulate male responsibility for family members, they preached temperance and promoted recreational activities that might involve entire families. Although used to differentiate the popular fronts from their right-wing opponents, these reform efforts also coincided with the moral sensibilities of elites.

From a different perspective, one closer to the grass roots, Socialist Party labor leader Roberto Pérez Núñez expressed the gendered coordinates of class collaboration in an article called "The Working Class and Its Future." Because (male) workers labored diligently to increase production and took care of their families, Pérez argued, they deserved better wages:

> On his way to work, the joyful, happy worker marches thinking of those he left at home, the little woman surrounded by their little children, or, an aged little Mother for whom he feels immense affection and because of them he wishes to arrive soon at work so that he can assure the Bread for his home.
>
> The day goes by and the laborer works full steam to satisfy his bosses, in this manner he wishes to demonstrate that he doesn't want to be reprimanded, he cares for the machines and the tools he is in charge of as if they were his own, because he is aware of his responsibilities and has a working-class consciousness. . . .
>
> That Capitalism which inspired [to do] something noble for Society, [and

which] wishes to serve the Patria, should leave aside pride and self-love and help the worker who knows his responsibilities and fulfills his obligations and respond by paying Wages which lift his morale and his living conditions to a level worthy of human dignity.

In Pérez's view, capitalist intransigence, which "drove [workers] into strike movements," harmed not only workers but also the nation. In contrast, because workers had "working-class consciousness" (and were patriotic family men), they obeyed their bosses and cared for capitalists' productive infrastructure![14] In this formulation—and in others like it—it was always necessarily manly men who furthered national well-being in the forms of productivity and class conciliation.

Significantly, when workers questioned the utility of class collaboration, they often invoked an alternative model of gender to justify their claims. Unsure that they would share in the benefits of national development and fearful that only capitalists would profit, laborers sometimes subscribed to an oppositional perspective that favored greater male autonomy from family and work responsibilities. From this point of view, class solidarity was more the result of male camaraderie than of allegiance to family. Consequently, some workers simply rejected family responsibilities, articulating a "wilder," less civilized masculine identity that was also explicitly anticapitalist—a way of expressing antagonism toward bosses, state officials, and popular-front political leaders who insisted that workers ought to get married and report dutifully to their jobs. In mining communities, for instance, the all-male nature of the workforce and the combative tenor of relations between workers and bosses (who were also often foreigners) stimulated a more unruly male culture of opposition. Indeed, miners who faced difficult working conditions and unsympathetic foremen or bosses frequently left one mining center to search for better employment opportunities in another. Their family ties were therefore fleeting. One social worker noted the "restless character" and "nomadism" of the Chilean worker, adding that "for this reason, his feelings toward the home are weak, and he does not hesitate to leave his home and family."[15]

Oppositional working-class standards of masculinity thus existed alongside hegemonic norms. Indeed, prevalent antimarriage maxims in the labor press clearly revealed a male, working-class rejection of stable married life:

All that is one's own seems better than one's neighbor's, except
  when it comes to one's woman.
[Todo lo propio parece mejor que lo ajeno, excepto la mujer.]

The only difference between marrying [*casarse*] and getting tired [*cansarse*]
  is one letter.
[De casarse a cansarse no hay más diferencia que una letra.]

Not even the tamest dog would let himself be tied up for his whole life.
[Ni el perro más dócil se dejaría atar para toda la vida.]

In the majority of cases, a man marries a woman and a woman marries
  a solution.
[En la mayoría de los casos, el hombre se casa con una mujer y la mujer
  con una solución.]

"Family life" is usually the most difficult.
[La "vida familiar" suele ser la más difícil.]

Death leads to something agreeable: widows.
[La muerte hace algo agradable: viudas.]

Black is worn to marriages and funerals. There must be a reason.
[Al matrimonio y a los funerales se va vestido de negro. Por algo será.]

What that longtime bachelor thief hated most was wearing handcuffs
  [*esposas,* handcuffs and wives].
[Lo que más sentía aquel ladrón, soltero empedernido, era que le colocaran
  las esposas.][16]

In short, not all male laborers collaborated fully with popular-front initiatives aimed at disciplining and domesticating workers. Yet as I show in
the next section, leftist activists who shared in the popular-front project for
national advancement and especially members of left political parties generally did not sanction this more defiant masculine identity, choosing instead to collaborate with state officials and employers in regulating male
workers at home and at work. Still, by insisting that the state and employers avoid repressive means of enforcing "proper" masculine behavior
and by refiguring the meaning and effects of discipline, they tried to make
disciplinary measures seem less onerous to working-class men. And be-

cause left leaders believed disciplined males would be better activists, they also participated in moralizing campaigns to consolidate their own political organizations. At home and at work, they argued, restrained masculine behavior was the best way for workers to express their class solidarity. Significantly, these leftist leaders saw male responsibility for their family members, especially male economic responsibility, as crucial to the consolidation not only of the popular-front project but also of a working-class solidarity rooted in family. They thus proposed a distinct view of masculinity that, although at odds with certain forms of popular resistance to capitalist abuse, retained a distinct working-class character even as it converged with elite disciplinary efforts.[17]

State Campaigns

Popular-front state officials took wide-ranging measures to discipline males, making them simultaneously into good workers, good providers for their families, and good citizens. Hard and consistent workers were good providers, state officials put forth; thoughtful and dependable heads of households made excellent workers. Thus, work and family became two inextricable elements of the masculine identity promoted by the state. "The desire to be a good family member, a good worker, and a good citizen gives life an inappreciable value," admonished *Vida Sana,* a health education magazine published by the Caja de Seguro Obligatorio (cso, Obligatory Insurance Fund), the social security agency for blue-collar workers.[18]

Although the often coercive recommendations of state officials were tainted with a good deal of elitism, working-class men who complied were offered important rewards: they would gain the rights of full citizenship, a say in the destiny of the nation, and material benefits. Popular-front officials portrayed the provision of health care to workers, for instance, as a *right* won by workers through their economic and political contributions to the nation. In this context, workers could, as citizens, legitimately contest not only state health policies but also the staffing of medical agencies. Indeed, widespread acknowledgment of the legitimacy of worker influence tempered the elitism of state authorities: worker organizations consistently argued that health professionals should avoid paternalism toward their clients, and worker representatives on state advisory boards worked to ensure that medical professionals acted more like friends than like parents.[19] Popular-front state officials did not always heed worker recommendations, but they did recognize those proposals as appropriate.

Moreover, popular-front state officials understood campaigns to reduce alcohol consumption and promote "healthy" forms of recreation as fundamentally educational and not punitive. This approach, too, facilitated popular influence. Aguirre Cerda's most famous motto was: "To govern is to educate and give health." Thus, he indicated *how* the popular fronts would govern—principally through prescription and incentive, not through punishment or policing. Concurring with this orientation, the head of the social service division of the CSO saw social workers' actions as "essentially pedagogical." Similarly, *Vida Sana* saw its role as "purely educational." Although more repressive means reinforced and complemented approaches aimed at convincing and building consensus—throughout the popular-front period, arrests for drunkenness remained the single largest category of detentions, constituting more than 40 percent of all arrests—popular-front leaders decidedly preferred to reward and prompt rather than to punish. Within all levels of the bureaucracy, leftists were particularly vocal in denouncing reform efforts that relied on punitive measures.[20]

Stressing abstention, restraint, and family values, the state took far-reaching measures aimed at domesticating men and making them efficient workers. One of the state's most aggressive campaigns sought to eradicate immoderate drinking. Drunken men, according to state officials, distastefully shouted obscenities on city sidewalks, beat their wives, picked fights, and were prone to debilitating diseases. Limiting male consumption of alcohol, state agents asserted, would make men better workers, better fathers, better husbands, and better citizens. Indeed, overcoming an addiction to liquor was a sign of the self-discipline that marked true manhood and furthered national development. Alcoholics, on the other hand, were retrograde "beasts." Equating alcoholism with animal instinct, *Vida Sana* chided, "Who can think, then, that alcoholism makes a man more manly? On the contrary. We must proclaim this out loud. The personality looks toward evil, and the instincts surface just as they were among primitive men." A didactic parable published in another issue of the magazine detailed the story of Gregorio Segundo Mesa Alarcón, "an exemplary citizen and a worker." Mesa Alarcón's adult life, like that of many other workers, did not begin auspiciously. As a child and adolescent, he had learned mistaken ideas about what it meant to be a man:

> The child grew, and in no time he had to feign manhood to conquer his work. Manhood also meant sharing with his *compañeros,* having the same distractions, not striking a sour note. And he frequented the tavern.
> He learned of heated discussions, of fights in murky surroundings, and of delayed anger about misspent money.

Suggesting that bad habits could be changed, the story detailed how this exemplary citizen "struggled with himself" until one day he visited the doctor. Heeding the physician, he gave up drinking. Two years later he would proclaim eternal gratitude to the doctor. His wife and children were also thankful. Mesa Alarcón had become a good citizen, worker, and husband: a true man.[21]

Through antialcoholism campaigns, state agents repudiated male battering and improper spending, both of which they saw as disruptive of family life. A man who liked to drink was not only a bad worker but also an insufficient husband and provider. Because drunk men had a propensity to beat their wives, state-employed social workers and physicians suggested, they provoked harmful conflict that divided the family. Husbands who spent their wages in bars, like those who squandered their earnings on bets, could not be good providers either. According to one social worker's survey of marital disputes among one hundred blue-collar municipal workers and their wives, alcoholism was at the root of the disagreements in 78 percent of all cases. Fifty-two families had economic problems, and in thirty-six cases alcoholism aggravated financial difficulties. In this social worker's view, when wives tried to reform their alcoholic husbands, the men resisted, and marital disputes ensued. To avoid these perils, she suggested the passage of legislation allowing wives to request that a judge legally prohibit their husbands from buying alcohol. Experts thus validated the concerns of working-class wives and sought to restrict male autonomy in the attempt to create a disciplined male citizenry. "He is a drunkard. What will become of the wife and children of that ill-fated man?" asked *Vida Sana.*[22]

State bids to extirpate alcoholism drew upon eugenic reasoning and therefore furthered popular-front efforts to promote progress by bettering the Chilean "race." A heavy drinker could not be an adequate father or a biologically fit progenitor. His offspring would be weak, disease-prone, unproductive members of the nation. They might even inherit their father's addiction. In 1939, Minister of Health Allende explained:

> It is equally useful to note that the act of conception often takes place while the man, at least, is in a state of drunkenness, and the effects of an acute alcoholic intoxication, as well as of a chronic intoxication, on the products of conception are well known.
>
> An alcoholic inheritance, determined by the influence of the toxic substance on the sexual cells of both parents, or of one of the parents, can be recognized, from the point of view of the [resulting] physical characteristics, by diverse types of dystrophies and even monstrosities. Notable mental characteristics include: mental retardation, idiocy, moral debility, a propensity toward neurosis (hysteria, epilepsy, dipsomania, etc.).

Moreover, because alcohol debilitated a man's organism, his ability to work properly as well as his civic capacities would be diminished. He might become a criminal or lose his mental capacities. A government publication reminded workers: "Do not forget that it is indispensable that every good citizen conserve a mental lucidity and perfect control over his nervous system at every moment of his life."[23]

To assure the success of its campaign against alcoholism, the state sought the cooperation of employers, who collaborated because they believed alcohol consumption generated absenteeism and accidents at work. As employers knew, San Lunes—Saint Monday—was a widespread "holiday" among Chilean workers. After a weekend of bingeing, laborers were often too hung over to attend work on Monday. When workers went to work still drunk, the probability of costly slip-ups increased. The state itself often lamented the economic losses caused by alcoholism. Acting in conjunction with state efforts, employers accorded bonuses to steadfast and abstemious workers and opened the gates of mining camps and factories to authorities preaching temperance.[24]

Many entrepreneurs also favored married over single workers and promoted temperance in order to turn men into proper husbands. These employers believed that by encouraging men to marry, they could decrease turnover and create a more stable workforce. As we have already seen, employers—especially in mining establishments, which had all-male workforces—faced the problem of Chilean workers' "natural inclination to move about from one mining center to another," which was harmful to companies that saw finding and training replacement workers as costly. Entrepreneurs increasingly saw the transitory nature of male employment as an impediment in their race for riches. Rather than substantially improve work conditions, however, companies chose to encourage worker stability by granting family allowances and other welfare benefits (such as the provision of housing for married workers). Married workers, they believed, would be less likely to pick up and leave if their families lived with them in mining communities—and because of the pressures of supporting a family, less likely to protest or go on strike if they were unhappy. Companies also felt it necessary to rid workers of certain "bad habits," such as drinking and gambling, that made them irresponsibly squander money that should properly be spent on their families. Company social workers, whose moralizing mission began in the family, were hired to make men into dependable breadwinners and abstemious, disciplined workers.[25]

A proper man, then, did not drink. He heeded the advice of his physician, attended work regularly, and led a settled life alongside his family. Along with these prohibitions, state officials promoted attractive alternative habits for men. A medical social worker noted with pride that she had convinced a young worker to give up his "incipient alcoholism" and join a sports club. On a more global level, diverse state-run programs gave workers recreational options compatible with their responsibilities to family, nation, and work. In fact, to foment healthy diversions in which the whole family could participate, President Aguirre Cerda set up a new agency, the Departamento de Defensa de la Raza y Aprovechamiento de las Horas Libres (Department for the Defense of the Race and Enjoyment of Free Time). According to the decree that set up the department, its objectives were:

To cultivate a consciousness of our national value and of patriotic honor;
To practice physical culture as a means of obtaining the vigor and aptitude required for work;
To practice hygienic habits;
To worship work, peace, and human solidarity;
To stimulate a feeling of individual dignity and excellence within civic and home life.[26]

Along with a sister program developed by the cso, the Defensa de la Raza built soccer and basketball courts and swimming pools; set up vacation areas for workers; established libraries; worked with unions and other workers' organizations to stimulate theater and music groups; and counseled Chileans, especially Chilean men, to desist from drinking and to take up sports. The cso and the Defensa de la Raza contributed to the creation of recreational centers such as the Hogar Pedro Aguirre Cerda (Pedro Aguirre Cerda Home) in the Santiago suburb of Conchalí and the Centro Cívico y Cultural Valparaíso (Valparaíso Civic and Cultural Center) in the port city. In these centers, neighbors could find game rooms, ping-pong tables, popular restaurants, or milk bars. The centers sponsored boxing, soccer, and hockey teams; housed theater groups; taught handicrafts, domestic arts, and literacy; gave talks and showed movies. Community, union, and women's groups held their meetings there. At the Centro Valparaíso, however, dances and alcohol were expressly forbidden, as were card games and dice.[27]

Although private groups promoting "healthy" amusements had existed before the state began its recreational project, prior initiatives had been inefficient and ineffective, according to cso publications. Those private sports clubs and artistic groups simply had not promoted a vision of the sportsman-citizen. State control, in comparison, assured that recreational organizations would articulate and propagate a vision of a disciplined male citizenry. When a youth club was set up at the Beneficencia-run Casa de Socorro, a kind of settlement house in Puente Alto, the social worker in charge stressed the development of good manners as a prime advantage of playing sports. Good manners, she emphasized, facilitated understanding between the sexes and between social classes. Like those popular-front officials who set up the Defensa de la Raza, she saw exercise and recreation as national imperatives.[28]

Proper citizens, in short, were proper workers and proper family men; day-to-day, those hardworking family men displayed temperance and good sportsmanship. Through antialcoholism and recreational campaigns, popular-front state agents made sure that the promotion of "national" interests would not remain empty rhetoric. The national character of state disciplinary campaigns was reflected in the promotion of gendered family values attractive not only to entrepreneurs, who saw them as good for business, but also—as indicated in the next section—to working-class men. By linking progress to popular economic and political participation, and both of these to gendered forms of worker discipline, popular-front state officials charted a distinctive path of class compromise. They also revamped gender relations.

Working-Class Masculinities

By trying, on balance, to educate and cajole rather than to repress and punish, the popular-front state tried to assure popular acceptance of its program. But the success of state campaigns was also conditioned by the way they converged with longstanding elements of working-class culture. In fact, within working-class organizations, the notion that working-class men should lead orderly, controlled, viceless lives predated socialist participation in the popular-front coalitions. Eduardo Herrera, for example, grew up in the socialist milieu of Valparaíso in the 1920s, a milieu that he later described as "fanatical." That fanaticism manifested itself in the fervor with which Herrera and his comrades attended meetings, distributed pamphlets, went on strike, and watched over polls on election day. It was also apparent in the zeal with which socialists regulated the familial and social life of their community, making sure that children were mindful of their parents, that Sunday luncheons were alcohol-free, and that dances were chaperoned to ensure that party-goers danced with moderation—no charleston allowed.[29]

In the days before 1938, this more austere working-class culture—like the more militant masculine identity advocated by others—cemented opposition to ruling elites. The socialist press hounded on the theme of capitalist immorality, exposing the exploitation of bosses and the shameful feats of dissipate and lazy bourgeois dandies who raped women and drank excessively. For workers and their families, socialist propaganda posited a proletarian honorability.[30] But as the left increasingly sought participation in the national community and made itself part of the popular-front project of state building, an emerging emphasis on the ways proletarian honorability converged with that of other social sectors facilitated the left's alliance with other political forces. Leftists decreasingly characterized discipline as a way of distinguishing correct proletarian behavior from incorrect capitalist conduct, and socialists' rejection of spontaneous, impulsive expressions of opposition to bosses and rulers facilitated the emergence of a national-popular project that stressed dialogue over confrontation. The oppositional nature of a separate socialist morality became less pronounced. Still, socialist morality continued to mark the boundaries of a distinctly leftist working-class identity, to solidify socialist organizations, and to function as a way of critiquing the bourgeoisie. It was most likely the continued association of masculine restraint with working-class opposition to capitalist abuse, as well as its convergence with elite disciplinary projects rooted in notions of progress, that facilitated the political displacement and marginalization of more unruly forms of masculine identity.

Both before and after 1939, left accounts commonly stressed that ideal socialists were austere and led orderly, viceless lives. Good socialists worked arduously and treasured culture and education. Advocating the practice of sports as a way of ensuring health, the socialist youth bulletin *Acción Social* (*AS*) reminded readers to "concern yourselves with sports as well, with life outdoors, with health and the equilibrium of all our biological functions." Although this working-class insistence on hygiene and health drew on and reproduced eugenic prescriptions emanating from the state, it rebutted elite perceptions that the poor were unworthy because they were dirty and complacent. In propagating good habits, subalterns emphasized their ability to alter and govern their own lives. Moreover, a recognition of the need for personal action in the face of adversity did not prevent left activists from pinpointing the material limitations subalterns faced as they strove for personal control. In signaling economic restrictions, militants reinforced an oppositional relation to the economically dominant class that impoverished them and to the experts that promoted moralizing campaigns instead of granting economic benefits. Socialists considered personal improvement necessary and beneficial, but recognized it could only go so far.[31]

The useful triumph of human will and rationality over base behavior constituted a constant subtext of socialist moral prescriptions. In an article titled "Habit: Precious Ally or Dangerous Enemy," *AS* differentiated good, liberating habits from bad ones that bound and reduced the will of the individual. Elsewhere, propagandists repudiated alcohol, because it made men lose their reason and was a "principal factor of mental narrowness [*estrechez*]." In contrast, the ultimately emancipatory development of good habits implied—at least initially—thought, caution, and a rejection of impulse. The worker press applauded the "habit of work" and sexual as well as political restraint, and it called on left organizations to encourage reading and establish libraries.[32]

Calls to moderation and personal betterment were part of an essentially masculine code of honor: the vices socialists tried to correct were largely masculine habits, such as smoking, drinking, betting, and womanizing—all animal-like impulses that, as another publication put it, made men into sacks of vices who shunned their obligation to fortify themselves physically and morally and to care for family members and comrades. Stressing the theme of improvement and its virile nature, the Socialist Militia, defense groups organized within the Socialist Party, stipulated that participants should avoid bars and "other places" (such as, most probably, whorehouses) where "far from improving himself, the *miliciano*'s life, which should be healthy and have a strong and virile quality, might be shortened."[33]

Although this orientation toward personal improvement and autonomy may have carried artisanal concerns with independence inherited from the past, it remolded them to fit the concerns of industrial workers in capitalist labor relations. In Volodia Teitelboim's novel, *Hijo del salitre,* based on the life of Communist Party founder Elías Lafferte, the protagonist rejects a job offered to him by Jacinto, an independent laborer contracted by the nitrate company for which they both work. He also turns down the coca leaves Jacinto proffers, explaining that because he is under the supervision of foremen, he cannot chew coca leaves on the job. Free to work or drug himself as he pleases, Jacinto sees Lafferte as a sellout lacking in autonomy. But even when Jacinto calls Lafferte a coward and questions his manhood, Lafferte holds out his own conception of freedom and manliness. As Teitelboim's narrator comments, "Elías didn't want to be a man of the *lluta* and the coca. He did not want that liberty. Was there no better liberty in life?" Countering Jacinto, Lafferte asks, "Is that your liberty, your right to that tiny heroic drug?"[34]

Whereas employers and state officials emphasized the productive losses caused by alcohol-loving workers, socialist organizations decried the detrimental effects of male vices on working-class unity. Worker publications decried the laziness and indifference of workers who spent leisure hours in bars and worried about the politically demobilizing effects of a deadened will. Thus, an "interesting letter from a compañera" to the union newspaper *El Obrero Municipal* lamented the political apathy of booze lovers and chastised husbands who thought only of "satisfying deathly vices that only poison the heart and atrophy the brain." Similarly, *Obrero Textil*'s "war on alcohol" aimed to lift laborers from "the mud" in which they were submerged and "at the same time reinforce our union cadres." In another skirmish in the textile workers' "war," the union newspaper bemoaned the fact that "nothing, not even the great poverty they suffer, has been enough to make the brains of many compañeros, who above all adore alcohol, work." Going on to link personal care to class consciousness, the article continued, "We are no longer able to attend to our own person. I ask, then, if we continue like this, will we be able tomorrow to defend our rights in the coming struggle?" Another union publication complained that while union leaders worked "night and day," sacrificing themselves for their co-workers, laborers carelessly sullied the reputations of their leaders in gos-siping conversations oiled by liquor. Besides, *Obrero Textil* noted, drunken fights undermined solidarity among coworkers.[35]

For communist Clotilde Villarrica, men with vices openly betrayed their class. "I never understood," she said in a 1993 interview, "why a worker would declass himself. Why, for example, a Party militant, being a miner would up and take the bourgeoisie's vices. . . . Taking the bourgeoisie's vices, taking another woman. Leaving his wife, his children, things like that. Well, getting drunk. Things—Well, that I don't understand." Villa-rrica saw drinking and womanizing as bourgeois vices for which working-class men should not be pardoned. Moreover, she equated a man's loyalty to his class with his devotion to his wife and family. Like state agents, em-ployers, and working-class leaders, she noted the distasteful effects of male drinking on family finances and of male camaraderie on family unity.[36]

After the popular fronts took power in 1939, leftists combined a focus on moralizing as a means of class unity and opposition to capital (and on class unity as a means of moralizing) with a discourse that stressed the promo-tion of proper masculine habits as also beneficial for the national commu-nity. Because leftists saw the health of workers and the strength of their organizations as fortifying the nation as well as the working class, they claimed that worker restraint contributed to a national grandeur that capi-talists sought to sabotage. Exhortations not to drink, bet, or visit bars began to emphasize not only the detrimental effects of these activities on personal health, working-class organizations, and family, but also the way they weakened the Chilean "race" and nation. A quite typical article in a socialist publication characterized alcohol consumption as "the principal social blemish" and stressed that the promotion of abstention would "save the race and return to the family the father who is today lost." It further noted that men who drank "lost a notion and a sense of the necessity of union Organization and of the defense of their own particular interests and those of the community." Linking personal improvement, family duties, and defense of the nation in a comparable way, another issue of the same newspaper described a drunk man as being in a subhuman state that allowed the diabolical, foreign-born owner of the bar he frequented to take advantage of him. What happened after he and his friend left the bar was even worse: the man provoked a fight; his friend was stabbed while trying to defend him; the man himself ended up in jail; and "His wife and older daughters cried this misfortune with grief and pain." Thus, drinking harmed the man himself by reducing him to an animal state; it harmed the nation by enriching the indecent foreigner who owned the bar; it harmed his friend (and potential political ally); and it harmed his family.[37]

Because vices were simultaneously detrimental to individuals, to families, to working-class organizations, and to the nation, the left sanctioned and helped carry out a multifaceted struggle to control depravity and corruption. Along with calling for personal restraint, they therefore granted authority and legitimacy to state regulation and claimed their own community as a proper regulatory instance. Even as leftists sought to curb excessive drinking themselves, they asserted that the state should campaign against alcohol consumption, encourage citizen health and good habits by promoting sports, and provide resources for the building of sports facilities. Many representatives of the working class, from union leaders to Socialist and Communist Party municipal counselors, embraced prohibition for the sake of family and community. When the mayor of Valdivia saw fit to prohibit the sale of liquor at union events, for example, the local socialist newspaper applauded him. Valdivia's *Palabra Socialista* added that in order for the measure to be truly effective, the sale of liquor in the areas surrounding union halls ought to be prohibited as well. The newspaper also denounced the authorization of liquor sales on Independence Day in the otherwise dry town of Corral. Referring to the problem of alcoholism, the Communist Party even went so far as to suggest in one publication that "in many cases the use of restrictive methods is indispensable to avoid or diminish the exacerbation of this problem."[38]

In other cases, however, the punitive fashion in which dry laws were enforced provoked the ire of workers and left leaders, so although the left continued to preach temperance, it also opposed certain prohibitionist measures. As early as 1940, for example, *El Despertar Minero,* a miners' union newspaper, complained about the extreme and punitive manner in which the Braden Copper Company applied dry laws. More generally, as diverse localities implemented prohibitionist measures, often at the insistence of workers' organizations, the difficulties inherent in delegating regulatory power to the state and enforcement to the police became more apparent to many. At least in relation to alcohol, leftist calls for state regulation became less frequent by the mid-1940s. Leftists continued to call for disciplinary state action but simultaneously affirmed their control over antialcoholism campaigns. The fight against alcoholism, a newspaper of the CTCH labor confederation put forth, "is not only the job of a State agency but a privileged task of Chileans who are clean of heart and who sincerely wish a complete improvement of the nation."[39]

Leftists further insisted that men of the popular classes drank to forget their misery and because they did not have access to healthier recreational pursuits. They thus shifted the emphasis of the antialcoholism campaign away from punitive and restrictive measures aimed at male laborers. Instead, they championed restraint of the rich and, like state officials, increased recreational opportunities for the working class. According to representatives of organized popular sectors, capitalists were the main instigators of the excessive consumption of inebriants. The rich profited from the sale of wine and spirits, and aspired to subdue subalterns' rebellious spirit by keeping them drunk. In response, popular organizations suggested that producers and distributors of alcoholic beverages should be taxed. One physician writing in *La Crítica* proposed that those involved in the elaboration of alcoholic beverages be banned from holding public office.[40]

Although leftists were suspicious of state-sponsored recreational activities such as those organized by the Defensa de la Raza, fearing that state officials would manipulate sports clubs for their own ends, they approved of the state's promotion of healthy diversions for workers. The Socialist Party's *La Crítica,* for example, hailed the personal and civic benefits to be derived from the practice of sports: "For modern statesmen and women, it is no secret that sports have a preponderant influence on *las buenas costumbres.* A sports-loving people is a people that can be easily channeled, directed, or oriented toward a sense of solidarity and social benefit. Sports create a morality that contributes to smoothing egotism and leveling men. And it keeps them away from the canteen." The practice of sports would not only uplift the race, but also diminish class conflict, the newspaper suggested.[41]

At the same time, leftists articulated recreational activities into their class-based political project. With increasing diligence beginning around 1935–36, leftists gave theater and music groups, dances, and sports a socialist intentionality and vied for control of leisure pursuits. Accenting the camaraderie of sports and social events—not the value of competition—they articulated these activities into a left discursive field that stressed class solidarity. This articulation not only took place on a rhetorical level but also involved concrete organizational and mobilizational practices. By playing in or creating sports teams at the workers' places of employment, leftists sought to supplant employer-sponsored clubs and to recruit members for their own organizations. Noting that many youths were not interested in politics, *AS* counseled members of the Federación de Juventud Socialista (FJS, Socialist Youth Federation) to participate in sports clubs. "By giving these clubs a strong spirit of collegiality and sportsmanlike sobriety," *AS* suggested, "the FJS will be doubly fortified. In its bodies as a result of sport, and in its ranks by attracting new and valuable elements."[42]

Not surprisingly, left attempts to discourage male vices were never fully successful. Men routinely went drinking after soccer games and even after union meetings. Although these practices were never publicly sanctioned by the left, they persisted and even contributed to a sense of class belonging and political unity. Noting the ways in which male socializing and politics went hand in hand, a social worker with anticommunist intentions attributed male vices to "pernicious influences of a communist nature that in uncultured minds produce a disorientation that has nefarious effects on an honorable and tranquil existence." But reproducing in oral testimony a very different notion of propriety, communist militants frequently characterized a politically committed male relative as *"tranquilo"* or *"de casa,"* a family man who was not interested in the excesses of male get-togethers.[43] By seeking to replace purportedly unhealthy forms of male sociability, leftists helped marginalize and repress alternative, raucous forms of masculinity and to shape a novel form of class compromise. Although the emerging form of class compromise generated a normative male identity linked to the consolidation of the nuclear family and capitalist production relations, and therefore to national prosperity, the promotion of such an identity also worked to cement an oppositional working-class culture and a form of nationality rooted in that culture. It also validated working-class women's efforts to do away with forms of masculine deportment that jeopardized the subsistence of their families.

Conclusion

As I have shown in this essay, although working-class and elite conceptions of masculinity diverged in some ways, they converged in many others. Agreement on certain norms of masculine deportment both depended on and helped secure national identity and state building. Yet convergence around certain norms of masculinity was not simply the result of the repressive efforts of "experts" intent on disciplining popular classes for the sake of capitalist modernization. Elites' attempts to incorporate certain sectors of the working class into a project of nation-state building was conditioned by popular-front methods that allowed dialogue between state officials and popular groups: popular-front politicians preferred education and incentives—better wages, enhanced political influence, control over dependent family members—over policing. In addition, the popular fronts garnered popular support precisely because their project coincided in many ways with certain popular norms of masculinity and popular forms of discipline, including those of working-class housewives. Concurrently, agreement over gender norms cemented cooperation not only between political leaders and working-class activists, but also between both of these groups and certain sectors of the economically dominant class. Notions of masculinity, progress, discipline, and nationality were elastic enough to at least partially accommodate each of these groups.

The convergence between popular-front leaders and popular classes, solidified by state incentive and invective, undoubtedly changed popular notions of what it meant to be a "proper" man. The coming together of popular leaders and state officials helped rout—although it did not obliterate—a more rowdy and nomadic masculine identity that shunned family responsibilities in favor of a more homosocial class identity. But popular adherence to "tamer," more "civilized" forms of masculine identity also gave male workers a sense of agency and efficacy and fortified their sense of class belonging. Thus, workers who cooperated with state officials and their campaigns could do so without losing a sense of their own specific culture. Even as they strove to further the interests of the nation, they did not fully relinquish their autonomy, and they would continue to complain about and haggle over precisely how disciplinary campaigns were carried out.

Undoubtedly, not all processes of state building are as open as the one that took place in Chile in the 1930s and 1940s. Elsewhere in Latin America, popular organizations had fewer options available to them, and national leaders exercised power more unilaterally. Even within Chile, not all potential citizens participated equally in determining the shape of the nation. "Retrograde" and uncultured men as well as women had fewer venues of influence.[44] Yet it is only by looking carefully at the tensions and nuances of sharing and conflict—tensions and nuances such as the ones that expressed themselves in Chile around issues of temperance and recreation—that we can gauge the openness of state-building projects. Otherwise, we condemn ourselves to vague and demobilizing generalizations about "the state."

Notes

Versions of this essay were presented at the Latin American Labor History Conference, Duke University, April 1998, and at the Maxwell Latin America Forum, Syracuse University, March 1998. I am grateful to the participants in the Labor History Conference, especially Greg Crider and Daniel James, and to my colleagues at Syracuse University for their gracious and incisive comments. Funding for this project was provided by a Fulbright Grant.

1 Formed in 1936, the coalition that elected Pedro Aguirre Cerda to the presidency in 1938 and persisted until 1940 called itself the Popular Front. However, I use the term *popular fronts* and the adjective *popular-front* (which I do not capitalize) to designate the Popular Front and subsequent governing coalitions in which sectors of the center and left, and eventually sectors of the right, participated. I take this usage from Tomás Moulian, "Violencia, gradualismo y reformas en el desarrollo político chileno," in *Estudios sobre el sistema de partidos en Chile,* ed. Adolfo Aldunate et al. (Santiago: FLACSO, 1984), 13–60.

2 Mary Kay Vaughan, "Modernizing Patriarchy: State Policies, Rural Households, and Women in Mexico," this volume; Laura Gotkowitz, "Commemorating the *Heroínas:* Gender and Civic Ritual in Early-Twentieth-Century Bolivia," ibid. On populist coalitions elsewhere in Latin America, see Daniel James, *Resistance and Integration: Peronism and the Argentine Working Class, 1946–1976* (Cambridge: Cambridge University Press, 1988); Samuel Baily, *Labor, Nationalism, and*

Politics in Argentina (New Brunswick: Rutgers University Press, 1967); Marjorie Becker, "Torching La Purísima, Dancing at the Altar: The Construction of Revolutionary Hegemony in Michoacán, 1934–1940," in *Everyday Forms of State Formation: Revolution and the Negotiation of Rule in Modern Mexico,* ed. Gilbert Joseph and Daniel Nugent (Durham, N.C.: Duke University Press, 1994), 247–64; Jan Rus, "The 'Comunidad Revolucionaria Institucional': The Subversion of Native Government in Highland Chiapas, 1936–1968," in ibid., 265–300; Barry Carr, "The Fate of the Vanguard under a Revolutionary State: Marxism's Contribution to the Construction of the Great Arch," in ibid., 326–52; Barry Carr, *Marxism and Communism in Twentieth-Century Mexico* (Lincoln: University of Nebraska Press, 1992); John D. French, *The Brazilian Workers' ABC: Class Conflict and Alliances in Modern São Paulo* (Chapel Hill: University of North Carolina Press, 1992). On Chile, see Paul Drake, *Socialism and Populism in Chile, 1932–1952* (Urbana: University of Illinois Press, 1978); Moulian, *Estudios sobre el sistema;* María Angélica Illanes, *"En el nombre del pueblo, del estado y de la ciencia (. . .)":* *Historia social de la salud pública, Chile 1880–1973* (Santiago: Colectivo de Atención Primaria, 1993).

3   Edda Gaviola et al., *Queremos votar en las próximas elecciones: Historia del movimiento femenino chileno, 1913–1952* (Santiago: CEM, 1986).

4   My view of state formation draws on Philip Corrigan and Derek Sayer, *The Great Arch: English State Formation as Cultural Revolution* (Oxford: Basil Blackwell, 1985); Antonio Gramsci, *Selections from the Prison Notebooks,* ed. and trans. Quintin Hoare and Geoffrey Nowell Smith (London: International Publishers, 1971); Joseph and Nugent, eds., *Everyday Forms;* Ana María Alonso, *Thread of Blood: Colonialism, Revolution, and Gender on Mexico's Northern Frontier* (Tucson: University of Arizona Press, 1995).

5   "En vibrante manifiesto el candidato de las izquierdas expresa al pueblo de Chile que se hace responsable de los postulados del F. Popular," *Unidad Gráfica,* 9 October 1938, 1; "Editorial," *Acción Social* 10, no. 81 (September 1939): 1–4. Unless otherwise noted, all newspapers and periodicals were published in Santiago.

6   Salvador Allende, *La realidad médico-social chilena* (Santiago, 1939), 5–8, 195–98, and passim.

7   For the Communist Party, the shift away from a revolutionary strategy was prompted by changes in the Comintern line and the loss of strength the party had suffered in the 1920s and 1930s. See Carmelo Furci, *The Chilean Communist Party and the Road to Socialism* (London: Zed, 1984); and the essays in Arturo Varas, comp., *El Partido Comunista en Chile* (Santiago: CESOC / FLACSO, 1988).

8   For references to leftists in government service see *Chispa* (Iquique), second fortnight March 1939, 5; *El Surco* (La Ligua), 28 December 1940, n.p.; ibid., 4 January 1941, 2; *El Progreso* (Arauco), 27 February 1941, n.p.; ibid., 6 March 1941, 3; interview with Marta Rojas, 14 June 1993 (all interviews were conducted by

the author in Santiago; pseudonyms have been used); Drake, *Socialism and Populism*, 239. On popular representation on the advisory boards of state agencies, see *Chispa* (Iquique), February 1939, 7; *La Crítica*, 6 November 1939, 10; *Combate*, first fortnight February 1943, 2; "Texto del discurso pronunciado por el líder de los empleados y obreros de la Federación de Beneficencia," *Noticiario Sindical*, 31 January 1949, 10; "La Caja de Seguro Obligatorio," *Boletín Médico-Social de la Caja de Seguro Obligatorio*, nos. 117–19 (July–September 1944): 205–13; María Mora Campos, "Protección a la familia obrera" (Memoria, Facultad de Ciencias Jurídicas y Sociales, Universidad de Chile, 1944), 135; Flora Meneses Zúñiga, "La ley 4054 de seguro obligatorio de enfermedad, vejez e invalidez" (Memoria, Facultad de Ciencias Jurídicas y Sociales, Universidad de Chile, 1936), 17; "Apóstoles del movimiento sindical," *CTCh*, 10 September 1943, 2; "El consejo superior del trabajo y el derecho social chileno," ibid., 1 May 1946, 13. Unless otherwise noted, all translations are mine.

9   *El Progreso* (Arauco), 24 April 1941, 1. Partido Comunista, "Estatutos del Partido Comunista de Chile aprobados por el XIII Congreso Nacional celebrado en 1946" (Santiago, n.d.), 37.

10 "El pueblo no come, no viste, no habita," *Bandera Roja*, fourth week September 1936, 1. "El problema de vivir," *El Despertar Minero* (Sewell), 1 August 1939, 2. *La Crítica*, 4 November 1939, 13.

11 "Resignación," *Rumbo* (June 1940): 88. "Como antifascistas censuramos el decreto de 'Defensa de la Raza'," *Combate*, 9 September 1939, n.p.

12 See Eugenia Rodríguez, "Civilizing Domestic Life in the Central Valley of Costa Rica, 1750–1850," this volume; Donna Guy, "Parents Before the Tribunals: The Legal Construction of Patriarchy in Argentina," in ibid.; Ann Varley, "Women and the Home in Mexican Family Law," in ibid.; Mary Kay Vaughan, "Modernizing Patriarchy." "En vibrante manifiesto el candidato de las izquierdas expresa al pueblo de Chile que se hace responsable de los postulados del F. Popular," *Unidad Gráfica*, 9 October 1938, 1; *Vanguardia Socialista* (Yungay), 16 October 1938, 1; "Destructores del hogar y de la fe," *La Crítica*, 8 November 1939, 3.

13 Karin Rosemblatt, "Gendered Compromises: Political Cultures, Socialist Politics, and the State in Chile, 1920–1950" (Ph.D. diss., University of Wisconsin–Madison, 1996).

14 "La clase trabajadora y su porvenir," *Noticiario Sindical*, 1 May 1949, 16.

15 Thomas Klubock, *Contested Communities: Class, Gender, and Politics in Chile's El Teniente Copper Mine, 1904–1951* (Durham, N.C.: Duke University Press, 1998). The quotation is from Graciela Alvarez Pacheco, "El servicio social ante el problema de la madre soltera" (Memoria, Escuela de Servicio Social, Ministerio de Educación Pública Concepción, 1944), 68.

16 "Máximas," *Vanguardia Hotelera*, March 1948, 4; ibid., October 1947, 4; *Juventud en Marcha* (Concepción), 5 June 1937, 2.

17 Popular acceptance of elite norms of masculinity obviously varies across time

and place and is conditioned by the pressure women exert, both collectively and individually. See the essays in this volume by Rodríguez, Guy, Vaughan, and Gotkowitz.

18 *Vida Sana* (Valparaíso) 2, no. 9 (January 1943): 6.

19 Rosemblatt, "Gendered Compromises," chap. 5.

20 For Aguirre Cerda's motto, see Allende, *Realidad médico-social,* 5. The quotations are from "El papel de la visitadora social en los servicios de la Caja de Seguro Obligatorio," *Boletín Médico-Social de la Caja de Seguro Obligatorio,* nos. 117–19 (July–September 1944): 347–52, quotation on 347; "Nota editorial," *Vida Sana* (Temuco) 1, no. 1 (November 1938): 1. On arrests for drunkenness, see *Estadística Chilena* 18, no. 12 (December 1945); ibid. 23, no. 12 (December 1950): 720–21. On leftists in the bureaucracy, see Rosemblatt, "Gendered Compromises," 347–62 and passim.

21 "El alcohol y las enfermedades venéreas," *Vida Sana* (Valparaíso) 2, no. 10 (February–March 1943): 3. "Ciudadano ejemplar," *Vida Sana* (Temuco), second period, 1, no. 6 (June 1941): 3.

22 Lucia Ponce Ponce, "Desavenencias conyugales en el hogar del obrero municipal" (Memoria, Escuela de Servicio Social, Ministerio de Educación Pública, Santiago, 1945), 11–16, 61. *Vida Sana* (Valparaíso) 2, no. 9 (January 1943): 5. On male drinking, domestic violence, and attempts to promote domestic harmony see also Rodríguez and Vaughan in this volume.

23 Allende, *Realidad medico-social,* 122. "El alcoholismo," *Boletín del Ministerio de Salubridad, Previsión, y Asistencia Social* (January 1940): 30–32, quotation on 30.

24 "Cruzada anti-alcohólica y anti-venérea," *Aurora de Chile,* 7 October 1949, 15; "Responsabilidades individuales y nacionales del alcoholismo," *Vida Sana* (Valparaíso) 2, no. 9 (January 1943): 3.

25 The quotation is from Graciela de Alvarado, "El servicio social en la industria salitrera," *Servicio Social* 11, no. 4 (October 1937): 224–53, quotation on 243. On the role of company welfare departments see Thomas Klubock, "Sexualidad y proletarización en la mina El Teniente," *Proposiciones* (Santiago), no. 21 (1992), 65–77, particularly 66–67; *Revista del Trabajo* 5, no. 10 (October 1935): 52–53; "La compañía de Refinería de Azúcar de Viña del Mar," ibid. 7, nos. 5–6 (June 1937): 129–30; "Compañía de gas de Valparaíso," ibid., 130–32; "Algunos aspectos del problema de la habitación obrera," *Servicio Social* 9, no. 3 (July–September 1935): 177; ibid. 9, no. 4 (October–December 1935): 305–7; ibid. 11, no. 4 (October 1937): 224–53; "Labor realizada por el servicio social en la compañía salitrera Tarapacá y Antofagasta de 1936 a 1941," ibid. 18, no. 2 (May–August 1944): 6–9; "Servicio social industrial en Concepción y sus alrededores," ibid. 20, nos. 2–3 (May–December 1946): 31–39; "ASIMET y el servicio social," ibid. 29, no. 3 (September–December 1955): 17–29; "El Departamento de Bienestar Social," *Pampa* (January 1949): 7; Olga Cárcamo Lastra, "Servicio social en la manufactura de metales 'MADEMSA' " (Memoria, Escuela de Servicio Social, Ministerio de Educación Pública, Santiago, 1948), 9–11.

26 Nora Ortega Fuentes, "Acción de la lucha antivenérea en Concepción" (Memoria, Escuela de Servicio Social, Ministerio de Educación Pública, Concepción, 1947), 58. Chile, Dirección de Informaciones y Cultura, "Recopilación de las disposiciones legales y reglamentarias sobre los servicios que integran la Dirección General de Información y Cultura" ([Santiago?], 1943), 202. See also *Alianza Democrática,* 11 October 1946, 4.

27 *¿Qué Hubo?* 1 August 1939, 30; "Horas libres y vacaciones," *Acción Social* 10, no. 84 (December 1939): 3–4; "Editorial," ibid., 10, no. 81 (September 1939): 1–4; "Un ensayo sobre biblioteca popular campesina," ibid., 12, no. 109 (February 1942): 2–10; "El aprovechamiento de las horas libres de los obreros," *CTCh,* second fortnight July 1939, 10. On the Hogar Pedro Aguirre Cerda, see "Liga de consumidores no. 7," *La Voz de Conchalí,* second fortnight June 1947, 5; and "El Hogar Pedro Aguirre Cerda al goce de la defensa de la raza," *El Centinela,* 4 March 1944, n.p. On the Centro Valparaíso, *Vida Sana* (Valparaíso) 1, no. 8 (December 1942): 1, 4–6.

28 "Horas libres y vacaciones," *Acción Social* 12, no. 84 (December 1939): 3–4. *Servicio Social* 19, nos. 2–3 (September–December 1945): 26–32.

29 Interview with Eduardo Herrera and Irma Salazar, 4 June 1993.

30 Ibid. On socialist morality in this period, see also Tomás Moulian and Isabel Torres, "Concepción de la política e ideal moral en la prensa obrera: 1919–1922" (Santiago: FLACSO, Documento de Trabajo no. 336, 1987).

31 "Sugerencia a la FJS," *AS,* no. 5 (n.d.): 5. Interview with Flor Valenzuela, 5 April 1993; Diego Muñoz, *Carbón* (Santiago: Editora Austral, 1953), 23.

32 "El hábito," *AS,* no. 3 (n.d.): 1. *Ahora* (Iquique), cited in *Obrero Textil,* 30 June 1937, 3–4.

33 Ibid. See also Sindicato Industrial Obrero Andes Copper Mining Co. y Potrerillos Raylway [*sic*] Corp., "Pliego de peticiones presentado a los Sres. gerentes y sub-gerentes generales" (c. 1937), n.p. The quotation is from Partido Socialista, "Reglamento nacional de defensa" (Santiago, 1940), 33.

34 Volodia Teitelboim, *Hijo del salitre* (Santiago: Editora Austral, n.d.), 131–32. Moulian and Torres, "Concepción de la política," posit the emphasis on education and control as reflecting the artisanal roots of the Chilean labor movement.

35 "Una interesante carta de una compañera," *El Obrero Municipal,* December 1936, 2; "¿Queremos tener una potente organización?" *Obrero Textil,* 4 December 1936, 3; *Ahora* (Iquique), cited in *Obrero Textil,* 30 June 1937, 3–4; "Labor ejemplar de las esposas de los obreros municipales," *El Obrero Municipal,* May 1939, 3.

36 Interview with Clotilde Villarrica, 6 April 1993. On women's collusion with state officials, see also Rodríguez, Varley, and Vaughan in this volume.

37 "El alcoholismo, la primera lacra social," *CTCh,* October 1945, 3. "Camarada, vas por mal camino," ibid., July 1946, 5.

38 "Un llamado a los deportistas," *El Despertar Minero* (Sewell), second fortnight August 1943, 6; "Campos deportivos, gimnasios, piscinas para la juventud" and

"El Parque Centenario que se entregue a los deportistas," *Mundo Nuevo,* third period, 1 March 1941, 6; "Los obreros se han adelantado a los deseos del gobierno para la implantación del antialcoholismo," ibid., 26 October 1939, 10; Sindicato Industrial Obrero Andes Copper Mining Co., "Pliego de peticiones." The quotation is from Partido Comunista, "Informes y resoluciones: Política parlamentaria; política municipal; cultura, prensa, y propaganda" (Santiago, 1940), 22.

39 "Alcoholismo y deporte," *El Santiago Watt* 3, nos. 38–39 (March–April 1946): 14; Partido Comunista, "¡Adelante por el cumplimiento del programa del Frente Popular!: Sesión plenaria del Comité Central del Partido Comunista de Chile" (Santiago, 1941), 44; "¡Ah la ley seca!" *El Despertar Minero* (Sewell), 30 April 1941, n.p.; "El problema del alcoholismo en el carbón restringe mayor producción," *El Siglo,* 4 July 1943, 5; "El alchoholismo, la primera lacra social," *CTCh,* October 1945, 3; "Nuestro gremio y la ley de represión al alcoholismo," *Vanguardia Hotelera,* second period, January 1938, 1. On drinking and the application of dry laws in El Teniente, see Klubock, *Contested Communities,* 59–61, 122–23, 155–64. The quotation is from "Una campaña de salvación nacional," *CTCh,* October 1945, 8.

40 Allende, *Realidad médico-social,* 119; *Liberación* (Tomé), 16 September 1939, 2; "Hambre y alcoholismo," *El Progreso* (Curicó), 25 November 1944, 2; "Diputados viñateros rechazan impuesto al vino," *Claridad,* 23 December 1937, 1; "Breves reflexiones patrióticas," *La Crítica,* 14 September 1942, 3.

41 The quotation is from "Por la salvación de la raza," *La Crítica,* 17 November 1939, 3, and is a virtual paraphrase of the decree that set up Defensa de la Raza, published in "Editorial," *Acción Social* 10, no. 81 (September 1939): 1–4.

42 Partido Comunista, "Informes y resoluciones," 21; *Tribuna Juvenil,* July 1935, 3; interview with Clotilde Villarrica, 6 April 1993; *Rumbo* (January 1940): 19; "Sugerencia a la FJS," *AS,* no. 5 (n.d.): 5.

43 For evidence of "deviant" male socializing, see "Alcoholismo y deporte," *El Santiago Watt* 3, nos. 38–39 (March–April 1946): 14; interview with Blanca Leiva, 25 March 1993; interview with Clotilde Villarrica, 6 April 1993. On the discrepancies between the pronouncements of left organizations and working-class customs, see also Klubock, *Contested Communities.* The quotation is from *Servicio Social* 9, no. 4 (October–December 1935): 305–7. Interview with Flor Valenzuela, 5 April 1993; interview with Blanca Leiva, 25 March 1993; interview with Ignacia Parada, 20 April 1993.

44 See Vaughan, Gotkowitz, and Varley, in this volume and Rosemblatt "Gendered Compromises," who also explore how women played into this process.

Maxine Molyneux

State, Gender, and Institutional Change

The Federación de Mujeres Cubanas

We have gone through three periods since the revolution: in the first we looked to the state to solve all of our problems, and we managed more or less OK. In the second, from 1988, we found the state couldn't meet our needs, and we were unable to meet them ourselves. Since 1993 we no longer rely on the state because we know that it cannot deliver what we need. But at least now we can begin to provide for ourselves.—[former FMC functionary, then working for an NGO, in an interview with the author]

The 1990s was a time of particular uncertainty in Cuba—a crisis associated, on the one hand, with the collapse of the Soviet system and, on the other, with the emergency associated with the "Special Period."[1] When, in 1990, Cuba was officially declared to be in the "special period in peacetime," it was a signal that the campaign of *rectificación*,[2] begun in 1986, had ended and that a new era of even greater austerity was at hand. As subsidies and trade with the Eastern bloc plummeted after 1989, the Cuban economy, already faltering throughout the latter part of the 1980s, suffered a severe if anticipated shock. The years 1989–93 registered the lowest growth rates since the revolution in 1959, a near 50 percent fall in global social product (GSP).[3] The crisis was reflected not only in the sharp contraction of the economy, but also in the acute shortage of basic goods and energy supplies that hit the Cuban population hard.[4]

While government policies, foreign investment, and tourism had brought some alleviation of the worst hardships from the middle of 1994 onward, there could be little doubt that the political and economic model espoused for the past thirty-seven years was in crisis. Among the population was a widespread recognition that the system had to yield to the forces of change, while the political leadership was preoccupied with controlling the pace and direction of such change. That this process had accelerated beyond what was initially foreseen was evident in the legalization of the dollar in 1993, followed in 1995 by the passing of a revised property law, the legalization of small businesses, and the introduction of new taxation measures in January 1996. The spread of markets throughout the island and of informal sector activities—most notable in Havana in the rapid expansion of the *paladares* or semiprivate eating houses and in the omnipresent *jinoteras* in the tourist areas—were evidence of the multifaceted nature of the move toward a greater role for the market, signaling major changes in state-society relations.[5]

For any society, the removal of its ideological and strategic patron and a collapse in national output over a five-year period would be challenge enough. Combined as these problems were with an unrelenting and vengeful pressure from the United States and with an apparent inability of the regime itself to take any political initiatives, the situation was especially acute.[6] Yet in this situation of protracted crisis, in which the dangers of a violent upheaval and of the loss of the very considerable social gains of the revolutionary period were ever present, a debate opened up on the future of the Cuban political system in which, for the first time since the triumph of 1959, the possibility of political reform was creatively explored. Both in Havana and in Miami, voices were raised that sought to chart a course for Cuba that would navigate the worst dangers facing it. Such a course would avoid the imposition on Cuba of "shock therapy," to be compounded by the revanchist proclivities of returning exiles, but would also demand from the regime a political change consonant with the economic reforms it was introducing.[7]

Examples of such views can be found in material produced within Cuba during the 1990s by semiofficial and independent groups, and in analyses attuned to such changes produced abroad.[8] One Cuban contribution, written from a position that stressed the achievements of the revolution, argued that political liberalization was both urgent and possible in contemporary Cuba.[9] The author, Haroldo Dilla, had little time for the argument that political change should be postponed until the economy had recovered or for the view that democratic and constitutional politics were not "appropriate" to Cuba. Although critical of U.S. hostility, he also dismissed the claim that the confrontation with Washington made such a democratization impossible.

Dilla's argument was instead that economic change of the kind associated with the "special period" could not be disassociated from political reform—that is, democratization. The crisis of the Cuban system was not just a result of events in the USSR or of U.S. pressure: it was a result of the changes brought about by the revolution itself: "Civil society has changed. In the first place, its popular sectors are today more educated, with better political formation and greater ability to participate. New generations have entered political life carrying a message of political commitment, but demanding new spaces and renovated forms in which to exercise it. Half of the population, women, is hoping for greater opportunities to express its aspirations in an autonomous manner against a patriarchal order weakened, but not destroyed, by more than thirty years of revolutionary life."[10] The crisis of the Cuban Revolution had, therefore, occurred at the time when Cuban society was best able to respond creatively to it.

The discussion that follows is a reflection on the changes under way in Cuba—ones that have placed the Cuban system of state socialism under pressure to reform. I focus in particular on one of the mass organizations, the Federación de Mujeres Cubanas (FMC, Federation of Cuban Women), and on the changing place of gender issues within the Cuban Revolution.[11] I locate the discussion of the FMC in the context of the arguments summarized above, linking the issue of political change and liberalization to the impact of social and economic change, and examining the degree to which the FMC has been able to adapt to the new realities it has faced.

The "Woman Question" and the Revolutionary State

The FMC in 1990 was one of the largest of the mass organizations in Cuba, claiming a membership of 3.2 million, or 80 percent of the adult female population.[12] An analysis of the federation is of interest for three main reasons. The first is that in membership terms it is not only the largest mass organization in Cuba, but the largest women's organization ever seen in Latin America.[13] Second, its record raises questions about the nature of the regime and its legitimacy in the eyes of its constituency.[14] The record of the Cuban Revolution in regard to "women's emancipation" is an achievement celebrated both internally and to some degree externally as evidence of socialism's superiority over capitalism. The FMC and the Communist Party are jointly credited with achieving above average levels of progress for the Latin American region on key indicators such as female mortality, educational levels, legal rights, health care, and employment. This progress is argued to have provided the regime with legitimacy and considerable support among the female population. If this latter claim were to be substantiated, then the Cuban case differs from the experience of Eastern Europe and suggests a greater degree of support for government institutions than prevailed there; it also suggests that the FMC may enjoy a correspondingly greater degree of effectiveness in responding to the needs of its constituency.

A third reason for focusing on the FMC is that its membership and constituency contain a high proportion of those who are most likely to be adversely affected in the short to medium run by any process of adjustment that eventuates from attempts to resolve Cuba's economic crisis. As studies of the social effects of adjustment have shown, the move toward a greater role for the market can be expected to exacerbate social inequalities and to deepen gender divisions. In Cuba's transition, too, there is already evidence that women suffer a disproportionate burden of the costs of economic crisis, and this trend is likely to accelerate. If the current regime is to avoid the fate of the Sandinistas in the Nicaraguan elections of 1990, when "the largest block of sentiment" against them were women,[15] it will have to address the fact of the gendered nature of economic restructuring and take adequate measures to offset them. Much depends, then, on the character of the FMC.

The official account of the FMC attributes its origins, in a predictable but by no means inaccurate manner, to socialist principle combined with what must in rather more critical terms be characterized as paternalism. According to these accounts, "Fidel himself" set up the Federation of Cuban Women in 1960 and appointed his sister-in-law Vilma Espín as its head, a position she has enjoyed ever since.[16]

The FMC was set up to organize and mobilize women for the defense and consolidation of the revolution. In function as well as in structure, it followed the pattern established in other socialist states, operating as a "mass organization" under the general direction of the party and acting, in Lenin's terms, as "a transmission belt." Its leadership was drawn from the handful of women who were close to the guerrilla command in the 1950s and who, like Vilma Espín herself, had been active in the prerevolutionary struggles. The authority of the revolution was thus present at the apex of the organization, as formal endorsement but also as hegemonic control.

In its goals, organization, and ideology, little differentiated the FMC from women's organizations elsewhere in the communist world. It sought to achieve the political mobilization of women in order to consolidate political power and to implement a socialist program of economic and social transformation.[17] These goals were expressed in terms of an ethical commitment to "women's emancipation," premised on women's entry into work, formal juridical equality, and social rights to health and education.[18]

Like its counterparts elsewhere, the FMC was charged with the task of helping to improve women's situation and to work for equality within the context of carrying out party policy. It was responsible for channeling demands and grievances to the leadership and could, therefore, perform the role of a mild pressure group. Most of its efforts were directed toward political and ideological work among women, which in the early years aimed to mobilize them into campaigns to extend basic health and literacy to the population and into voluntary work schemes.[19] It was also involved in popularizing legislative change such as the Family Code (1975) and the socialist Constitution (1976) and in helping to realize other aspects of government policy that directly affected women and the family.

While claiming to represent women's interests and acknowledging that women did, indeed, have distinct concerns, it sought to define these interests in terms of party goals. In reality, such official women's organizations had little scope for independent initiatives, but in some cases they successfully challenged party policy on a limited range of issues. In two much cited examples, the FMC opposed attempts to follow the Soviet practice of banning women from more than three hundred jobs on "health" grounds and successfully lobbied to permit men to attend to family members in hospitals where previously only women had been allowed.

Integral to the issue of the FMC's capacities and program are the character of the revolutionary state itself, more generally what concepts can be used to describe the socialist regimes of Europe and the Third World, and, in this particular context, the degree to which Cuba can be assimilated to them. It is not possible here to discuss these issues in detail, but two points can be made. First, although not "totalitarian" in the sense of wholly monolithic or unchanging and at least for a time enjoying some popular support, the socialist regimes of the communist bloc did exhibit a high degree of centralized control by the party elite through the bureaucracy of party and state. The reality sometimes fell short of their aspiration, and an autonomous civil society continued in some measure to exist (in the family, churches, underground intellectual groups, and informal, often illegal economic activity). But these were authoritarian societies in which citizens had few if any civil rights. Moreover, while the ruling parties themselves sought to explain and legitimate their activities through appeals to the masses and to engage in various forms of "participatory democracy" (elections, mobilizations, mass meetings, consultations, etc.), these measures in no instance altered the fact of party rule. In overall terms, the party leaderships put through policies that were designed, in addition to guaranteeing their own power, to promote economic development and social change. They implemented a broad top-down program of socialist modernization that was supposed to lead to the emergence of a superior form of social and political existence. This idea of progress sustained the revolutionary elites, just as it justified repression of alternative views and policies. Policies on all issues, women included, need to be seen in this context.

Writers on Cuba have been divided both as to the nature of this model and as to how far Cuba fits the standard identified above. The reasons for stressing difference have been expressed often: the Cuban Revolution initially had a popular, nationalist, and democratic character, and in its first phase was devoid of overt Leninist authoritarianism and direct Soviet influence; the revolution enjoyed a high degree of participation and widespread support on patriotic and social grounds; despite widespread and continued violations of internal norms of legal and human rights practice, the regime's level of coercion was significantly less than in other communist states;[20] not least, the regime in Cuba survived the collapse of communism elsewhere. As far as gender relations were concerned, Cuba also exhibited less of the puritanism of other Soviet bloc states, an aspect of the island's society that outside observers have too often interpreted as evidence of women's emancipation. All these arguments are important and relevant; they do not, however, gainsay the fact that the post-1959 Cuban state, for a combination of necessity and choice, came to exhibit, where it did not do so from the start, many of the distinguishing features of such regimes.

The character of the Cuban Revolution owes much to the particularities of Cuban history and is often presented as a singular, autonomous occurrence, but it needs also to be understood in its conjunctural context; it was born at the end of a decade that had witnessed the accelerating momentum of the Cold War and itself became embroiled in the confrontation between East and West in the missile crisis of 1962. The tense international situation helped to lock Cuba into a path, as an ally and showcase of the Soviet Union, which had profound effects on its population as a whole—effects that were clearly gendered in character. Although enjoying considerable popular support, which continued for some time after the initial confrontation with the United States, the Cuban leadership had nonetheless set in place by the mid-1970s a system that, modeled on the USSR, was premised on centralized, bureaucratic control and, without Soviet subsidies, was economically unsustainable. The Cuban Communist Party (CCP), founded in 1965, was a highly centralized body, modeled on the Communist Party of the Soviet Union. The Cuban press was as controlled as any in the socialist bloc. The party bureaucracy, dominated by men, sought to direct all social and political life; if the secret police were less evident than in the USSR and its allies, other bodies—notably the CCP itself and the Committees for the Defense of the Revolution (CDRS)—performed analogous functions. Despite a greater use of mass meetings, the charismatic power of its leader, the system of *poder popular*,[21] and a more sustained commitment to participation through voluntary labor in the development efforts of the state, the political process was broadly similar. If this was true of the party and state in general, it was also true of policy on what, in conventional socialist terminology, was referred to as "the woman question" and of the ideological and organizational forms this policy took.

The FMC in the 1980s: Adaptation and Resistance

The combined effects of Cuba's insertion into the Soviet bloc, the reformulation of Cuban political and cultural activity along Eastern bloc lines, U.S.-enforced international isolation, and the regime's own controls over intellectual life all but succeeded in insulating the revolution from the major international currents of social and political thought until the early 1980s. It was then that in response to a variety of related circumstances— some internal, some international—a measure of opening up began to occur. The exodus of 125,000 Cubans from Mariel in 1980 was followed by a loosening of some control over economic and social life, with a small private sector being allowed to develop in the service and agricultural domains, and a greater—if still limited—measure of contact being permitted with the Western world. The FMC was perhaps more exposed to these processes than were some of the other mass organizations, if only because the United Nations Decade for Women of 1975–85, along with the Latin American presence within it, became an important and new focus of its international activity.[22]

By the later 1970s, it had become evident that the FMC was no longer operating within the official socialist policy universe and that it existed in tension with two complementary forces—one coming from outside, from a self-confident international women's movement that had strong regional counterparts in Latin America,[23] the other generated internally by women's increasing expectations and self-assertiveness. In retrospect, it can be seen that the UN Decade was a defining moment for the debate on women's place in society in the communist states.[24] As these states saw it, they had a "superior record" on women's rights and social indicators preferable to most of the capitalist states; the UN Decade presented them with an opportunity to make their case and to make a bid for a share of the resources that became available during the decade. Many an official women's organization declared itself to be a nongovernmental organization for the purposes of this exercise, and the FMC, too, duly followed suit. It was in the context of regional meetings for Latin America that the Cuban delegates encountered the diverse currents of activism within the women's movements of Latin America, including one current for which they hitherto had little but contempt—feminism.[25]

As far as feminism was concerned,[26] the FMC had since its inception maintained an attitude of open hostility to it, and this attitude remained unchanged throughout the 1970s. The official position of the FMC, in keeping with the standard Soviet line, attributed women's subordination to capitalist imperialism, a system against which both men and women should unite. Feminism was seen as bourgeois and divisive, and in its insistence on autonomous organizational forms, it was considered at variance with the FMC's acceptance of "democratic centralism" under overall party control. Feminist writings were therefore banned, and there was never any serious engagement with feminist theory within the FMC or beyond it. Vilma Espín insisted that the FMC was a "feminine rather than a feminist" organization and clarified the difference on the eve of the UN Decade for Women, explaining that "We never fought for partial demands; we were always conscious that the problem of women is a part of the whole society and integrally related to the struggle of all the people for their liberation, to men and women together sweeping aside the very foundations of capitalist society to build a new life."[27]

In 1977, however, rather than offering a blanket denunciation of feminism, Espín was careful to identify the main enemy as its North American variety—that is, liberal, nonsocialist, and radical feminist: "We have never had a feminist movement. We hate that. We hate the feminist movement in the United States. We consider what we are doing is part of the struggle. We see these movements in the USA which have conceived struggles for equality of women against men! That is absurd! For these feminists to say they are revolutionaries is ridiculous!"[28]

The FMC was, however, unable to sustain this negative stance. As feminism began to attain greater support within the Latin American left and even to acquire a popular following in the region, official policy shifted to one of co-optation. The policy process gradually began to absorb feminist issues, urged on by women's advocacy within the UN. A handful of younger women sympathetic to feminism began to work within the FMC, and later a few were even sent to Europe, some to England, to study gender issues. At the same time, pressure from within the island had been mounting. By the midseventies, it was evident that the Cuban record on women's emancipation was, in its own terms, in need of improvement. Women's participation in the organs of institutionalized power, particularly in those positions with any real authority, remained at strikingly low levels.[29] Moreover, daily life for women in shortage economies was hard, all the more so where there was reliance on a considerable degree of mass participation and voluntary work. These problems had become all too apparent from within as well as from outside because of the growing international scrutiny to which Cuba was subjected in feminist fora in Latin America and in the activities of the UN Decade.

In contrast to several countries of the Soviet bloc, no dissident feminist groups or writing emerged in Cuba itself, but the leadership was prompted into a growing awareness of the problems women faced everyday in work, in political life, and in the family. As the seventies progressed, public disillusion set in, although the U.S. embargo took much of the blame, and skepticism about the FMC's role in regard to women grew. The party had counted on the substantial involvement of women at the base of the political pyramid—in the institutions of popular power and in the CDRs. Here, women carried out the tasks of community management and *vigilancia* (neighborhood watch), and those who were *integradas* helped to mobilize women to participate in national campaigns.[30] These women, too, voiced their grievances against the system, making persistent demands for improved childcare, housing, and transport, and for longer opening hours for shops. These issues, neglected in what was in many other respects an exemplary record of public provision, had been far from the concerns of the FMC.

From the midseventies, galvanized perhaps by participation in the UN Decade, there occurred some shift in party policy toward the achievement of greater sexual equality and the enhancing of women's political participation. The Family Code of 1975, modeled on the East German legislation passed a year before, laid the basis for a campaign to increase male responsibilities within the household. This phase of greater awareness of the need to address the problems women faced—dubbed the "revolution within the revolution" by one analyst[31]—saw a greater emphasis on improving women's situation overall, an emerging critique of gender divisions in everyday life, and a revised FMC agenda showing more sensitivity to the kinds of issues that had been raised within women's movements. In 1984, Cuba hosted the preparatory regional meeting for the Women's Conference marking the end of the UN Decade. Many Latin American feminists attended the conference, some of international repute; a few, known to have a position of critical support with regard to Cuba, were granted an audience with Castro himself. One participant recalled that this meeting seemed "indicative of some kind of reconciliation with feminism, yet how much this was a genuine accommodation and how much window-dressing is hard to say."[32] In any event, the FMC's Congress of 1985 seemed to many observers to show signs of a greater sensitivity in its handling of gender issues than had been evident in the past.

None of these events, however, were accompanied by significant changes in the style of work performed by the FMC or in the internal character of the organization, which continued much as before. The 1980 Congress had noted that local-level work in the delegations and blocks was unsatisfactory and that attendance was falling in the study circles.[33] This decline continued throughout the 1980s; in 1985, Espín had to defend the very existence of the organization in the face of harsh attacks on its performance, exciting speculation that it might cease to function. There appeared to be a disjuncture between the revitalization taking place within official discourse and the practice of the organization itself.

The character and priorities of the FMC could not, however, be detached from general trends in society as a whole. In the mid-1980s, the limited process of economic liberalization was halted. In one of those sharp countermoves characteristic of socialist states, Castro turned against the farmers' markets and closed them down, arguing that they had led to the emergence of social inequalities and, worse, a corrupt, parasitic sector that was undermining the revolution. This move did not at first have a great impact on the FMC's agenda, and the organization appeared to maintain a commitment to the tenor of the 1985 Congress. Yet in response to pressures of a quite different kind, it was called upon to undergo a revitalizing transformation that came from dramatic changes in the policies of the Cuban state as a whole: just as the Soviet bloc was embarking on its reforms, and indeed to some extent perhaps because of this very fact, Cuba took a very different path—a "rectification of errors" campaign marked by a return to earlier policies and to slogans designed to fortify the revolution against its internal weaknesses.

Rectificación occasioned much affirmative rhetoric from within and was greeted by at least some writers abroad as proof of the vitality of the Cuban Revolution. It gained some popular support because of its attack on bureaucratic inertia, privilege, and corruption, and because of the opportunity it afforded for greater public discussion about the social problems Cubans faced. On the other hand, the suppression of the nascent private sector was accompanied by a political clampdown designed, in part, to preempt infection from the growing mood of reform in the USSR. The hidden agenda of the rectificación period was evident in the critical manner with which the Cuban press reported or often failed to report events in the USSR and Eastern Europe—one that contrasted with the regime's support for the Chinese party in its suppression of the Tienanmen demonstrations in June 1989. Signs of political unease within the regime were also evident in the trial and subsequent execution of senior military officers and close allies of Castro.[34]

If judged by economic indicators, the consequences of rectificación were a failure in that the general orientation of the economy did not change substantially in this period, and the policies pursued did little to halt the coming crisis. At best, the rectificación merely staved off, in the name of a return to an unattainable socialist purity, the broader reforms that Cuban society needed; at worst, it fostered political discontent and postponed economic reform. Trade and other links with Eastern Europe were maintained until 1990, while the economy as a whole returned to the more centralized, unresponsive, but still functioning mode of the 1970s.

As far as women were concerned, there was evidence of a continuing commitment to address some of their needs and some of the social problems that they faced: following demands made at the 1985 Congress, measures were taken to increase childcare provision, and a greater stress was placed on the need to share housework in line with the 1975 Family Code. There were increased provision of contraception and renewed efforts at sex education in attempts to reduce the high rate of teenage pregnancies. At the same time, more efforts were made to incorporate women into economic activity, with the result that their participation in the labor force grew.[35] In terms of policy, it could be argued that the FMC and the Cuban state in general maintained a gender-aware policy stance in the rectificación period,[36] and its rhetoric reflected some of the concerns of its constituency. But against this positive interpretation, other considerations should be registered: the overall concern of rectificación was to improve the productivity of the labor force and to mobilize large numbers of "voluntary" workers. This mass mobilization was not without its social costs, specifically what Cubans call "a crisis in time management" as people struggled to fulfill the multiple demands made upon them. "Participation" there was, but to what extent it could be taken as a sign of support for the regime is difficult to say. Volunteering for such work was often the only way to gain a promotion at work, housing points, or access to scarce goods. Arguably, considerations of regime survival, above all, determined the policy of the FMC in this period as in others. Whether in regard to the increase in the number of childcare centers and women in work or the efforts regarding teenage pregnancies and abortion, these policy responses reflected above all the concerns of a state worried about the deepening economic and social crisis it was facing.[37]

This social crisis was reflected above all in the increasing desire of many Cubans, particularly the young, to flee the country by any means, legal or illegal.[38] This was the context in the second half of the 1980s, with the FMC reputedly the most unpopular mass organization on the island, unable to halt declining attendance at meetings or to address the growing dissatisfaction arising from a deteriorating economic performance. Despite its evident efforts to assimilate some of the debates about women's place in society and the resultant modernization of its rhetoric and improved policies on some issues, the federation had failed to achieve a strong political profile. For some analysts, this failure was because it did not seek to mobilize around issues of a feminist or controversial kind and rarely contested official policy. Its main periodical, *Mujeres,* avoided difficult (that is, interesting and relevant) questions, preferring "to stick to recipes." Certainly it was widely acknowledged to have failed to attract younger women into its ranks, and its own cadres responded to this problem by denouncing the increasingly depoliticized youth as morally bankrupt and frivolous. By the end of the decade, the organization was seen as having lost momentum, and there were again calls for it to be disbanded.[39]

This contradictory evolution was evident by the time of the Fifth FMC Congress, held in 1990. A random survey of one hundred women taken a week before the Congress revealed a striking indifference to the FMC's activities. Seventy percent of respondents did not know that the Congress was taking place, and only 6 percent had great hopes regarding its outcome. An ambitious agenda had been promulgated and discussed prior to the Congress itself, but at the Congress it was overruled by a more traditional stress on mobilizing women in defense of the revolution (under the old patriotic slogan "Socialism or Death") and was as a consequence never realized. The Congress ended with a unanimous vote of confidence for Castro, described as "the Father of all Cubans, and guide to all Cuban Women."[40] In the words of one Latin American feminist in Cuba for the preparatory regional meeting of the Cairo Population Conference, "the atmosphere had changed, the old guard were back, the ones who were sympathetic to feminism seemed to have disappeared."[41]

In the period that followed the Congress, the main determinant of women's position was not any shift in FMC attitudes to feminism, but the crisis that engulfed the whole Cuban regime and society as a result of events in Eastern Europe. The precipitate decline in the economy exposed the population to extremes of deprivation they had never dreamt of, and while women struggled to cope as best they could, the FMC was unable to protest publicly about official policies or offer much in the way of support to its membership. Instead, women were once again called upon to defend the revolution by redoubling their efforts. Thousands entered the microbrigades to build houses or volunteered to work in the agricultural sector.

The FMC in the 1990s

The 1990s held out the prospect of even greater challenges to the FMC that threatened further to detach it from its remaining supporters. The consultative efforts prior to the 1990 Congress had led the organization to develop what its officials described as a somewhat more "feminist" approach and to seek a more visible role among its constituency.[42] These imperatives, however, came at a time when the demands placed both on the organization and on its members were acknowledged to be particularly severe. The FMC had faced a difficult situation during the years of rectificación, and the "special period" placed under renewed strain its dual function as a promoter of women's equality and arm of the party. Partly in response to this new situation, the FMC renewed its attempts to refashion itself as an NGO, a status few outsiders were prepared to credit, given its ties to the party and one that it did little to confirm in its rhetoric.[43] The Sixth Congress in 1995 reemphasized the principal role of the organization as "defense of the revolution," and the general secretary's speech once again invoked the heroic, militant, and nationalist past of Cuban women, placing the *federadas*[44] at Fidel's right hand in resisting the imperialist blockade and defending the gains of the revolution. The rearticulation of the themes of revolutionary nationalism, *lealtad,* and identification of the party with Cuba's national history, together with the invocation of a militant Cuban womanhood, underscored the political character of the FMC in a frank restatement of its priorities.

The combination of economic crisis and the policies adopted to deal with it nonetheless placed the FMC under pressure to justify its existence in somewhat different terms: to its existing functions it added renewed fundraising efforts in the international arena for its projects, ranging from health care delivery and social work to publishing programs. Yet, although it claimed to defend the cause of sex equality through governmental and policy channels, it acted less as a vehicle for advancing women's interests than as a means for managing female discontent and mobilizing increasing numbers of federadas into voluntary work.

On paper the organization maintained and even increased its organizational strength. In 1994, more than 3.5 million women paid their dues as a result of special efforts to increase membership and to collect the money on which the FMC depended for a substantial portion of its funds. In the same year, it claimed representation in 72,874 *delegaciónes* and 12,114 *bloques;* it had a paid staff of 1,327, and 242,008 voluntary leaders at the base of the organization.[45] Despite these impressive figures, FMC activity at neighborhood level was patchy, sometimes minimal, and as the CDRs declined in importance, so too did the FMC. Although the CDRs were to revive in some areas, by 1996 the FMC was widely regarded as irrelevant to the needs of Cuban women. Some acknowledgment was given to the fact that good people worked within the organization, but one woman expressed a common view that "the top layer is too rigid; everyone says that as an organization it has to change."[46] It had therefore not succeeded in acquiring a more positive image in the eyes of the Cuban public, a problem exacerbated by the fact that for the previous two years, as a result of a paper shortage, it had been unable to publish its periodicals, *Mujeres* and *Muchachas.* The general contraction of resources associated with the Special Period inevitably affected the overall organizational capacity of the federation as well as the morale of its supporters, be these its permanent staff on their dwindling real incomes or the large voluntary workforce of federadas whose time was already under considerable pressure from the demands of surviving in increasingly difficult circumstances.

From its own organizational perspective and from the vantage point of what were seen as the recovery years of 1995–96, the FMC had not only survived the worst years, but saw itself as well placed to play a key role in the changing policy environment. In early 1996, it was preparing to engage in an islandwide "consultation" process for feedback on the resolutions of the Sixth Congress, and it had already held a number of, in its view, successful sessions. With the easing of the paper shortage, *Mujeres* and *Muchachas* were to be revived, and a new periodical was planned for diffusion abroad, largely for fundraising purposes. The FMC magazines were to be aimed at a broader and younger readership, but with editorial control remaining in the hands of senior members of the revolutionary generation.

The organization counted among its successes the Casas de Orientación de la Mujer y la Familia (also known as Casas de la Mujer, or Casas), an idea loosely based on the "Women's Houses" supported by women's movements in Latin America and elsewhere, which offered a variety of services such as refuges from domestic violence and centers of advice and support. Following demands made at the previous congress in 1990, it had also expanded the number of childcare centers to a total of 1,156. Its activity in the field of health was given prominence and a new project, assisted by UN funds, was underway in which the FMC organized volunteer health workers for an extensive screening for cervical cancer.

The mobilization of women into voluntary work was an important aspect of the federation's response to the crisis, continuing in some measure the policy of the rectificación period. However, if voluntary programs were important in themselves and could provide the organization with a civic role in the transition, they also revealed some of the ambiguity of the FMC's dual function as a women's organization and as an arm of the state. This ambiguity was particularly evident in the FMC's social work program, which involved some fifty-three thousand volunteers. In keeping with its growing concern regarding what it saw as a crisis in the family, the federation directed considerable energy and resources toward "family support" initiatives, many of which aimed to help more than ten thousand single mothers and thirty-six thousand children in need. The FMC's volunteers assisted in locating absconding fathers for purposes of legal recognition of children and support, and in arranging subsidies and care for abandoned, abused, or distressed children.

Much of this work was channelled through the Casas de Orientación de la Mujer y la Familia, which by 1994 numbered 155 throughout the island. These Casas served as a vehicle for FMC initiatives at the local level: as such, they differed radically in conception from those programs established by women's movements in other countries. They were, as their name suggested, designed principally to "guide" (orientar) women; they offered a drop-in social, psychological, and legal advice service, and organized a range of courses, some of which aimed to help women to acquire a trade and set up their own small businesses. In 1996, the most important of these Casas, in the Municipio Plaza de la Revolución, located in Havana and serving a population of 171,000, offered courses in repairing bicycles, sewing, and hairdressing.[47]

However useful such services might have been, the manner in which they were delivered said much about the character of the FMC. The offer by the Casas de la Mujer of free advice from social workers and legal experts, for example, should have served as a useful resource for women, but because the FMC was perceived by its clientele as an arm of the government, its advice was not considered disinterested. Nor could those women visiting the Casa expect to find redress from the actions of the state itself. Those seeking help in handling difficult issues—such as drug dealing and abuse in their family, a jinotera daughter, a suspected AIDS infection, an alcoholic or violent husband, or a son considering the option of becoming a *balsero* (rafter emigrant)—knew that they would receive an official response that exposed the person seeking advice to a political lecture or, worse, to the possible involvement of the law, whether she wished it or not.[48] It is not surprising, therefore, that the rates of take-up among the population for the services on offer at the main Casa in Havana were strikingly low, with only 181 visits recorded for 1995.

In part, it was the very multifunctionality of the FMC as well as its lack of autonomy from the state that prevented it from effectively serving the needs of its constituency in this type of work. As an organization, it had always suffered from overloading, a problem that continued because it felt itself unable to disperse its activities to nonstate agencies. The FMC had both too much power and too little; as far as its role in the delivery of social welfare, it might have had more success if it had redefined its status, acting either as part of the welfare ministry—that is, as an acknowledged and adequately funded department of the state—or as an autonomous body, a genuine NGO. The only permitted women's organization and encumbered by its function as a party organization, it was constrained in developing an independent response to the changes that Cuba was undergoing and that would only accelerate in the future. Such was the view expressed by several former federadas[49] and confirmed to some degree by the FMC's initial response to the new economic conditions, which was to play down their effects on women and to join in the party leadership's condemnation of those who were "enchanted by capitalism." It did, however, acknowledge the extra strains endured by women in the special period; Vilma Espín made a point of praising the efforts of Cuban women in her speech to the Sixth Congress. Later studies by the FMC detailed some of the negative effects on women of the economic crisis. But, again, many of the most serious problems women faced—housing, poverty, job loss, sexual abuse, rape, or rising violence against women resulting from the overall crisis— were ones that the organization felt unable either to acknowledge publicly or to discuss except in familiar rhetorical terms. This inability resulted in part from the continuing role the FMC played in disseminating party propaganda both at home and in the international arena. In short, the federation was able to offer little in an epoch that called for remedial policies rather than slogans.

This was particularly evident with regard to female employment. The government announced its intention of reducing employment by half a million, and the number was expected to rise to a million over the course of 1996–97.[50] The FMC, however, painted an optimistic picture of the situation of female workers in the special period, arguing on the basis of 1994 data that no decline in female participation rates had occurred. A full 44 percent of Cuban women were in employment in 1993, constituting a female labor force of 3,203,904. One FMC study argued that far from falling, women's participation, in the areas designated "priority sectors" (tourism, agro-science, technology, and health) made them "a respectable force." Overall, whereas men's employment in the civilian state sector declined from 62.5 percent of the total in 1985 to 59.3 percent in 1994, women's employment rose from 37.5 percent to 40.6 percent. The authors of the analysis were able to conclude that "Cuban women have become a vital force in the country's economy," that they have been and continue to be "a vital factor in development."[51] If sustained, this status could cushion other trends that affected women's employment adversely. But the analysis presented a partial picture of female employment trends and avoided confronting the issue of the future role of women in the economy. It took little account of inconsistencies in the way employment and unemployment were defined, and ignored the fact that many women registered as employed were on extended "leave" from work to devote themselves to the daily tasks of survival for their families. In Havana in 1996, there was considerable evidence of female unemployment and underemployment. More than one stallholder in the craft market in Vedado was a young woman professional either out of work or unable to manage on what she earned: one nurse was supplementing her wage, which she could no longer live on; another twenty-three-year-old engineer reported that she had been sacked from her job and could find no other. Half a dozen women interviewed in Havana complained that they had been made redundant and then offered inappropriate or distant alternatives, which they declined—the latter typically for "family reasons." Young professionals expressed considerable discontent at a situation where they could not find jobs commensurate with their skills and expectations. Significantly, the FMC was not seen as able to offer any solution, useful training, or valuable advice to these women beyond referring them to voluntary work and putting them on a register, an option that was regarded with skepticism and that few seemed willing to try.

It is clear that under such circumstances, state agencies could not be counted on, as in the past, to provide the solution either to unemployment or to the declining standards of living that many already faced or would face in the near future. Other means of support and of satisfying expectations of social mobility had to be found: chief among these ranked the opportunities afforded by the market, specifically the expansion of the informal sector and petty trade.[52] Although many women entered this sector, whether as producers of goods or providers of services, this move in many cases entailed a deprofessionalization and consequent loss of earlier skills as architects, doctors, nurses, teachers, and other state sector professionals, unable to live on their earnings in the state sector and unable to sell their skills abroad, turned to the tourist sector for work and dollars. One recourse for women that reveals the less benign face of informal sector activity is prostitution, which, with the onset of the crisis, became a survival strategy for many women in the tourist areas of the island. Although not illegal per se, prostitution has always been discouraged in the conditions of the "special period"; it was officially tolerated as "the social price we pay for development" and subject to regulation by the authorities, ostensibly for reasons of public health.[53] For the women involved, it represented not only a means of obtaining dollars but, for some, the hope that it would provide a husband and a life abroad. For the older revolutionary generation, prostitution represented a return to a shameful past, and the unsound attitudes of "the youth" were routinely invoked to explain it. Yet for many *habaneros,* men and women, it was seen as resulting from economic necessity and gained a degree of tacit support from family members who were themselves dependent on the income it generated. Some FMC functionaries acknowledged the complexity of the issue of prostitution, but explained it as an inevitable effect of the blockade and consequent economic difficulties faced by Cuba. At the same time, they deplored the practice, insisting that many jinoteras were not pushed into it by poverty but by bad attitudes and sometimes greed, and they successfully lobbied the government at the end of 1995 to pass legislation banning sex workers from hotels. They also went to hoteliers, "explaining to them why this had to be."[54] Although such legislation might have reassured the promoters of family tourism in Cuba, it did little to address the problems of prostitution—let alone of the women engaged in it.[55]

The mixed results of these various government policies notwithstanding, there was evidence from early 1996 of some improvement in the overall economic situation as well as at household level. The state maintained its commitment to social expenditure, so the population enjoyed some protection from destitution,[56] but there could be little doubt that, overall, considerable hardship and insecurity continued. In such conditions, women's invisible and unpaid labor on behalf of the household tends to expand. Their responsibilities in the domain of reproductive work involve an extension of their work time in the home, either preparing food or performing services of various kinds (cleaning, caring for the elderly and children, washing clothes, and gardening) that might previously have been paid for or were provided by the state.[57] With prices high for scarce goods, time must be spent hunting out bargains, and as numerous studies attest, it is generally women who are involved in negotiating exchanges of goods and services and short-term loans through local networks and kin ties. Cuban surveys show that the traditional sexual division of labor in domestic work remained virtually unchallenged by years of FMC efforts to raise awareness of the problem or by the 1975 Family Code. Women bear the main burden, whether or not they are in employment.[58] The declining quality and accessibility of public services creates a redefinition of the boundaries between the public and private realms, with greater responsibility being devolved from state to family. In a context where the availability of good quality childcare is threatened and where there is a growing population of elderly whose overall security is diminishing, female kin step in to fill the gaps in public provision. The granting of special leave to women workers for "family reasons" is one indicator that they are already doing so; their earnings and career patterns are on the line, however, and will be affected by such practices in the short as well as in the longer run. These issues are given little consideration in the current context: indeed, the *absence* of public debate and public policy on these issues is striking.

These are some of the ways in which gender asymmetries acquired a new salience in Cuba's "special period." At the broadest level, this novelty is given by the gradual redefinition of state-society relations which has begun to create new social divisions, new economic agents, and new vulnerabilities for much of the female population. The processes set in train in the move toward marketization have contradictory effects on women—acting to the detriment of many of those in employment and especially those who constitute the working poor, but providing others with the means to become new economic agents. It will be some time before the long-term trends are more clearly visible, but in the meantime the issue is whether the significance of these gender asymmetries has been absorbed into public policy arenas and responded to with appropriate policies that succeed in reaching the most vulnerable groups. The FMC has so far shown that it has been slow to offer an adequate response to these processes. As a government organization, its capacity to operate as an effective advocate of particular group interests has been constrained, and its work is not supported by other, independent NGOs. The FMC remained the only women's organization legally permitted on the island and, particularly pertinent here, was still the only NGO licensed to deal specifically with women's issues.[59] The only independent feminist organization to emerge in postrevolutionary Cuba, MAGÍN, was founded in November 1994 but closed down after a brief flowering.[60] NGO activists who wanted to work with women tended to do so as a part of larger nongender-specific projects; one Cuban woman said, "if we want to work with women, we avoid the FMC. It is better to work without them. They are still stuck in old ways of 'macro-thinking'; they need a new perspective."[61]

Gender, State, and Revolution: Conclusions

After more than three decades of socialist policies, the Cuban population as a whole had achieved greater access to health and education, and the poorest sectors of society had seen a marked improvement in their standard of living. With regard to women, Cuban socialism had presided over their mobilization into considerable activity at all levels of public life, but had imposed a toll on daily life, one common to shortage economies, and the social division of labor retained its essential inequalities as far as the gender order was concerned. Thus, the decades of communist rule, for all that they did bring changes in social relations, only had a limited effect on the balance of power between the sexes in the home and in the public realm.

The role played by the FMC in this process was in many ways a contradictory one: it was an authoritarian organization that took its orders from above and allowed little internal dissent, let alone public debate of policy issues. Its senior members were never—any more than any other officials of the party or state elite—subject to a genuine electoral process. Its input into policy, even as a mild form of pressure group on behalf of women, was hampered by its primary allegiance to the party and by the latter's control over budget allocation and overall policy. It had relatively few resources to undertake research on issues relating to women; the result was that even if it had wished to, it had limited means of arguing for or against policies on the basis of their popularity, effectiveness, or likely impact on women's lives beyond what its officials reported.

Yet the FMC was supposed to represent more than just a mouthpiece of the party, and it did provide a space, albeit one within determined limits, for activities and discussion around issues of gender equality. Any attempt to assess its significance is bound by larger considerations about the meaning of the revolution and the socialist project itself. For those who see the entry of women into the public sphere—their education and employment—as a good in itself, the federation clearly assisted in achieving this entry. For those who stress the negative terms of that involvement, placing the emphasis on the federation's lack of autonomy and authoritarian character, the gains are diminished as an effect of instrumentalist policies or the inevitable processes of modernization.

Within the prevailing political context, there can be little doubt that the FMC played an important role in helping to realize government goals in relation to women. Women's emancipation constituted one of the ideological platforms of state communism, and the women's union had a legitimate role in promoting these principles. Advancing the project of women's emancipation and hence improving the lot of its female citizens were achievements of which the regime was particularly proud. It certainly made available abundant evidence of the benefits that Cuban women enjoyed under the patronage of the state in terms of education, health, and expanding employment opportunities. But there is another reading of this history of progress that is not captured by the statistics and that places these gains in a more negative light.[62]

Ultimately, such judgments in the case of Cuba will have to wait until the emergence of an internal feminist critique and until this critique is, in turn, put into perspective by history. It is often said by Cubans themselves that the FMC did play a useful role in the early period of the revolution and enjoyed support by virtue of its positive association with a popular revolution. The latter brought tangible benefits to many who had suffered under the previous system, bringing them a measure of upward mobility. As a women's organization dedicated to sexual equality, the FMC may even have benefited from Cuba's long and distinguished history of activism by women's movements,[63] although it chose to distance itself from that past, preferring to attribute to the revolution of 1959 the key role in women's struggle for emancipation.

Whatever its failings, Cuban socialism created a distinctive kind of women's movement, albeit one that was a creature of the state. The FMC represented a sustained and in some ways successful attempt to legitimate an institutionalized women's movement, just as populist regimes in Latin America had played an innovative role in shaping an institutionalized labor movement. The Cuban Communist Party sought to construct new gender-state relations, and the women's movement it created was authorized to represent and pursue women's interests, officially defined. In a myriad of ways, by mobilizing women, creating a female constituency, funding a women's organization, and diffusing an official discourse of women's rights and sexual equality, the leadership effectively legitimated women's claims on the state and against certain structures of authority and discrimination. But in return for policy initiatives supporting women, the state expected complete loyalty to the party line and brooked no rivals.

The successes as much as the failings of the FMC as a women's organization cannot be understood, therefore, without taking due account of its relation to the state and that state's evolution in Cuba over the forty years of its existence. After the excitement of the first decade and despite some enlargement of its agenda, the FMC became, as many observers have indicated, increasingly ossified: along with other mass organizations, it was criticized by its membership for its bureaucratic character, which had placed evident limits on its pretensions to act on behalf of that membership.

Much feminist criticism of the FMC and of the Cuban record with regard to its policies on women has focused on the resilience of patriarchal privilege, sexual inequality, and machismo, and the social and gendered divisions of labor, with the implication that the women's union and the state could and should have devoted more efforts to "transforming society." Although it is undoubtedly true that the organization could have done more to address these issues, the problem may have been the reverse—namely, that *too much* or *the wrong kind* of intervention occurred, that too much energy was expended in attempts to force a diverse population into conformity with the party line. The FMC's lack of autonomy and its instrumentalism may have enhanced its effective capacity to bring about change in some areas, but it seems also to have generated some resistance to conformity. This resistance was evident in declining support for the FMC, in the falling proportion of women in most political institutions, and in young people's boredom with the old rhetoric—all of which may have symbolized a more general dissatisfaction and retreat from an increasingly exhausting public domain.

In the special period, extra strains were placed on women and on the state institutions that were charged with their protection. As Cuban socialism faced increasing pressures for democratic reform, the leadership set its face against it.[64] Many on the island wanted change but feared its consequences: the market promised opportunity, but could not provide protection against the risks it brought. The evolution toward a regime that is politically democratic and socially just and that embodies the positive legacy of the revolution depends on many factors, both external and internal. Among the former, a change in the policies of the United States predominates; among the latter can be instanced the development of civil society to complement the space occupied by other institutions and practices intrinsic to democracy. As a site of female activism, civil society is particularly important, be it in the form of NGOs, publishing initiatives, neighborhood associations, or other unofficial groupings. In regard to both social preconditions—and what people within the island are themselves aware of and willing to encourage—the opportunity for a move toward democratization, consonant with a preservation of Cuba's independence and the social values of the revolution, is in the realm of the possible. It remains to be seen what role Cuban women choose to play in such a process. Women have historically been in the forefront of struggles for social rights and have looked to the state for their delivery. Whether Cuban women perceive their interests to depend not just on the development of civil society but also on the creation of a transformed, democratic state in which they can achieve much greater and more independent articulation is a question that their experience of socialism and of its crisis has posed in especially acute form.

Notes

The author would like to thank Ruth Pearson for productive discussions about shared concerns, Margarita Velázquez and Fred Halliday for comments, and Jean Stubbs and Emily Morris for their help with materials. This essay is an abbreviated version of ILAS Research Paper no. 43, which appeared in March 1996. All interviewees have been anonymized, and all translations except where otherwise indicated are by the author.

1 The policies of the special period, inaugurated in 1990, were a response to the foreign exchange and fiscal deficits caused by the cessation of economic support from the Soviet bloc. They stressed self-reliance, rationing, across the board cuts, and moral incentives. See Manuel Pastor and Andrew Zimbalist, "Waiting for Change: Adjustment and Reform in Cuba," *World Development* 23, no. 5 (1995): 705–20.

2 On the campaign for the "rectification of errors," see ibid.; Susan Eckstein, "More on the Cuban Rectification Process: Whose Errors?" *Cuban Studies* 21 (1991): 187–92.

3 Cuban economists estimate that the aggregate fall in the GSP between 1989 and 1993 was around 45 percent. Julio Carranza Valdés et al., *Cuba, la restructuración de la economía: Una propuesta para el debate* (Havana: Editorial de Ciencias Sociales, 1995), 17. The global social product (GSP) differs from gross domestic product (GDP) as a measure of economic growth. Among other things, it excludes nonproductive sectors such as health and education.

4 In the second half of the 1980s, the Cuban economy stagnated, with an average growth rate of less than 0.2 percent. Pastor and Zimbalist, "Waiting for Change," calculate that the real GDP growth rate in 1990 was −3.1 percent, in 1991 −14.0 percent, and in 1993 it was −20.0 percent. However, by 1994 there were signs of recovery, with GDP rising by 0.7 percent, then by 2.5 percent in 1995.

5 *Paladar,* literally "palate" or "taste"—that is, a semiprivate eating house; *jinotera,* literally "female jockey," denoting a form of casual prostitution.

6 The legislation of the Torricelli Bill and the Helms-Burton Act have arguably set back the prospects for Cuban democracy in several respects: economically it has retarded Cuba's recovery process; politically, it has enabled the Cuban leadership to entrench more repressive policies with respect to civil society.

7 For a discussion of this reform current and of exile politics, see my "The Politics of the Cuban Diaspora in the United States," in *The United States and Latin America: The New Agenda,* ed. Victor Bulmer-Thomas and James Dunkerley (London: Institute of Latin American Studies, and Cambridge, Mass.: David Rockefeller Center, 1999), 341–69.

8 Thinking along these lines, from within Cuban research institutes, can be found in a volume of papers presented at an international workshop on democracy held in Havana in 1994: Haroldo Dilla, ed., *La participación en Cuba y los retos del futuro* (Havana: Ediciones CEA, 1996), and Haroldo Dilla, ed., *La democrácia en Cuba y el diferendo con los Estados Unidos* (Havana: Ediciones CEA, 1995).

9 Dilla's essay in *La Democracia en Cuba* is entitled "Cuba: Cuál es la democracia deseable?" 117–29.

10 Ibid., 180.

11 This study draws on two research visits to Cuba—one in 1981, the other in January 1996—as well as on other comparative work, referenced below, on social policy and regime transition in socialist states.

12 Other than the FMC, the most important interest groups represented in mass organizations are La Asociación Nacional de Pequeños Agricultores (ANAP), the Comités de Defensa de la Revolución (CDRS), the Central de Trabajadores de Cuba (CTC), and the Unión de Juventud Comunista (UJC).

13 Eva Perón's Peronist Women's Party, founded in order to mobilize support for the Argentine regime in 1949, had on the eve of the 1951 elections 500,000 members, with 3,600 branches in the country as a whole, at a time when Argentina's total population was substantially larger than that of Cuba in the 1980s, the latter being under 11 million. For a discussion of how to differentiate between varieties of women's movements, see my "Analyzing Women's Movements," *Development and Change* 29, no. 2 (1998): 219–45.

14 The unexpectedly rapid collapse of the former Soviet bloc has shown how difficult it is to make assumptions about the way that the effects of state policies are experienced by their populations. Claims regarding the legitimacy of communist parties cannot be tested and are therefore based on speculation rather than on hard evidence: although it is probable that, despite the denial of political freedoms, such regimes can, for social and patriotic reasons, enjoy legitimacy, it is also evident from the Eastern European experiences that over time stagnation in the political field can undermine this legitimacy and that much of the regime's support can disappear once possibilities for social advance other than through the party become available.

15 The Sandinistas gained 41 percent of the vote in the 1990 elections, a drop of 22 percent on their 1984 results. Roger Lancaster discusses the reasons why many women defected to the opposition in *Life Is Hard: Machismo, Danger, and the Intimacy of Power in Nicaragua* (Berkeley, Los Angeles, Oxford: University of California Press, 1992), 291.

16 Espín had been active in the revolutionary movement, but she was at first unconvinced about the need for such an organization and later recalled wondering, "Why do we have to have a women's organisation? I had never been discriminated against. I had my career as a chemical engineer. I never suffered." Sally Quinn, "Mother of a Revolution," *The Guardian* (Manchester and London), 14 April 1977.

17 *Memoria: II Congreso Nacional de la Federación de Mujeres Cubanas* (Havana: Editorial Orbe, 1975).

18 For comparative perspectives on women and socialism, see Barbara Wolf Jancar, *Women under Communism* (Baltimore: Johns Hopkins University Press, 1978), and my "Women's Emancipation under Socialism: A Model for the Third World?" *World Development* 9–10 1981): 1019–37. The strategy of "emancipating" women by drawing them into the labor force was justified by reference to the theories of Engels on capitalism and the division of labor, wherein women's oppression derived from their exclusion from the labor market.

19 The literacy campaign of 1961 involved thousands of FMC members who acted as "loving mothers" to seventy thousand literacy workers, performing such tasks as delivering their mail, making their beds, and cooking, as well as replacing schoolteachers who were involved in the campaign.

20 The Cuban record on repression is not, however, without its gendered elements; the persistent persecution of homosexuals, many of whom were sent to the Unidades Militares para el Aumento de la Producción (UMAP) labor camps, is among the most reprehensible instances.

21 The system known as "popular power" was established in the 1970s and comprised local assemblies with elected bodies, first at the provincial and then at the national level. It achieved a degree of local involvement in decision making, but fell far short of democratic change. The upper echelons of the system, at both provincial and national level, were under CCP control. The significance of the National Assembly can be gauged from the fact that it met for only a short period every year. It was noticeable that the phrase repeatedly used to identify the function of this system was "canalizar las inquietudes de las masas" (interview with Jorge Hart Davalos, member of the Asamblea Provincial, Havana, March 1981).

22 Hitherto, much of the FMC's international activity was developed within the context of two concerns. One arose from its membership with the Soviet bloc and involved exchange visits by delegations from "fraternal" states and membership of international communist organizations. Vilma Espín had been active in the Soviet controlled International Federation of Democratic Women, established in 1960, and acted as vice president for a time. The other regional concern was Latin America, where efforts were directed at developing solidarity for revolutionary currents approved by the Castro leadership. See Francesca Miller, *Latin American Women and the Search for Social Justice* (Hanover and London:

University Press of New England, 1991), one of the few analysts who has examined the importance of international links in the Latin American women's movement.

23 The FMC at first had remained aloof from the regional feminist Encuentros, but their members began to attend from 1988 when four delegates went to the meeting in Taxco, Mexico. There they were exposed to a variety of different feminisms (including that of the Sandinista delegates from Nicaragua), at a time when a less orthodox left was also emerging, one more sympathetic than its predecessors to feminist ideas.

24 I have argued this at greater length in "The Woman Question in the Age of Perestroika," *New Left Review* 183 (1990): 23–49. Other developments of the time—noticeably the increased concern of states with human rights, something to which the USSR and its European allies also had to pay lip service—played a parallel role.

25 See N. Saporta Sternbach et al., *Feminism in Latin America: Identity, Strategy, and Democracy* (Boulder, Colo.: Westview, 1992), for a discussion of Latin American feminisms and for details of the Encuentros.

26 That there are different feminisms as well as different women's movements alerts us to the heterogeneity of women's interests and to the varying ways in which they are socially constructed. But what most definitions of feminism agree upon is that as a social movement and body of ideas, it challenges the structures and power relations that produce female subordination.

27 Vilma Guillois Espín, *La Mujer en Cuba* (Havana: Editorial de la Mujer, 1991): 100.

28 Quinn, "Mother of a Revolution."

29 Women constituted 23.91 percent of party members in 1988 and 18.21 percent of the Central Committee. Until 1985 there were no women in the Politburo. Sheryl Lutyens, "Reading between the Lines," *Latin American Perspectives* 22, no. 2 (1995): 100–24, 104 cited.

30 Activists in one of the mass organizations or in the party.

31 Jean Stubbs, "Cuba: Revolutionising Women, Family, and Power" in *Women and Politics Worldwide,* ed. Barbara Nelson and Najma Chowdhury (New Haven and London: Yale University Press, 1994), 189–209. See also Sheryl Lutyens, "Remaking the Public Sphere: Women and Revolution in Cuba," in *Women and Revolution in Africa, Asia, and the New World,* ed. Mary Ann Tétrault (Columbia: University of South Carolina Press, 1994), 366–93.

32 Interview with author, London. 1996.

33 Lois Smith and Alfred Padula, *Sex and Revolution: Women in Socialist Cuba* (Oxford: Oxford University Press, 1996).

34 This was one of the most dramatic moments in the internal history of the Cuban Revolution. The truth of what occurred in the Ochoa trial is not yet known: that something serious was wrong and that Ochoa was shot in order to emphasize the need for unquestioning obedience of the regime were not in doubt.

35 As part of this effort, the FMC established a homeworkers' program that in 1989

involved some sixty-two thousand women, many of whom were seamstresses and none of whom enjoyed the social protection enjoyed by employees. The FMC did seek redress on this issue, but without success. Padula and Smith, *Sex and Revolution*, 138.

36 See Lutyens, "Reading between the Lines," for a positive assessment of this period. Lutyens also claims that the situation of Cuban women in the rectification period contrasts with the deteriorating conditions of other postsocialist women (106). The point, however, is that Cuba and Eastern Europe cannot be compared because they were not at comparable stages of the adjustment process; indeed, Cuba's had not yet begun.

37 It cannot be excluded that at least part of the shift in Cuban policy was influenced by the growing discussion within the Soviet Union of how neglect of women's concerns was linked to rising social problems—marital instability, delinquency, absenteeism, crime.

38 Carollee Bengelsdorf, *The Problem of Democracy in Cuba* (Oxford: Oxford University Press, 1994).

39 Bengelsdorf, *The Problem of Democracy*.

40 Smith and Padula, *Sex and Revolution*, note how those who dissented from this paternalism could be treated: "In 1991, María Elena Cruz Varela, a 37-year-old award winning poet, socialist, and mother of two, publicly renounced Castro as 'not my father' and protested in an open letter to the commander in chief the lack of democracy and respect for human rights in Cuba. In response, a 'rapid reaction Brigade' dragged her from her Havana apartment, beat her, and made her physically swallow some of her own writings" (534). She was imprisoned for eighteen months.

41 Interview with author, Havana, January 1996.

42 FMC official, interview with author, Havana, January 1996.

43 The report on Cuba in the *Mujeres latinoamericanas en cifras*, ed. Teresa Valdés and Enrique Gomariz (Santiago: Instituto de la Mujer/FLACSO, 1992) series contains an insert from the FMC leadership criticizing the authors for what it sees as errors and bias in the interpretation. Among the points made is the following "Queremos apuntar que resulta un error insertar a la FMC bajo el rubro de Acción Estatal, cuando se trata de un ONG" (Santiago de Chile: Instituto de la Mujer/FLACSO 1992). It is worth noting that at the Fourth United Nations Conference on Women (Beijing, 1995), the FMC was represented at both the NGO forum (the *only* Cuban women's NGO) *and* at the governmental meeting.

44 *Federadas* is the Cuban term used to denote FMC members.

45 The percentage of adult women nominally affiliated to the FMC rose from 74.0 percent in 1974 to 82.3 percent in 1994. In 1994, the total number of federadas was 3,657,220—the largest percentages made up of housewives at 42.5 percent and workers at 38.9 percent. Students (10.5 percent), pensioners, and others accounted for the rest. *Estadísticas sobre las mujeres cubanas* (Havana: FMC, 1995).

46 Former FMC member, interview with author, Havana, January 1996.

47 This information is based on a meeting with the director, a member of the FMC for twenty-five years, and several staff at this Casa, Havana, January 1996.

48 When I asked the director of the Casa de la Mujer in Havana what advice a woman would be offered in the case of drug abuse or domestic violence, she replied, "It's simple; it is a legal offense" (January 1996). Such an approach does not encourage use of services, let alone the enhanced capacity of individuals to deal with their problems. One official's response to my inquiry about violence against women was that "the greatest violence is that of the blockade."

49 Interview with author, 1996. As one explained, "The FMC not only lacks analysis, it also lacks a sense of its own purpose: this is why it is perceived as irrelevant by the mass of Cuban women whose lives have changed so dramatically."

50 Anonymous Cuban economists, interviews with author, Havana, 1996.

51 Carolina Aguilar, Perla Popowski, and Mercedes Verdeses, "El periodo especial y la vida cotidiana: Desafío de las Cubanas de los 90" (Havana: FMC mimeo, 1994), 4.

52 By January 1996, more than 160,000 people were registered as self-employed, and markets of various kinds were doing a brisk trade in agricultural produce, meat, and crafts. Small shops selling snacks and drinks had also appeared outside people's houses, mostly run by women, as had the ubiquitous paladares, officially permitted so long as they did not exceed twelve dining places. Attempts were subsequently made by the authorities to regulate and restrict these activities, resulting in a sharp decline in numbers.

53 Carlos Lage, in 1993, quoted in Carolee Bengelsdorf, "(Re)considering Cuban Women in a Time of Troubles" (mimeo, 1995), 24. Castro, too, is reported to have said that women who prostitute themselves "do so on their own, voluntarily and without any need for it." Ibid., 25.

54 Senior members of the FMC, interview with author, Havana, January 1996.

55 Apart from its other costs, prostitution represents a deskilling of a highly trained and educated female population. The evidence is that in the worst phase of the recession, qualified professionals engaged in it along with other groups.

56 See Ruth Pearson, "Renegotiating the Reproductive Bargain: Gender Analysis of Economic Transition in Cuba in the 1990s," *Development and Change* 28, no. 4 (1997): 671–706, for an analysis of Cuba's "crisis in reproduction."

57 This had, in effect, occurred in the household where I was staying in Vedado, Havana. The wife had given up her job because it was too far away and underpaid, and because she was looking after a sick relative. She still had a cleaner who came everyday (informal domestic service is widespread in Cuba), but now did the gardening herself and spent a considerable amount of her time in doing household activities, shopping, and negotiating for scarce resources and services.

58 Valdés and Gomariz, eds., *Cuba: Mujeres latinoamericanas,* 50. There are considerable disparities in the available data on social indicators of all kinds. Data for this section have been taken where possible from sources originating from the

Centro de Estudios Demográficos at the Universidad de La Habana, and from the Instituto Nacional de Investigaciones Económicas, *Situación Social en el Ajuste Económico* (Havana: mimeo, 1995).

59 This was still the case in early 1999.

60 MAGÍN, an association of women in communications, described itself in its founding document in the following terms: "MAGÍN es una simbiosis de los conceptos de *imagen è imaginación,* vinculados estrechamente con el quehacer de sus integrantes como creadoras y difusoras de mensajes y con la reconocida capacidad de las mujeres para sentir que hay un cielo sobre nuestras cabezas." MAGÍN, *Programa de Desarollo* (Havana: mimeo, 1994).

61 Interview with author, Havana, January 1996.

62 This is suggested by the experience of the former Soviet bloc in relation to "the woman question" and may bear upon considerations of the prospects of the Cuban regime's institutions and its own survival into the next period. With regard to the Cuban record on women's emancipation, it is impossible to say whether popular attitudes will turn out to be significantly different from those that emerged in other parts of the postcommunist world. In Russia and Eastern Europe, there was considerable criticism of the nature of the official project of "emancipation" in general, of the many shortcomings of the project even in its own terms, and of the attempt to realize it through state intervention, from above, via state-sponsored women's unions. Such a program of emancipation, for all its undoubted social achievements, redounded less to the credit of these regimes than was supposed by many analysts, especially under conditions perceived as dependent on an unacceptable concentration of political power at the center. For a discussion of the backlash effect in the former Soviet bloc, see Nanette Funk and Magda Mueller, eds., *Gender Politics and Post-Communism: Reflections from Eastern Europe and the Former Soviet Union* (New York and London: Routledge, 1993), and my "Women's Rights and the International Context in the Post-Communist States," in *Mapping the Women's Movement: Feminist Politics and Social Transformation in the North,* ed. by Monica Threlfall (London: Verso, 1996), 232–59.

63 See Lynn C. Stoner, *From the House to the Streets: The Cuban Women's Movement for Legal Reform 1989–1940* (Durham, N.C.: Duke University Press, 1991), for a history of women's rights activism in Cuba.

64 After the general crackdown that occurred in 1996, the emerging debate over democracy in which Dilla and others had played such a central role was silenced and the scope of NGO activity on the island was increasingly curtailed. Dilla's institute, the Centro de Estudios de Europa, was temporarily closed and some of its leading members (including the director) were moved elsewhere. Following Raul Castro's speech to the National Assembly in March 1996 after the downing of the planes piloted by exiles, and following the passage of the Helms-Burton Act, NGOs were seen as a fifth column working to undermine Cuban society from within.

Jo Fisher

Gender and the State in Argentina

The Case of the Sindicato de Amas de Casa

Debates on the role of the state in promoting gender-based social change were not just theoretical issues for the women's movement in Argentina in the 1980s and early 1990s. On the eve of the country's return to constitutional rule, women's organizations had to make very real decisions about the kind of relationship they would seek with the new government. In the early 1980s, this meant asking questions not only about whether the state could advance women's interests, but also about the extent to which it could re-create itself as a democratic body after seven years of repressive military dictatorship. As in the 1940s, with the emergence of the Peronist women's movement, the issue divided women and led to acrimonious debates within their organizations.

Through interviews with its leadership and grassroots members, and an analysis of its publications, this chapter looks at the development of the Sindicato de Amas de Casa (SACRA, Housewives' Trade Union) from 1983 to 1995, a working-class women's organization with feminist roots that came to develop a close relationship with the Peronist state from 1989. The significance of SACRA lies in its numerical strength—formed in 1984, but by 1995 claiming a membership of five hundred thousand women. Although this figure may be wildly exaggerated, more sober estimates of approximately fifty thousand still make it a potentially significant bloc within the organized trade union movement and certainly identify it as Argentina's largest working-class women's organization. Its significance also lies in the radical nature of its demands, on paper at least, and the political implications of those demands for the position of Argentine women. In particular, its objective of organizing housewives into a trade union represents a unique attempt at drawing together a dispersed and scattered workforce that has had no place in the traditional world of trade unions. By its nature, a housewives' trade union poses a number of potential challenges to traditional trade union movements in terms of both the form of organization (territorial as opposed to workplace) and the issues of concern (primarily reproductive). This study considers how far SACRA represents a genuinely new current in the Argentine working-class women's movement and how far it is an effective vehicle for promoting the interests of women in the face of the growing feminization of the workforce and of poverty in the 1980s and 1990s.

SACRA and the State: The Legacy of Eva Perón

The Sindicato de Amas de Casa represented the first significant attempt to organize working-class women since the Partido Peronista Femenino (PPF), the women's branch of the Peronist Party that was formed in 1949 and that, like SACRA, claimed a membership of half a million, predominantly working-class women. The populist governments of Juan Perón (1946–55) had a seemingly progressive gender politics that was the result of the particular characteristics of the populist state. Populism emerged as a challenge to the traditional oligarchical state thrown into crisis by the world depression of the 1930s and the collapse of world markets for Argentina's agricultural exports. The crisis presented the emerging industrial bourgeoisie with an opportunity to forge a new development project— import substitution industrialization—aimed at promoting national industry. The project required a restructuring of class relations in which the national industrial bourgeoisie sought allies in the working class and urban middle class. Perón saw that the success of the project depended on the organization of the working class so that it would become a powerful counter to the traditional oligarchy, and his main strategy in relation to labor involved a complete renewal of its leadership so that it would become dependent on state patronage. He also recognized that women, still without the vote and making up a substantial section of the labor force, were an untapped political resource. In the same way as Perón removed independent labor leaders who might have threatened his position, the Peronist women's movement under Eva's leadership effectively dislodged the old feminist leaders and appropriated their cause. This movement represented a sharp break from the earlier women's movement, which had been predominantly middle and upper class in composition and had related to the state as opposition pressuring the government for change. Under Perón's 1946–55 governments, with his wife Eva as spokesperson for women's affairs, the women's movement became the vehicle for the state's efforts to mobilize women for the Peronist cause. Although Eva spoke of the need for women to organize themselves, she also emphasized their subordination to Perón, telling the women of the PPF that they "could only aspire to the honour of placing themselves at the orders of their leader and struggle until the last breath for his work and for him."[1]

In terms of its relationship with political parties and the state, the development of its demands, and its form of organizations, SACRA represented a potential departure in the working-class women's movement in Argentina. Although it identified with many aspects of Peronism, unlike the PPF, SACRA was not formally part of any political party and, according to its leaders, was open to all women: "They may have different religions, affiliation to different political parties, but this doesn't bother us. Ours is a broad movement."[2] It originated from the non-Peronist left and the second-wave feminist organizations that emerged in Argentina in the 1970s. In response to the discrimination women faced within the party and their lack of representation in leadership posts, it evolved from a women's group created in 1974 on the fringes of a small left-wing political party, the Frente de la Izquierda Popular (FIP). It aimed to link class and feminist politics to create a "popular feminism." In 1975, the majority of the group's membership left FIP to establish the Centro de Estudios de la Mujer Argentina (CESMA) as an independent feminist collective. CESMA was one of only two feminist organizations to survive military rule.

Apart from equal political representation, central themes that dominated the debates of Argentine feminism in the early 1980s were reproduction, and, in particular, housework. For CESMA, housework became the key issue with the potential to unite both working- and middle-class women. According to Elida Vigo, a former member of CESMA and now SACRA's president, "In our political discussions we aimed to find an issue which was common to all women. . . . In CESMA we reached the conclusion that housework was the key issue that affected all women, especially poor women."[3] These discussions led not only to the decision to create a trade union, but also to the shedding of CESMA's feminist profile. In 1983, just as new feminist groups began to appear in Argentina, CESMA disbanded, and the majority of its members began the process of forming a housewives' trade union.

The move away from feminism was accompanied by a shift toward Peronism, and although the union's discourse echoed that of socialist feminists with its emphasis on the productive nature of housework, it also drew on Eva's speeches. It was from Eva that SACRA's leaders claimed their inspiration for wages for housework: "We must have in the home that which we go out to seek: our small economic independence. . . . A salary paid to the mothers by all the nation."[4] In the words of SACRA's president, "The Housewives' Union has its roots in the history of Argentine women themselves in the search to find a way that achieves equality in society. In the 1940s in Argentina, there was a woman who represented the fight to conquer these rights, and that woman was Eva Perón, but because of the high level of development in Argentina at that time, the need to respond to this proposal wasn't clearly seen."[5]

Although portrayed as the natural development of Eva's thought, SACRA's discourse represented a potential shift in terms of the representation of women's interests. As a section of a political party, the PPF's achievements were constrained by the wider political requirements of 1940s Peronism, which ultimately determined gender policy outcomes. Concerns about the falling birth rate in the 1930s and 1940s led to a primary preoccupation with the role of women in the private sphere. Peronist population policy was designed to promote demographic growth, which led to measures that Marysa Navarro argues implicitly defined women with the fundamental social function of "maternity at the service of the nation."[6] The policy was accompanied by a gender discourse based on essentialist ideas about women. Eva constantly praised them for their special qualities of gentleness, fortitude, and self-sacrifice, and although she urged women to take an active role in public life, she defined their spiritual role in the family as their major sphere of influence. The idea that women were essentially different from men was not unique to Peronism and had been a strong theme in most sections of the Argentine women's movement since the mid–nineteenth century. Demands for equality were made in terms of protecting these differences, particularly women's reproductive role.[7] It was precisely because of these innate qualities that women's suffrage was seen as a historical necessity. Women's public participation was seen as an extension of their domestic role into the public sphere; they would bring their special qualities to this sphere and act as the moral guardians of the political process.[8]

Although SACRA's chief concern was women's domestic role, its discourse emphasized women as workers with rights, not as wives and mothers carrying out their work out of love and duty. "It's considered that women are naturals for housework—we say it's got nothing to do with nature—it's a cultural question."[9] The union argued that because the whole of society benefited from the work of housewives, the state should be regarded as their employer and therefore pay wages and provide social security benefits. Its main objectives were to gain society's recognition of housework as socially necessary, productive work and of housewives as workers with a right to their own union, wages, health insurance system (obra social), and pension.

Despite SACRA's claim that it promoted the interests of all women, its demands—particularly those for improved social security provision for women—were a response to the practical gender interests of working-class women, concerns that became critical from the mid-1980s with the adoption of neoliberal economic measures. Unlike middle-class women, who had domestic servants and private health care and pension arrangements, working-class women were the most severely affected by the growing levels of male unemployment, falling standards of living, and the collapse of the state social security system that characterized the 1980s and early 1990s. Both the state pension system, which worked through obligatory contributions by employees to a pension fund, and the union-run obra sociales covered only those members of the population in standard employment. Women's shorter working lives, irregular career patterns, and concentration in sectors not covered by social protection meant they were less likely than men to have contributed sufficiently to funds, and married housewives not in paid employment were dependent on their partners having contributed. Studies have confirmed an increase in inequalities between working women of different social classes. According to Rosalía Cortés, the female workforce was becoming increasingly polarized between a growing sector of highly qualified and highly paid female workers, particularly within the financial and service sectors, with full labor protection, and an expanding proportion of women in the least-qualified employment sectors, with no protection at all.[10]

That SACRA's campaign for social services responded to the needs of working-class women was clear from interviews carried out at a branch of SACRA in 1991 in the province of Buenos Aires.

Question: What does SACRA offer you?

Respondent 1: The obra social is very important. Most of the women and many of the men work by the hour, and we have no obra social. We have to travel a long way to get to the public hospital, and we have to queue for hours to be seen and often there are no antibiotics or even bandages.

Respondent 2: Most of us had no health cover—many of the women and men in the neighborhoods are in casual work and aren't covered. We believe in SACRA's campaign for women's rights, like the pensions for older women. When we look around our neighborhoods and see how many old and destitute women there are, of course we can see how important it is for us. The health scheme and the pension campaign are the main reasons we are in SACRA.

Respondent 1: We believe in the union's demands and especially the fight for automatic pensions for older women. That's only fair—a woman works all her life, and without a pension she has to work until she drops.

SACRA also represented a new departure in terms of the organizational networks of working-class women's participation. The PPF was organized separately from the Peronist union movement and was seen as the appropriate place for the organization of women. Despite her influential role in the Confederación General de Trabajo (CGT), Eva did little to promote women or gender issues within the trade unions.[11] For SACRA, trade union status was crucial, not only to enable it to carry out functions normally associated with Argentine trade unions, such as the administration of an obra social, but also to obtain social recognition of the value of housework, which would enable women to take their place as workers alongside men in the union movement. According to one of its leaders, "We emphasized a union of workers, not just a housewives' association. The essential point was to change people culturally and ideologically to show them that what housewives do is real work."[12]

SACRA and Democratic Opportunities

During the election campaign of 1983, political parties made attempts to attract the female vote by incorporating women's demands into their electoral platforms and by raising issues rooted in feminist thinking and advocated by women's organizations. Issues such as divorce, the reform of family law, and peace appeared repeatedly in the speeches of the candidates of the Radical and Peronist parties. Under Raúl Alfonsín's Radical Party government (1984–89), the Subsecretaría de la Mujer (ssm) was created and given the role of formulating a coordinated, nationwide policy on women. However, although the theme of gender permeated many new areas of social life—including neighborhood organizations, political parties, and trade unions—the failure of the autonomous women's movement to act in a coordinated way in relation to the new constitutional government gave the initiative to the state, whose contradictory motivations in its approach to gender circumscribed any advances. This problem was particularly evident with regard to the ssm.

From the beginning, the functioning of the ssm experienced a number of problems, which suggested that its creation was more an act based on the need for state modernization and the search for a First World profile than a response to the demands of the women's movement, political parties, or unions.[13] One of its major difficulties was that it had few links with women's organizations. It received little cooperation from feminist groups, which remained suspicious of dealings with the state, and its middle-class profile made contact with the working-class movement difficult. Its location within the state apparatus also created problems. Not only was it situated in a Christian Democratic secretariat of a Radical government, thus alienating it from both Peronist and Radical women, it was also isolated from macro-policymakers and decision-making arenas. In addition, it was located within the Secretariat of Human and Family Relations, which emphasized the "promotion and protection of the family," associating it with assistentialist state policies aimed at supporting women in their role as mothers.

As a working-class women's organization with links to Peronism, SACRA had few contacts with the Alfonsín government. Together with the majority of the Peronist union movement, it took an oppositional stance to the Radical government. It also rejected many of the gender reforms as biased toward the middle classes, particularly the ways in which the divorce and equal paternity rights laws were framed. As SACRA's president pointed out, "Don't forget that during the entire administration of Alfonsín, SACRA was never received by a single national functionary, not even by those who occupied the Subsecretariat of Women."[14] The principal advances made by

SACRA under Alfonsín were at a provincial level, where Peronists held power. In Misiones, SACRA won automatic state pensions for old and destitute women, benefiting some twelve hundred women, and in six other provinces, partial versions of a pension system were instituted.

Carlos Menem's election in 1990 marked the beginning of a completely new relationship between SACRA and the state. From 1987, SACRA worked closely with Menem, supporting his campaign for the governorship of the province of La Rioja and his program for the "defense of housewives," which included pensions and wages for female heads of families with no economic resources. In 1988, SACRA began its national campaign of support for Menem for the coming presidential election, launching a campaign based on two demands—the creation of a national ministry for women and the recognition of domestic work, starting with pensions for housewives—that Menem agreed to support. The union saw the Peronist state as a vital mechanism for achieving its objectives: "It's important to analyze our links with the state. . . . This link will make possible the conquest of more rights."[15]

The links were formalized with SACRA members standing for government in Peronist coalitions. One of SACRA's explicit objectives was to win posts in provincial and municipal legislatures. Elida Vigo stood as a candidate for a Peronist-dominated coalition and later became a national parliamentary deputy for the northern province of Misiones. Another SACRA member was elected deputy for Salta, several were elected to councils across the country and others were appointed to provincial and national executive posts. Elida Vigo was also appointed to the Consejo Nacional de la Mujer, the Peronist successor to the SSM, and then to the Cabinet of the President's Women Advisors in 1993. Menem regularly sent messages of support to SACRA's national congresses, choosing its Fourth Congress to commemorate forty-five years of female suffrage. At this congress, SACRA's president reiterated its support for Menem, saying "You can count on 500,000 militants who are going to march all over the country. . . . We need your government's support to win pensions for housewives."[16]

Such active support of Menem's government directly contradicted the union's position on a number of fundamental issues. First, its close relationship with the government brought into question its claim to political independence and its ability to represent women from all political persuasions. Moreover, Menem was elected on a populist platform that promised employment and improved living standards for the working class; the series of International Monetary Fund (IMF) and World Bank–backed austerity measures he embraced on taking office, as well as a closer relationship with the United States and increased dependence on international financial institutions, clashed with SACRA's nationalist position. At the same time, some of the consequences of Menem's policies—unemployment, increased social inequality, cutbacks in social services, and a series of anti–trade union laws, were in direct conflict with SACRA's basic objectives.

Organizational Structure and Status

Support for the close relationship with the state was not universal among SACRA's membership, but its leaders were able to maintain what became in some quarters an increasingly unpopular position only through tight control of the organizational structures. Despite representing a potentially radical new strand of trade unionism, SACRA adopted a centralized structure of organization that resembled more traditional Peronism than new feminist or neighborhood groups, which often chose loose, informal structures. According to its president, "Our organization has been structured so that it's absolutely centralized. But at the same time it's democratic centralism. . . . [To be recognized,] the leader has to prove that she can organize a group of women."[17] According to the statutes, all members had the right to choose and be chosen for representative posts. However, the information available on elections is vague and suggests that only one election for the national leadership took place between 1983 and 1995, in 1992. Responses to questions in 1991 about internal democracy suggest that some of SACRA's grassroots members did not support such close collaboration with Menemism: "The leaders—we have differences with them. They seem a very closed group to us, who don't share our ideas," or "They say Eva represents them as women, but they're not Peronists in the way we are. They're from some small political party," or "There's no democracy. The whole question of meetings and elections is very closed."[18] The association with the government, together with the union's active campaigning for Menemist candidates encouraged attempts to unseat the leadership. One branch failed in its attempts to form an alternative list of candidates for the leadership elections of 1992, and in that year the branch left SACRA, not only because of their failed attempt to oust the leadership, but more seriously because of the collapse of SACRA's first obra social, which left thousands of paid-up members with no health coverage. Amid accusations of mismanagement of finances, several of SACRA's leaders, including the treasurer, were expelled. The president and the union's political orientation, however, remained in place.

The issue of elections was also linked to SACRA's legal position. The organization's main dealings with the state under Alfonsín were through its attempts to gain legal trade union status. These applications were all rejected by the courts on the grounds that because there was no recognizable employer—the essential prerequisite of the employer-employee labor contract—the "relationship of dependency" did not exist, and thus there could be no legal recognition of the organization as a trade union. As an intermediate measure, SACRA registered itself as a civil association in 1986. Although this measure was a long way from its objective of winning recognition of the housewife as a worker or from enabling it to carry out trade union functions, it allowed the establishment of a form of obra social. However, because no identifiable employer had been established in law, SACRA was no closer to winning wages for housework, which meant the union was forced to survive on voluntary contributions from its members to fund the provision of health services, as opposed to the normal situation where regular union dues were deducted from wages and placed in a fund to which employers also contribute.

The position remained the same under Peronism, despite the personal intervention of President Menem. Failing to convince the Ministry of Labor, responsible for the registration of new trade unions, in April 1993 Menem signed Decree 673 by which a new category, *personería social* ("social status"), was invented, largely for the benefit of SACRA. The decree applied to all associations whose objectives were the protection, training, health, and social security assistance of housewives, and these associations would now be registered at the Ministry of Labor. As expected, SACRA was the first housewives' association to be registered. Although personería social still fell short of trade union status, the decree specifically permitted housewives' organizations to administrate private pension systems and obras sociales. Crucially, however, the Labor Ministry's normal function of monitoring free and fair elections in trade unions was not applicable to organizations with personería social.

Significantly, SACRA's claim to trade union status represented a challenge not only to the law, but also to existing trade unions. From the beginning, SACRA's relationship with the organized labor movement was ambiguous. "At first a lot of people thought we were crazy. Some unionist friends lent us rooms to meet, thinking that at any moment we'd give up and go back home."[19] The organization was taken more seriously when its capacity to mobilize women became evident. It took part in CGT actions and demonstrations, including strike rallies against the economic policies of the Alfonsín government. "They took us seriously because we mobilized thousands of women for strikes in the time of Alfonsín."[20]

However, SACRA was not a full member of the CGT and had no voting rights at CGT congresses: "the fact that we're not integrated [into the CGT] of course puts us in a weaker position. If we had full union status, we could vote, and considering that we have five hundred thousand members, we would have had the right to have a seat on the national executive."[21] In reality, there were many areas of potential conflict between SACRA and the established trade union movement. Many unions were still committed to the idea of the "family wage" and saw payments to housewives as a mechanism for depressing wages. Some also saw SACRA's "dual membership" policy as encroaching on their potential membership. According to SACRA, under this resistance was the perceived threat to the power of established trade unions; with a claimed membership of five hundred thousand, the union would have rated among Argentina's largest. "It's a struggle against the union world, which is a masculine world. . . . We've got as many members now as the biggest trade union. They're afraid of being challenged for the leadership, but we want to be there, and we will."[22]

Paradoxically, despite its claim to challenge the masculine world of trade unions, SACRA's support for Menem aligned it precisely with the sector of the labor movement that was the most traditional in gender terms. The women's department representing the Menemist trade union current was reluctant to offer SACRA its full support. According to one of SACRA's leaders, the department "could have a more explicit recognition of housewives as unionists. . . . there are about twenty members, and SACRA is not there."[23] Other women trade unionists, particularly those from alternative union currents, remained suspicious of SACRA's close links with Menem's government: "they don't like women who unionize as housewives, so there's a kind of competitiveness with us. They say that women should join the union in their workplace, and we say they should unionize in all the places they work."[24]

SACRA, Government Policy, and the Political Representation of Women's Interests

It was not only conservatism on the part of established trade unions that made the relationship with SACRA difficult; the union itself often took an ambiguous position on women in the paid workforce. This ambiguity was just one element in a discourse that increasingly resonated with essentialist ideas about women. The more radical demands, such as wages for house-work, gradually became a low priority in SACRA's campaigning activities. Under Menem, this demand often disappeared from the campaign litera-ture. It did not feature in the campaigns of 1989, 1992, or 1995, and there was an implicit acceptance of Menem's position that economic circumstances did not permit increased public spending.

The significance of this is that SACRA relied on wages as its chief weapon in combating unequal gender power relations: "with wages a woman will have a different relationship with her partner because she won't depend on him or the eldest child to bring in the money. There will be more equality in family relations."[25] Without the wages demand, little real attempt was made to address this crucial issue, and what was left was a discourse close to that used by Eva Perón and consistent with Menem's ideas about women. Although Menem's speeches emphasized women's rights, they did so only within a framework of traditional Peronist thinking about women, which included antifeminist sentiments. When the SSM was dismantled, the femi-nists went with it, and its successor, the Consejo Nacional de la Mujer (CNM), was created with a structure that made it directly responsible to the president. As events at the Fourth UN Women's Conference in Beijing were to show, the CNM was strictly under his control.[26]

Although some of SACRA's leaders pointed to the establishment of em-ployment training programs as evidence of their concern with paid work for women, most appeared to share Eva's concern that women should not be "masculinized" by employment: "there is this idea that a woman has to compete in the labor market on the same terms as men . . . training her for nontraditional jobs. But you can't simply see her as a plumber or electrician. For us that's nothing more than a return to a devaluation of the work she does in the home."[27] The union leadership argued that attaching value to housework through wages would increase the value of this work in the paid labor market and lead to a greater recognition of these skills. In the words of one of the union's former leaders, "We believe in equality inside the differences. The issue is to give equal value to the differences."[28]

The idea of extending women's traditional role into the public sphere also featured in SACRA's promotion of women in politics. The union campaigned for positive discrimination in political parties through a quota system and a women's ministry to formulate national government policy for women. Just as Eva spoke of the creation of a "new kind of politics" by women, SACRA suggested that women should bring their special qualities to the public world: "Women should be in government so that policies are closer to social reality, instead of grandiloquent ideas that lead to nothing."[29] It argued, "housewives in politics can change the way of seeing reality. This could be because we are the transmitters of life. It's something natural."[30]

The union's position on the sexual division of labor within the home was also underpinned by essentialist ideas about the proper role for women. Although it challenged the image of housewives as inactive and passive, it failed to challenge the very notion of women as housewives. SACRA presented a parliamentary bill calling on national, provincial, and local government to provide affordable communal facilities such as creches, public canteens, and laundrettes, but it did so not as a challenge to the traditional sexual division of labor, but as a method of assisting women with the burden of their domestic work. Similarly, there was little emphasis on sharing domestic responsibilities with men. Indeed, inherent in the idea of wages for housework was that transforming traditional roles in the home could leave women redundant, and this contradiction was evident in the discourse and literature of the union. Some members defended housework as women's work and were insulted by the suggestion that men should participate in it: "they [traditional feminists] put forward the idea that men should wash their own shirts, and this is our area. We are the housewives, and we want to be recognized for our work."[31] For others, the sharing of housework was a desirable, but slow process: "The transformation required for men to take on housework as their responsibility is slow and can only be achieved by women organizing and gaining more consciousness," not through challenging men. "We've never proposed or accentuated the contradictions with men. We believe they're just as much workers as women, and the idea is to strengthen the union movement and transform the whole of society, not to turn it into a personal, individual struggle."[32]

Not only did SACRA's leaders fail to challenge the traditional sexual division of labor within the home, but several came close to prescribing it as the appropriate division of roles between men and women. In words reminiscent of Eva, "We believe that women are the focal point of the home. . . . it doesn't matter how much a woman negates her condition as housewife. . . . she is always dealing with what happens in the home. . . . And as much as we want to pass it on to men, we're different, and we're always going to be different."[33]

The dropping of the demand for wages for housework was also significant because the achievement of SACRA's other key demands were contingent upon it. Without wages, a union health insurance policy and pension fund required voluntary contributions from members, with no equivalent contribution from employers. As SACRA leaders pointed out, this was one reason why there was such a low take-up of their obra social (estimated at under 10 percent of members). Instead, pensions for housewives became associated with the government's policy of promoting private pensions and family savings: "with the changes in the economy we had to bring [our proposal] up to date and adapt it to the private pension system."[34] In 1997, a new law was passed to enable housewives to contribute to a private pension fund as self-employed workers. The value of the pension depended on the number of years of contributions, and those who benefited most were women under thirty-five years old—which excluded a large proportion of SACRA members. From a sample of members registered at the Ministry of Labor and Social Welfare, the average age of SACRA members was forty-three.

At the same time, SACRA became increasingly involved with policies that did little to meet their demands for social security provision for women, but instead were more oriented toward housewives themselves providing these services. After Menem's election in 1989, SACRA's leadership encouraged its members to take advantage of government social programs designed to satisfy basic community needs, such as health, sanitation, communal allotments, income-raising projects, and community centers. This approach laid SACRA open to criticisms that it was collaborating with the huge cuts in health and social services provision and with their replacement by cheaper community-run services. Increasingly, SACRA's activities also became associated with housewives in their role as consumers, encouraging them to participate in the protection of consumer rights, a specific aim of Menem's Plan Social.

The success in legislative terms of SACRA's strategy of support for Menem's government was therefore questionable. Although it claimed some credit for the 30 percent quota for political parties and the establishment of a women's ministry, it can be argued that SACRA gained little from Menem's government that it did not have under Alfonsín. As one of SACRA's leaders herself admitted, "In these first years [of Menem's government], we haven't gained much in terms of specific policies."[35] None of SACRA's principal demands for the recognition of housewives as workers with a right to a wage was achieved, and the new pension and health insurance systems offered little to the poorest housewives, precisely the group that SACRA had aimed to represent. The union achieved some success, however, in raising public awareness of housework. The presence of Menem together with huge numbers of SACRA members at public meetings did not go unnoticed by the press. There was also some recognition by the courts of the role of housewives. A 1987 resolution fixed an economic value on the work of a housewife at half the monthly wage of a husband in paid work because, according to the same SACRA leader, the tasks of a wife allow the husband to "dedicate himself to his business without doing domestic tasks." In November 1995, the civil courts in Mar de Plata also put a value on housework by ordering compensation of US$320,000 to the family of a woman who died in an accident.

The following interview, carried out in 1994, shows how SACRA's leaders typically justified their support for Menem.

Question: Why does the union support Menem?
Respondent 1: Because of the things he's done for women. The 30 percent female quota for political parties, for example, and the number of women now in parliament.
Question: What about SACRA's other demands?
Respondent 1: The president inherited a dramatic crisis that was the result of thirty-five years of counterrevolution against the Peronist heritage. . . . All this has meant that he's had to postpone some social policies, and he has had to do unorthodox things.

Question: Such as?

Respondent 1: All the talk of free markets and competition . . . but for the first time, he has attacked the culture of tax evasion. He's begun to change things.

Respondent 2: It hasn't been spectacular, but at least there's some kind of stability now. . . . Before, with inflation, people couldn't plan anything.

Respondent 1: In his second term of office, when things are sorted out, he'll be able to concentrate on social policies.

SACRA, the Argentine Women's Movement, and the State

According to the Chilean feminist Julieta Kirkwood, two of the key *nudos* or difficulties facing the women's movement in the 1970s and 1980s were the relationship with the state and the relationship between the nonfeminist and feminist movements.[36] The controversy and division these issues caused in the 1980s were not new to the Argentine women's movement, and most notably they had surfaced in the early 1940s with the emergence of Peronism. The refusal of the early feminist organizations to work with the Peronist state, even regarding suffrage, which they saw simply as political opportunism on the part of Perón, laid them open to charges of elitism and irrelevance to the interests of working-class women. At the beginning of the 1980s, the new Argentine feminist movement was facing similar criticism.

The decision to abandon feminism was based on criticisms that it was a small middle-class movement, oriented toward Europe and the United States, and unrepresentative of working-class women. These criticisms echoed those of many other popular women's organizations in Latin America, where rigid social structures made class a crucial constituent of gender interests. But although in some other Latin American countries, popular women's movements and feminist organizations managed a working relationship, this was not the case in Argentina. Part of the reason for the distinctive development of Argentina's women's movement in the 1970s and 1980s, as Sonia Alvarez has shown, was the exclusionary, antistatist, neoliberalist model adopted by the military in Argentina, which meant that Argentine women did not experience the same kind of contradictions in their everyday lives as those in Brazil, Peru, and Mexico, where state capitalist development was vigorously pursued.[37] Argentine census reports show an almost static level in women's economic activity during the 1970s and 1980s;[38] at the same time, economic crisis arrived later in Argentina, so it was not until after the mid-1980s that self-help neighborhood organizations began to establish themselves.

Instead, the principal contradictions that arose in women's roles in Argentina during the 1970s and early 1980s were primarily political and ideological.[39] The Argentine military's emphasis on the sanctity of the family was strongly supported by the church, but was contradicted by the gender-specific consequences of its political repression. The policy of mass disappearance of political opponents, mainly young people, had a dramatic impact on women in their roles as carers of their families and was seen as a direct assault on the families of the mothers whose children had disappeared. It prompted the growth of women's organizations such as the Madres and Abuelas de Plaza de Mayo, which were able to gain moral legitimacy from the powerful image of motherhood they themselves evoked and to challenge openly the military's claim to be defenders of the family.

As well as structural factors, micropolitical variables also shaped the development of Argentina's women's movement—particularly the lack of organizational networks.[40] The dominant sectors of the Argentine church collaborated openly with the military, refusing to support human rights or community organizations; nor was the left, destroyed in Argentina rather than defeated as in Chile or Brazil, able to fulfill the role of organizer of neighborhood groups. The speed of the transition to constitutional rule made the reorganization and participation of civil society more difficult in Argentina than in Brazil, where, as Fiona Macaulay shows in her chapter, women's movements were able to significantly influence the political process. At the same time, military vacillation in the face of the Madres and Abuelas enabled these women's organizations to establish themselves and survive military rule, whereas other women's groups—in particular, feminist ones—were targeted and intimidated in the months after the coup.[41] Unlike the widespread self-help networks that grew up in the poor neighborhoods of Santiago or São Paulo, the Madres had little impact on the everyday lives of other Argentine women. It was an organization strictly composed of and run by mothers of disappeared children, and for most of the period of military rule, although they achieved international recognition, they remained invisible to the majority of the population.

If structural and micropolitical variables did not favor the development of working-class women's movement, neither did they favor the development of a strong feminist one. Although Argentina was among the first Latin American countries to establish "second-wave" feminist groups, military repression meant these groups disappeared between 1976 and 1980, and it was only during 1980–83, with few international contacts and little access to new feminist literature, that groups of mainly middle-class Argentine women began to set up small organizations. On the eve of constitutional rule in the early 1980s, feminism reached only a very limited sector of the population, mainly in Buenos Aires, and had not produced an interclass women's movement capable of uniting around a diverse platform of demands.

Argentine feminism was also weakened by divisions over both theory and practice. The clearest differences were centered on the relationship with the state and with the nonfeminist women's movement. Until the 1980s, most sectors of the Argentine women's movement had engaged with the state not to promote gender equality, but to provide social welfare. The women's movement that emerged in the 1970s and 1980s however, featured a strong element of hostility to the state. This hostility was particularly evident from the small feminist and nonfeminist organizations such as the Madres de Plaza de Mayo. In the case of feminists, the insistence on autonomy meant that most organizations were reluctant to work with women from political parties and so became increasingly distant from contemporary concerns. According to Haydée Birgin, the feminists "were absent from the country's struggle for democracy,"[42] and Magui Bellotti has suggested that open support for human rights and participation in the antimilitary struggle were the exception, rather than the rule. Until 1985, most groups "oscillated between indifference, some individual participation, and the view that [nonfeminist movements] reaffirmed the traditional role of women and therefore had no connection with feminism."[43] "There's a lack of communication between women of the middle and working classes."[44] The result was that Argentine feminism failed to link gender with class issues. The economic crisis that followed Argentina's return to constitutional rule was a crucial issue for working-class women, but rarely featured in the debates or concerns of the feminist movement. "Feminism hasn't yet understood the basic needs of other women, those who are not intellectuals, and because of this they don't know how to reach these women."[45] This situation sharply contrasted to the case in Brazil, where, as

Macaulay shows, Centro Feminista de Estudos e Assessoria (CFEMEA) gained political legitimacy precisely because of its active participation in the struggle for democracy and its joint activities with working-class women.

Linked to the failure to take on working-class demands was a second criticism of feminism by Argentine working-class women: its emphasis on gender as representing the key division of interests in society inevitably led to a mistaken strategy—fighting against men. For SACRA, the wide and growing class divisions in Latin American societies meant that working-class women identified more with men of their class than with middle-class women. According to SACRA's leaders, in order for women to improve their situation, they must work with men on class and dependency issues: "The struggle of women has to be linked to the struggle of the whole society for the liberation of the country."[46] As one SACRA leader put it, "Many feminists are born hating men, and it's not about hating the other sex. It's about making a better world."[47]

Although in its "wages for housework" position, CESMA drew on a radical strand of European socialist feminism, it found itself at odds with the dominant current of Argentine feminism. The decision to create a union prompted a public debate in the press between members of SACRA and several notable feminists who questioned the members' assertion that housewives were workers and their demand for a wage. Increasingly, SACRA hardened its position against feminist organizations, finding a more receptive framework for its ideas in Peronism—particularly in the ideology expressed by Eva Perón and in her calls for the dignification of housework.

The union's decision to reject feminism should be seen in the context of criticisms of the feminist movement, but also against a background of the strong identification of working-class women with Peronism and the historical antagonisms between Peronist and feminist organizations. Increasingly, SACRA's antifeminist stance came to echo Eva Perón's view of feminists as women of the oligarchy and manhaters who failed to take account of working-class women. One SACRA leader stated, "I think feminist groups in Argentina are very European-based. I'm not putting down the struggle of European women, but it corresponds to another reality."[48] Another explained, "In Argentina, feminism has never been a mass movement. Feminism was always a small group of women who employ other women to do their housework."[49]

Nor did SACRA develop links with other women's organizations. The need for pensions was the only issue on which SACRA worked together with the two other principal housewives' organizations in Argentina, the Liga de Amas de Casa and Amas de Casa de País (ACP). It was not a member of the Women's Multisectorial, formed in 1984, a loose association of women from political parties, trade unions, feminist organizations, human rights organizations, and housewives' committees who agreed on a core of basic demands to put to the government. Moreover, it took no part in the National Women's Meetings, held yearly from 1986 and attended by a wide range of women's organizations. The inclusion of pensions for housewives in the demands of the latter two organizations was a result of the participation of the ACP.

Conclusions

The case of SACRA illustrates the complexity of state-gender relations. Elections—particularly elections after long periods of military rule when political parties were keen to attract women's votes—proved key access points to the state for Argentine women's movements. Under both Menem and Alfonsín, important advances were made toward legal equality for women, including laws against discrimination against women, reform of family law, as well as divorce and political party quotas (although the latter was not fully implemented). The success of women's movements in promoting their demands, however, was conditioned by a number of factors. One was the character of the new governments. For historical as well as ideological reasons, different regimes favored different women's organizations. The opposition Alfonsín's government encountered from working-class organizations such as the unions made the participation of working-class women in agencies such as the SSM difficult and led to criticisms that working-class interests were being ignored in legislation affecting women. Under Menem, working-class women and their organizations, such as SACRA, had greater access to power and state institutions, but feminist organizations were alienated by a gender discourse heavily inspired by both traditional Peronist ideas and the Catholic Church.

Access to governments, however, may not be the determining factor in gender policy outcomes, however, and SACRA's close relationship with

Menem's government did not guarantee the achievement of its demands. Broader policy requirements under both Menem and Alfonsín circumscribed the direction of gender policy. Both presidents presented themselves as modernizing forces. Under Alfonsín, the search for a liberal, modern, First World image after years of barbaric military rule focused on the defense of civil and human rights, and bringing gender legislation up to date was one element of this process. Important gains were made, but there was no coordinated gender policy. The more controversial demands of the women's movement, such as abortion, were left untouched, and state agencies set up to coordinate gender issues were underresourced and had little access to key decision-making arenas. Menem projected himself as an economic modernizer, partly to gain acceptability from international financial institutions. He needed women's support not only to counter the potential opposition from organized labor to proposed antiunion legislation, but also arguably to soften the blows of massive welfare cuts imposed under IMF aid packages. Women's work could replace the collapse of neighborhood and community services.

Prevailing assumptions and ideologies about the role of women may permeate different state departments and institutions, and contradict state intentions to modify gender relations. Social welfare programs in the 1980s and 1990s, for example, were aimed at mothers or women in their role as dependents or care givers, reflecting the difficulty of incorporating gender into state policies as a political issue, rather than as a social one. This attempt produced contradictions not only in policy—which promoted equality, on the one hand, and a dependent role for women, on the other—but also in the real lives and roles of women.

The case of SACRA also shows how the character of the civil society of which an organization is a part affects the extent to which social movements can influence the outcomes of state gender policy. Several factors affected the development of the relationship between the state and SACRA. The first was the distinctive nature of the women's movement in Argentina, which was not conducive to the growth of a widespread cross-class, feminist-influenced movement as in other Latin American countries. This factor influenced SACRA's decision to reject feminism and adopt ideas more closely associated with Eva Perón. The attempt to gain acceptance as a trade union necessitated an emphasis on working together with men, made it cautious about developing relationships with other women's organizations, and blunted its radicalism and ability to challenge gender power relations. At the same time, its failure to gain recognition from the established union movement limited any potential for changing the movement and reinforced a direct relationship with the Peronist state. This relationship influenced its progressive adoption of orthodox Peronist positions on a number of gender issues, which necessitated compromising several of the organization's key demands. Instead of offering a radical alternative to traditional working-class women's organizations, SACRA came increasingly to reproduce the discourse, forms of organization, and state relations that had been characteristic of the Partido Peronista Femenino.

Notes

1   See C. Llorca, *Llamadme Evita* (Barcelona: Editorial Planeta, 1980), 119. All translations unless otherwise indicated are by the author.
2   Elida Vigo, interview with author, Misiones, 1991.
3   Ibid.
4   Eva Perón, *My Mission* (New York: Vantage, 1953), 190, 192.
5   Elida Vigo, interview with author, Misiones, 1991.
6   Marysa Navarro, *Evita* (Buenos Aires: Planeta, 1994), 233.
7   For a comprehensive account of the early women's movement, see A. Lavrin, *Women, Feminism, and Social Change in Argentina, Chile, and Uruguay, 1890–1940* (Lincoln: University of Nebraska Press, 1995).
8   Susana Bianchi and Norma Sanchís, *El Partido Peronista Femenino, primera/segunda parte* (Buenos Aires: Centro Editor de América Latina, 1988), 62.
9   Laura Rubio, interview with author, Buenos Aires, 1991.
10 Rosalía Cortés, "Marginación de la fuerza del trabajo femenina? Estructura de ocupaciones 1980–1993," in *Acción pública y sociedad: Las mujeres en el cambio estructural,* ed. Haydée Birgin (Buenos Aires: CEADEL, Feminaria Editora, 1995), 83–101.
11 There is little evidence to support the claims of Peronist activists such as Elena Palmucci that Eva set up a women's department in the CGT in the 1940s. See *Ensayos de y por mujeres* (Buenos Aires: FEPESNA, 1995), 68–81. See also Nancy Hollander's claim in "Si Evita viviera," *Latin American Perspectives* 1, no. 3 (1974): 42–57, and those of contemporary Peronist women activists that Perón introduced labor legislation specifically to improve the position of women in the paid workforce in 1946–55. Navarro, *Evita,* 232, and Susana Novick, *Mujer, estado, y políticas sociales* (Buenos Aires: Centro Editor de América Latina, 1993), 108–114, found no specific labor laws affecting women in this period; rather, women benefited from general working-class gains.

12 María Lucila Colombo, interview with author, Buenos Aires, 1994.

13 See Mabel Bellucci and Adriana Rofman, "Mujeres: Entre el movimiento social y el estado: Historia y balance de la Subsecretaría de la Mujer de la Nación (1984–1989)," *Todo es historia* (Buenos Aires, 1990), and Mabel Bellucci et al., *A manera de balance: La Subsecretaría de la Mujer de Argentina* (Buenos Aires: unpub. report, 1990).

14 Elida Vigo, "Fue reeligida Secretaria General del SACRA," *Periódico del Sindicato de Amas de Casa de La Republica Argentina* III, no. 6 (August 1990): 6.

15 Elida Vigo in ibid., p. 6.

16 Elida Vigo, in SACRA publication, Año 1, no. 1 (January 1993): 7.

17 Elida Vigo, interview with author, 1992.

18 From interviews with branch members of SACRA, Lomas de Zamora, 1991.

19 María Lucila Colombo, interview with author, Buenos Aires, 1994.

20 Graciela Escobar, interview with author, Buenos Aires, 1991.

21 María Lucila Colombo, interview with author, Buenos Aires, 1994.

22 Laura Rubio, interview with author, Buenos Aires, 1991.

23 María Lucila Colombo, interview with author, Buenos Aires, 1994.

24 Ibid.

25 Elida Vigo, interview with author, Misiones, 1991.

26 See "El día después," *Mujer / Fempress,* nos. 168–69 (October–November 1995), 3.

27 María Lucila Colombo, interview with author, Buenos Aires, 1994.

28 Laura Rubio, interview with author, Buenos Aires, 1991.

29 María Lucila Colombo, interview with author, Buenos Aires, 1994.

30 Ardonso, interview with author, Buenos Aires, 1995.

31 Ibid.

32 Laura Rubio, interview with author, Buenos Aires, 1991.

33 Ardonso, interview with author, 1995.

34 Nélida Parra (national deputy and member of SACRA), "El Congreso preve sancionar la ley de amas de casa," *La Nación,* 2 January 1997.

35 María Lucila Colombo, interview with author, 1994.

36 See Julieta Kirkwood, *Ser política en Chile* (Santiago de Chile: FLACSO, 1986).

37 Sonia Alvarez, "The Politics of Gender in Latin America: Comparative Perspectives on Women in the Brazilian Transition to Democracy" (Ph.D. diss., Yale University, 1986), chap. 11.

38 Subsecretaría de la Mujer, *La situación de la mujer en la República Argentina* (Buenos Aires: Ministerio de Salud y Acción Social, 1988), 10.

39 See Jo Fisher, *Mothers of the Disappeared* (London: Zed, 1989); Juan M. Villareal, "Changes in Argentine Society: The Heritage of the Dictatorship," in *From Military Rule to Liberal Democracy in Argentina,* ed. Monica Peralta-Ramos and Carlos H. Waisman (Boulder, Colo.: Westview, 1987), 69–96.

40 See Alvarez, "The Politics of Gender," chaps. 3, 11.

41 See Magui Bellotti, "El feminismo y el movimiento de mujeres," *Cuadernos del Sur,* no. 10 (Buenos Aires, 1989): 11–41; Inés Cano, "El movimiento femenino

argentino en la década del '70," *Todo es Historia* 183 (Buenos Aires, 1982): 84–93; María del Carmen Feijoó, "The Challenge of Constructing Civilian Peace: Women and Democracy in Argentina," in *The Women's Movement in Latin America,* ed. Jane Jaquette (Boston: Unwin, 1989), 72–94.

42 Haydée Birgin, "La igualdad es una asignatura pendiente," in *Transiciones: Mujeres en los procesos democráticos, Isis,* edición no. 13 (Santiago de Chile, 1990), 33–49.

43 According to Bellotti, only Asociación de Trabajo y Estudio sobre la Mujer (ATEM), formed in 1982, took an active role in human rights and the struggle for democracy until 1985. See "El feminismo y el movimiento de mujeres," 41, n. 19.

44 Magui Bellotti in Sylvia Chejter, unpublished manuscript (Buenos Aires).

45 Gloria Bonder in Chejter, unpublished manuscript (Buenos Aires).

46 Graciela Escobar, interview with author, Buenos Aires, 1991.

47 Ardonso, interview with author, Buenos Aires, 1995.

48 Laura Rubio, interview with author, Buenos Aires, 1991.

49 Alicia Donadio, interview with author, Buenos Aires, 1991.

Fiona Macaulay

Getting Gender on the Policy Agenda

A Study of a Brazilian Feminist Lobby Group

One of the primary activities of the state is the regulation of social relations: between capital and labor, between citizen and the state, and between men and women. Gender relations are constantly constructed and reconstructed, regulated and policed by agencies of the state, both in the so-called private sphere of the family and in more public arenas, to employ the misleading dichotomy of the rubric of liberal discourse. However, the state is not monolithic. Composed of a diversity of actors and structures, it is susceptible to influence and vulnerable to pressure from both domestic and international interest groups and lobbies.

The Brazilian state itself was relatively impermeable to women's political lobbying until the 1980s. The absence of strong, organized parties, the dominance of tiny, closed political elites who relied on personalistic and clientelistic relations, and the influence of the corporatist system established under Getúlio Vargas in which the centralist state formulated social policy from the top down drastically reduced the number of access points. Even those actors who were privileged insider players, such as organized labor and business,[1] found it difficult enough to negotiate the corporatist bureaucracy that had become insular, self-serving, and self-replicating. Until the political opening and the crafting of a new democracy in the 1980s, women's organizations, along with other social sectors, remained outsiders with respect both to the insider players and to the structures of the state itself.

However, in the 1990s, a new feminist lobbying organization was formed in Brazil, the Centro Feminista de Estudos e Assessoria (CFEMEA, Feminist Research and Advisory Center), which established new modalities of interaction between the organized women's movement and the state apparatus. An examination of the way CFEMEA evolved and operated, by comparison to earlier attempts by women's groups to achieve similar ends, is revealing of the way the women's movement has changed its view of and approach to the state. It also demonstrates the increased porousness of the state to gender issues and to effective lobbying on behalf of a broad-based issue network. A nongovernmental organization (NGO), set up in 1989 in Brasília, CFEMEA provided a bridge between women's entities, on the one hand, and the legislative process and the wider political system, on the other. It lobbied legislators for changes in laws and the Constitution, monitored the progress of bills through the National Congress, consulted women's groups regarding policy formation, kept them informed about current legislative developments, and worked very closely with an all-party group of women deputies who generated the bills in consultation with women's NGOs and the women's movement in Brazil. In particular, it collaborated with Congress on revision of penal and civil codes and lobbied the legislature with regard to the implementation of the Beijing Platform for Action.[2] Its emphasis on skill and knowledge sharing through its monthly newsletter (Fêmea, or "Female"), movement-based consultation, and specialist briefings to legislators underscores its unique pivotal function between one sector of Brazilian society and the state apparatus. During the 1980s, the organized women's movement came to have more leverage over the political system, and some became insider players as politicians or policymakers, albeit in relative isolation. It is the novelty of CFEMEA to play an intermediary role between an active yet diverse and dispersed women's movement and the political system. It is this hybrid status and the ability to combine intimate, acquired insider knowledge of the rules of the institutional game with representation of the interests of an autonomous organized movement that distinguish from previous attempts by women in Brazil to change public policy in the direction of greater gender equality.

This chapter examines the ways in which the women's movement in Brazil has come to organize itself so as to exert maximum, effective lobbying pressure on particular points of the Brazilian state in order to get gender-sensitive legislation and policy formulated, debated, and passed. The chapter begins with historical perspectives on how the women's movement approached the state in Brazil prior to and during the transition to democracy in the 1980s. The formation and modus operandi of CFEMEA are described, and a number of theoretical models are explored for understanding both the new forms of organization that have emerged within the

Brazilian women's movement and the movement's relationship with a Brazilian state undergoing some profound structural changes at the end of the twentieth century. In broad terms, the content of the public policy areas around which women organize has not necessarily changed dramatically. However, this chapter argues that what has changed is the *way* in which women's and feminist lobbying has taken advantage of transformations in the state and political structures and has entered into a more interactive and dynamic relationship with those structures.

Historical Perspectives

The Brazilian state has regulated gender and social relations in many different ways—through legislation (penal, family, labor codes), through foundational political texts such as the constitutions, and through social legislation and policy, whether promoting modernization, public hygiene, or modifications to family structures and life. The state's approach and effectiveness have inevitably been conditioned by national peculiarities such as extreme regionalism, now reflected in a strengthened federal system, and by the legacy of corporatist and clientelistic relations. Brazil suffered from two prolonged authoritarian periods in the twentieth century: the Estado Novo instituted by President Getúlio Vargas (1937–45) and collegiate military rule (1964–85). Literally "New State," the Estado Novo was an authoritarian, corporatist regime, a legal hybrid combining elements of Salazar's Portugal and Mussolini's Italy. Periods of democratic rule from 1889 to 1985 were characterized by institutional instability and an elitist, personalist style of politics. For a women's movement to have an impact on policymaking required a capacity for organization and mobilization to give the movement some leverage on institutions. A degree of continuity and permeability was also necessary within political institutions, including political parties. These conditions were absent until the 1980s, which heralded crucial structural changes in the state, such as advent of the New Unionism and a rupture in the corporatist nexus between the Ministry of Labor bureaucracy and pro-government unions. The growth in "new social movement" activity in the 1970s and 1980s brought new actors, agendas, and alliances onto the political scene.

Women's activities in the late nineteenth century and much of the twentieth century were highly stratified by race and social class. The continental size of the country, high levels of illiteracy, and egregious social inequalities militated against the possibility of wider cross-class female or feminist coalitions around common goals such as women's suffrage or workers' rights. A number of women's organizations and federations did emerge, with a focus on suffrage and on women's economic status in particular. During the 1920s and 1930s, the Federação Brasileira pelo Progresso Feminino (FBPF, Brazilian Federation for Women's Progress), the major feminist organization of the time, spearheaded the campaign for women's suffrage and legal rights.[3] Founded in 1922 by Bertha Lutz, a powerful, charismatic upper-middle-class professional woman, it claimed to speak on behalf of a diversity of women's organizations—professional, civic, charitable, and pro-suffrage—gathered under its umbrella. Its membership, however, consisted of schoolteachers and civil service employees, but very few factory women.[4] The leadership of professional women turned not to the grass roots for influence, but to the domestic elite and to foreign allies. The suffragists sought support from senators and deputies of a liberal disposition in the Congress[5] who sponsored bills out of personal, not party ideological, disposition.[6] Winning the vote in 1932 did not afford women leverage in the political system. Highly restricted for both men and women until the postwar period, suffrage was not a subject of widespread political mobilization, and there were no mass-based parties whose electoral fortunes depended on widening the electoral base by wooing women's ballots. The Estado Novo ensured that women did not actually exercise the vote until 1946.

The leadership of the FBPF was, however, adept at seizing opportunities offered by new political conjunctures, such as changes in the composition of the ruling masculine elite. Following the October 1930 Revolution, Lutz was appointed to a commission responsible for drafting the 1934 Constitution, which granted a number of new rights to women related to suffrage, political office, public positions, labor law, the protection of the family, and social welfare. In this regard, it foreshadowed the 1988 Constitution. The difference lies, however, in the process of formulation. The 1934 Constitution was formulated by a small group of experts: no women were elected to the Constituent Assembly, and there was no women's mobilization around these issues. Attempts to modify the civil and penal codes were debated widely, but came to nothing. The Estado Novo rolled back many of the legislative gains, excluded women as political actors, and foreclosed all space for civic organizations to exert pressure on the authoritarian state.

Until then, the few women elected did actively champion women's rights in this institutional arena, but without the backing of the organizational resources and programmatic commitment of a political party and without a critical mass of fellow women politicians. Carlota Pereira de Queiroz, the first woman elected deputy in 1933, and Bertha Lutz, elected *suplente* (as a stand-in) in 1936, became active legislators—presenting bills on education, marriage law, aid to poor families, protection for mothers and children, practical and legal guarantees for working women, entry into the professions, and constitutional guarantees for women. However, the impact these women legislators had was modest and their institutional foothold weak. Ordinary women had no input or influence on gender-related policy because there existed neither the institutional channels and opportunities nor the mobilizational capacity of an organized movement. Change, when it occurred, was delivered from the top. However, the Brazilian state never organized and incorporated women en masse either via state-sponsored women's groups, as did the Centros de Madres (Women's Centers) in Chile, or via a subsidiary department of a dominant ruling party, as in the case of the Peronist Party in Argentina or the Federation of Cuban Women. In the latter case, as Maxine Molyneux demonstrates in this volume, patronage by the ruling state party has hampered the federation's capacity to focus on its constituency's needs and act effectively on its behalf. None of the women's organizations that emerged in the 1940s in Brazil had any staying power or significant influence on national politics.[7] The issues addressed by these groups—cost of living, democracy, and peace—prefigured the spectrum of concerns around which women's groups in the 1970s and 1980s would later coalesce. However, no clear focal point crystallized around which women could organize across class differences. They mostly formed reactive, localized campaign groups.

The improvement of women's status was conceptualized in the 1930s and 1940s as an element in the wider corporatist project of nation building and modernization. Vargas's corporatist Consolidação das Leis Trabalhistas (CLT, Consolidated Labor Laws) of 1943, aimed at controlling labor, contained protectionist legislation regarding women's working conditions—equal pay for equal work, anti–sexual harassment provisions, paid maternity leave and benefits, job security during pregnancy, time off work for breastfeeding and after abortion, and a requirement for all firms with more than twenty employees to provide a crèche.[8] The corporatist system persisted into the democratic period of 1945–64 and was strengthened under the military in 1964–85. The women's movement of the 1980s therefore built on a base of existing legislation and rhetoric about women's rights in the workplace and public sphere. The core issues concerning the women's movement in Brazil have not changed radically since the early decades of the twentieth century: implementation of the CLT labor laws, civil and political rights, and economic survival of the family—although the feminist agenda has expanded to include reproductive rights and sexuality. However, tangible progress has been made. Revisions to civil and penal codes prepared by a new wave of feminist specialists were under debate in Congress by the late 1990s. Electoral legislation requires a quota of up to 30 percent women candidates in all elections,[9] and women have secured some key welfare rights.

What changed was the strategy and the discourse adopted by women activists in the 1980s and 1990s when certain structural changes in the state allowed them greater leverage over a wider variety of access points. The organizational *strategies* chosen by women activists in the first decades of this century were shaped inevitably by the political and institutional environment. Public policy was delivered top down, largely unaffected by or with the aim of controlling grassroots mobilization. Political institutions were closed to women, as were arenas for policymaking, such as ministries. Contacts with politicians were made on a personalist rather than party political level, and politicians' consultation with women's groups was sporadic at best. Debate over gender policy was clearly lively within women's groups, but without institutionally stable interlocutors in the system, such debates had little direct effect on elite policymakers.

Transformations:
The Brazilian State and the Women's Movement

The 1980s and 1990s saw the organized women's movement exert influence on the state apparatus and the formal political sphere as never before, both in degree and method. A qualitative shift occurred in the 1980s during the transition to democracy,[10] as a number of factors converged that opened up multiple sites and levers of influence for feminist activists. These factors in turn created the political conditions within which CFEMEA later emerged. The women's movement broadened to encompass a multiplicity of territorially, ideologically, sectorally, and thematically based groups. Success in influencing the political system was no longer restricted to urban professional women, but extended to working-class women. Knowledge about the mechanisms and access points of the political system was much more widely disseminated. There also existed at least one political party, with significant clout in the system, that was committed ideologically to women's equality and that had strong organic links with the women's movement through the "double militancy" of its members. The number of women in Congress rose to a critical mass and produced a female cross-party backbench grouping. I elaborate below on the role of "doorkeepers" in the political system, played by parties and elected representatives, as well as on the importance of knowledge sharing within a heterogeneous women's movement in a political system with multiple access points.

The first key factor was the leverage the women's movement was able to exert on the political forces emerging in the transition period. The movement's bargaining power enabled it to gain institutional footholds. The biparty system, which was the creation of the military government and survived in modified form until the late 1980s, produced a centrist opposition party, the Partido do Movimento Democrático Brasileiro (PMDB, Party of the Brazilian Democratic Movement), which sought to attract new electoral constituencies in order to consolidate its already considerable victories in a number of key elections. At its political zenith during the transition, it looked to women who had been involved in organizing against the military regime for support for its pro-democratic platform. In exchange, the more politically progressive elements in the party responded to women's movement demands for new forms of representation of women's interests. In the mid-1980s, a number of Women's Councils were established in PMDB-governed states, to represent women's views and to advise government on appropriate gender-sensitive public policy. In the best cases—for example, in São Paulo—the authorities committed themselves to public spending on tackling violence against women, set up women's police stations, offered women's health services, and signed up to the principles and commitments of the United Nations Convention on the Elimination of all Forms of Discrimination against Women. Set up in 1985 within the Ministry of Justice under the PMDB-led federal administration of President José Sarney, the Conselho Nacional dos Direitos da Mulher (CNDM, National Council for Women's Rights) received a relatively high degree of political and financial support until 1989.[11] It was staffed by experienced feminist activists who were skilled in public policy formulation and political lobbying, and who benefited from high credibility, good currency with the PMDB, and the political support of the government. However, as the decade wore on, the CNDM fell victim to political maneuvering that displaced the centralized initiatives into other arenas, nongovernmental rather than government spheres, and into locally generated rather than nationally initiated activities. The collapse of the CNDM is instructive of the central dilemma facing feminist activists in approaching the state: balancing trade-offs between the goals of maximizing democratic input from within the women's movement, on the one hand, and achieving effective policymaking via targeted leverage exerted by a body of policy specialists, on the other. The 1980s saw the women's movement in Brazil divided between maintaining autonomy and gaining an institutional foothold. The CNDM, with only advisory powers, nevertheless achieved many public policy advances in the first four and a half years of its life, particularly in the Constituent Assembly. Jacqueline Pitanguy, its president during that period, commented, "It doesn't really matter what you call it, a council, secretariat, whatever, if you have political space to execute policy, as we did. We behaved as if we were in fact a deliberative body."[12] The CNDM had no operational staff and no budget of its own: staff were seconded from other ministries, and the budget was allocated by Congress out of the national budget and stood at US$3 million, making it easier to co-opt and control. Political support dissipated toward the end of the Sarney government, whose justice minister suddenly cut the budget without warning. There then followed a period of dramatic deinstitutionalization as the members of the board and a series of presidents, most of whom were unknown in the women's movement, were shuffled and replaced, and the budget was decimated. Ironically, CFEMEA, perhaps the continent's most effective feminist lobbying group, emerged as a result of the Brazilian state's historical tendency to co-opt and absorb initiatives that derive from social mobilization into its clientelistic networks.

Frustration with the purely advisory capacity of the Women's Councils and the ease with which they could be co-opted and controlled by politicians led feminist policymakers in the late 1980s to enter the decision-making executive branch of the state. Generally within the municipal or state administrations of the Partido dos Trabalhadores (PT, Workers' Party), women's secretariats were set up, or they were designated subministries with much wider remit, powers, and operational budget. Women activists in the PT justified work inside the state apparatus as a way to address the intersectoral public policies required to respond to women's needs.[13] Access to resources would ensure that commitments were actually implemented. In general, the secretariats were successful in influencing public policy from within. However, it became clear that councils and secretariats fulfilled complementary functions. The councils had an advisory and representational role, composed partly of delegates elected by local women's groups. On the other hand, their institutional clout was minimal. The secretariats ran a converse risk of becoming either party political tools or excessively technocratic, filled with the career feminists or "femocrats"[14] who could not by virtue of their position in any sense "represent" local women. The challenge of combining wide consultation with effectiveness in a complex state bureaucracy also undoubtedly influenced CFEMEA's working model.

A second factor in opening up opportunities for feminist activists was the growth in the organizational capacity of the women's movement under military rule, around the three axes of human rights, economic survival, and a feminist agenda. These axes increasingly overlapped, making cross-class coalitions and the formation of common agendas possible. A multiplicity of local grassroots women's groups worked on a range of issues—from daily survival issues ("reproductive" issues in Marxian terms) such as crèches, cost of living, housing and health care—while women mobilized in trade unions, within political parties, and in the church. Those with a more feminist agenda focused on violence against women and reproductive rights. For the first time, women had acquired a national voice in the CNDM, and certain issues were taken up as a common agenda across class lines, such as the campaign against violence against women. The place of the CNDM was then taken by a network of state and municipal councils on women, which provided a loose national policy network grouped together as the Forum of Heads of State and Municipal Councils for Women, whose influence and sphere of activity was primarily subnational and local. A number of other important women's networks grew and consolidated during the 1980s: some based in a particular geographical area, such as a state;

some based around occupational groupings, such as women rural and domestic workers in the two trade union peak organizations, the Central Unica Trabalhadores (CUT) and Força Sindical; some grounded on personal identity, such as black women and lesbians; some based on ideological grounds, such as those affiliated to political parties; and some based on shared campaign issues, such as those concerned about reproductive rights, violence against women, or health issues. The small number of feminists within public administration and Congress also began, tentatively, to form informal networks. It is this richness and diversity of women's organizations that made CFEMEA both possible and necessary, and that has required them to develop flexible forms of consultation, skills sharing, and alliance building.

The 1988 Constitution provided a conjuncture during which the hundreds of women's groups and organizations were able to have an input into policymaking across a wide range of issues. Channeling women's debates around the new Constitution was possibly the CNDM's finest hour: the Constituent Assembly catalyzed the women's movement and provided a concrete reason for women's groups to transcend political differences. It represented a discrete utopian moment in which women's groups could build their own wish list for gender equality with a prospect of real results. This experience proved that it was possible to identify a common agenda to unite diverse groups and interests, and that the state was now more receptive to women's demands. It also utilized women activists' invaluable practical experience in lobbying legislators and navigating the rapids and backwaters of parliamentary and legislative procedure.

Third, party political factors played a part in altering the situation for women activists as new political actors entered the stage. Political parties are gatekeepers between civil society and the state, mediators of societal interests, and thus prime interlocutors of the women's movement. They formed part of the post-transition institutional-political terrain that feminists and others had to navigate in pursuing changes in public policy, allocation of state resources, and the conditions of entry for women. The PMDB's dominance faded, and the party itself fragmented. It thus became virtually useless as a conduit for women's demands because of its now internally fractionalized and personalistic structure. Initially it had embraced a wide range of centrist to left-wing sectors, but increasingly took on catch-all characteristics, devoid of a coherent ideology, which diluted its earlier commitment to women's equality. However, a radical new political force, the PT, was fast emerging during the 1980s as an important left-wing alternative.[15] It encompassed and supported a number of social movements within its rainbow coalition and gave these new actors a voice as well as direct access to political institutions. After 1982, the PT elected to Congress trade unionists, metal workers, rural women activists, active feminists, and former domestic workers among others—marking a qualitative change in Brazil's political system and breaking the monopoly of the old dynastic and clientelistic elites. Erstwhile "outsiders" now became "insiders." The PT therefore possessed three important characteristics as far as feminist lobbying was concerned. First, it had a strong legislative presence. Second, it was highly disciplined internally, so individual legislators toed the party line, which was determined at national conventions. Third, it had a significant feminist presence within the parliamentary party, as well as at the grass roots, which resulted in a strong ideological support for a broadly feminist agenda. In Congress, PT deputies orchestrated a cross-party women's coalition with which CFEMEA was able to work closely.

The numerical increase and the changing characteristics of women elected to Congress were also crucial to CFEMEA's project. Before the 1980s, the percentage of women in Congress never topped 1.5 percent. It rose sharply as a result of feminist organization, from 1.7 percent in 1983 to 5.3 percent in 1987 for the Constituent Assembly, and stood in 1998 at 6.6 percent. The women elected in the mid-1980s tended to fall into two categories: women who had come the familiar, personalistic route on the coattails of male relatives who preceded them in elected office, and women in the center-left parties with identifiable constituencies and often a feminist political agenda. However, once these women were in office, differences often melted away, in large part because of the unideological and opportunistic character of most of the Brazilian parties. Women elected for the Partido da Frente Liberal (PFL, Liberal Front Party), Brazil's major right-wing party, did not necessarily hold the kinds of attitudes on gender issues often identified with conservative politics. CFEMEA produced two in-depth surveys of two consecutive parliamentary intakes in order to test the receptivity of senators and deputies toward certain pieces of gender-related legislation.[16] The study concluded that although the center-left was predictably consistent on such issues, allies might be found in the most unlikely of places on the political right, and that there was little consensus within party blocs, ideological groupings, or economic credos.[17] Thus, in the 1980s, the potential for a cross-party coalition—the so-called lipstick lobby *(lobby do batom)*, as the cross-bench women's grouping *(bancada feminina)* is known—was greater than it would have been in a more ideologically structured party system. The right- and left-wing parties were more likely to clash along ideological lines on "mainstream" political differences such as economic policy. Gender issues were not party politicized as they were in Chile, for example, where the very lack of fundamental disagreement between government and opposition, all vying for the same consensual middle ground on economic and foreign policy issues, meant that political differences were constructed around the private sphere—that is, around gender relations in the family and in society.[18]

The Formation of a Feminist Lobbying Group

Rising from the ashes of the CNDM, CFEMEA became a high effective centralized lobby. It relied for its support and credibility, however, on parallel networks, such as the Forum of Heads of State, and on the thematic networks involved in women's health, reproductive rights, violence, and race issues. Carmen Barroso's comments on women's lobbying around health issues in the 1980s explain CFEMEA's success: "Two factors were important in generating political clout for feminists—their technical competence, that is, mastery of data on public policies and women's situation, and political legitimacy acquired through their active participation in the general struggle for democracy and the joint mobilization with grassroots organizations."[19] With access to a good-quality technical base acquired in the thematic policy network, CFEMEA won legitimacy from the reliability of its briefings and from its position in the women's movement as a hub of information exchange and networking, and as an opinion former for the opinion formers. It enjoyed a high level of acceptance in Congress, even from those who most disagreed with its agenda. Although CFEMEA is not in any sense formally representative of women's interests, legislators came to see it as a key interlocutor in this area.

The organization was founded by a group of four women on secondment to the CNDM from a variety of government agencies in Brasília, to which they returned when it was wound down. They became de facto the women's movement's only source of information in the seat of federal government about the course of gender-related legislation, such as modifications to penal and civil codes that would make a reality of promises tendered by the new Constitution. The need for an entity such as CFEMEA was created in part by the characteristics of the Brazilian political system, which suffers from a snowstorm of legislative initiatives. In 1992, 180 bills affecting women's status were pending in Congress. In 1994, during the constitutional revision process initiated, 17,246 proposals (with 12,614 amendments) were tabled, of which 956 concerned the chapter on social rights and would have affected women's rights in the areas of work, health, family, and education. Of the latter, 90 percent were in favor of maintaining the current provisions. Those threatening to reduce women's gains revealed the right's primarily financial objection to areas of social spending, such as maternity leave and crèches.[20] The women's movement had achieved 80 percent of its objectives in the drafting of the 1988 Constitution, which remained frustratingly inoperable because legal statutes were frequently not brought into line with the new constitutional principles so that archaic discriminatory laws remained in effect.

The four women persuaded sympathetic deputies to lend their offices and mailing facilities. In 1991, funding from the Ford Foundation enabled them to set up a formal project, the Programa Direitos da Mulher na Lei e na Vida (Program for Women's Rights in Life and Law). Accommodated by the gender studies department at the University of Brasília, and later in its own offices, CFEMEA was at last institutionalized with full-time workers, and the first newsletter, Fêmea, was mailed out in May 1992. The print run rose to six thousand a month, sent out to approximately eight hundred women's organizations across the country.[21] These numbers indicate the diversity and level of grassroots activity within the women's movement as well as the huge potential this diversity represents for lobbying at national, state, and municipal levels. It also demonstrates the servicing needs of these groups in terms of centrally available information and networking. The information service of CFEMEA has broadened over time to include electronic-mail lobbying, urgent action bulletins,[22] and special series of newsletters such as the one that mobilized women around the proposed revision of the Constitution.[23] It tracked the enabling legislation following the 1988 Constitution and supported two parliamentary commissions of inquiry into violence against women and into the forced sterilization of women. The organization offered a focal point for debates across the country prior to the NGO forum of the Beijing Conference and afterward formed the information hub of the specialist groups and networks that took on one of the fourteen priority areas identified at the conference—for example, women's health or education. Successes so far have included legislation on quotas for women in party election lists. In 1997, a presidential veto on a family planning law was removed, the result of a campaign initiated by CFEMEA soon after President Cardoso took office in 1995. Social security rights, including paid maternity leave, have been won for rural women and for domestic workers. The organization has pushed proactively for new and extended rights, as well as defensively when existing rights have been challenged. It spearheaded two successful campaigns on abortion. The first, viewed by CFEMEA as its most intensive lobbying effort to date, was the defeat in 1997 of a proposed constitutional amendment that would have eliminated women's existing rights to legal abortion. At the height of their campaign, begun in 1995, CFEMEA mailed bulletins daily to all the members of Congress and weekly updates to their affiliates in the women's movement. Some sixty thousand women sent in postcards to lobby Congress. The second campaign aimed at consolidating and implementing an existing law. In 1940, abortion was made legal if the pregnancy was a risk to the mother's life or a consequence of rape. In practice, however, no public hospital provided legal abortions. It has taken local initiatives, the passing of by-laws by municipalities, and changes to state constitutions to begin to provide an already legal service. Following this lead, in 1997, CFEMEA and the women deputies initiated national legislation to remove the last possible legal objections. They encountered stiff opposition from church-linked deputies, although the proposed legislation did not even broach the issue of decriminalization of abortion.

It also intervened in budgetary debates, pressing the federal government for earmarked funding for projects to combat violence against women, and showed women how to secure funding for gender projects within state and municipal budgets.[24] Although CFEMEA is a national, centralized body, it appreciates the potential of the federal system for securing rights for women at a subnational level. The text of draft or approved bills on key issues is reproduced in the monthly magazine for copying, adapting, and submitting to state assemblies and municipal chambers. The 1988 Constitution strengthened federalism, allowing states and municipalities to formulate parallel, "local" constitutions and laws, and thereby automatically multiplied the number of focal points on which local women activists and networks could concentrate their lobbying. Institutional blockages at the federal level have been circumvented—mainly by local PT women activists and legislators—in part by the creative use—of these parallel legal instruments to implement rights granted in the Federal Constitution, such as the provision of workplace crèches and statutory provision of municipal services for female victims of violence.

Therefore, CFEMEA performs a vital function in providing both the technical backing and data to deputies who wish to promote certain pieces of legislation. Although politically the women in CFEMEA are identifiably center-left in orientation, they can cross party lines because the organization can aggregate an otherwise disparate women's movement and is not identified with factions, tendencies, or political parties. Despite some hostility from evangelical Christian deputies, the organization has a strong and respected profile in Congress. Opponents on certain issues—abortion, for example—will support them on others, such as quotas. The "feminist" label appears to elicit much less resistance than in other Latin American countries. Another key aspect of the CFEMEA's success is the relationship between it and the PT, which now spearheads legislative initiatives on women in Congress. Women's movements have often had a tense and contradictory relationship with political parties—for example, during the struggle for suffrage and during the debates over double militancy in the 1970s and 1980s—so such collaboration represents a shift on the part of the left both with respect to designing and implementing gender policy and to legislating for social change. Aware of the way in which the PMDB co-opted the CNDM, CFEMEA has been careful to avoid overidentification with the PT. Its policies have not been distorted by proximity to a political party, as Jo Fisher outlines in her account of the rapprochement of the Housewives' Union to a Peronist agenda in Argentina. Unlike SACRA, CFEMEA targeted a number of different access points in the state, and it was not forced to trade political support for policy concessions. The model in Brazil is an effective three-pronged one: the women's movement debates and mobilizes; CFEMEA provides technical backing and a central point of articulation, and carries out targeted lobbying of legislators; the women elected representatives draft bills and lobby inside parties and parliamentary committees. A keystone of its success has been the presence of the bancada

feminina, which came to exert considerable influence in Congress, drawing members and sympathizers from among the male deputies. The
powerhouse behind it in 1994–98 was the flamboyant and energetic PT
deputy Marta Suplicy, a former television sexologist and an outspoken feminist, active in legislating particularly on sexuality issues such as abortion
and civil rights for homosexuals. As such, she is a key opinion former and is
constantly in the public eye. It is perhaps significant that she is closer to the
women's movement than to her own party. The close relationship between
CFEMEA, her, and the bancada has made it possible to raise the public profile of a particular issue by skillful use of the media. The bancada claims the
solid support of around 80 percent of the thirty-three women deputies
elected in 1994, and all women deputies and senators are nominally members. Differences of opinion derive from personal convictions rather than
from any party political or party ideological convictions. Within the bancada, interest in pushing certain agenda items springs often from personal
background and expertise rather than from any party line: Jandira Feghali,
a doctor from Rio and Communist Party deputy, is a respected authority on
health issues; Fátima Pelaes, a PFL deputy, legislates on work and family;
Marilu Guimarães focuses on violence against women, having chaired the
parliamentary commission on the subject; Rita Camata of the PMDB takes a
special interest in children and the family.

Several campaign issues in particular illustrate CFEMEA's modus operandi when mediating between the legislative, policymaking sphere and
sectors of the women's movement. The strength, maturity, and coherence
of the women's networks is highly variable and determines to what extent
CFEMEA can take a lead role in the consultation process and in crafting
recommendations for policymakers. The networks of women's health activists, women rural workers, and domestic workers are relatively strong,
in the last case due to mobilization over a period of years around a bill that
was eventually approved in Congress. When a number of overlapping and
conflicting bills were presented on family planning, CFEMEA organized a
number of roundtable debates with the relevant feminist networks in order
to come up with one consensual, compromise bill on which legislative
efforts could be focused. Although violence against women has long been a
core concern for the feminist movement, in Brazil the issue network is still
in its formative stages, and CFEMEA has played a key role in assisting the
network to begin to identify a common policy agenda around the policy

objectives. Without a clear consensual line on an issue, CFEMEA cannot play its lobbying and intermediary role to its fullest effect—that is, to articulate a single position on behalf of the movement for the benefit of legislators.

This brief overview of CFEMEA's major campaigns underscores the organization's strengths and explains its success and wide acceptance. The novelty of CFEMEA's approach to the state in Brazil stems from the fact that there was no useful model for it to copy. None of the original staff was a trained lobbyist or had any experience of elected office or parliamentary procedure, so they learnt through experience.[25] The relationship that CFEMEA has established with congressional representatives is unprecedented in Brazilian politics, for although many lobbying organizations are active in Congress, no other interest-group lobbying body is dedicated full-time to tracking legislation. Moreover, CFEMEA does not represent any organization as such, and it covers a very wide range of issues within its potential ambit because so much legislation affects gender relations directly or indirectly. It has no aspirations to become a substitute for the women's movement or to act as its leader or representative. Instead of speaking on behalf of the movement, it facilitates communication and acts as an axis between the very diverse elements of the movement, legislators, and the executive branch of government. It functions as a clearing house that can offer specialist advice and training on the mechanics of the legislative process and on tactics to take in a particular situation. It views its remit as one of demystifying the political system and of empowering and educating women to engage with that system. Its publications give detailed profiles of women legislators and members of key commissions, and, after each election, they offer full contact details for every deputy, thus increasing both accountability and access within the political system. Straddling both organized civil society and state institutions, CFEMEA is neither completely an insider nor an outsider to the institutions of the state. In this matrix, the executive branch remains the weak link. The CNDM still functions within the Ministry of Justice, and although a respected feminist, Rosiska Darcy, was appointed by President Cardoso to head it in 1995, it has failed to acquire greater resources or political clout. The CNDM remains marginal within the government, with a skeletal staff and no budget, thus rendering it incapable of carrying out its ambitious objective to "mainstream" gender issues within the work of the ministries. It is also marginal to the women's movement and its allies in Congress, specifically because of fundamental differences over the movement's strategy vis-à-vis the state apparatus: many feminists and CFEMEA lobbied the president elect to reconstitute the CNDM as a full secretariat or subministry, but Rosiska Darcy argued for structural change from within. In the event, CNDM lost the leverage with which to insist on extra resources, so CFEMEA continued to fill a vacuum created within the state apparatus, where women's increased expectations were not met by the government.

Feminist Policy Networks and the State

If CFEMEA is novel in Brazil and Latin America, how might it be characterized, and how do CFEMEA and the women's movement now stand in relationship to the Brazilian state? Political science, international relations, and policy studies offer a number of models for conceptualizing CFEMEA's unique role and function.

The term "interest group" is not particularly useful in understanding and analyzing women's mobilization and lobbying strategies because it implies that women have definable objective interests by virtue of their gender, which is by no means evident.[26] To characterize CFEMEA simply as a lobbying organization does not do justice to the dense interrelationships between women's organizations of different kinds in Brazil, inside and outside the state. It also does not capture the complex vertical interactions between the international, regional, national, and local ambits of women's mobilization and policymaking. In Congress, CFEMEA's legislative work on violence against women draws on United Nations activities,[27] on regional initiatives such as the Inter-American Convention on Violence against Women, and on subnational policy experiments such as the setting up of women's refuges and women's police stations, and the allocation of budget lines to gender-specific policies within the constitutions and bylaws of a number of states and municipalities.

Lobby groups also measure their success in terms of legislative outcome and generally represent a sharply defined interest group with a narrow political agenda or objectives. The women's movement is neither. Women's organizations and groups exist within a much looser, heterogeneous, principled-issue network, which in turn encompasses smaller, much more highly integrated subsets of women such as the policy and issue networks mentioned above. The range of experience CFEMEA has in working with a number of thematic women's networks in Brazil—domestic workers, rural workers, women against violence against women, women working for abortion and reproductive rights—illustrates vividly the varying degree to which elements of the women's movement have or have not identified clear policy goals and "interests," depending both on the subject matter and on the circumstances under which the issue network has evolved.

CFEMEA focuses not just on the *outcome* of lobbying campaigns, but also on the *process* of policy definition. It assists the women's movement in defining policy goals, in reaching a compromise consensus as bills are amalgamated and amended, and in training and educating women's groups to replicate CFEMEA's legislative initiatives at municipal and state levels. Great emphasis is placed on empowering, replicating, sharing skills and the expert advice from the women's networks for the content of bills, and offering the political savoir-faire of the women's bancada for questions of political strategy.

The global women's movement fits the criteria of an international principled-issue network, defined as "a set of organizations, bound by shared values and by dense exchanges of information and services, working internationally on an issue."[28] There is interest in replicating CFEMEA's model in other Latin American countries (Paraguay, Mexico, Chile, Argentina). The domestic women's movement constitutes an issue network within which CFEMEA and its parliamentary allies form part of a policy network[29] that includes its feminist advisors, many of whom belong to policy communities on labor, health, reproduction, and legal concerns. Both CFEMEA and the domestic women's movement form part of this wider international principled issue network.

Conclusions

The Brazilian state is characterized by its size, bureaucratization, corruption, and inefficiency. It is decidedly leaky in terms of the misdirection of resources and the privatization of supposedly public ends. Overgrown and unwieldy as it is, it also finds itself in flux, permeable not just to individual influences but also to new collective interests. The state should be viewed not as a coherent, if contradictory unity, but rather as a spatially and politically diverse set of institutional and discursive arenas that play a crucial part in organizing power relations such as gender relations. Thus, a number of strategic possibilities are available at any one time. During the period of transition to democratic rule, the Brazilian state opened up to a much greater plurality and capacity for grassroots input.

The feminist response to the failure of the centralized, federal CNDM was to create a policy network and specialist groups or policy communities within that broad network. The federal system means that the technical and strategic information on gender legislation is not aimed wholly at a centralized legislature: it can be used and replicated at state and municipal levels. As an independent NGO, CFEMEA is not prone to the pitfalls facing state feminism such as partisanship or the creation of a distant, technocratic elite.[30] Its success lies precisely in its strategic position at once outside and inside the state apparatus. It has been able to avoid the fate of co-option and clientelism that befell the CNDM, yet has enjoyed access within the centralized decision-making locus of the state. Its wide contacts with the women's movement and its methods of communication and consultation have guaranteed legitimacy, backing, and a "multiplier effect" elsewhere in the state apparatus. Its experience has provided a new mode of effective engagement with respect to the Brazilian state.

Notes

1 Organized labor within the formal sector was a privileged interlocutor of the corporatist state established by Vargas. The system, controlled at the top by the Ministry of Labor, exercised control over labor but also created a space in which dialogue was possible. The degree of leverage that labor was able to exert on politicians within such a tightly regulated system is a matter of debate among historians of the period.

2 A set of recommendations to governments to achieve women's equality resulting from the Fourth United Nations World Conference on Women, held in Beijing, China, in 1995.

3 There were also other "feminist" strands at the time, such as anarchist and libertarian feminism and conservative Catholic feminism. See Susan K. Besse, *Restructuring Patriarchy: The Modernization of Gender Inequality in Brazil 1914–1940* (Chapel Hill: University of North Carolina Press, 1996).

4 The fullest account of the suffrage movement is given in June Hahner, *Emancipating the Female Sex: The Struggle for Women's Rights in Brazil 1850–1940* (Durham, N.C.: Duke University Press, 1990).

5 Deputy Basilio de Magalhães was supported as a candidate by women. Juvenal Lamartine, the governor of Rio Grande de Norte, unilaterally gave women the vote in the state, and thus the first woman elected to public office was Alzira Soriano, who became mayor of the municipality of Lages.

6 For comparative perspectives, see Francesca Miller, *Latin American Women and the Search for Social Justice* (Hanover: University Press of New England, 1991), and Asunción Lavrin, *Women, Feminism, and Social Change in Argentina, Chile, and Uruguay 1890–1940* (Lincoln: University of Nebraska Press, 1995).

7 For a fuller account, see Fanny Tabak, *Mulher e democracia no Brasil* (Rio de Janeiro: Pontificia Universidade Católica, 1987); Besse, *Restructuring Patriarchy;* and Hahner, *Emancipating the Female Sex.*

8 Conselho Nacional dos Direitos da Mulher, *Mulher e trabalho 4: A legislação e o trabalho feminino* (Brasília: CNDM, 1986).

9 For the federal and state elections of October 1998, a quota of 25 percent was applied, thereafter 30 percent. A quota of 20 percent was first applied to municipal elections in 1996.

10 For an account of the transition to democracy, the rebirth of the women's movement, specifically their campaigns on health policy, and the setting up of the Women's Councils, see Sonia E. Alvarez, *Engendering Democracy in Brazil: Women's Movements in Transition Politics* (Princeton, N.J.: Princeton University Press, 1990).

11 Vice President Sarney took power in 1985 when the president elect, Tancredo Neves, died before taking office. The elections for president were democratic, but indirect and conducted under a college vote system in Congress. Both men were elected on a PMDB-headed ticket.

12 Jacqueline Pitanguy, interview with author, Rio de Janeiro, 24 October 1995. Unless otherwise noted, all translations are by the author.

13 For a case study of the PT administrations, see Fiona Macaulay, "Gender Politics in Brazil and Chile: The Role of Parties in Local and National Policy-Making" (D.Phil. diss., Oxford University, 1997), and " 'Governing for Everyone': The Workers' Party Administration in São Paulo 1989–1992," *Bulletin of Latin American Research* 15, no. 2 (1996): 211–29.

14 Suzanne Franzway, Dianne Court, and R. W. Connell, *Staking a Claim: Feminism, Bureaucracy, and the State* (Cambridge: Polity, 1989); Sophie Watson, *Playing the State: Australian Feminist Interventions* (London: Verso, 1989), and her "Femocratic Feminisms," in *Gender and Bureaucracy,* ed. Michael Savage and Ann Witz (Oxford: Blackwell, 1992), 186–204.

15 The PT has grown exponentially at each election, with the fifth largest number of deputies in Congress in 1994, and has been the main center-left challenger for the presidency since 1989.

16 CFEMEA, *Direitos da mulher: O que pensam os parlamentares* (Brasília: CFEMEA, 1993).

17 Individual PFL deputies have introduced bills to decriminalize abortion and to give land rights to women in land reform.

18 Fiona Macaulay, "Localities of Power: Gender, Parties, and Democracy in Chile and Brazil," in *Empowering Women: Illustrations from the Third World,* ed. Haleh Afshar (London: Macmillan, 1998), 86–109.

19 Carmen Barroso, "The Women's Movement, the State, and Health Policies in Brazil," in *Towards Women's Strategies for the 1990s: Challenging Government and the State,* ed. Geerte Lycklama à Nijeholt (Basingstoke: Macmillan, 1991), 52.

20 "Revisão ameaça os direitos da mulher," *Rede Revi / Fêmea,* January 1994, 4–5.

21 Iáris Ramalho Cortês and Guacira César de Oliveira, interview with author, Brasília, 23 January 1998.

22 Brazil has one of the highest percentages of NGOs "on-line," due in part to the country's own information technology industry, but mainly to the vision of IBASE, a leading research and social policy NGO in Rio that set up an NGO e-mail network in the late 1980s. As a result, a relatively high number of women's NGOs are on-line or have access. Electronic communication is particularly important in a country with the geographical dimensions of Brazil.

23 They produced *Rede Revi,* a bulletin for the National Women's Movement Network on the Revision. The Constitution was completed and ratified in 1988; however, there were so many internal discrepancies that a five-year period for its revision was established. The process began but was interrupted by scandals and elections so was never completed.

24 Violence against women has been designated a priority area by the National Secretariat for Human Rights, a subministry within the Ministry for Justice, where the CNDM is still located. However, the women's movement has had to battle each year to get a budget allocation. So that the issue would not be "overlooked" again, CFEMEA and others lobbied in 1997 to get a specific budget line opened up within the federal budget. However, they failed in this first attempt.

25 Their backgrounds are in law, sociology, and economics.

26 Kathleen B. Jones, and Anna G. Jonasdóttir, eds., *The Political Interests of Gender: Developing Theory and Research with a Feminist Face* (London: Sage, 1988).

27 For example, the Beijing Platform for Action, the Convention on the Elimination of the Forms of Discrimination against Women (CEDAW), and the United Nations Special Rapporteur on Violence against Women.

28 See Katherine Sikkink, "Human Rights, Principled Issue Networks, and Sovereignty in Latin America," *International Organization 47,* no. 3 (1993): 411–41.

29 It forms such a network insofar as it maintains a stable relationship with parts of the state machinery, interacts with bureaucrats, represents an interest group, and has a cooperative and interdependent relationship with politicians.

30 See Dorothy McBride Stetson and Amy Mazur, eds., *Comparative State Feminism* (New York: Sage, 1995).

Contributors

ELIZABETH DORE is Reader in Latin American History at the University of Portsmouth (UK). She has written extensively in the fields of modern history, gender studies, and social theory, focusing on the processes of capitalist transitions. She is author of a monograph on the Peruvian mining industry and of a forthcoming book on rural Nicaragua, and serves on the editorial boards of NACLA's *Report on the Americas* and *Latin American Perspectives*. She worked for a number of years on the staff of several development agencies that specialized in gender issues and currently acts as consultant to NGOs active in Latin America. She is editor of *Gender Politics in Latin America: Debates in Theory and Practice* (1997) and author of *The Peruvian Mining Industry: Growth, Stagnation, and Crisis* (1988) and the *Myth of Modernity: Rural Nicaragua, 1840–1979* (forthcoming).

MAXINE MOLYNEUX is at the Institute of Latin American Studies, University of London, where she teaches and writes in the fields of gender theory, political sociology, and development studies. As a comparative sociologist with a critical interest in socialist states, she is the author of monographs on the Ethiopian Revolution and on South Yemen, as well as of articles on Cuba, Nicaragua, Eastern Europe, and the USSR. She was a cofounder of *Feminist Review* and acts as a consultant to several UN agencies and other NGOs. Since joining the Institute of Latin American Studies in 1994, her research has focused on issues of citizenship rights and rights-based approaches to development in Latin America. She is coauthor of *The Ethiopian Revolution* (1981), author of *State Policies and the Position of Women in the People's Democratic Republic of Yemen, 1967–77* (1982), and coeditor of *Gender and Justice in Latin America* (forthcoming). Her next book, *Women's Movements in International Perspective: Essays on Latin America and Beyond,* will be published by ILAS / Macmillan.

MARÍA EUGENIA CHAVES is a researcher at the Ibero-American Institute of the University of Gothenburg, Sweden.

REBECCA EARLE is Lecturer in History at the University of Warwick and author of *Spain and the Independence of Colombia* (2000), and *Epistolary Selves: Letters and Letter-Writers, 1600–1945* (1999).

JO FISHER is the author of *Mothers of the Disappeared* (1989) and *Out of the Shadows: Women, Resistance, and Politics in South America* (1993).

LAURA GOTKOWITZ is Assistant Professor of History at Swarthmore College. She is working on a book on citizenship, race, and motherhood in Bolivia.

DONNA J. GUY is Professor of History at the University of Arizona. She is the author of *Argentine Sugar Politics: Tucuman and the Generation of Eighty* (1980); *Sex and Danger in Buenos Aires: Prostitution, Family, and Nation in Argentina* (1991); and coeditor of *Sex and Sexuality in Latin America* (1997) and *Contested Ground: Comparative Frontiers on the Northern and Southern Edges of the Spanish Empire* (1998).

FIONA MACAULAY is an Associate of the Center for Cross-Cultural Research on Women, Queen Elizabeth House, Oxford University. She is author of *Gender Politics in Brazil and Chile* (2000).

EUGENIA RODRÍGUEZ S. is Associate Professor of History at the University of Costa Rica. She is editor of *Entre silencios y voces: Género e historia en América Central, 1750–1990* (1997) and *Violencia doméstica en Costa Rica* (1998), and author of *Hijas, novias, y esposas: Matrimonia, Familia, y relaciones de género en el Valle Central de Costa Rica, 1750–1850* (forthcoming). She was awarded a research grant from the Harry Frank Guggenheim Foundation in 1999.

KARIN ROSEMBLATT, Assistant Professor of History at Syracuse University, received her Ph.D. in history from the University of Wisconsin—Madison. Her book on gender, labor, and the Chilean popular-front coalitions of the 1930s is forthcoming from the University of North Carolina Press.

ANN VARLEY is Reader in the Department of Geography at University College–London. She is coauthor of *Landlord and Tenant: Housing the Poor in Urban Mexico* (1991); editor of *Disasters, Development, and Environment* (1994); and coeditor of *Illegal Cities: Law and Urban Change in Developing Countries* (1998).

MARY KAY VAUGHAN is Professor of History and Latin American Studies at the University of Illinois–Chicago. She is author of *The State, Education, and Social Class in Mexico, 1880–1928* (1982) and *Cultural Politics in Revolution: Teachers, Peasants, and Schools in Mexico, 1930–1940*, which was awarded the Latin American Studies Association's Herbert Eugene Bolton Prize for best book in Latin American history in 1997. She is coeditor of *Creating Spaces, Shaping Transitions: Women of the Mexican Countryside, 1850–1990* (1994).

Index

Cabildo Eclesiastico (Cartagena), 109

Caja de Seguro Obligatorio (CSO), 271–72, 275–76

Calatayud, Alejo, 222

Cali, 134

Camata, Rita, 361

Campaña Admirable, 133

Canon law, 13

Capitalism, 8, 17–18, 34; agrarian, 86; development, 265; free-market, 195; industrial, 176

Cárdenas, Lázaro, 50, 52, 54, 197, 203, 240

Cardoso, Enrique, 359, 362

Carranza, Venustiano, 242

Cartago, 89

Casas de Orientación de la Mujer y de la Familia (Cuba), 306

Castas, 10, 109–10

Catholic Church, 5, 6, 9, 13, 17, 21–22, 44, 50, 69, 88, 153, 198, 338, 341

Catholicism, 85, 209. *See also* Anti-religiosity; Secularization

Central America, 16, 18, 19, 20

Central Unica Trabalhadores (CUT), 355

Centro de Estudios de la Mujer Argentina (CESMA), 324

Centro Femenista de Estudos e Assessoria (CFEMEA), 66, 340, 346, 352; formation, 347, 353, 354, 357–78; modus operandi, 347, 358, 361–63

Centros de Madres (Chile), 350

Cepeda y Ariscum, Alfonso, 113

Chaco War, 225, 227

Chamorro, Fruto, 15

Chiapas: Palenque, 246; Tuxtla Gutierrez, 243, 245, 246, 250, 252; Yajalon, 246

Chihuahua: Namiquipa, 242

Child labor, 177–78

Child mortality: in Mexico, 206

Children, 12, 23, 48, 60, 62, 163, 183, 187, 199, 306, 350; abuse of, 23, 173, 179, 185, 190; equal governance over, 173, 174, 176, 328 (*see also* Custody); errant, 186–87; illegitimate, 174, 177, 182, 190; rights of, 12, 13, 49, 187–90; orphaned, 179; violence toward, 172, 185

Child support, 162, 163, 184–85, 262, 302, 306, 310, 351

Chile, 14, 18, 44, 50, 55, 62, 65, 66, 69, 131, 198, 262–85, 338, 357, 364

Church. *See* Catholic Church

Citizenship, 10, 16, 35–36, 37, 43–44, 45, 49, 51, 56, 57, 60, 64, 67, 68, 69, 141, 196, 217, 271, 276

Civic roles, 130, 306; and responsibility, 141

Civil codes, 18, 19, 22, 46; in Argentina, 173–74, 175, 176, 177, 178, 185 (*see also* Ley Agote); in Mexico, 25, 51, 53, 242; in Nicaragua, 156–58, 162, 164; in Uruguay, 189

Civil society, 34, 36, 38, 52, 64, 65, 67, 68, 296, 338, 342, 355, 362

Class, 7–8, 20, 35. *See also* Dominant class; Elites; Plebe, the; Working class

Cochabamba, 215, 216, 220

Codigo General de 1841 (Costa Rica), 89, 90, 92, 94

Coffee economy: Nicaragua, 147, 149, 150, 159, 165–66

Cofradías, 150–51

Colina de San Sebastián. *See* Coronilla, the

Coll, Jorge E., 188

Colley, Linda, 130

Colombia, 127–42

Colonial government, 108–19

Colonias proletarias. *See* Housing

Comité Ejecutivo de las Fiestas del Centenario de 1912, 219, 223

Committees for the Defence of the Revolution (CDRS), 297, 300, 304

Labor (*cont.*)

nized, in Chile, 265; shortage of, 163, 176; systems of, "unfree," 9, 18; unions, 55, 348 (*see also* Hijas del Pueblo; Sindicato de Amas de Casa); voluntary, in Cuba, 295, 297, 299, 302, 304–6; waged, 8, 25, 203, 240, 325, 333–34; waged, family, 56. *See also* Employment; Housework; Slavery

Ladinoization, 21, 153

Ladinos: in Nicaragua, 151, 166

Lafferte, Elías, 279

Landes, Joan, 127, 137

Landholding, 11, 17–19, 20–21; in Mexico, 21, 50, 201, 202, 204; in Nicaragua, 149, 150, 151, 156; in Nicaragua, female, 56. *See also* Property

Land privatization, 9, 17–18, 19, 21

Land reform, 197, 201

Las Casas–Sepúlveda debates, 11

Law, 37, 44; civil, 242, 349, 351; criminal, 242, 348, 349, 351; family, 4, 6, 18, 242, 295, 300, 302, 310, 328, 341, 348, 359; marital, 13; property, 4, 6. *See also* Property

League of Nations, 196

Legal rights, 294

Legal tradition: Anglo-Saxon, 12, 19

Lesbians, 355

Lewis, Oscar, 251

Ley Agote (1919), 174, 178

Liberal Contract, 15

Liberal reforms, 5, 6, 17–18, 20, 45–46, 47

Liberal (oligarchic) state, 41, 42–50; in Bolivia, 219; in Costa Rica; centralization of, in Costa Rica, 89; formation of, in Costa Rica, 86–88; in Nicaragua, 156

Libros semanales, 240, 254

Liga de Amas de Casa (Argentina), 341

Literacy, 44, 53, 206, 226, 278, 295 n.19, 349

López, Santiago, 163

López del Carril, Julio, 189

Lowenthal Felstiner, Mary, 13

Lutz, Bertha, 349–50

Machismo, 239, 240, 254, 314

Madres and Abuelas de la Plaza de Mayo, 62–63, 338, 339

MAGIN, 311

Male authority, 9, 56, 202

Male camaraderie, 269, 280, 283

Male discipline: Chile, 270, 271–75

Mallon, Florencia, 21

Mann, Michael, 35

Manumission, 113

Mariel exodus, 297

Marital abuse, 23, 59, 92, 243, 307, 308; typologies, 93–94

Marital disputes, 273; resolution of, 89

Marital home, 9, 243, 244, 248; abandonment of, 50, 53, 238, 243, 246, 248, 253. *See also* Patrilocality

Marital rights, 6

Market women: in Cochabamba, 215, 216, 217, 221, 224–30

Marriage, 8, 13, 21, 36, 53, 58, 87, 242, 243–47, 253, 350; allegations regarding, 88, 91, 92–94; companionate, 87–88, 90, 96; ideals of, 23, 24, 87, 90, 94; interracial, 109, 110–11; patriarchal, 87, 88; patterns of, 86; and property, 154, 157, 161; volition in, 13. *See also* Nonmarriage

Married women. *See* Wives

Marshall, T. H., 35

Masculine domination. *See* Patriarchy

Masculinity, 5, 173–74, 182, 190, 269; working class, in Chile, 263, 270–71, 277–84, 280, 283–84; working class, in Mexico (*see* Machismo)

Masiello, Francine, 139

Mass culture, 253

Mass society, 53, 196

Master-slave relationships, 112, 113; and possession, 117–18

Maternity, 49, 57, 162; leave, 49, 350, 358, 359

Mejoras, 150

Melo, Carlos, 178

Menem, Carlos: administration of, 66, 329–33, 336, 341–42

Meseta de los Pueblos. *See* Nicaragua

Mestizaje, 109, 217

Mestiza/os, 10, 12; in Bolivia, 216, 217, 221; status of, 109. *See also* Market women

Mestizoization, 197

Mestizos de casta, 109–110

Mexican Revolution, 42, 47, 50–53, 54, 194, 197, 208, 239

Mexico, 9, 16, 18–19, 20, 23, 25, 44, 46, 47, 48, 50, 65, 132, 173, 194–210, 250, 337, 364

Mexico City, 245, 248

Michoacán, 252

Migration, 42, 43, 44, 49, 302, 307. *See also* Labor; Mariel exodus

Military rule, 60–64. *See also* Argentina; Brazil; Chile

Miscegenation, 12

Misiones (Argentina), 329

Misogyny, 62

Mobilization, 25, 39, 52, 53–54, 57, 59–60, 132–33, 136, 199, 204, 217, 262, 300, 302, 332, 354, 363. *See also* Feminist movement; *individual organizations;* Women's movement

Modernity, 39, 43, 45, 46–47, 59, 67, 71, 207, 239; fantasies of, 204; social, 48

Modernization, 13, 42, 50–51, 55, 254–55, 264–66, 342; narratives of, 240; socialist, 296

Morality. *See* Domestic morality; Masculinity: working class

Mortality: female, in Cuba, 294

Motherhood, 14, 22, 45, 49, 58, 62, 70, 141, 164, 189, 221, 225, 263, 338

Mother-in-law, 244–47

Mothers, 57, 60, 200, 325, 328, 338; "single," 23, 56, 161, 162, 164, 176, 177, 178, 179, 188, 207, 242, 306; and custody cases, 183, 188. *See also* Household: heads of

Mother's Day: in Bolivia, 215–16, 217, 225, 231

Mulatta/os, 9, 10, 12

Municipal government: of Diriomo, 150, 154, 162; as Ladino sphere in Diriomo, 151, 164

Municipal politics, 165–66

Mutual Aid Societies, 226. *See also* Hijas del Pueblo

Myth, 6, 11–12

Namier, Lewis, 21

Napoleonic Code, 39, 43

Napolitano, Valentina, 247

Nariño, Antonio, 131

National Confederation of Popular Organizations (Mexico), 52

National identity: in Chile, 264, 266

National imaginary: military, 61

National memory, 217

National Peasant Confederation (Mexico), 52

National Revolutionary Movement (MNR), 216, 228

National symbolics, 11, 138–39. *See also* Familial imagery

National Women's Meetings, 341

Nationhood, 37, 42–43, 61

Navarro, Marysa, 325

Nazarri, Muriel, 20

Neoliberalism, 35, 37, 63

Nicaragua, 15, 21, 23, 59, 60, 147–66

Nongovernmental organizations, 64, 65, 298, 311, 347, 365

Nonmarriage, 12, 149, 153, 159, 160–61

Normative para la declaración de mestizos (Bogota 1764), 110, 111, 116
Nuevo Leon: Monterrey, 248, 252
Nutini, Hugo, 247
Nutrition, 200, 206

Oaxaca: Juchitan, 249, 250
Obra social. *See* Social security; Welfare
O'Donnell, Guillermo, 34
Older generation: authority of, 238, 240–41, 247–49, 253, 254
O'Malley, Ilene, 239
"Order and Progress," 5, 20
Orphans. *See* Children

Panama, 128
Paraguay, 225, 364
Parental authority, 18, 23, 176, 242, 248. *See also* Older generation
Parental rights. *See* Children; Custody
Parents, 13; errant, 174; unfit, 178. *See also* Fathers; Mothers; Older generation
Partible inheritance, 12, 19, 156–57
Partido da Frente Liberal (PFL), 356
Partido do Movimento Democrático Brasileiro (PMDB), 352, 355, 360
Partido dos Trabalhadores (PT), 354, 356, 360
Partido Peronista Feminino (PPF), 322, 323–25, 327, 343
Partido Revolucionario Institucional (PRI), 52, 206
Party of the Revolutionary Left (PIR), 228
Pateman, Carol, 16, 36
Paternity, 22, 162, 163, 177, 182, 328
Patria, 61
Patria potestad, 12, 23, 24, 43, 45, 65, 176, 178, 179, 182–83, 185, 188, 190, 242
Patriarchy, 10–14, 39, 45, 50, 59, 68, 90, 91, 100, 132, 154, 164, 166, 173, 174–75,

190, 204, 206, 209, 239, 241, 314; authority of, 16, 18, 24 (see also Power: naturalization of); authority of colonial, 9, 11, 13–15; modernization of, 22, 24, 40, 47, 68; modernization of, in Mexico, 24, 51, 194–210, 238, 240, 241–42; paternalistic, 10, 238, 254, 294; and property, 150–56, 161; "Republican," 14–16; restoration of, 62. *See also* Familial imagery; Fatherhood; Households
Patrilocality, 247
"Patriotic development," 52, 199, 239
Patriotism, 131, 138–39; in Chile, 266; and civil ritual in Bolivia, 216, 225; in Cuba, 296; and the family, 141, 225–26
Patronage, 166
Patronato Nacional de Menores (Argentina), 178
Peasantry, 9, 18, 19, 208–10; "domestication" of (Mexico), 197
Peasant women: image of, 209–10
Pelaes, Fátima, 361
Pensions: in Argentina, 326, 329, 335–36, 341
Pereira de Queiroz, Carlota, 350
Pérez Núñez, Roberto, 268–69
Perón, Eva, 57–58, 66, 189, 323–24, 325, 327, 333, 340, 342
Perón, Juan: administrations of, 54, 57, 188, 189, 323–24
Peronist women's movement. *See* Partido Peronista Femenino
Personería Social, 331
Peru, 44, 54, 65, 337
Pimping, 185
Pinochet, Augusto, 62
Pitanguy, Jacqueline, 353
Plebe, the, 119, 128, 129, 137, 218, 222, 223, 225
Polygamy, 157
Poor men, 172

Poor women, 64, 153, 154, 162, 175, 308; and landholding, 158–59

Popular-front coalitions: Chile, 262–63, 264–65, 267–72, 276–77, 280, 284

Popular mobilization, 216

Popular sectors, 91, 154, 218; in Chile, 262–63, 264

Population, 201, 209–10

Potestad, 114. See also Patria potestad

Poverty, 311; feminization of, 159, 323, 325

Power, 6–7, 35, 36, 37, 38, 39; in rural Nicaragua, 165–66; naturalization of, 8, 11, 16, 148–49. See also Patriarchy: authority of

Priests, 154–55

Primogeniture, 12

Privacy, 101

Private sphere, 34, 36, 346, 357. See also Domestic sphere

Programa direitos de Mulher na Lei e na Vida, 358

"Progress," 266

Promiscuity, 200

Property, 9, 11, 20, 43, 147, 149, 292; common, 17, 20–21, 150–56; private, 9, 17–19, 22, 25, 156–60, 160–62; and redistribution, 197

Prostitution, 8, 137, 292, 307, 309–10

Public administration, 87

Public sphere, 4, 15, 37, 39, 45, 46, 51, 218, 222, 241, 325, 334, 346; activity in, 60 (see also Civic roles; Mobilization); dissuasion from activity in, 15, 133; and honor, 11, 153–54; and secular authority, 149, 153

Puebla, 251

Race, 8, 9, 10, 13, 20, 47, 108–11, 197; and Brazil, 349, 357; and Chile, 264, 273, 280

Racial: criteria and social structure, 108, 110; designations, 109–10; hierarchies, 12; identity, 11; separation, 109; typologies, 109

Radical Party (Argentina), 328

Rape, 62, 69, 134–36, 153, 185, 205, 308, 359

Raza, 109

Recreation, 199–200, 203–4, 206, 262, 272, 275, 282–83

Reproductive practices, 205. See also Knowledge: female

Reproductive rights: politics of, 49, 52, 60, 62, 64, 69, 208–9, 323, 324, 325, 351, 354, 357, 364. See also Abortion

Republicanism, 14–16, 127, 132, 137

"Republican Motherhood," 141

Restrepo, José Manuel, 134

Royal Decrees (Real pragmatica), 11, 22

Salamanca, Daniel, 219, 223

Salamanca, Sara, 219, 220, 221, 223

Salavarrieta, Policarpa ("La Pola"), 139–40, 141

Sanción Pragmática (New Spain 1778), 110–11, 116

Sandinista Revolution, 166, 294

San José, 89

San Luis Potosi: Matehuala, 245

Sanzetenea de Terrazas, Teodosia, 229

Sarney, José, 353

Sayer, Derek, 8, 35, 87, 148

Schooling. See Education

Scott, Joan, 3

Secularization, 5, 6, 13, 17, 21–23, 25, 42, 44, 50, 155, 198, 199, 200, 201, 253

Seduction. See Breach of Promise

Separation, 184, 242

Sepúlveda debate. See Las Casas-Sepúlveda debates

Servant role, 250–51

Sexual abuse, 154

Sexual contract, 16, 36

Sexuality, 21, 22, 46, 49, 69, 361

Sexual practices, 8

Sexual regulation, 153, 157, 162. *See also* Domestic morality

Sexual relations: and property relations, 162

Siles, Hernando, 223

Sindicato de Amas de Casa (SACRA), 58, 65–66, 322–44, 360; and feminism, 337, 338–31; formation, 324; and Menem government, 329–333; and Partido Peronista Femenino, 323–25; status of, 331–32

Skocpol, Theda, 194

slavery, 9, 10, 11, 114–15, 132, 137, 176; women in, 112, 116–17, 119. *See also* Chiquinquirá, María

Social assistance. *See* Welfare

Social exclusion, 35, 43, 45, 68, 111, 116

Social hygiene. *See* Health

Socialism, 59–60, 265. *See also* Cuba

Socialist morality, 277–78

Socialist Party: Chile, 263, 266, 279

Socialist state, 41, 59–60. *See also* Cuba

Social order, 10, 13, 37, 171–74, 176; regulation of, 10, 47, 149, 164, 166. *See also* Domestic morality

Social policy, 4, 48; in Brazil, 358; in Mexico, 196–99

Social relations, 9, 33, 34, 36, 38, 45, 51, 59, 70, 244, 283, 346, 349. *See also* Patriarchy

Sociedad de Beneficiencia (Buenos Aires), 179, 180, 186

Soto, Bernardo, 86

Soviet bloc, 59, 63, 293, 297, 299, 301

Sterilization: forced, 358–59

Stern, Steve, 14, 240, 251, 252, 254

Subsecretaría de la Mujer (Argentina), 328. *See also* Consejo Nacional de la Mujer

Suffrage: female, 25, 44, 45, 51, 52, 53, 54, 240, 243, 263, 325, 329, 337, 349, 360

Suplicy, Marta, 361

Supreme Court of Justice (Mexico), 238, 241, 243–44, 249, 252–53, 254

Tamaulipas: Ciudad Madero, 245, 249, 252

Taylor, Diane, 61

Teachers, 200, 205, 206

Tecamachalco, 203, 204–5, 206, 207, 308

Teitelboim, Volodia, 279

Temperance. *See* Alcohol

Terror, 61, 62

"the commons," 150

Thompson, E. P., 88

Tribunals. *See* Courts

Turner, Bryan, 35

Tutelage. *See* Custody

United Nations: Convention on the Elimination of all Forms of Discrimination Against Women, 352; Decade for Women (1975–1985), 63, 298, 299, 300; First Women's Conference (Mexico City), 63, 242; Fifth Women's Conference (Beijing), 66, 333, 347, 359

Urbanization, 252, 253–54

Uruguay, 19, 46, 47, 49, 51, 59, 189

U.S.-Cuban relations, 292–93, 299

U.S.-Mexican relations, 198; cultural influence of, 253

Usufruct rights, 150, 151, 158

Uxoricide, 23, 69, 157, 177, 241

Vagrancy, 8, 64, 262

Vargas, Getulio, 54, 57, 346, 348

Vice, 93, 239, 279–81. *See also* Alcohol

Victims and victimization, 134, 135, 136

Vigo, Elida, 324, 329

Villarrica, Clotilde, 280

Villarroel, Gualberto, 216, 225–31

Violence, 9, 23, 69, 204–5, 240, 241, 247, 250, 254, 308, 352, 354, 357–60, 361, 363–64. *See also* Domestic Violence

Library of Congress Cataloging-in-Publication Data

Hidden histories of gender and the state in Latin America /
edited by Elizabeth Dore and Maxine Molyneux.
p.   cm.
Includes index.
ISBN 0-8223-2434-2 (alk. paper). — ISBN 0-8223-2469-5 (pbk. : alk. paper)
I. Sex role—Political aspects—Latin America—History. I. Dore, Elizabeth.
II. Molyneux, Maxine.
HQ1075.5.L29H53   2000
305.3'098—dc21   99-36543